BETWEEN TWO FIRES

Between Two Fires

GYPSY PERFORMANCE

AND ROMANI MEMORY

FROM PUSHKIN TO POSTSOCIALISM

ALAINA LEMON

DUKE UNIVERSITY PRESS DURHAM *&* LONDON 2000

© 2000 Duke University Press

All rights reserved

Printed in the United States of America on acid-free paper ∞

Typeset in Galliard by Keystone Typesetting, Inc.

Library of Congress Cataloging-in-Publication Data appear on the
last printed page of this book.

CONTENTS

ACKNOWLEDGMENTS

I want to express gratitude first to those Roma in Russia who made time for me, namely the Jankeschi family, and to the Saporronji and Rruvoni, to whom I owe hospitality and grateful thanks. I am also beholden to Lev N. Cherenkov, Vladislav Petrovich Demeter, Nadezhda Demeter, and Olga Stepanovna Demeter. I am especially grateful for the guidance of Irena Tarasova and the companionship of her family. The Russian State Humanities University (RGGU) sponsored me as a scholar, and the Moscow Romani Theater generously allowed me access to the auditorium and backstage. Thanks there go to the Theater's director, Nikolaj Slichenko. I want to also thank musicians Lena and Oleg Novoselov in Perm, for all manner of help there, and in Moscow, Alena Tsvetkova and Aleksej Uxlovskij.

Romologists Ian Hancock and Thomas Acton offered invaluable advice and comments at many stages of research and writing. I want to convey my deep gratitude to all the members of my dissertation committee at the University of Chicago for originally encouraging me in this project: Sheila Fitzpatrick, Victor Friedman, Paul Friedrich, Michael Silverstein, and finally Sharon Stephens, who is missed greatly. I much appreciate the labors of others at the University of Chicago who read later drafts; they include David Althshuler, Matti Bunzl, Keith Brown, Piya Chatterjee, Lauren Derby, Kriszti Fehervary, Susan Gal, Anne Lorimer, Dale Pesmen, Catherine O'Neil, Stephanie Platz, Katherine Trumpener, and Miklós Vörös. Enormous thanks to all those who read chapters or papers: Marjorie Balzer, Richard Handler, Caroline Humphrey, Valdemar Kalinin, Martha Lampland, Maria Montoya, Gloria Goodwin Raheja, Peter Rutland, Daniel Segal, Michael Stewart, and Bonnie Urcioli. I am also indebted to commentators at conferences: Judith Irvine, Elizabeth Povinelli, Alfred Rieber, and again Martha Lampland and Dan Segal. The participants of the 1995 Social Science Research Council (SSRC) Summer Workshop in Soviet Studies gave the work rigorous attention, and I thank most particularly Barbara Anderson, Elena Ivanova, Michael Kennedy, and Yuri Slezkine. I am grateful to the Center for Russian and East European Studies at the University of Michigan, especially Jane Burbank, William Rosenberg, and Katherine Verdery. Warm thanks go to participants in the Linguistic Anthropology lab at the University of Michigan, especially Lisa Lane and Bruce Mannheim, and to students in the University of Michigan Anthropology Department, in particular Helen Faller and Morgan Liu, who read drafts. For pressing me to frame this work in a way that can communicate across disciplines, I am obliged to the Michigan Society of Fellows, especially Paul Anderson, Jochen Hellbeck, Barbara Ryan, Adam Smith, Michael Szalay, and James Boyd White. Finally, I am most warmly beholden to Midori Nakamura, who codirected and coproduced our documentary *T'an Baxtale*. And immense thanks go to Maria Lemon and Lee Lemon, for reading drafts but mainly for many other things.

The work leading up to field research for this project was supported by a graduate training fellowship from the Joint Committee on Soviet Studies of the Social Science Research Council (funded by the Soviet and East European Research and Training Act of 1983, title VIII). Fieldwork was supported by both long-term and short-term grants from the International Research and Exchanges Board (IREX), with funds provided by the National Endowment for the Humanities, the United States Information Agency, and the U.S. Department of State, which administers the Russian, Eurasian, and East European Research Program (title VIII), and a U.S. Department of Education Fulbright-Hayes Doctoral Dissertation Research Abroad Fellowship. Writing in the dissertation stage was sponsored by the Joint Committee on Social Sciences of the SSRC, and at the manuscript stage by the Michigan Society of Fellows. I thank all of these organizations for their financial support.

Part of chapter 4 was previously published in a different form as "Hot Blood and Black Pearls: Society, Socialism, and Authenticity at the Moscow Romani Theatre," in *Theatre Journal* (Johns Hopkins University Press) 48, no. 3 (December 1996): 479–94. All photographs were taken by the author, unless otherwise indicated in the caption line. All persons who wished to be publicly known through this publication are named in the text as they prefer to be called. Others remain anonymous or appear under changed names.

NOTE ON ORTHOGRAPHY AND TRANSCRIPTS

Because of the need to transliterate both Russian and Romani with the least amount of confusion, transliteration follows the guidelines of the American Association of Teachers of Slavic and East European Languages (AATSEEL), except for conventional spellings, such as "Maxim Gorky," and bibliographic entries, which reproduce Library of Congress entries if they exist. Other exceptions include (in Romani only) an H following the voiceless stops K, T, or P, to mark aspiration; (in both Russian and Romani) an H after Z, S, or C, which stands in for a hachek diacritic [ˇ] to indicate strident and velarized fricatives or affricatives; an "Hj" after these same letters stands in for a [´] to mark mellow palatalization of consonants (following Russian orthography as applied to written Romani). Some dialects of Vlax-Romani (such as Kelderari) deploy variant pronunciations of rolled and uvular *r* (marked respectively by "r" and "rr"), and of stop and fricative *g* (marked by "g" and "gg"). These variations are marked in transcripts, but not in already conventionalized spellings ("Roma") since not all dialects in Russia (such as Lovari and Xeladytka) would deploy them.

In transcripts containing both transliterated Russian and Romani, roman typeface indicates the matrix language (speakers' "original" choice of language for the situation), italics the language code-switched into. Transcripts and translations from both tape and video as well as from dialogue reproduced from field notes appear throughout. These are distinguished from each other by parenthetical remarks, such as "audiotape interview," etc. Not all dialogue gives the original Russian or Romani: excerpts that illustrate code-switching between Romani and Russian, or that include special poetic or performative speech, give original Romani and Russian transcripts as line-by-line translation. A double slash (//) in some dialogues signifies a point where the speaker is interrupted or resumes speaking. The author is responsible for all translations, with special thanks to Ian Hancock and Victor Friedman.

Introduction

In winter 1992, the Moscow Romani Theater staged a Sunday matinee of a musical drama entitled *Gypsy*. The play had been in the repertoire for years, having been adapted from a 1960s novel that also spun off a film and more than one television series.[1] The hero of *Gypsy* is a Gypsy World War II veteran, Budulaj. A Nazi tank killed his wife eighteen years ago, and now he travels the Russian countryside, seeking kin and army comrades, along the way fighting prejudice and enlightening the "wild" Gypsy nomads. The story is well-known, and while it incorporates relatively progressive images of "New Soviet Gypsies," it also weaves in familiar ones that typecast the Gypsy as a natural performer. At the matinee, a small audience of Russian pensioners hummed along with the familiar melodies. One of them exceeded the nostalgia of the rest, however, by trying to physically enter the mythic, recent past on the stage: he drunkenly stumbled through the dark down the central aisle, waving his arms and crying out, "Budulaj, Budulaj!" Ignoring stairs on the side, he swung his leg up onto the floorboards and staggered over to embrace the actor playing Budulaj. He was stopped, "Go back to the audience — you are disturbing the work of the collective," cried the actor playing a Russian journalist. The other actors nervously improvised an exit, while an usher led the credulous drunk down the stairs, past the marble proscenium arch, which in 1992 still was carved with Soviet airplanes and stars.

The Problem: Representation and Memory

By the mid-1990s, those decorations had been removed from the proscenium. But less visible performance frames — or, more important, assumptions about what they are and how they separate "life" from "art" — continue to inform social categories, as do "transgressed" frames. Pan-European ontologies posit an infinite regress of prosceniums, one that I argue underwrites many social and racial distinctions. In Russia, this regress and those distinctions intersect a peculiarly forceful engagement with "Gypsy performance." In some ways, this engagement distinguishes being Romani in Russia from being Romani in the United States or in nearby Eastern Europe. Oppositions between what is "staged" and what is "real life" buttress social and racial distinctions to structure Soviet and post-Soviet stereotypes about Gypsies (and behavior toward Roma) in particular ways. As far as Roma themselves are concerned, these oppositions and stereotypes have catalyzed certain kinds of Romani self-consciousness, but to fixate upon them would exclude more particular accounts of experience and memory.

I first noticed the relevance of intersections between performance and social categories in 1988 in the city then known as Leningrad, where I heard Russians speak with ambivalence about Gypsies. On the one hand, they would exalt them as "nature's poor sons," citing poetry by Alexander Pushkin that they said "captured Gypsy song," as if transcending the everyday. On the other hand, in speaking of Gypsies outside the realm of poetry or theater, they would curl their lips and speak of smells, bare feet, lies, and fingers reaching for money.[2] This book treats such images of Gypsy song or street life not as organizing truths but as threads of encounter among many others. Even as hegemonic images in public discourse, these threads are ones that Roma alternately internalize, reject, or are indifferent to.

While such images dominate public representation and limit Romani self-representation, ultimately there is also another story to tell about Roma in 1990s Russia. Several demographic and political factors differentiate that story from the one told about Roma elsewhere in Europe. To start, Roma are fewer and more widely dispersed in Russia than in East Europe, where they comprise a sizable portion of the population: the 1989 Soviet census numbers almost 153,000 Roma in all of Russia (Liegois [1994:34] estimates 400,000), compared to, say, 600,000 in much smaller Hungary.[3] In Russia, racist groups are more likely to attack Africans or Abkhazians, whereas in Ukraine, Romania, the Czech Republic, and elsewhere, skinheads target specifically Roma. Perhaps because of these differences, it is possible (for now) to write a book about Roma in Russia that, while addressing processes of discrimination, does not dwell on the supposed helplessness of a "cast-off" people, but instead treats Romani agency in everyday social life seriously by concentrating on metadiscourse about that life.

Though grounded in the present, much of that metadiscourse evokes memory, whether remembered events or remembered texts. Gypsies are usually depicted not only as people "without history" but as indifferent to recollection, living in an "eternal present." For instance, the fact that the world knows so little about Nazi liquidations of Roma is blamed on lack of Romani interest or even on alleged Gypsy taboos on remembering the dead. However, memory must be broadcast and magnified to become known, and not only have Roma lacked access to mass media, but most Roma who survived World War II have been living in states that prohibited memorials of atrocities that laid bare their racial logic.[4] Budulaj suffers, but he suffers as does any other Soviet veteran, not *because* he is a Gypsy. In the Soviet Union relevant layers of Romani memory, whether they find a place in public media or not, span numerous shifts in Soviet policy. In the 1920s, for example, the USSR was the first state to cultivate written Romani, only to neglect it by the late 1930s. And though it continued to nurture Romani intellectuals and performers, it forbade them to attend World Romani Union conferences until 1990. All of these events, and memory about them, work their way into Romani discourse about social life.

Such events, policies, and stereotypes have impressed themselves upon Romani communities in Russia in particular ways. Usually, Gypsies are typecast as untouched by any government, as rebellious wanderers always at the borders of nations and centuries, to which Gypsies relate as "parasites." This typecasting, even in Russia, often goes so far as to deny any local Gypsy commitment, religious or national. Yet, although Roma are mostly marginal to state politics and circles of elites, and though they are dispersed across every country colonized by Europe, Roma nevertheless are and speak of themselves as connected to local places and pasts. This may be a banal point, but it is one lost in nearly every novel and newspaper article about Gypsies, even in many scholarly monographs. While many scholars would no longer assume that only state-controlling majorities comprise "real" (or "host") societies, it remains commonplace to *define* "Gypsy culture" only by features or practices that seem to isolate Gypsies from a majority. This book, by contrast, grounds Romani social life within the borders of Soviet and post-Soviet Russia.

Impressions of uprootedness are propped up by the way in which Romani histories are usually told in public media, that is, as only adjunct to the histories of states. For instance, at the Moscow Romani Theater, a musical titled *My — Tsygane (We Are Gypsies)* traces the Romani migration from India to Persia, across the Balkans, up through Western Europe, and finally eastward back to Russia. Along the way, Bizet's (or Mérimée's) Carmen represents fiery Spain, and Hugo's Ezmerelda, clerical Italy. The beckoning voices of a Russian folk choir herald the Gypsies' arrival to their "second homeland," Russia. Such scenes mark out European political boundaries, using Gypsies as emblems for diverse nation states rather than tracing the lives and acts of particular Roma at the various sites of diaspora. But without such particular histories, we cannot understand what it means to be Romani; there never actually lived an abstract Gypsy, "nowhere and everywhere." The image of wandering leads to faulty abstractions about diaspora: all humans travel and shift. The challenge may be less to construct a "nomadology" for Gypsies (cf. Deleuze and Gautteri 1987:23) than to see that Roma, too, belong to places. Particular histories, and the numerous quotidian discursive performances that recent and distant memory narrate, make it apparent that Roma do not see themselves as mere guests; they *earnestly* see themselves as simultaneously Romani and a number of other things, be it Russian, Soviet, Orthodox, or "black."

I stress "earnestly" because Gypsies are hardly ever depicted as sincere players. Gypsies have instead been ascribed a reputation as natural performers. Pan-European tropes of stage performance characterize stereotypic Gypsy occupations (fortune-telling, violin playing, begging), which are all described as sorts of playacting. Meanwhile, Roma who do *not* engage in such work are seen to be assimilated or as no longer authentic. Performance, both as a category of cultural activity itself and as a trope extended to other social practices, is thus a crucial lens through which to understand Romani life in Russia.

A few words are in order on the politics of representation, in both senses of the term. Roma lack representatives in Russian political bodies as well as the means to visibly represent themselves in the media; they have little power even to name themselves in such media. In Russian, Roma are often lumped in with several other peoples, all as *tsygane*. This term, along with German *Zigeuner*, Hungarian *Cigany*, and various others throughout Europe and Turkey, derive from the Greek *atsinganoi*. Its etymology is uncertain, but one often proposed is that it derives from the name of a heretical sect to whom Roma may have been likened. In English, Roma and other groups, such as Irish Travelers, are lumped together under the name "*Gypsies,*" the English term being a derivative of "Egyptians." Roma who arrived in Western Europe in the fifteenth century were mistakenly thought to come from Egypt; the fact that Romani is an Indic language had yet to be discovered. Roma in East European countries only began to name themselves "Roma" in public in the late 1980s, and the mass media switched only in the mid-1990s from variations of "tsygane." In Russia, however, despite the existence since 1931 of the Moscow Romani Theater—with "Romani" prominently on its façade—"tsygane" was still used in the press to the exclusion of "Roma" even as late as 1997.

The label "tsygane" can deprecate in a way that "Roma," used in Russia in the 1990s *only* by Roma, cannot, though the word has less derogatory force in Moscow, where some people color it "romantic," than in Bucharest, for example. Roma sometimes speak of themselves as tsygane, whether ironically, or to cater to non-Romani interlocutors, or with indifference. In this book, rather than eschewing the words "tsygan" or "Gypsy" as potential slurs, or interchanging "Gypsy" and "Romani" randomly, as some authors have done (some perhaps confused by the fact that Roma use both), I use both to convey subtle shadings in discourse, for the shifts are not arbitrary. I use either term in quotes to report direct speech, tsygan or Gypsy without quotes to indicate stereotypy, and Roma (plural), Romni (feminine singular), Rom (masculine singular), and Romani (adjective) to denote individuals or collectives. In this way, I can more faithfully describe verbal interactions, to untangle what speakers express by preferring certain terms in certain situations.[5]

Fieldwork and Networks

My observations are drawn from three years of fieldwork with Roma and other Soviet (and then post-Soviet) peoples in Moscow, in Moscow suburbs, in villages just beyond a 100-kilometer-radius around Moscow, and in the Urals. The period extends from 1988 to 1997, the longest stay being two years from August 1991 to 1993. Fieldwork was supplemented with archival research and mass media surveys; from 1995 to 1996 I worked in Prague monitoring the East European press on Romani issues. I rely heavily on transcripts and on interactions that included me; I do not introduce this material for autobiographical reasons but because my presence as a foreigner evoked explicit discourse about performance and authenticity and about particular kinds of foreignness, topics key to understanding intersections of performance frames with social kinds.

My "fields" were networks of Roma and others and covered city, suburbs, and countryside. The research was thus "multi-sited" (Marcus 1995) and was neither a "village ethnography" nor a broad survey. Methods were also multiple. In addition to interviewing, attending ritual events, accompanying people on errands, and so on, I combed state archives and collected media recordings to translate with various consultants. In 1993, I videotaped for two weeks and watched the resulting documentary (Lemon and Nakamura 1995) with participants.

As it turned out, I conducted fieldwork during a time that many Soviets were describing as "catastrophic" and "transitional."[6] During this time, the country went through an attempted coup and several elections, referenda, and changes of currency. Metro stops and streets were renamed; the guerrilla iconoclasm already familiar in broadcasts from Eastern Europe since 1989 sprang up in Russia, too, though its monuments were not eradicated so cleanly as elsewhere in that region. This book, however, does not privilege crisis and contestation; even images of social chaos mined decades-old layers of memory, habit — and TV reruns. For instance, the repertoire at the Romani theater, with its run of plays dramatizing socialist assimilation, *did not change* until the mid-1990s, and even then most of the old productions were retained, though located differently in public culture.

Public culture is more than mere scenery backing Romani social life. This became clear to me in 1989, when I met Roma in Chicago. On Saturdays, in exchange for a language lesson in Kalderash Romani (one of the Vlax dialects), I cleaned and later helped with cooking (readers who may be convinced that Romani pollution rules would forbid this will note that even *gazhje* [non-Roma] can be taught). These Roma lived in a second-floor apartment carpeted in white plush, owned a VCR, microwave, and dishwasher, and wore Izod shirts and Keds — *and* they also spoke Romani, socialized with Roma, and felt the events of their lives to unfold *Romanes* (in the manner of Roma). Their America overlapped mine: Hollywood films, Halloween costumes, the fate of "our boys" in Iraq mattered to them, too. That overlap, and the fact that they connected their words to broader cultural landscapes like anyone else, did not make them less Romani.

This also implied to me then that being Romani in the Soviet Union must be different from in the United States. Very little ethnography, whether in the USSR[7] or in the West, has dealt with differences among Roma or with how state policies contributed to those differences, even within a single state. For instance, the Soviet state treated Romani groups that had lived in Russia for five hundred years one way and those that had arrived from Eastern Europe at the cusp of the twentieth century another. European policies often have articulated a gradient social scale from "our Gypsies" to "foreign Gypsies" (see Hubschmannova 1998:234).

Though I address how Roma and non-Roma construct these differences and relate them to policy, public culture, and performance, I do fail to describe *all* self-named Romani groups in Russia. Groups such as Xeladytka (Russka) Roma,[8] for instance, are represented here only by urban performers or intellectuals; Crimean or Muslim Roma hardly at all; while Vlax Roma may seem overrepresented. Though my research extended over several years and various groups and families, I chose to limit field "breadth" to achieve greater ethnographic "depth" over time.

Romani groups in Russia are not distinguished in the press, but scholars label them according to dialect and political geography. Russian-language sources (Ploxinskij 1890; Barranikov 1931; Demeter and Cherenkov 1987; Druts and Gessler 1991) describe three periods of Romani immigration into the Russian Empire. Roma had already been in Western Europe since the early fifteenth century, about half a millennium after the first proto-Romani speakers left India; they had moved west and north, with some then turning east into Russia. The first period saw Roma move from the Balkans and Wallachia into Ukraine in the mid-fifteenth century, and also from Poland into Belarus and the Baltics by around 1501. About two hundred years later, more Roma moved from Germany and Poland into the Baltics and central Russia. Most Roma who settled in the north came to be called Russka or Xeladytka Roma; in the south, Ukrainska or Servi Roma. A third wave in the nineteenth century included Roma from Wallachia, Moldova, and Austro-Hungarian lands, groups such as Lovara and Kelderara (together with later-arriving Ungri and Machvaya groups) labeled Vlax Roma. Some Vlax were counted in imperial territory, starting with the annexation of Moldova, but they began appearing in central Russia mostly after the 1860s abolition of slavery in Wallachian lands. A series of smaller, disparate migrations continued throughout the twentieth century, clus-

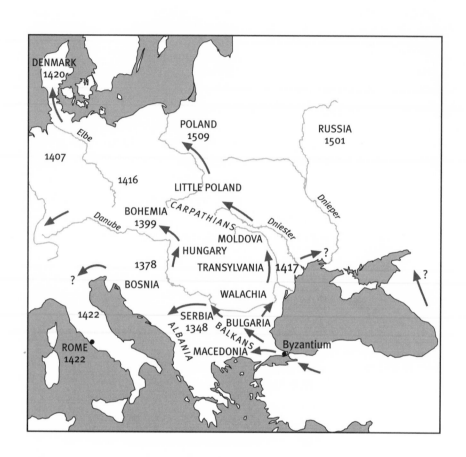

DENMARK
1420

Elbe

1407

1416

POLAND
1509

RUSSIA
1501

LITTLE POLAND

Dnieper

BOHEMIA
1399

CARPATHIANS

Danube

Dniester

MOLDOVA

HUNGARY

1378

TRANSYLVANIA

1417

?

BOSNIA

WALACHIA

?

1422

SERBIA

BULGARIA

ALBANIA

1348

BALKANS

ROME
1422

MACEDONIA

Byzantium

8

tered around the two world wars, after the Revolution, and again from the late 1970s. These were mostly Vlax Roma, but there were also non-Vlax, including families of Sinte from Germany and non-Romani speaking Beash Gypsies from Moldova.

Predecessors of Romani-speaking people left northwest India about one thousand years ago. Media and literature have consistently portrayed these migrations as expressing inherent nomadism rather than as historically motivated. Since the nineteenth century, accounts of original movements have assumed that Roma must have descended from "wandering" criminal and untouchable castes of entertainers and refuse carriers, projecting current Romani poverty in Europe onto all moments of a Romani past.[9] To support such theories, many cite the phonetic correspondence of the ethnonyms, *Rom, Lom, Dom* with the Sanskrit *Domba,* or cite Firdausi's poem chronicling a fifth-century gift by the king of Sindh of twelve thousand musicians (called Luri) to the Persian ruler.[10]

However, Romani and Indian scholars argue that the original diaspora was a mixture of upper-caste warriors, perhaps Rajputs, with mixed-caste and Dravidian camp followers (Hancock 1995a:16–25 and 1999; Kochanowski 1968). They place the proto-Romani movements later (as do most scholars) and show that it could have been motivated by early-eleventh-century military incursions of Afghani and Turk forces, the Mahmud of Ghazni.[11] Moving west after Ghaznavid incursions, they argue that these mixed groups coalesced and perhaps absorbed other traders or refugees along the Silk Road. Roma then lived for centuries in Persia before migrating into Byzantine, Caucasian, and Balkan lands. Far from being aimless wanderings, their movements into Europe were likewise probably motivated by military invasions, this time by Ottoman Turks.[12]

The image of drifting nomadism, however, persists even though most Roma in the Balkans and Carpathians[13] and in Ukraine and Russia were settled by the eighteenth century or earlier. In 1990s Russia, most Roma of my acquaintance had lived their entire lives in a single city, village, or house. Even those Vlax families who had been nomadic until forced settlement in the late 1950s had lived in villages or towns near extended family since then. It was not they, but I who moved between regions and cities—not to mention across Soviet and then Russian borders. As a foreigner researcher, and a moving one, my presence evoked questions about the borders I crossed; I was variously identified as "the American," "from Moscow," or even "just back from visiting Kelderara." These identities and affiliations facilitated some relationships but blocked others, evoked certain genres of question, and performed certain kinds of relations.

Some people warned me that, because I was a foreigner, no Gypsy would ever speak openly to me. "Aren't you afraid?" Russian friends would bait. But this was perhaps a particular twist to a generalized xenophobia; the Soviet state had long negatively sanctioned connections abroad and kept track even of many internal social connections. Even in 1993, some post-Soviets behaved as if this were still so, taking care not to identify acquaintances by surname. Still, both Russian and Romani intelligentsia character-ized Gypsies as *particularly* "closed." Many post-Soviets added to the image of Gypsy exclusivity one of clannish interconnection, a single low-tech network of gossip, the "Gypsy post office" *(tsyganskaja pochta).* Soviet eth-nography and journalism linked such "clannishness" with primitivity and criminality, and Roma were aware that being branded as clannish rendered them suspect. They also knew that the state had kept records of family relations (not only those of Roma) to identify "class background," and some knew that Nazis had collected Romani genealogies (commissioned from anthropologists, to establish degrees of racial "purity").[14] Thus older Roma perhaps *were* even less inclined than other Soviets to reveal social and familial relations, but for reasons of history, not clan consciousness.[15]

All the same, even coming in the wake of decades of arrests for associa-tion with bourgeois foreigners, as an *amerikanka* I shared the counter-system cachet of foreign commodities, was a potential trading partner, a useful trophy acquaintance, a translator of Stevie Wonder lyrics, and an interesting interlocutor from a faraway place, especially for people under forty. That is, Roma were not so "closed" as I had been warned.

Still, meeting Roma through networks was more comfortable for every-one than approaching Roma at random or alone (say, on the street). The first time I chatted with a Romani woman at a bazaar, she did not return the next day as promised. Machvane women begging outside the Central Tele-graph office once invited me to visit them and joked about arranging a marriage with one of their brothers, but the police drove them away as soon as I stepped into the Telegraph to post a letter. Beash along the Arbat (a central Moscow tourist drag that has preserved its antique buildings and cobblestones) or outside McDonald's would not respond to questions in Romani or in Russian, whether Romani acquaintances or I tried to speak to them. The streets may be a typical backdrop against which Gypsies are depicted, but this was not where I usually met Roma.

But even social dead ends were instructive. Each time someone introduced me to a new person or group — or refused to introduce me — I learned something about how well they trusted both me and each other, something about their solidarity or dissociation. One person might forbid me to speak to his own close kin, while another would readily introduce me to wide circles of acquaintances. Some showed me off as an American acquaintance, while others passed me off as a visiting cousin "to avoid awkward questions." Intellectual Roma tried to cloister me at home, reluctant to release me to the bazaar, where I might see "uncivilized Gypsies." Other Roma tried to recruit me to come work at the bazaar, even if they, too, asserted their status as "civilized" over other Roma they saw there. In the infrequent public contexts where Roma from different groups came together, people remarked upon those others with whom I sat, spoke, or laughed.

I started fieldwork at the Moscow Romani Theater. Like the streets, the Theater was a highly visible site of "Gypsiness," though also atypical for the Western imagination of Gypsies, being an occupational home for urban Romani intellectuals. In addition, the Theater, as an institution that produced and publicized Gypsy performances, connected more Roma from across the country than could any mythic tsyganskaja pochta. Moreover, the interest of a foreigner in theatrical performance was perhaps seen as less potentially controversial than nosing about semilicit street markets.

Still, many people discouraged me from beginning research at the Romani Theater or with the Romani urban intelligentsia: they were not "authentic." I would not meet "real Gypsies" if I wasted time at the Theater, declared two Russian folklorists I met briefly in early spring 1990. They together had collected and published several volumes of Gypsy songs and stories, and a historical survey based on archives and oral accounts (Druts and Gessler 1985, 1988, 1990, 1991). During that first and only meeting, they grilled me on Russian Gypsy choral music, showed exotic photographs of impoverished villages, and stressed that I would get nowhere without their help. They promised to take me to see the "wild" *(dikije)* Gypsies of a "real Gypsy camp" — on the condition that I first read a number of nineteenth-century musicologists and bring them some batteries.

Some Romani intellectuals shared criteria of authenticity with the folklorists, dividing Gypsies into two kinds ("wild" and "civilized"). They too did not consider the Romani Theater to be real, and defined genuine Gypsy folk art as rooted *either* in the countryside or in the urban past of tsarist-era Gypsy choirs; even some whose relatives worked at the Theater said so. In winter 1990 I met Nadezhda Demeter, a Romani ethnographer, and she invited me to visit her family; that fall I stayed with them for a month. During this stay I began to feel the heat surrounding questions of who controls representation of Roma. Such questions are salient throughout Eastern Europe, especially since the late 1980s, because many Roma see non-Romani involvement in Romani issues as intrusive and mercenary. Indeed, none of the nongovernmental organizations in Europe that dispense funds or influence policy affecting Roma are headed by Roma. In Moscow, the Demeters accused Russian folklorists of stealing cultural texts, such as song lyrics, to skim cash similarly from their publication.

Still, Demeter's 1988 dissertation, though limited by Soviet policy discourse, also divided Rome into two kinds, assimilated vs. nomadic. Based on interviews with her relatives and finished just as glasnost was gathering steam, like much Soviet ethnography it urged the liquidation of particular kinds of customs, while asserting that the October Revolution already had transformed life. By the time I met her, however, Demeter was arguing for cultural revival of certain prerevolutionary practices. A video of her son's arranged wedding in 1991 pointedly recorded the public display of bridal virginal blood, her *patjiv* (honor), though the dissertation had taken pains to show that the Revolution had erased such rites. For a "native ethnographer" in the Soviet Union, the issue of what constituted a "real Gypsy" was personal as well as scholarly, and not easily resolved (see also Balzer 1995): "civilization" threatened the erasure of "culture" (*kul'tura*) but also promised status and "culturedness" (*kul'turnost'*). These concerns dovetailed with many late-Soviet cultural revivalisms and anxieties about cultural loss.[16]

Worry that "civilization" contradicted cultural "authenticity" plagued not only Romani intellectuals, but Romani performers, too. Those who spoke Russian at home worried that doing so entailed wholesale "loss of culture." Those living with standard Soviet decor (Central Asian carpets on the sitting-room wall; glass cases for china, books, and knickknacks; plastic chandeliers in tiny kitchens, maybe a crystal one in the living room; lace curtains; television and VCR) marked their flats as Romani with portraits and photographs of famous Romani singers (often kin), calendars with pictures of horses, a seven-string guitar, and picture books and scholarly tomes written about Roma. Such people were concerned that I form impressions of the right Roma in the right settings, in ways that seemed to me inconsistent. Some offered to introduce me to "authentic, wild Gypsies" in their "camps" (actually, their villages) while warning me to avoid what may have been the very same Roma at the bazaars. Others would introduce me only to Romani scholars and professionals and take me to the Romani Theater and to restaurant performances, but then discourage me from research at the Theater or with intellectuals because they were not "authentic."

To escape these problematic limitations, I tried to be introduced to actors at the Romani Theater via multiple routes. First, I attended performances on my own, having in 1990 obtained the gracious permission of the main artistic director, Nikolaj Slichenko, to speak to actors. I was occasionally given free tickets and allowed into the dressing rooms, but could not witness rehearsals; as actors later complained, the repertoire had not changed in years, so there were no rehearsals. Despite permissions, backstage interviews rarely transcended official rhetoric about the Romani Theater as a place to "achieve internationality" or to "perform the Russian classics with a Gypsy flavor." This was not because Roma in particular were "closed and clannish" but because Soviet theater politics were, as elsewhere, tangled by censorship and cronyism. Romani actors especially could not afford to provoke the administration—the Romani Theater was an ethnic "ghetto," and there were no other theaters where Romani performers could find work.

I met my most helpful Theater consultant through a Russian academic who brought me to the home of one of the lead actresses in 1991. She described herself as "half" Gypsy and was married to a Russian man; in her home there were none of the usual portraits of Romani performers or emblematic Gypsy horseshoes. Still, the first time we visited her house, she played the "Gypsy singer." Assuming that my interest in "Gypsy culture" was driven by a thirst for the exotic, she exclaimed that "we must provide you some colorful material" and began a tale about a grandfather horse thief. But as I began to visit her regularly, she spoke more often about the stage as a profession and sometimes took a distant stance toward other

Roma, speaking of "them" in the third person plural. Over the years, she filled me in on backstage gossip, explained dancing and singing techniques, and gave her own subtle interpretations of "Gypsy stage style."

In time, several non-Roma introduced me to Roma, although often these Roma turned out to be related to those I already knew. For instance, a Russian who taught Indian dance in the Moscow Children's Gypsy Choir and who danced in other Gypsy ensembles (even passing onstage for a Gypsy) took me to visit Romani villages south of Moscow where the Roma had kin in other villages I knew north of the city. She also introduced me to elderly performers with whom she had studied dance, one of whom, Olga Stepanovna Demeter, turned out to be a relative of the ethnographer. Olga insisted I take lessons with her too, and in 1997 gave me a copy of her memoirs (Demeter-Charskaja 1997).[17]

Gradually, a few other Theater actors invited me to safer ground at home. For instance, in the spring of 1992, an older actress asked me to visit and read through her mother-in-law's personal papers, for she had been buried a full year and the appropriate time had passed to sort her things. The deceased had been a Romani activist in the 1920s and early 1930s who translated textbooks and socialist pamphlets from Russian into Romani on topics from hygiene to the emancipation of women from patriarchal, "rigid" customs. Along the way, her son and his wife gave me still another veteran actor's angle on Theater gossip and performance styles.

Occasionally, when acquaintances learned that I was visiting others, they voiced anxiety or tension. Similar tensions about loyalty pervaded sites of stage performance and rehearsal themselves, sometimes among Roma, sometimes between Roma and gazhje. In the summer of 1992, Theater acquaintances invited me to observe several weeks of a film shoot featuring seasoned actors from the Theater or their relatives. On the set, the actors and the crew were polarized, more so than at the Theater, it seemed, perhaps because the Theater was at least publicly headed by a Rom. The Russian crew were troubled when I ate with the Romani actors; and similarly, the Romani actors seemed uneasy after I spoke a long time with the Russian director.

Away from the stage, spending time with Romani nonperformers similarly complicated relations with Romani performers. I met many of these nonperformers, in fact, on the grounds of the Romani Theater. Adjunct to the theater was an acting studio for adolescent Roma. (Despite images of

FIGURE 1   Gilorri. A young dancer listens to advice a few minutes before an outdoor performance, her mother standing close by. Audience members on this occasion in 1991 (as on others) questioned whether she was an "authentic Gypsy" because she had blond hair. Sometimes the choir director addressed such doubts publicly before appearances.

naturally expressive Gypsies, the next generation needed to be trained. Their teachers appealed to method principles, although they told half-hearted children to "turn up the emotional pitch a notch" to portray a "real Gypsy," a decidedly non-Stanislavskian direction).[18] They were mostly children of performers — but not exclusively. The Moscow Children's Gypsy Ensemble, Gilorri ("Little Song" in Romani), also rehearsed at the Romani Theater, and many members were performers' children. But several were brought in by Romani mothers with aspirations of upward cultural mobility. There were even a few children brought in by Russian mothers eager for their girls to learn "Gypsy dance." Gilorri was directed by another relative of Nadezhda Demeter, her cousin Vladislav Petrovich Demeter. The children performed "Gypsy stage," "Romani folk," and "Indian-style" dances, staging them at Houses of Culture, local township celebrations near Moscow, and even at the Palace of the Soviets. By late September 1991, I was attending rehearsals twice a week, taking photographs for the director to use for publicity, and teaching English, a role that continued through 1993 at the Romani Sunday school. Urban Romani intellectuals and performers, concerned that their children were "losing their culture," had established the Sunday school with funding from UNESCO, and it was attended mostly by the members of Gilorri.

The parents or older kin who brought the children to rehearsals sometimes would argue with the ensemble leaders over how to represent "Gypsiness" on stage, as when the director wanted to remove a Romani word for vodka (*brvinta,* in Russka dialect) from a song to render it appropriate for children, while the mothers, concerned about tradition, would not hear of such lexical meddling. But more often, while the children rehearsed, their mothers and grandmothers would sit in an adjoining room and lament pan-Soviet problems — prices, the 1991 coup attempt, the many varieties of sausage available "before perestroika." They would discuss minority issues, such as the treatment of "blacks" by police and thugs on the streets. Sitting with these women, listening to their nostalgic discussions, and asking advice about how to find food led to further introductions and hospitality — even after one of the directors warned me not to accept invitations, adding ominously, "You don't know what a Gypsy, especially a Gypsy woman, might do."

These acquaintances snowballed: one grandmother from the performer / intellectual contingent took me to meet her sister, a retired performer who had also worked as a consultant for film crews and who was hoping to render similar services to me. At our first meeting, she read aloud her screenplay dramatizing a feud between "civilized" and "wild" Gypsy in-laws during World War II. She took pride both in being educated and in "maintaining ties with the wild Gypsies in the *tabor* [Rus. camp]." Herself a child of parents who claimed origins in several different Romani groups, and having a Russian ex-husband, she described authentic identities roiled by transgressions of ethnic borders, tradition polluted by modernity. The screenplay then twisted around what was to her a familiar motif of conflict over rules regulating gendered behavior, the difficulty encountered by an urban Romani *bori* ("bride," "daughter-in-law," "sister-in-law")[19] who must adjust to the "stricter" rules in a nomadic Romani family.

To make the film, she needed capital; I lacked it and could offer only to interview her and pay her for interviews "American style," as she put it (she had been burned in the past by nonreciprocal foreigners, and preferred calculation up front). Over the next several months she would dictate recollections (her own and her parents') of traditions, and on holidays take me to "see the customs of real Gypsies" living near Moscow. She was herself gathering impressions of "beautiful customs" to use in the film, and her visits to the *tabor* both reinforced fictive kin ties (she was godmother to many) and gave her the opportunity to collect what she called "ethnography" for her film. Actually, our first such trip fell together without her planning. In the autumn of 1991, I was interviewing her cousin about the evacuation of the Romani Theater from Moscow during World War II, when the telephone rang.[20] A Moscow television program had called looking for someone to "take them to the Gypsies" to shoot a documentary spot. After hanging up, the cousin proposed that I come along with my camera to take photographs for him. On the appointed day, however, he fell ill and sent his cousin in his place.

At what turned out to be a Kelderari village, the consultant established distant kin ties with the eldest grandmother and explained that the Russians wanted to film them. At first, the Kelderara mistook me for her relative and my awkward Romani for an American dialect. I clarified that I was a Gazhji from the United States, which piqued their curiosity — a few pried me away from the TV crew to feed me and request songs in English ("Feelings" and anything by Stevie Wonder). Far from being "closed" to the outside world, they posed numerous informed questions: Do Americans really eat dry flakes of crunchy pressed grain with milk for breakfast, as on TV? How much does a Ford Escort cost? Do you go to church? Do you think Bush or Clinton will win the election?

I began visiting that village on my own, taking the electric train from Moscow for several days at a time, especially for celebrations at Christmas, the New Year, and Easter, and the godparent tributes staged on the days after. On such days, each house displayed a table with pyramids of oranges, roast chickens, and clustered bottles of fruit liquor, vodka, and cognac. Each family would visit its godparents' homes, following behind the accordion, criss-crossing the snow (on Christmas) or the mud (at Easter): the best-tramped paths marked the way to the most popular godparents. "Ordinary" days I spent with those women and children left home after other women had gone to work selling small items at the bazaar or reading palms at the train station. The men would either be outdoors in welding suits, driving commissioned repair work back to clients, or getting new orders.

The women would come home at the end of the day with plastic bags full of medium-grade sausage, bread, potatoes, more rarely some chicken or beef. Whether with Roma in the city or in the village, gendered divisions of the social world affected with whom I could speak alone and with whom only in company; in the village, the evening return of the women drew me more fully into adult interactions (though I slept in the children's room). An ideology of male authority accompanied notions of proper visibility of women and interaction across genders (though sometimes the feminine was nonetheless foregrounded in expressions of village identity, as in family photographs or the retellings of the eldest matriarch's biography). In the village, gender more than ethnicity structured ideas about "front- or back-stage," of what should be visible and what not.

At any rate, a year after my first stay with Romani intellectuals and actors in 1990, I was spending more and more time with Roma distant from professional performance, even though most had heard of the more famous performers, and some were even personally acquainted with them. But though I visited the Romani Theater less frequently, talking about theatrical and media performance remained a way to prompt Roma to compare themselves to Russians, to other Soviets, or to other Roma, and it was often in reference to the Theater that they would anchor their memories to state histories or to literary texts.

Whether I presented my main research focus as "performance" or "ordinary life," many people rejected the idea of a study of Gypsies that would connect the two. Once, in the spring of 1991, during a break at the studio during which teenage Roma had grilled me about Michael Jackson and Prince (whom they had heard was half-Gypsy), the assistant music teacher, a young Russophone Armenian, inquired what so interested me about Gypsies. Used to assumptions that my main interest should lie in Gypsy music, I told her that to the contrary I was also interested in Romani "daily life" (Rus. *byt*) offstage. She raised an eyebrow: "What for? All they do is speculate." Such dismissal of the social realities surrounding performance or of the ways representations echoed in daily life was a common reaction.

By August 1991, I already had begun to speak to such "speculators." At first, I had only hoped to ask how they interpreted stage imagery and how they evaluated the performers. The former question did not evoke much interest, since the nonperformers did not often check their own actions against stage images. However, they did describe a "really Romani" way of interacting, but differently than did the performers. These differences seemed connected to ways they imagined lines to be drawn (or not drawn) between the categories life and art.

Recognizing those differences in borders forced me also to rethink how "tradition" was framed and performed in social life. For example, in summer 1991, a teenage Romani girl (a beginner at the studio, who soon quit) invited me to a birthday party beyond the Moscow suburbs; I stayed at the party for two days, not yet knowing the way back to the city. So that she could guide me there, the day of the party we met at the first Moscow McDonald's, the one across from Pushkin's monument—she appeared wearing short lycra bicycle pants, and I was shocked, because until then Roma I had met always insisted that Romani women never wore pants or short skirts. I had seen exceptions rarely, and usually only at home. Only later, when she caught sight of male cousins approaching through the gate of her house's courtyard, did she bolt upstairs to change into a long skirt; neither the gaze of the male gazhje in the city or of her own brother at home had catalyzed such action. What framed her self-presentation was not gendered identity alone, but the ways her understanding of its moral imperative contingently intersected her social location.

In this family and in other Vlax families, men and women lived more separate lives than Romani urban intellectuals (or even Vlax families in Chicago), spending most of their time in separate rooms (for instance, a few months later, at a large funeral party held in the same girl's house, the women cloistered in the kitchen, leaving the dining room to the men). Still, these separations had to be performed, were sometimes transgressed, and thus often became topics for reflection and comparison to other people.

By early December 1991, other Roma, in particular Vlax Lovara, began to take up much more of my time than any other Roma, with the result that I devote the most attention to Lovara in this text. I met Lovara also first at the Theater. Several Lovara children came sporadically to Gilorri rehearsals, although their mothers kept aloof from the others, not joining the discussion circle on sausage and, as I discovered later, irritated that the directors instructed in Russian. They bridged this distance in the falll of 1991, when I attended a press conference on minorities at the Palace of Soviets where Gilorri and several other Romani groups entertained. One of the Lovari mothers saw me translate there for Romani delegates from Romania and decided to invite me home.

FIGURE 2   Draga and Rubinta with a granddaughter, dressed for Easter in 1992

She and her sister lived a few kilometers apart, just outside the suburbs of Moscow. Their households were headed respectively by her mother-in-law and their mother, both widows, who commanded the loose allegiance of dozens of descendants. However, it was the middle-aged sisters (also widowed) who actually performed this alliance through their own daily cooperation in arranging commerce and celebrations. There was much movement between the households; younger people and children often spent the night at each other's houses, ten minutes away by car. One house was actually a two-house compound — the younger widow, her three children, and a son-in-law in the main house; the matriarch in the back house with her younger, living son, their *bori*, two grandchildren, and an unmarried daughter (other sons lived in Ukraine). The compound at its smallest consisted of ten people, but when relatives visited, featherbeds cushioned the floors and there was room for more than twenty.

These households, both headed by women, were not altogether typical. First, they were relatively wealthy for Roma, even among Lovara in Russia, and second, men were present irregularly, and not as fathers or husbands but as brothers, sons, and sons-in-law. However, the lack of male heads of family had not in the least decreased family prestige. The matriarchs were honored at large ritual functions; their houses always included on ritual holiday visiting rounds; the women easily organized market labor; and their daughters had suitors. There was no pressure on the widows to re-marry; on the contrary, widows were to consider themselves eternally wed to the deceased. When one actually did, several years after my original field-work, her kin were enraged. Despite similar constrictions, participation in Romani communal life did not require maleness, and despite gendered hierarchies, women could visibly lead. To be sure, when we videotaped for two weeks in 1993, younger women hid from the camera—but their hus-bands, too, displayed "shame," and women with grown children and grand-mothers did not hesitate to direct younger men how to speak or behave before the camera.

The shifting value of gendered ideals in relation to other ones shows the contingent ways cultural and social bonds are performed not only despite, but *through* what seem to be transgressions. For instance, one Lovari girl eloped with a Rom from a poorer family (the family thought the couple might be hiding in my Moscow apartment, until they surfaced in Ukraine a few months later). The mother had been hoping to match the girl with Lovara from New York City.[21] Yet the elopement was not long a scandal— afterward, to her younger cousins it became a heroic adventure; they spoke about wanting to elope like she had. In the long run, more important than her one-time transgression was her ongoing, performed deportment of herself as a cool character, savvy bargainer, stylish dresser, and so on.

What fell under scrutiny as "really Romani" was not always adherence to idealized culture, on stage or in rules. Differently framed words and prac-tices mattered just as much; people recognized them as "authentic," less be-cause they compared them to the theatrical, the literary, or the explicitly "tra-ditional" but because they could connect them to various sorts of memory.

Framing Performance

Three rationales drive the focus on performance. First, for contingent historical reasons, particular Roma became famous in Russia as stage per-formers, which structured "class" relations with those Roma who did not. Second, pan-European ideologies about performance and dramaturgic models of interaction are all too often transposed into accounts of Romani culture; these transpositions have obscured our understanding both of the social lives of Roma who are not performers, and of the social relations surrounding the stage. Third, social thought about performance and performativity, though partly limited by dramaturgic and theatrical models, offers ways to understand how and why people divide what they see as staged from what they see as everyday life or authentic politics, and ways to illuminate the import of such divisions to racial and national ideologies.

In much of Europe, "Gypsy life" is depicted as ongoing song and dance, from the castanets of Bizet's opera *Carmen* to the musical vignettes of Gatliff's film *Latcho Drom* (1994). However, in Russia the force of the mythology surrounding Gypsy performers is differently positioned than elsewhere. Choral singing began to emerge as a "Gypsy occupation" at the end of the eighteenth century, when Gypsy serf choirs were instituted on noble estates; this was the only occupation that allowed Roma to settle within the cities. Similarly, Soviet Romani elite occupational structures emerged later in and around the Romani Theater. Even in the 1990s, singing and dancing was the only high-prestige career open to most Roma, and for Roma who were not professional performers, claiming relatives at the Romani Theater was one of the only forms of symbolic and social capital they could lay claim to.

Hardly a day passed in early 1990s Russia without a Gypsy ensemble appearing, however fleetingly, on television or in film cameos.[22] There, as in much of Europe, theatricality is metonymic of Gypsy culture, writ large. Because Gypsies are defined as essentially performers, as naturally, without rehearsal or notes, in touch with the musical muses, it is all the simpler to transpose tropes of performance into descriptions of all Gypsy life. Even Roma who are not professional performers are described in theatrical terms, as born or raised with special talent for masking: the real Gypsy is a liar, and all Gypsies naturally counterfeit. The image parallels those in the United States that combine black musical talent and tricksterism, as well as many other ethnic stereotypes, such as Jewish "calculation" in Europe. But in the case of Gypsies it has important historical particularities.

Ideologies about performance condition assumptions about what separates performance from the rest of social life, yet dramaturgic models handily leak into areas of life supposedly separate from the stage. They leak in at the points where they intersect other ideologies and practices of personhood, agency, and authenticity (see Agnew 1988). These ontological leaks and intersections are signaled, in part, by overlapping terms for performance which signify both "doing" and "displaying." In English, Russian, and sometimes in Romani, the same terms oscillate between false and sincere agencies, real and counterfeit persons. For instance, the Russian verb *ispolnjat'* ("to fulfill, fill, carry out") works both in a "practical" phrase like "*ispolnjat'* a promise," but also in a "theatrical" phrase like "*ispolnjat'* the role of Hamlet," and in its metaphoric extension back to "reality," to "*ispolnjat'* a role in history." Similarly, in English one can both "execute an order" and "execute a role." The Russian *vystupat'* ("to come forward, appear") likewise works both in "break into a sweat" and in "appear on stage," while a *vystuplenije* refers to a particular staging, and a *massovoje vystuplenije* is a "mass action." "Play" in English, *igrat'* in Russian, and *khelel* (also "dance") in Vlax Romani all combine in phrases like both "play a part" (*igrat' rol', khelel p'estrado*) as well as "play with fire" (*igrat' s ognem, khelel-pe jagasa*).

The polysemy reflects a pan-European tendency, at least in late-20th-century Russia, to frame performance as separate from real life while also claiming that "all the world is a stage," and fretting that nothing is unstaged. The proscenium poses a problem of surfaces, surfaces assumed to be ontologically different from "depths" (see Clark 1995).

Among Western social theorists, Erving Goffman (1986) systematized the proscenium metaphor to describe "our western" ordering of social reality as a gradient from "pure" theater to "mixed" social interactions (work, ritual, play). Along this gradient, boundaries between performers and audiences become more or less porous (126). Following Bateson (1972), Goffman focused on "keyings" and "fabrications," modes by which people signal to each other whether they see ongoing interaction as more or less formally modeled upon some other, "original" event, as displayed, ironized, or falsified. Some original actions resist reframing, while other moments of social reality are especially vulnerable to reframing. That is, some frames are slippery and open to contestation (this is what Bateson called the "labile nature of the frame") while others resist "frame breaking," moments when one such contextual order intrudes upon another.

As Goffman recognized, the trope of the proscenium is just that, a trope, but one that carries with it cultural and historical connections with categories of agency and authenticity. In Russia, as in the West, this trope is alive, but not always and not for everyone: my interlocutors *variously* perceived "frames" or their transgression as socially significant. While many of my consultants wanted to exclude "staged" from "real" life, not all of them always did. Even during our documentary taping, although people behaved differently, and although this difference illuminated both what they saw to be appropriate performance frames and what their expectations were about social categories (people came to the fore who were not my usual interlocutors, for example), they did not maintain such frames throughout, even when they spoke as if they thought they should.

Social theory has diverged *and* overlapped precisely along lines laid out by common senses of "perform" that oppose and continue its sense as "to display" and its sense as "to do." In the ethnography of speaking, for instance, performances are moments of "verbal art" set apart from "ordinary talk," when speakers are responsible to display discursive skill (see Bauman 1977; Friedrich 1986:22–39). Many of the same ethnographers simultaneously treat performance as "doing," as a mode of social "emergence" (see Bauman 1977), revising ideas from philosophy of language about the *performativity* of speech acts. By performative speech, J. L. Austin had in mind those speech acts that, given proper institutional support, enact themselves by their utterance, such as "I now pronounce you man and wife" if uttered by a priest (Austin 1975). Symbolic anthropologists following Victor Turner have also reworked Austinian performativity to analyze ritual as enacting and producing social *roles,* while literary criticism and cultural studies have taken up performativity to describe social *identities* as made through utterance *and* display (see Butler 1990, 1998).

Not everyone writing about "performance" is always careful to separate senses of "displayed" or "framed" performance from that of "performativity." Perhaps this is right. Perhaps analytic senses of "performance" *should* run together where they *are* conflated in practice. Austin, however, was himself adamant that the two were incompatible, that ["a performative utterance is . . . when uttered on stage rendered hollow and void" (1975:22)]. As criticisms of Austin run (e.g., Derrida 1988; see also Lee 1997:49), the problem is that performatives work because they are conventional, and conventions can only become such through framed repetitions — through *performances.* Nevertheless, when necessary throughout this book, the terms "theatricality" and "performativity" will distinguish main analytic senses of "performance."

Still, to assert their separation can be misleading: how to account for any "real-world" effects of stage performance? How to avoid defanging performativity within performance? Handler and Segal (1989) for instance observe that the characters of Jane Austen's *Mansfield Park* make just this mistake when they rehearse a romantic play, and reconfigure their actual romantic relationships. Taken in by the "superficial appearance that the play is just a play," they simultaneously are "carried away by the romantic attachments performed within the frame of the play" and fail to see how the creation of performance affects their subjectivities (334) and sense of agency.

Thus, while embedding a performative utterance into a bit of theatrical business certainly *changes* its force, it nonetheless has *some* force, some social reality on both sides of the proscenium.

To both differentiate and connect performance and the performative involves unpacking ideologies about what frames them. Attention to framing necessarily involves attention not just to the "content" of stereotypes or to "images" but to their ordering and to their *indexical* meanings. Basically, indexical signs "point" to things or relations "in context" (including the frame), rather than naming or describing them. Not all signs are merely descriptive, or *referential* (see Jakobson 1960; Hymes 1974; Silverstein 1976, 1979). The American pragmatic philosopher C. S. Peirce sliced types of meaning into a trinity: icon, index, symbol. Roughly, symbols refer by convention alone; they are "arbitrary" in Saussure's sense (e.g., the word "map"). Icons and indexes are less arbitrary, more motivated — icons because they resemble their referents (an actual map, onomatopoeia); full indexical signs because they point to some thing or relationship connected to the context of their production ("east," "then," "you") — their meaning can only be determined through knowledge of relevant context. Relevant context, of course, is not limited to the "real-time" here and now but can include knowledge about the past, about social hierarchies, or about cultural and generic associations (see Hanks 1987; Duranti, Goodwin, 1992).

For an example of indexical meaning, in a 1950s play at the Romani Theater, a Gypsy stage character mispronounces the Russian "sotsializm" as "sushulizm"; the form of the "mistake" indexes, or points to the character's distance from both Russian language education and the Party line, without explicitly describing either. For an illustration of iconic meaning, consider the following: Russian folk groups wear costumes identical in color and trim, and dance in precise unison. By contrast, Gypsy ensembles wear varied colors and cuts and dance individually; their dress and movements iconically figure the winds of "free will," and also ostensibly index the loose social relations that many post-Soviets imagine to characterize the "freedom" of Gypsy society. In fact, Gypsy stage talent itself is seen as a visible manifestation of freedom and innovation, as if performance were itself always revolutionary.[23]

Because indexical signs point to social relations and contextual borders, attention to them *and to their reframings* helps trace the significance of those social relations and borders for various people. We have already considered briefly one peculiar example of such a reframing: at the Moscow Romani Theater Sunday matinee, when Budulaj's Russian fan broke up the performance, his drunken address to the actor sent indexical signs flying in unusual trajectories: "You are disturbing the work of the collective," rang the reproof. Perhaps a different ensemble might have absorbed the snafu, engaging the drunk and addressing him as "you" differently, within the play's framing of relations. But this was not what happened, and instead more habitual relations were insisted upon among audience and actors. To recognize relations indexically is to perform them, often in ways more forceful than what explicit, descriptive statements about people can accomplish.

Particularly key in recognizing reframings are discursive *shifts* and *switches*[24] in code, topic, genre, footing and voice.[25] Throughout, for instance, I discuss numerous tape-recorded conversations in which Roma code-switched among Romani, Russian, and sometimes English.[26] A *codeswitch* is often defined as a change, within or across utterances, from one code (whether classified as a language, dialect, or register) to another. Such switches, as Hill (1985), Irvine (1989), Woolard (1989), Gal (1987), and others have recently elaborated, are always evaluated within a political economy in which people have variable access to linguistic resources and in which competing language ideologies define hierarchies of codes. So, for example, officially, Russian is lionized as the language of Lenin and of Pushkin, while Romani is rarely recognized by most post-Soviets as a language at all. A code-switch is usually distinguished from a *shift* (though a shift can signal a change in code and vice versa). Indexical forms called "shifters" are what scholars such as Jakobson (1957), Friedrich (1966), and Silverstein (1976) have identified in culturally significant ways to include personal pronouns, verbal tense, and spatial deictics — the "you" that becomes "I." Here, I pay special attention to shifts and switches that signal changes in topic and more importantly, shifts in *frame* or *footing*. A "frame," to recall Bateson (1972) and Goffman, is metacommunication that tells participants what kind of interaction is ongoing — a wink modifies the threat into a joke, it reframes it. "Footing" is the attitude or stance that participants take vis-à-vis each other or to what they see as relevant context (Goffman 1974 and 1979).

However, far from delimiting clear-cut borders around "genuine Romani" realms, such apparent switches require more layered interpretation (see Hymes 1974; Hill 1985; Urciuoli 1991 and 1995). This book, therefore, does not focus on linguistic form alone, but on how both shifts and more "stable" texts were embedded within social relations, places, and practices, how they circulated through and were channeled by cultural and political institutions (see Gal 1987 and 1989; Irvine 1989).

Paying attention to indexical meaning also flashes beams onto what people perceive to limit relevant social context. Indexicality thus illuminates how my consultants constructed (or ignored) frames around (and gaps between) the "staged" and "real." These concerns had a great deal to do with how even Roma who were not performers related to the Romani theater, to the state, to Russians, and to each other, in everyday displays of verbal skill or even much more mundane talk.

Finally, indexical meaning is important because any one performance (whether a theatrical display or a formulaic performative utterance) evokes comparison with past performances. They point to memory because they cite older forms as authority, or they improvise upon them, or they attempt to overturn them (see Voloshinov 1978; Hymes 1974; Bauman 1977; Briggs 1988; Silverstein and Urban 1996). People hook their words not only to real-time, physical contexts, but to past texts and events. Since performance indexes memory especially, attention to it *can* (despite the ways theatricality connotes masking and performativity can connote improvisational "freedom" — motifs running throughout racial stereotypes about Gypsies) open up more historical ways to understand what matters to Roma in the ongoing present.

This book then moves from realms of theatricality, from representation in literature and media, to more diffuse performances and performative moments in everyday interaction, to track how ideologies about performance reproduce social, and especially racial, categories.

Chapter 1 opens with the performative power of remembered texts, of literary and mass media depictions of Gypsies, especially of Gypsy performers, to underwrite racial categories. Precisely through their historical connection to the works of canonized Russian poets, these categories have been subsumed within Russian and Soviet imperial hierarchies since the nineteenth century. Romani musical talent was not recognized as a good in itself, but instead, Gypsy song was seen as a conduit for Russian national, poetic genius. By the early 1990s, Russians and many Romani elites (drawn to these narratives because they confirmed a natural, divine origin for talent) continued to cite heavily from nineteenth-century literature, linking Gypsies to nostalgia for prerevolutionary grandeur, a time when poets frequented "Gypsy choirs." Descriptions of Gypsies continued to trigger shifts both into poetry and into nationalist discourses. All the same, by the mid-1990s, the press began to use the old literary texts to new ends, to denigrate Roma, belittle their stage performances, and exclude them from the post-Soviet Russian nation. Roma are familiar with all these discursive twists (many themselves quote Russian poets from memory).

While most Soviets were enchanted by literary Gypsy songstresses, they kept a distance from the other, "wild" Gypsy hawkers or fortune-tellers, pictured against a backdrop of semilicit city markets. As Chapter 2 shows, the distinction between "two kinds" of Gypsies depended on an ideological, proscenium-like separation between art and daily life (*byt*). Nevertheless, while denigrating the streets as a realm of byt, many post-Soviets simultaneously read them as though peopled by stage characters — characters recalled from past visions and spectacles as much as "experience." Many non-Roma I spoke to assumed that they could map all the "types" there, such as "shifty Gypsies." But from the point of view of *some* Roma, they walked there hidden in plain view, misrecognized as other non-Russian "blacks," whose dark faces in the 1990s supposedly ciphered political disruption and economic decline.

"Shifty" Gypsies often are described as secretive, and many a writer, this one perhaps not excluded, hopes to tear back the curtain on Gypsy culture, maybe to reveal curious and restraining customs, even another set of inner veils, "a thicket of taboos" (Kobak 1995). Roma who disappoint the fantasy of penetrating backstage (Romani intellectuals, for instance) are often described as deracinated, alienated from the "real Gypsies." It is as if, to remain genuine, Gypsies must live only in gutters or in poetry. Chapter 3 unravels how models of the proscenium and images of segmentary clans weave crude taxonomies of Gypsy "kinds," as if all difference among Roma were based in endogamous taboo. This chapter's discussion of Romani communities and of ways Roma in my study spoke about differences among them is set against the preceding chapters' romanticism and racial logic. It takes up Romani reflection on these issues as moored to pan-Euro/Soviet categories of "civilization," "wealth," or "gender." Roma lack access to media that would allow them either to represent these moorings as legitimate ones or to articulate their significance in relation to ways by which the Soviet state executed variant policies toward diverse Romani groups.

Although Gypsies are typecast as natural performers, Gypsy performance in Soviet Russia in fact has required material and symbolic investment by the state. Chapter 4 outlines the institutional history of the Romani Theater and its ongoing connections to film and documentary production in the 1990s. Established in 1931, the Moscow Romani Theater was intended to entice Roma to "become civilized" and to debunk stereotypes, though it ultimately intensified them. In part because of the Theater's assimilative mandate, urban Romani performers by the 1990s were suspected of having given up true, rebellious "Gypsy natures" by acclimating to city and stage. Romani intellectuals and performers themselves spoke of experiencing cultural identity "complexes."[27] The problem of authenticity was complicated also by the fact that stage performance was conceived to harbor both genuine Gypsy talent and its antithesis, Gypsy "kitsch." The chapter ends with two short ethnographic sketches of film production that trace how Romani performers and Russian directors negotiated the seeming paradoxes of authenticity through struggle for control over performance frames.

Chapter 5 dislodges Soviet (and European) assumptions that define authentic Gypsy cultural identity as lacking both memory of the past and commitment in the present. Ideologies about performance scaffold these lacks. The chapter takes up dramaturgic metaphors of the proscenium where they structure state archival accounts of Gypsy misdeeds, and contrasts them to Romani oral histories and moral tales. In 1993, I found criminal case files on the grandfather of a Romani family I had known since 1991. For the state, the issue had been concealment of loyalties and exchanges. Its witnesses contrasted "true selves" to hypocritical backstage actors, and set Gypsy actions against sinister, "ethnographic" scenery of "tradition." His Romani descendants, however, interpreted the archives by connecting them to biographical narratives in ways that, while indexing troubled loyalties, did *not* always divide social commitments into "real" versus "staged."

Chapter 6 dissolves strict determinations of inauthenticity by asserting that while Roma often distinguish between themselves and gazhje, they also align themselves with some gazhje, even if just to reflect upon Romani culture. Many scholars have argued that a binary Roma/gazhje opposition is key to Romani culture — even that the opposition *causes* their social and political marginality. Coupled with the metaphor of the proscenium, this division divides the social world into realms of "sincere" versus "staged" interaction. However, to reproduce that opposition performatively is not automatic. Moreover, even distinctions from gazhje are in fact fed by Soviet-European hierarchies of value. Finally, even when distinctions become habitual, Roma may still reflect on them; they are *not* "incarcerated by culture" (Appadurai 1992). Many Roma strongly claim belonging in Russia, know and believe in landmarks of Soviet history and society, speak of patriotism, cite Pushkin (some even Stalin). Their accounts of their own actions are set within real and imagined contexts which cannot be isolated from Russia as a place or as a past.

The conclusion refolds these layers within a final description of an interaction involving Roma, Russians, and an American. In this interaction, difference emerged through ways each participant connected utterances of the others less to the moment, as to remembered performance frames and political discourses, and to imagined, faraway places. In order to make these connections, certain sorts of performance and performativity are denied to certain "types" of persons. Social difference, paradoxically, is figured dualistically as both "staged" and as "natural."

Thus the binarism of this book's title, *Between Two Fires*. First of all, it quotes the title of one of the first plays staged at the Moscow Romani Theater in the 1930s, a play written in Romani which depicted a Gypsy camp poised to choose between the authentic promises of the Red Army and the wicked deceptions of the White Army (see dialogue excerpt in the appendices). But second, it comments on the myriad, impossible dualities that plague not only definitions of Romani culture, or oppositions of Romani culture to "European" culture, but discussions of culture and of social difference in general. I do not presume to think I have succeeded in transcending such ways of looking at the world merely by examining them. However, I hope at least to draw attention to some of the deceptively brittle ways "Culture" as "Art" and "culture" as "life" are sundered, and the ways the so-called autonomy of art in fact informs the interdependencies of people.

· 1 ·

Pushkin, The Gypsies, and Russian Imperial Nostalgia

In Russia, media incarnations of the Soviet war hero Budulaj fanned the spark of exotic difference that set him apart from Russians and "closer to nature." That spark was signified by musicality: in the late 1970s TV series, *Vozvrashchenije Budulaja (The Return of Budulaj),* Budulaj loses his memory, but when he plays his harmonica he recalls, if not all the events of his life, at least his true Gypsy self. The ubiquity of similar depictions of "Gypsy song," the tautness of their intertextual links, loaned such moments in the TV show a forceful authenticity.

This chapter traces how forms of art, especially theatrical and musical art, attach to forms of identity in ways reinforcing national and racial ideologies. As one might expect in Herder's Europe, Soviet *and* Russian national ideology both subsumed the singing Gypsy and opposed itself to him. Crucial here is Pushkin's Byronic 1824 poem *Tsygany (The Gypsies;* Pushkin's spelling). Or rather, what is crucial are readers' receptions of it as a source of truth about Gypsies. Russian imperialism, Soviet internationalism, and finally post-Soviet Russian nationalism have each embraced and excluded Gypsies by citing such "classics." In their deployment, these texts have performatively transfigured political and social life by naturalizing social relations between Roma and non-Roma, interpellating Roma as "the Gypsy"; that is, the repeated citation of poetic lines in particular contexts limits the terms of discursive interaction.

"Either Gypsy Art or Gypsies Themselves"

Fascination with the Gypsy saturates several European national imaginaries, such as those of Spain or Hungary, but the Russian romance with

Gypsies has no equivalent force in most other countries, where Roma are a much larger, much more visibly impoverished minority, such as the Czech Republic, Slovakia, or Romania. In Russia, the figure of the Gypsy is elaborated through Russian romantic literature from the nineteenth century onward (see Hamill 1943; Scherbakova 1984; Janicki 1989). In the 1980s and 1990s, late- and post-Soviets continued to invoke nineteenth-century authors (especially Pushkin) to underwrite first Soviet internationalism and then Russian nationalism.

Literary texts thus figure importantly as sources for both theatrical and real-time performative citations. The method I use in tracing these literary invocations recalls Said's *strategic formation,* "a way of analyzing [how] groups of texts, types of texts, even textual genres acquire mass, density, and referential power amongst themselves and thereafter in the culture at large" (1978:20). In theme the chapter departs from literary critic Katie Trumpener's perception that in Western European literature, images of Gypsies act "as figurative keys to an array of literary genres and to the relations between them" (1992:873). This was so in Russia as well; moreover, writings about Gypsies keyed slippages between categories of art and those of everyday cultural identity.

I met few Soviets who did not perform such slippages when quoting or even mentioning poetic "Gypsy" texts. For instance, in 1993 after I had been teaching English at the weekend class for children of Moscow Romani performers for nearly two years, we taped a case of such a conflation of Gypsies' art and identity, one keyed by familiar images and by allusion to Pushkin. The class was attended mostly by members of the troupe Gilorri, though a few Russian girls participated. While taping a class, we interviewed one of these Russian girls, a six-year-old named Katja, about two pictures of "Gypsy girls" that she had painted with tempera. The child was shy about speaking in front of the camera, and so her grandmother, in her sixties, whispered prompts. The end of the interview turned to questions of identity:

> Author: And you yourself, who are you?
> Grandmother [prompting]: I'm Russian.
> Katja: I'm Russian [pause].
> G [prompting]: But I really love Gypsy—
> K: But I really love Gypsy . . .

G [prompting]: Art.

K: Art.

G: Louder.

A: Why?

K: Because there *[tam]* there is much joy, because there *[tam]* there is always merrymaking . . . there *[tam]* it is very nice.[1]

A: Would you like to be a Gypsy?

K: Yes.

(Lemon and Nakamura 1994, videotape transcript, translated from Russian)

The girl's projection of wishful identity onto a painted world "there" (*tam,* "over there") had itself been projected into her speech. Just after this interview, the grandmother admitted to the camera that, regarding love of Gypsies, "It's as if I've transferred my own inner feelings to my granddaughter." Whence was such a projection launched into a six-year-old's consciousness, or for that matter, into her grandmother's? Certainly not from immediate contextual surroundings at the school, where the Romani children wore jeans and wrote English words into notebooks, but from textual memory, memory of past performances and citations. Earlier in the interview, the grandmother phrased her prompts as if they referred to the girl's paintings, but in fact they described things not visible within that imaginary frame: "Say that she is dancing and that the moon is shining on her," she said, though the girl had painted no moon. Such utterances evoked familiar imagery from film, literature, and the stage.

There is nothing necessarily sinister in such ventrilocution — in many speech communities such orchestrations are seen as caring ways for elders to involve children in talk (Briggs 1984). More important to note here is not the mere transmission of images, but the particular, repeated intersections among categories: culture with ethnicity, ethnicity with place, culture and ethnicity with art. For instance, the grandmother fills in a pause after Katja has claimed Russian identity ("I'm Russian") by opposing Russianness to love for Gypsy art ("But I love Gypsy . . ."). The grandmother then expected her granddaughter to fill in the blank, but again intercedes to provide the object of love ("art"). Later, however, Katja required no prompting; she moved by herself from the abstraction "art" to describe a place, a mythic "there" (*tam*), where "there is always merrymaking." She had already learned that "art" encapsulates Gypsy sociality as a separate place, another world free of cares.

This slippage was pervasive and general. When I first began to tell Muscovites that I study "Gypsy culture" they would assume that by *kul'tura* I meant "art." I had in mind everyday practices and categories and the patterned understandings people have of them. The gaps between our understandings of culture were not so different from those across which American anthropologists face both thinkers from some other disciplines and the public, for whom "culture" often means "high culture," "national cultural," or "culturedness," or more rarely, "custom." The potential sense of "culture" as "civilization," as a complex of manners and hygienic practices (see Elias 1978), thus made sense to them, but not in this context, Gypsies being, by definition "wild" and *nekul 'turnyje*.

It was culture as art that defined Gypsies; it was manifest in Gypsy song and dance because *Russian* literature found it there.[2] Thus Soviets would advise me to go to Bessarabia to do my project, not only because many Roma lived there, but because Pushkin had been inspired to write about them there. And thus the Russian grandmother, a few minutes after we had interviewed her granddaughter, likewise fused the objects of her admiration, or rather, admitted that she confused them — "Gypsy art" with "the people themselves" with Pushkin:

> I lived in Western Ukraine where we had a lot of Gypsies. This memory from childhood . . . that is, to this day, the presence of Gypsies in my childhood has never been blotted out. That is, I always — well, where there are Gypsies, *there it's good, there it is merry*. Well, you know, well, Gypsies, they are a very tempestuous people, very merry people. Especially, of course, their art is unique! Can't compare it with anything! They are so liberated! Songs, unforgettable songs! Of course, what can I say, except that we, well, if even the great poet Pushkin, *he* was crazy about Gypsies, then of course! Therefore, either it's Gypsy art or the people, Gypsies themselves. (Lemon and Nakamura 1994, emphasis added)

The grandmother's shift, from personal memory to citation of Pushkin and general stereotype, pivots on the same phrase that occurred (without prompting) in her granddaughter's speech, evoking a vague sense of *place* ("there it's merry"). This topic and voice shift accompanies a shift in style; dislocated, relatively inarticulate phrases shift to fluent cliché. The final deferral to Pushkin and his poem *Tsygany* (1824) disclaims personal knowledge,[3] as though really knowing Gypsies were beyond the reach of ordinary persons in ordinary society, such knowledge accessible only to transcendent genius such as Pushkin's. Simultaneously, reference to the poet dramatized personal fantasy and experience, but in a broadly familiar way. Pushkin thus serves as a discursive hook, one that anchors the logic of attraction and difference: "*Therefore,* either it's Gypsy art or the people, Gypsies themselves."

Turning Gypsy: *Volja* and Imperial Nostalgia

The plot of Pushkin's famous poem is this: A non-Gypsy outlaw (Aleko) falls in love with a Gypsy woman (Zemfira), who brings him home to her camp. They live happily until she tires of him, favoring then a Gypsy like herself. Her father understands this as natural, asserting to Aleko that women love only fleetingly, "like the moon visiting clouds." Aleko cannot accept this and kills both Zemfira and her new lover. The Gypsies decline to punish him with violence but leave him sitting alone on a rock, telling him, "You want *volja* [free will/freedom] only for yourself." Volja is that ideal inherent to Gypsies that Aleko cannot grasp, and is also a potential source of tragedy.

Critics have debated to what extent Pushkin qualified approval of the Gypsies, to what extent was Aleko a self-portrait, and so on, but what matters here are not Pushkin's intentions but the ways in which the poem resonates through late-twentieth century public culture. For instance, some literary critics argue that Zemfira is not the real heroine, that the male characters are pivotal (Andrew 1990). This may be so, but it is Zemfira who captures the fancy of twentieth-century Soviets, and it is Zemfira, not her father, whom *they* most regard as the "Gypsy type."

Pushkin is significant because of the way he was canonized: he is described by many as able to transcend and bridge cultures by means of his art, able to understand "everyone." Through Pushkin's mediation, art brings cultures together. But as a corollary to that, Pushkin, liberal exile though he may have been, also came to stand for empire and expansion, both tsarist and later. As a Stalin-era issue of *Pravda* read, "Pushkin is equally dear to the hearts of Russians and Ukranians, Georgians and Kalmyks. . . . Hundreds of millions of people began to speak for the first time through Pushkin's lips" (*Pravda,* February 10, 1937, quoted in Sinjavskij 1975:36).

Pushkin reigns as authority on the "Gypsy soul" because he was lauded, both under Stalin and under the tsars, as the titan of imperial poetry, a creator of "Russian soul." Though his cult irritated Futurist poets, dissident writers, and cynical university students,[4] his lyrical, light verse graced every Soviet literature textbook, and his monument stood on the most central Moscow avenue leading to Red Square.

Dostoevsky, in an 1880 speech at the unveiling of the Pushkin monument, first lionized the national genius: Pushkin would not only unite the Russian people,[5] he would unite the Russian people with the imperial subjects. "There has never been a poet with such a universal responsiveness as Pushkin. It is not only a matter of his responsiveness but of its amazing depth, the reincarnation in his spirit of the spirit of foreign peoples."[6] Key to Dostoevsky's argument was Pushkin's *The Gypsies,* and in developing that argument, he located art within the Gypsy soul—or rather, relocated the traces of "Russian genius" found in Pushkin's lines *about* Gypsies within Gypsies themselves. (Pushkin himself treats Gypsies as a conduit for art's transcendent genius; his Gypsies remember sheltering an exiled Ovid, inheriting his songs and tales.) Dostoevsky grounded Russian national destiny in the way the poem implicitly opposed elemental free will, volja, to mere *svoboda,* which implied a more structured liberty from social law. Citified, especially aristocratic Russians could only rebel, could only clamor against imposed order, while Gypsies, already in nature, already apart from society, knew authentic volja.

As social allegory, the poem extended Pushkin's earlier political themes on liberty. In it, authentic *volja* unfurls as art when Gypsy characters sing; Zemfira defies Aleko and hints that she loves another through song, for instance. However, the depiction of Gypsy *volja* was born not in Moldova at all, but in Moscow and St. Petersburg, where Romani choirs had become enormously fashionable among the aristocracy.[7] Pushkin amplified this fashion, and after him came scores of poets and writers on the same theme.[8]

The Gypsy choirs were mythologized as much for their intoxicating music as for the spectacle of seeing men extravagantly toss fistfuls of cash at the feet of Gypsy divas, in the hope of thus transcending mundane concerns. Such extravagance shows up in many tales, as in Leskov's *The Enchanted*

Wanderer, for instance, and the Romani Theater's adaptation *Grushenka*. "One will shoot himself (or hang or drown himself) from unhappy love, one will squander a million, having thrown it all at the feet of his Gypsy beloved, another will make a present of his palace, another a glass of diamonds" (Druts and Gessler 1990:183). Some accounts render the singer as a sort of prostitute, or geisha, although 1990s Roma contest this view, pointing out that choirs were run by families and that while individual singers were paid for songs by request (Rom-Lebedev 1990: 41), they were not allowed to go off alone with clients.

All the same, Gypsy musical performance offered Russian spectators a way to imagine themselves unfettered by civil order through controlled, emotional "surrender" to a social inferior. This was not the favored explanation in Soviet Russia: "The admiration of Russian aristocrats for Gypsy singers and dancers could be explained by a general rapture for their art. In the end, it even became fashionable to up and marry a Gypsy woman" (Druts and Gessler 1990:183). Such marriages became the topic of countless stories; even into the 1990s, texts about the fascination of aristocrats or poets with Gypsy singers remained immensely more plentiful than any sorts of detailed accounts of everyday Romani life.[9]

Gypsies represent the unpredictable forces of authentic desire — not an ordered liberty from rule (svoboda) but the free exercise of will and caprice, volja. Literary Gypsy women, "fiery and temperamental," personified volja more forcefully than their male counterparts (though their veins, too, flowed with "hot blood"). Volja is linked explicitly in Gypsy narratives with female, foreign sexuality.[10] Of course, such allegations are not unique to Russian views of Gypsies — Europeans have long imagined women of other cultures (and classes) as excessively lusty (see Levy 1991; Gilman 1993). The passionate, dark Gypsy woman is a trans-European motif, à la Carmen, in Mérimée's 1845 novella of the same name (influenced by Pushkin's *Tsygany*), but the Russian obsession with her takes on particular colors. Not only the repetition of a set of character relations (an aristocrat vainly courts the lowest of outcasts and everyone dies) but also their intertextual configuration give the genre its particular force.

The literary Gypsy woman defies possession; it is a tragic mistake to cage her. If she allows herself to be kept, she withers and dies, like Leskov's Grushenka in *The Enchanted Wanderer* (1873). In this tale, a noble purchases Grushenka from her Gypsy kin and keeps her on his estate, forcing her to sing over and over until he breaks her will. Just as she falls in love with him, he tires of her. The obvious resemblance is to Lermontov's *Hero of Our Time* (1840). The jaded, post-Byronic hero of that novel, a Russian noble on military tour in the Caucasus, steals a Chechen girl, Bela. Bela miraculously learns Russian very quickly and falls in love with her captor. But the Russian wearies of her apparent simplicity, and when she steps outside the Russian fort to soothe herself of his neglect, cooling her legs in a nearby stream, one of her own "hot-blooded" countrymen takes his vengeance on her honor by killing her.

Most fictional attractions between Gypsy and Russian likewise end bitterly, betraying anxiety about cultural or racial miscegenation. Historian Sunderland (1997) remarks that nineteenth-century Russians were not leery of miscegenation as long as the "end result was culturally Russian" (816), and this was still true in the Soviet-era tales and retellings.[11] The danger of the appeal was that, in most Gypsy tales, the Russian men attempted to throw off the bonds both of responsibility and of Russianness. They must fail, for their rash effort betrayed and undermined the ideals of Russification.

However, in *most* Russo-Gypsy "miscegenation" tales, the Gypsy woman usually rejects the Russian man. Zemfira tires of Aleko. Blok's hero in the poem, *V Restorane* (*In the Restaurant*, 1910), never even manages to approach the willful Gypsy singer. Emil Lotjanu's 1976 film, *Tabor Uxodit v Nebo (The Gypsy Camp Ascends to Heaven)*, a screen adaptation of Maxim Gorky's 1892 tale *Makar Chudra*, is the most well-known celluloid version of temporary mismating between volja and social norms. The story is set on the nineteenth-century border between the Russian and Austro-Hungarian Empires, in the Western Carpathians. A Hungarian aristocrat becomes infatuated with the Gypsy woman Rada when his feckless carriage driver nearly runs her down and she halts the horses with the power of her gaze. Later, the aristocrat drives to her camp, presents her with a lavishly trimmed dress, and asks her father for her hand. The father only defers to Rada. In reply, she flings the dress to the camp buffoon, who dons it over his own Gypsy tatters to dance after the retreating, humiliated noble. She prefers a Gypsy man willful as herself — but refuses even him obedience, making him promise to kiss *her* feet before all their kin. On their wedding day, she laughs when he refuses to bend before her and trips him with a whip. Shamed, he stabs her through the heart, and is in turn killed by her father.

Russian stories of courtships and marriages between aristocratic poets and Gypsy singers reveal more about Russian national ideology and identity than they do about Roma. As in many orientalist fantasies, fascination hoped to subsume, even become a Gypsy.[12] The wish to subsume is gendered; the adoring Russian is male, the Gypsy is female. This genderedness seems commonsense indeed. One female Russian journalist describes the appeal of unions between Russian men and Gypsy women in the subjunctive, using the masculine first person, as if it were already clear to readers that, as a Russian woman, such a coupling was not an option: "If I had been a *male* journalist, I would have married a Gypsy, as did the famous soccer coach Andrej Starostin. As did the dramatist Isidor Shtok, Pushkin's friend Pavel Voinovich Naschokin. Like count Golitsyn, like Tolstoy's brother, Sergej" (Loginova 1992:36).

There is a parallel gendered division of activities among non-Roma who coopt Gypsy identities, who pretend to "be" Gypsy. Russian women were more likely to "become" Gypsy by dressing up, or by learning Gypsy dance or song, as a kind of hobby or even a profession, doing stage impersonations.[13] Russian men more often turned their fascination into expertise, becoming folklorists, journalists, or freelance writers on Gypsy topics. One male who violated the usual gendered split in modes of appropriation was a mentally handicapped young Russian man who attended the Romani Theater several times a week during the early 1990s and who claimed to "be" Gypsy. He would stand in the foyer before curtain rise and dance, shimmying his shoulders (a feminine-marked dance move), and then stand outside the dressing room exit after curtain fall, begging departing performers each night for a new word in Romani.

In Pushkin's poem, Aleko tries to possess, but cannot become, a Gypsy. As Zemfira remarks, "He wants to be like us, a Gypsy," but he cannot accept her female freedom, he is not made for volja. Men remain Russian; few Russian women appear in most Gypsy narratives. Where they do, they represent the bondage of convention, as in Lev Tolstoy's *The Living Corpse* (1900), in which the male aristocrat is stifled by wealth, marriage, and social position and feigns his own death, freeing his wife to remarry, himself taking up with a Gypsy singer.[14] There is no place for Russian women in the fantasy of volja. To partake in it, they must instead mask *as* Gypsies.

The most famous literary exception occurs in the story of Budulaj, the Gypsy war hero. He falls in love with Klavdija Petrovna, a good-hearted

Russian woman who has adopted his son.[15] She fears him at first, says the narrator on the first pages of the book (Kalinin 1963:5–6). Budulaj overcomes that fear with his gentleness with horses, his musical talents, and his literacy (though a stumbling, accented literacy) in Russian. He, in fact, seems to prefer socializing with Russians and sermonizes to the nomadic Gypsies (even a settled Romani woman cannot win his heart). Still, he and Klavdija never come together — thugs savagely beat him out of consciousness just before he confesses his love to her.

Intermarriage was a Soviet trope of successful internationalism (see also Slezkine 1994a:307). As Budulaj remarks on the marriage of a kinswoman to a Russian, *"Byli vashi, byli nashi: sejchas Druzhba Narodov"* (There were "yours" and "ours": now there is Friendship of the Peoples). Accordingly, the persistence of the Gypsy siren has more to do with imperial interests (or ambivalence about the effects of imperial conquest) than with real erotic attractions born in actual intercultural interactions.

To see this, it helps to examine how categories besides gender and art intersect volja: namely, *space,* imperial space, expanse *(razmax),* and open space *(prostor).*[16] Literary analyses of *The Gypsies* usually overlook the epilogue, in which Pushkin recounts meeting Gypsies who inhabit the Russian imperial frontier, "where the Russian pointed out the sovereign borders to Stambul [Constantinople], where our double-headed eagle still sounds past glory." Pushkin's epilogue maps encounters with Gypsies onto newly acquired national lands, justifying their borders while drawing attention to the site of his own political exile. The acquisition of Moldova in 1812 by the Treaty of Bucharest increased the number of Roma on Russian territory, through annexation and migration (see Crowe 1995:159). At the border, Gypsies simultaneously were a sign of imperial expansiveness *and* of exile from the centers of power. Post-Soviets continue to link Gypsies with the vastness of Russian lands, lands extending to the east, lands that promised endless material resources, lands to which political prisoners were sent, from which they rarely returned.[17] As a middle-aged Russian journalist who had written about Roma for Soviet popular journals such as *Ogonjok* rhapsodized, via tropes of boundless space, "In Russia, there is much big space. Gypsies thus felt free here like nowhere else in the world. . . . They could even ignore state attempts to put them into reservations and enforce residency permits, though the government did send whole camps to the gulag, on any excuse" (interview from field notes 1992).

The journalist cites both Soviet-sanctioned accounts, in which Russia is the real, "second" Gypsy homeland, and a then fashionable discourse of resistance, in which immense Russian forests offered Gypsies a place to hide from imposed Soviet power. Imagined Gypsies, traversing expanses of terrain, could reclaim space and motion from the Soviets in ways that Russians could not. This journalist greatly romanticized the inclination and ability of Roma to hide in forests and on the frozen steppe, without papers and employment options, tools or capital. Most of the traveling Roma in Siberia were there because they had been sent there in trains to work camps, as were many other people. Although the speaker of these lines had had connections with a Romani community through a former wife, this did not prevent him from recycling literary stereotypes. Similarly, the few actual marriages between Romani singers and aristocrats and the public fascination with stories about such marriages, both real and fictional, did little to increase knowledge of Romani social life or to change political relations between Roma and non-Roma.

All the same, movement over territory seemingly begets volja in Gypsy song, so amenable to Russian ears. Quoting Russian author Kuprin, another Soviet journalist writes that the vocal decorations, vibrations, and glissando particular to the Gypsy style come of "the action of the movement of rolling caravan wheels on the voice" (Velexova 1972:88). All this occurs "naturally" *(ot prirody),* for "Gypsies do not read music" but sing "untrained." Gypsy singing style is not recognized as a technical genre but as an uncontrived effect, one that can intensify any song's emotional power (Kuprin 1964).[18] The singer is thus an organic, natural conduit for waves of national nostalgia, as if the melancholy and motion of the Russian soul passed from landscapes and roads through the body of the Gypsy singer. Once again, art makes of Gypsies a vehicle for idealized Russian national identity.

Western literary critics and Romologists have argued, to various analytic ends, that literary Gypsies throughout Europe figure nationalist nostalgia — they are envisioned as a kind of time capsule for storing national forms (music, folklore, traditions) and a simpler past (see Trumpener 1992:871; Hancock 1985). Soviet scholars, for their part, claim that Gypsy choirs became so popular *because* their repertoires contained half-forgotten Russian folk songs and ballads embellished in a "Gypsy style" (Rom-Lebedev 1990; Druts and Gessler 1985 and 1988). Trumpener (1992), however, demonstrates that in Western European literature this nostalgia is ambivalent. The appearance of "rootless" Gypsy characters signal a shift to an "obsession with memory visible mainly as amnesia" (861); Gypsies trigger narrative time to switch its flow from normal history into a suspended, vertiginously timeless present that melts with the past.

The pragmatic significance of Gypsy volja changed over time, even as Soviet theatrical, literary, and filmic productions recycled older texts or themes. Socialist-didactic plays such as *Hot Blood (Gorjachaja Krov')*, first produced at the Moscow Romani Theater in 1959 (still on the repertoire in the late 1990s), laud Gypsy song as a locus of authentic volja; "No one can take our songs away from us by any force. To the grave with them! Only in a traveling song — here all our adversities, all our Gypsy troubles are forgotten." In the play, dramatizing conflict between settled, socialist Gypsies and their relatives who still travel, song is the only "tradition" about which the feuding characters agree. Art, which cannot be taken away, is an essential quality shared by all Gypsies. Still, socialist discourse meanwhile adapted and tamed volja.

One Russian director at the Moscow Romani Theater claimed to me that under socialism he always had used Gypsy freedom to hide antisocialist themes, that Gypsies functioned rather like a "bourgeois white piano," a forbidden stage property signifying decadence. When a playwright feared the censors, said the director, he would throw something marked as being in bad socialist taste into the script, such as a white piano or girls in bikinis. The censor would hopefully be distracted, command only that the decoy piano or girls be deleted, and miss the more subversive subtext: "Gypsies work the same way. You can stage any social conflict you want, as long as you set it in a Gypsy camp." Gypsies were for him no more than a trope for antistate and antimodern nostalgia. This was crystal clear in the way the director described how he actually chose elements of Gypsy tradition for his scripts: "The audience wants to see customs, superstitions, something miraculous. When I pick up a book, I read about customs in ancient France and in India, where people are yet unspoiled by civilization. . . . I take a custom and gave it to the Gypsies. . . . Theater is the means to reach another world, when we are talking to God, . . . in any play, an exit to such a level is art" (interview from field notes 1991). Gypsies were his vehicle "to reach another world," separate from mundane life, "unspoiled" and more essential.

Whatever the value transcendent aspirations may hold for artists, depicting social conflict among people "unspoiled by civilization" is hardly a critique of socialism or even of society, as much as the director might have wanted it to seem so in 1991, when coming out as anti-Soviet was so chic. Little antiestablishment subtext actually appeared in the Romani Theater's repertoire, even by 1997, whether considered from an anti-Soviet or an ethnic minority point of view. Scripts had no clear reference to any specific political complaints (such opacity being not unusual in late-Soviet, cryptic magical realism or science fiction but rather less so by the end of glasnost). Rather, the texts on the theater's repertoire dovetailed well with official ideologies. From Russian imperialism to Soviet internationalism, the trope of Gypsy volja has been appropriated easily by every regime.

By the early 1990s, nostalgia for Gypsy volja refracted freshly through events at the fall of state socialism—often via the same texts as before. Russian media mobilized snippets of Gypsy song in a January 1992 television retrospective of the August 1991 coup attempt, to evoke volja. In the broadcast, 1991 events in Russia were montaged with 1989 footage of the Berlin Wall being dismantled, while in the soundtrack ran a famous "Gypsy romance," set to lyrics by Apollon Grigorjev: "*Dlinnaja doroga . . . gitara semistrunnaja*" ("a long road . . . a seven-stringed guitar," the seven-stringed guitar being a metonym for "Gypsy music").

Trumpener argues that in Western European literature Gypsies evoke a "dream of historylessness" *and* an "idealizing envy of Gypsy life seemingly outside of history and beyond the reach of the authorities" (1992:853). In late- and post-Soviet Russia, Gypsies have ciphered a lost, prerevolutionary past free of imposed state power. Though volja is ideally pure of such mundane sorts of freedom, indifferent to it, Gypsies stood against "imposed" state law, like aristocrats, priests, and certain literary figures. In 1993, a young, self-proclaimed monarchist, who identified himself as Russian but also claimed to have "one-quarter Gypsy blood," claimed that Russian aristocrats recognized and praised Gypsy volja because "Gypsies could not be made to bow down or to live as the state decreed. In this the nobles [given their position by the tsars] felt an affinity with them, especially with their pride. They were not like peasants, who work, or till, or market. Their laws are holdovers from a feudal warrior caste, who lived by taking and felt pride in it" (interview 1992). This modern monarchist did not tap recent Soviet past to stress the particular spatial and social experiences that Roma and aristocrats may have had in common (such as being excluded from the capital, being dispossessed of property, etc.), but instead idealized a time when nobles were still in power.

Such evocations of prerevolutionary Gypsies did not conjure, in the early post-Soviet imagination, the scent of romantic nostalgia that Pushkin breathed while writing. They resonated with memories of the recent past and the ongoing present in urban apartment blocks. The nostalgia they evoked was not that of bored, Byronic, aristocratic travelers, nor of landed nobility pining for the capital. Soviet and post-Soviet readers celebrated Pushkin's *Gypsies* not only because it pointed to liberty (however "anti-Rousseauvian" [see Andrew 1990]) but also because the text — and Gypsies themselves — had become suffused with the *author*'s aura, that of a prerevolutionary Russian imperial aristocracy, of the once-moneyed nobility who had patronized Gypsy choirs. Listening to a phonograph record of songs from even a Soviet Gypsy film could evoke talk about prerevolutionary times and national poetic genius.

Romani intellectuals were as conversant in these texts as any other Soviets — often more so, since they mattered deeply to them. Retired Romani performer Olga Demeter-Charskaja writes in her 1998 autobiography that during the Civil War, "Gypsies did not understand what the Russians were fighting for. . . . they were indifferent to who was in power. Just so long as there were peace and liberty [*svoboda*]." These words are quoted in the preface by painter Nikolaj Bessonov, who reads in them an allusion to Pushkin:

> That phrase rang like an aphorism — but not just that. They looked Gypsy through and through, but were somehow astoundingly seductive to the Russian ear. Soon I understood, that here was a hidden quotation, but could not remember where from. Suddenly it came to me — of course, those are Pushkin's lines: "On the earth there is no happiness, but only peace and freedom [volja]." The great Russian poet, like the Gypsies, considered peace and volja a worthy trade for happiness. That means that in the Russian and in the Gypsy soul, something exists that powerfully draws the two different peoples together! (10)

Although hybridity was often lauded as an official goal in Soviet nationalities policy (others saw in it a discourse of assimilation), Romani intellec-

FIGURE 3   Prerevolutionary Gypsy choir

tuals did most of the work to simultaneously stress both hybrid and particular Gypsy identity. Romani intellectuals themselves treasured accounts of volja, especially in stories wedding aristocrats to female singers, for they vividly confirmed the hybrid "interweaving" of Russian and Gypsy cultures. In addition, Roma could deploy marriage tales to increase their symbolic capital, both to index art and to index becoming "civilized."

Romani intellectuals sometimes explicitly articulated that Gypsies evoke and embody nostalgia, describing this feeling as a bond between Gypsies and Russians. Vladislav Demeter, choirmaster of Gilorri, for one, drew commonalities between the "fate of the Russian people" and that of Gypsies in just such terms, naming "nostalgia" as an agentive emotion linking Russians to Gypsies, an agency in turn driven by musicality. His interlocutor is the Russian philologist of Romani, Lev N. Cherenkov:

> D: By [means of] Gypsy singing, this nostalgia is directed not only
> backward, as a longing for a nonexistent homeland, for a common
> ethnic, geographic, and historic unity; this nostalgia is also directed
> forward, as a longing for an unobtainable ideal. The attraction to the
> Gypsy, this nostalgia, especially in Russian culture, in Russian

psychology, the tragic fate of the Russian people has so much in common with the historic fate of the Gypsies. Not literally, not in nomadism, but in that the Russian soul is constantly racing, constantly searching, constantly demanding. It is never in the present moment, it is always waiting for something. It is always searching for something. It is always unsatisfied because there has never been a normal life.

L: There never was, there never was!

(Lemon and Nakamura 1994, videotape transcript)

Demeter, too, conflates art with the image of the people and likens the actual movement of Gypsies *or* Gypsy song to the movement of the Russian soul, "constantly searching," as if the Russian soul and Gypsy song bubble up from the same source. He asserts that Russian audiences see the discontent of the Russian soul mirrored in Gypsy singing. His Russian interlocutor emphatically agrees that a "normal life" never existed in Russia, echoing a then widespread critique of life under socialism, and long-standing discourse about eastern backwardness vis-à-vis the West. Here lies a subtle difference between Russian and Western nostalgia about Gypsies. Likewise not "normal," Russians simultaneously expel Gypsies *from* civilization into nature, and identify *with* them against the "coldness" of the West.[19] Besides colonial guilt, a fear of losing their place among the nations, of being colonized, tinges this desire to subsume.

Gypsies cannot represent "normal life," since they lack "ethnic, geographic, and historic unity." This set of qualities uncannily echoes the three unities of classical drama (action, place, and time).[20] It is as though an ideology about proper theatrical form — about what makes characters and motivations work dramaturgically — in part structures categories of historical identity and agency: Gypsies are seen as playing no role on the stage of world history.

Citing Pushkin

Since its publication, Pushkin's verse often has been taken as "true," vested as "ethnographic." If not taken as literally true, then it has been taken as uncovering deeper, more essential truths than are apparent in reality. By the late-Soviet period, such readings had been elevated to official discourse, as uttered for instance by the director of the Romani Theater, Romani singer Nikolaj Slichenko, in a piece directed to an international audience: "Pushkin's rebellious Zemfira, Tolstoy's voluptuous Masha the Gypsy, Leskov's heroine Grushenka, the very incarnation of beauty, were not produced by their creators' imaginative genius. These are real people, alive and warm, who came out of their tents and their caravans and strode directly into literature" (1984).

Such investment in arguing for the unmediated connection between art and people seems at odds with how little Pushkin actually saw of the nomadic Roma of whom he wrote. Pushkin was exiled to southern Russian possessions from 1820 to 1823 — first to the Caucasus, where the imperial army was skirmishing with "mountain tribes" to secure the border with Turkey, and then to Moldova, recently ceded to Russia by the Treaty of Bucharest in 1812. On his return to central Russia, Pushkin turned out a cycle of poetry featuring Georgians, Turks, and tribes such as the Circassians of *Prisoner of the Caucasus.* Circassians he never encountered at all, imagining their villages from the tales of Russian expatriates. Before taking up pen to write *The Gypsies,* Pushkin had had only fleeting contact with Roma in Moldova (see Druts and Gessler 1990: 170–75).[21]

Pushkin's poem nevertheless continues to be "true" because it narrates a hegemonic account of Russian national identity that many find emotionally compelling. As a Russian intellectual at a 1991 Moscow dinner party declared à propos of my research topic, in tones of hushed ecstasy, "You have found the pearl of our Russian culture!"

Literary critic Susan Layton remarks that nineteenth-century Russian readers, besides enjoying poetry's sweet rhyme and prosodic fluidity, received poetry written about the Caucasus during imperial expansion as "true" because so little information from the South was published *at all* due to war censorship and the technical limitations of print. Poetry, in such a vacuum, could fill the functions of several genres, including journalism, geography, and ethnography (1994:19–21). *The Gypsies,* written during the same period, has been taken by readers as expressing a deep understanding of Gypsy life. While most contemporary, professional Pushkin critics do not take Pushkin's account as literally ethnographic,[22] many other readers did, and continue to do so. Pushkin's poem has even been described as "ethnographic." Pushkin biographers and literary commentators occasionally digress from biographical or literary exegesis into accounts of Gypsy customs (usually based on hearsay) as if discussion of the poem or the poet keyed a shift into an "ethnographic" genre.[23] Bits of Pushkin's verse turn up inside many Soviet ethnographies of other non-Russians, from the Caucasus to Siberia. As for other genres on Gypsies, few Russophone authors have touched Roma without mentioning Pushkin; his shadow presence not only weaves throughout texts and dialogs but also frames entire accounts, to various ends.

For a brief Soviet period, Pushkin's lines were contested: in the late 1920s, Pushkin's southern cycle was denounced as imperial, orientalist arrogance; and in 1931, when the Moscow Romani Theater was established, Pushkin's *Gypsies* (along with Bizet's *Carmen*) was excluded from its repertoire, then still composed entirely of Romani-language productions. But by 1934, the state had reappropriated Pushkin. The theater's preparations for the Soviet-wide Pushkin Jubilee of 1935 were well under way with a musical production of *The Gypsies* — in Russian. By this time, scripts began to feature more and more Russian characters, all benign or at worst prejudiced, their bigotry always overcome by the denouement. Pushkin stood as the bridge to such overcoming. In the 1935 film *The Last Camp* (which closely followed plots of the Theater's earlier plays), one of the pro-Gypsy characters, a Russian collective farmer, keeps a portrait of Pushkin next to one of Stalin on his wall. Gypsy girls visiting the collective giggle at this worker when he recites the poet while standing atop a collective horse; this awkward, yet friendly interaction only underscored that the "Friendship of the peoples" (Druzhba narodov) was mediated by Pushkin.

The idea that Russian literary art should mediate the art of the other Soviet peoples explicitly structured statements that Romani Theater performers first fed me in 1991. They explained the repertoire based on works by Tolstoy, Pushkin, Lorca thus: "Our theater portrays universal themes, through song, dance, and the Russian classics. . . . [t]he classics apply to everyone, and to Gypsies as well." Still, only those classics that traced explicit Gypsy themes were staged — there was no room there for "classics" in general.

For decades, writing about Gypsies entailed citing these classics. A 1972 article in *Sputnik* (a Soviet publication with a *Time/Life* flavor) begins with the Romani exodus from India but treats its history as an enigma with a poignant appeal to the Great Writers: "Cervantes, Mérimée, Pushkin, Dostoevsky, Tolstoy—who hasn't written about them?" Not only journalists practiced this; so too did the handful of Soviet ethnographers who wrote about Roma, framing scholarly articles with references to Pushkin or Lermontov. Even the post-Soviet, 1994 edition of *Narody Rossii* (*Peoples of Russia,* an ethnographic encyclopedia published, as in Soviet times, under the auspices of the Academy of Sciences Institute of Ethnography, with titles such as *Peoples of the USSR, Peoples of the World*) appeals to the canon for similar effect — "The Gypsy choirs enjoyed an amazing popularity, their admirers including Pushkin, Turgenev, Tolstoy, Leskov, Fet, Grigorjev, Polonskij, Ostrovskij, Blok and others"—as if to stress that these writers' interest legitimated an object of ethnography. The late Leksa Manush, himself a Baltic Rom, published a detailed article about Romani musicality in *Soviet Ethnography* in 1985 that began by invoking a list of "titles of poems by Russian poets of the past century" (46) to testify to the importance of Romani music. The first paragraph of the article reads:

> One of the most striking features of the Gypsy people is its exclusively inborn musicality. Musician, singer, dancer—these have long been considered the principal professions among Gypsies [Manush footnotes Soviet ethnographer Barranikov (1931) alongside poet and critic Apollon Grigorjev (1915)]. Gypsy music, song and dance has more than once had great influence on the creative work of various composers, writers and poets of those countries, in which Gypsies settled, and, if you will, on Russian poetry in particular. To this the mere titles of works by Russian poets of the last century clearly testify: "Gypsy Dance" (Derzhavin, 1805), "Gypsy Song," and "Gypsy Dance" (Shevyreva, 1828), "Gypsy Songs" (A. K. Tolstoy,[24] 1840) and "Song of the Gypsy Girl" (Ja. P. Polonskij, 1853), "Gypsy Vengerka" (A. A. Grigorev, 1857), "Gypsy Song" (A. N. Apuxtin).

Only after establishing that Gypsies inspired the art of others did he continue to write about Romani music itself.

In 1985, two Romani scholars, the ethnographer Nadezhda Demeter and her father Georgi Demeter, a historian of Soviet sport, jointly published an article in *Pravda*.[25] Its title, "Nature's Poor Sons?" quotes a line from Pushkin's *Gypsies,* but with a question mark. After listing persecutors from the Spanish inquisitors to Hitler, the article claims that Roma finally found their "second homeland" in Russia because Russians appreciate Gypsy music—"democrats" such as Pushkin setting the example. This marvelous musicality would have been lost, the writers continue, without the intervention of the Soviet state, who not only taught Roma to read Pushkin but who also established the Moscow Romani Theater. The authors, finding the Theater to be in decline, end by calling for more attention to "Gypsy art," since "preserving and developing" it would advance *all* the world cultures.[26]

When Soviet ethnographers, Romani or not, wrote for the press or for academic journals, they reiterated a schema in which the world's societies were interwoven and nested by means of art.[27] A few lines from a seminal article by Cheboksarov ("Problems of the Typology of Ethnic Units") published in *Sovjetskaja Ethnografija* lays out connections between culture and art that can be traced in many ethnographers' works: "The progressive creativity of Pushkin, Repin, Mendeleev are, first and foremost, inseparable parts of the treasury of Russian culture, and only through this culture do they become the property of all mankind" (1967:133).

The imagery of Russian culture as a *conduit* for exchange rather than as "treasury" is what matters here; as though only Russian culture offered clear such conduits ("only through this culture"). Roma are seen to possess no Pushkin of their own; having only fleeting lovely unwritten songs, how can they, alone, articulate themselves within the Soviet array of nations, to exchange with them, save by being subsumed within Russian culture? They become valued because they are appreciated by cultured Russian poets. Such poetic status was argued to offer Roma the opportunity to absorb spiritual substance and move to a "higher cultural level."[28]

Thus Roma themselves, especially Romani intellectuals and performers, whether speaking *about* or *as* Gypsies, have had to hook their own words to those of Pushkin and the other Great Writers. Performers at the Romani Theater had to be able to quote Pushkin from memory—substituting his words for their own was a job requirement. In 1992, I witnessed the audition of a young Romani woman from Siberia, who was asked to sing, dance, and then to recite Pushkin. She protested, "I don't know any Pushkin." "Shame!" several of the watching actors chastised. She did not speak much Romani (though neither did some working there), and, after a brief exposition of dancing skills, the director dismissed her: "You put me in an unpleasant position—you are absolutely not ready. Come back in two years, and learn both Pushkin and the Gypsy language in the meantime."

The significance for Roma of such ventrilocution, of voicing and citing such texts both on stage and in "ordinary" interaction, is profound, and I will have occasion to return to it in later chapters.

Shifting Keys: From Pushkin to Police Photos

Literary stereotypes about Gypsies in Russia cannot be dismissed simply because they are "inauthentic," because Roma themselves know them and cite them; they have become implicated in many self-representations. Moreover, 1990s press accounts and other narratives created by non-Roma, even when claiming to be firsthand, rarely based their authority on interaction with Roma but instead on these older, literary genres. And, as it turned out, the same genres through which Russian and Soviet imperial hierarchies subsumed Gypsies *into* themselves also could be deployed to opposite ends, to *exclude* Gypsies. This is what happened in the early years of postsocialism. By 1996, though journalists continued to refer to Pushkin's poetry, they did so differently. From July 1995 to April 1996, I collected thirteen articles on Roma from the Russian press, and, of these, six referenced the opening line to Pushkin's poem:[29] "Gypsies in a noisy throng wander Bessarabia." One such article quoted the entire first stanza only to dismiss it as a relic: "Yes, that word 'Gypsy' has long had a romantic aura. Pushkin wrote about them."[30] The article (archly subtitled as realism, "The Gypsies as They Are") decoupled Gypsies from art, ironically coopting Pushkin's lines as a pivot on which to turn an image of Gypsies into one in which they overwhelm the countryside, and "grow like weeds." The reference to "noisy throngs" is taken to literal extremes.

In an article written by a police captain, the phrase "Gypsies in a noisy throng" frames the assertion that Gypsies commit a disproportionate number of crimes, hinting at impending "genetic degradation." By 1996, the press no longer deferred to ethnographers but was instead calling on such police expertise to explain Gypsy behavior, or else relying simply on journalistic "field accounts."[31] The public ethnographic focus had shifted from Druzhba narodov to conflict between nations and criminality. Thus, another article bluntly states that "in the past we were internationalists . . .

but now we must call things by their own names" and describe "ethnic crime" as such. Pushkin's text, as a call to internationalism, is overturned.[32] The rest of that piece, sprinkled with police photos rather than ethnographic data, advises citizens to stay away from "women with a strikingly Eastern appearance."

The exotic willfulness of Zemfira is transposed into the antisocial, hypnotic powers of female beggars and thieves. Another article, titled "Don't walk off with a throng of Gypsy women to their nomadic tent," gives similar advice. Echoing the article by the police chief, this article's negative evocation of Pushkin in the body of the text reduces once transcendent and mediating art to mere "romanticism." "The Russian person has an ineradicably romantic relationship to Gypsies, raised on Gypsy ballads, the lines of Pushkin and prose of Gorky. But unfortunately, these days the Gypsy share of crime is 3% — a significant figure, considering that there are only 150,000 living in Russia" (*Moja Gazeta,* Samara, April 2, 1996).

From mention of Pushkin, the article immediately passes on to describe "clan" social structures, grounding anticriminal advice in something resembling ethnography. Such a digression from poetry into pseudo–social science recalls the ways in which nineteenth-century Pushkinologists took similar license. But Pushkin's positive rendering of Gypsy volja — and any notion of the Gypsy soul as connected, via his work, with art — is eclipsed; the poem retains only its capacity to key discursive shift into an "ethnographic" mode and to authorize that discourse. In the 1990s, intertextual arrows among earlier texts remained intact; but now the well-known stanzas were both debunked as misguided *and* used to underwrite quick ascriptions of criminality. Whereas before, mention of Pushkin's appreciation of Gypsies signaled a romantic ideal of affinity, now his poetry framed diatribes that *excluded* Roma.

Only one article, one which rephrased these opening lines as a question in its title ("As Before, in a Noisy Throng?"), marshaled Pushkin in the old fashion, to reference Gypsies and Gypsy art simultaneously, and as conduit to world culture. Not coincidentally, the author was Romani. Writing from Moldova, in Russian, the author deplores the "descent" of his people into crime but proposes that a theater be built to preserve Gypsy culture (a historically very Soviet solution for Roma, if not for other minorities) and to attract tourists from abroad,[33] Pushkin's poem having been set in Moldova, after all.

Some Roma, too, had become cynical about Pushkin's understanding of Gypsy volja. Consider this short conversation between the author and two retired Romani performers in 1992, Olga Demeter and her sister Nina Demeter, who criticized other, nonperformer, nonintellectual Roma whom they assumed (not so accurately) to be indifferent to politics:

O: I read that today [people] are screaming on Red Square. "Down with Yeltsin!" Well, to Gypsies nothing is that important. They only want to eat, sing, and get married.
A: Maybe they are right?
N: Hah—look, she defends them! "Free." Hunh. "The Great Pushkin understood them."
(Interview from field notes)

Nina quoted a well-worn cliché on how well Pushkin knew Gypsies, exhaling with ironic fatigue in her reference to the would-be internationalism of Pushkin's verse. Yet, caught between the two poles of extravagant myth and sordid press ethnographies, she did not shift the terms but challenged them by voicing others' words—all the more perhaps because speaking to an outsider assumed to know no other point of reference. Many of my Romani consultants seemed similarly constrained to pluck from alternating tropes of criminal asociality or romantic will.

Russian images of Gypsies have been described as dual (Druts and Gessler 1990). Indeed, most non-Roma I knew maintained dual attitudes of fascination with and disdain for Gypsies, switching enchantment with freedom for distrust of lawlessness. A single person, over the course of a single conversation, might laud "Gypsy art" and then spit on "Gypsy speculators." Some Russian authors have called this duality "balanced," especially since "nowhere was their contribution as integral to the national musical tradition as in Russia" (Chinyaeva 1997:1). However, this duality bears scrutiny; romantic Gypsy imagery has masked political inequalities and harsh repressions more than once (see Acton 1974; Hancock 1987; Mayall 1985). Under the Third Reich, jolly "Gypsy films" were produced as actual Roma were being exterminated (Trumpener 1992:854). Russian and Romani intellectuals alike are apt to overlook how Pushkinian depictions of Gypsy social life (whether romantically or cynically cited) elide histories of slavery, dispossession, and dislocation.

But many in Moscow, including Romani intellectuals, do not read the dual stereotype as flip sides of a powerfully performative and authorizing set of interlocking tropes. Instead, they see dual perceptions of *reality*. "Real," essentially Romani talents earn admiration, while "actual" but "regrettable" habits of "wild" Roma earn disdain. These perceptions are described as accessible depending on one's position in the social scheme of things. To illustrate, one Romani intellectual aligned the duality of Gypsy imagery with an ontological duality, one he saw as natural and universal, between art and the daily grind (byt), between transcendence and the sordid streets:

> We can perceive a Russian person through bums at the train station, an alcoholic, a man in line. Or, we can perceive the Russian nation through the image of a Lomonosov, a Turgenev, you see. . . . They are all various aspects. . . . [I] just do not understand why rank-and-file people live for a crust of bread, understand, I perceive everything through the eyes of a person of art, a person of thought . . . but that is my preference. In a similar manner a person might look at Gypsies. A person perceives us one way when his soul is close to poetry, to romance, to music — that is, [as] a thinking, individualistic person. But a rank-and-file person — a simple philistine, without a feeling for poetry, for the symphony, you understand, for elite art — he sees Gypsies via daily life, only as beggars, fortune tellers, thieves and so on. It all depends on what platform in life you find yourself. (Video recording, 1993, translated from Russian)

Romani performers and intellectuals spend great energy attaching themselves to art and distancing themselves from byt. They, too, have learned the ontological divide separating public from private, real from inauthentic, the sphere of elite art from that of daily life. But such "platforms" of "preference" are *not* actually selected vantages that reveal two actual, different, essential manifestations of Gypsies. The notion of "preference" masks not only how social positions *do* refract vision, but how those social positions are created. This is why few have asked how and why *some* Roma have come to be so visible in precisely the arenas of the stage or the street. What are the political structures of social visibility?

Having traced threads of volja in Gypsy song and theatricality, in the realm of Art, I probe next the realm of byt, on the stage of the street, the bazaar, the station. Myths about Gypsies as beggars and hawkers were spun against these backdrops; though less audible in Soviet media than those artful ones that echo Pushkin, they were nonetheless well known. By the late 1990s, they fell ever louder from the lips of post-Soviets, who, not quite echoing Aleko, continued to say that "we are becoming Gypsies," but in new ways.

· 2 ·

Roma, Race, and Post-Soviet Markets

I had waited two hours on the Tver' platform. The 12:00 commuter train to Moscow had been canceled, but no one had been told, as usual. I stood in the shade of a crumbling, concrete underpass exit, next to a pair of old women. The older one, missing a few fingers, found a seat on a gray, cement garbage urn. She was talking, running a familiar course from inflation to the accursed *demokraty*. A ratty bleached-blond wearing a black polyester miniskirt, probably only 18 but already with a terminal crease between her eyes, joined the crowd but did not melt into it. The old woman marked her, gestured, and turned her tongue to "these new fashions." Then she moved her gaze to my long skirt: "Well, *that* — that is all right. Normal, just plain."

A few meters away, a man slept drooping sideways over his baggage — a cardboard box tied with string and a tattered, striped, nylon bag. One tattooed and sunburned hand extended stiffly over his chest; the other awkwardly supported his dirty, massive head. Standing near him were, perhaps, his brother and mother. Maybe he had just returned from jail — those were prison tattoos. The "brother" pulled something out of the nylon bag without disturbing him, then they decided to protect his face from the sun by draping another rough, fabric bag over his head. In this way they stood over him. Some time later, an old, bemedalled veteran passed. He didn't like the sight, thought they were taking up too much space, and loudly said as much to the mother. They cursed each other even as the veteran moved slowly away, every few steps pivoting on his cane to fire a few more explosive words. The mother defended, to everyone and no one, "What difference does it make! He isn't bothering anybody!"

The old woman meanwhile had turned her complaints to the Gypsies. "They have become so brazen. Before, they didn't dare to tell fortunes right at the station!" When, soon after, two Romani women and a young boy appeared on the platform, the old woman said nothing. These Roma sat on the wooden box they carried with them and ate sunflower seeds. Nobody told any fortunes. (Excerpt from field notes, 1993)

The Street and the Byt: Visibility and Misrecognition

I extract this scene whole from my field notes precisely for its picturesque superficiality, its archetypes and public characters familiar to late and post-Soviets: the intrusive babushka, the sluttish dyed blond, the former convict, the Gypsies. Streets, stations, markets, the public sites of daily life, of byt, were superficial stages where pedestrians could gather quick impressions from which to metonymically extrapolate entire unseen social worlds.[1] Upon these extrapolations, people based equally quick interactive decisions. This pragmatic immediacy affords streets a greater sense of "reality" than the stage. But while interactions in such spaces may seem more visceral, they leave brief impressions with which pedestrians interweave memories of media or literary images to construct social hierarchies. Ethnographers are thus not alone in imposing readings on social activity. "Natives" of public places are equally guilty; in Los Angeles or Moscow they impose all manner of moral, social, biological, or political motives onto the visible doings of strangers.

But just as the social reality of the stage was in my experience often denied, street impressions were frequently based on the erroneous supposition that things were fully transparent; the foreigner was assumed to be local, the local Gypsies to be outsiders. To interpret social activity in such places, post-Soviets deployed ideologies of theatricality; that is, they read street encounters not against a historical knowledge or social relations but in dramaturgical terms (see Crapanzano 1992:18, 95–104), as "characters" or "types." Gypsies were often said to come in two "types," but the street was home to only one of them. In Russia, any single person might shift from waxing poetic on Gypsy art to disparaging Gypsies at the markets or on public transport. This discursive division into "two kinds" of Gypsies parallels the ontological separation between art and byt. This division is not clear-cut: theatricality could be seen as both rehearsed and transcendent, daily life as both real and riddled with artifice. But even with these twists, the separation surfaces in numerous post-Soviet discourses about racial authenticity and market accountability, discourses that performatively entrap Roma in situations where they are misrecognized.

The division between art and byt[2] *partly* overlaps the one between "public" and "private," although both have a place in both realms:[3] byt can describe both binding social habits (everyday customs) and a solitary daily grind, while art can unfold both in transcendent solitude and on the most public of platforms. Of interest here are the more derogatory descriptions of byt as "public," when daily grind rubs elbows within crowds.

Gypsy myths mirror the ways in which public spaces are marked out as settings for social action,[4] and Gypsies are racialized through being mapped onto particular such settings. Racial hierarchies in turn come to seem natural because they are anchored to specific, familiar places. These hierarchies shift as the values and meanings of places shift. Racial categories certainly existed, though not officially, under Soviet socialism and were already linked to spaces such as street markets, but by the early 1990s, Soviets were deploying race in new ways to make sense of economic and political changes, and of the loss of empire. And while some post-Soviets continued to envision a romantic, literary Gypsy as companion to the Russian soul, itself described by Russian philosophers and poets from Berdaev to the Symbolists as "restless," "nomadic," these references also were changing, as we have seen.

In the 1990s (and earlier), the streets were where the "real," the "wild Gypsies" were said to be found. The street was described as if it were their natural habitat, though a degraded one, since modern-day Gypsies in central Russia lacked picturesque tents or wagons — journalists had to travel to the far reaches of Siberia to photograph sightings of the "last camp."

Many Roma did pursue street occupations (hawking, trading, begging), occupations that the socialist state frowned upon — these were the most visible Roma. Although non-Roma would not have recognized them, different groups monopolized different commodities: in the late 1980s and early 1990s, Russka (or Xeladytka) Romani women cornered the outer margins of bazaars wearing gray, goat-wool scarves, hawking vodka, chocolate, and cigarettes (the domestic, second-class Java brand, neither the first-class Kosmos nor the harsh Belamor). In the pedestrian underpasses, Lo-

FIGURE 4   Kelderara at a Moscow bazaar near Kiev train station in 1997. These women live a few hours outside Moscow and come into the city all together several times a week, either to trade or, as here, to tell fortunes to passersby.

vara, Ungri, and Russka (all women) alike tended card tables loaded with cotton shirts from Korea and angora sweaters from China. More Lovara women braved the packed bazaar crowds at the Children's World Department Store, selling fluffy, colorful men's scarves. The Vlaxura sold gold-colored costume rings and earrings cheaply, just outside some of the metro stations. Kelderara women did not usually trade — they stood in bazaars near train stations, or walked the suburban trains, carrying babies bundled in pure white cloth, reading palms. Near the tourist stretches of the Arbat and the Kremlin, by the McDonald's and Hotel International there were the beggars, Moldovanurja and Machvaja — usually not more than a few dozen in the capital at a time (one could recognize the same faces day in and day out), but highly visible at central tourist spots.

Although many Roma then (as now) were ordinary workers or professionals, their labors were invisible.[5] Likewise invisible — to non-Roma — at the bazaars were Romani men. Only Gypsy women and children were described against the backdrop of city streets and markets as "packs" or "flocks," indistinguishable from each other, shrieking in a "senseless" language. Russians were unaware that the Romani women worked in such groups because they were afraid of Russian crowds, of drunken Russian men, and of police who demanded bribes. Not knowing such details, non-Roma collected only brief, visual and visceral material to fuel entire theories of Gypsy culture and social structure. They authorized those theories not only by citing familiar texts, as we have seen, but also by mapping physical detail onto the stage of mundane, "public" settings.

Everyone has a Gypsy story, everyone has a narrative that begins on such a stage: "One time, at the bazaar, a Gypsy. . . . " Take, for instance, a vignette published in a 1990 monograph titled *Gypsies*. The scene, intended by its Russian authors to illustrate progress in Soviet assimilative battles, is set inside a Moscow Metro car:

> In the Metro, at the station Sokol'niki, two old Gypsy women entered the wagon. Each had at her back a sort of sack holding babies who could barely support their own heads, which, like balls, bounced with the jerking of the wagon. . . . Suddenly, a young black-haired fellow in a severe gray suit rose from a seat near us and, attentively peering into the Gypsies' eyes, uttered a few sharp words in Gypsy. The old ladies went dumb and became meek. They got out at the next station. . . .
>
> We approached him:
>
> "Please forgive our indiscretion, but what did you say to them?"
>
> "I am a worker, a smith, my father was a smith. We always worked for a living and never begged. But those — they are used to begging, their heads are fogged, they don't even understand that they shame themselves and all of us. I told them 'Your children must study, go home and wash them.'" (Druts and Gessler 1990:311)

This text appears in the closing pages, thus framing the entire book. The mundane, "realist" Metro setting embeds the "Gypsies" within sensual detail, merging physical character with place — the babies' heads jerk in unison with the lurches of the metro wagon, anchoring these Gypsy bodies to the car.[6] The passengers, representing society, merely observe, and thus reinforce the line between civility and impropriety. The "wild" Gypsies, ignoring public observation and judgment, flee also the opinion of their "own kind" when he is too civil — all this dovetails with Gypsy "asocial" behavior.

The authors report a conflict about assimilation as occurring in a "public" space — rather than reporting any debates that may have occurred at, say, a Romani wedding or in a Romani home. Because the setting was defined as a particular sort of public, the Russian authors could better maintain the narrative conceit of being accidental, objective witnesses to a spontaneous interaction. Placing reported action and speech in a "public" arena "deplaced" it, as usually occurring and easily verified, just as "devoicing" bolsters a speaker's authority.[7] They thus were able to avoid explaining social relations and policy that had mediated the conflict and to present it dramaturgically as a dyadic clash between "cultured" and "wild" Gypsies, the "two kinds."

Public transit was a common setting for reworking images of suspect non-Russians (see Lemon 2000), even more so as the 1990s progressed. Gypsies were not the only non-Russians upon whom were fixed anxieties about change, projected as fears of crime in the public streets. Hatred for Gypsies was not a political platform for young fascists in Russia as it has been in Romania or the Czech Republic, or even western Ukraine, although there have been a few violent incidents.[8] Gypsies were considered less well organized and less fierce than other non-Russians, such as Chechens. Moreover, their transgressions were gendered: Gypsies' petty theft and swindling were pictured as feminine, while Caucasian armed robbery, smuggling, and racketeering were seen as masculine efforts. Still, racialized activities were mapped onto public spaces in ways not wholly unique to Gypsies. Any "black" face there was suspect.

The press and many ordinary post-Soviets spoke of Caucasians, Central Asians, and other non-Russians as staging an "invasion" from outlying points of the former Soviet Union, just when the republics had seceded; the phrase "They are turning Moscow into a little Caucasus," reverberated in headlines and in kitchen conversations. People assumed that "blacks" were motivated to "invade" not by historical or economical forces (they were not always recognized as refugees or entrepreneurs) but by racial-psychological ones, by greed and "hot blood." Conflicts in the non-Russian republics were relocated internally, as "character" — not read in relation to demands for economic or cultural autonomy. Accounts of these people's presence in the capital elided the Soviet and imperial states' roles in those conflicts. The plots of media narratives echoed the fatalism of Greek revenge cycles, as if Caucasian culture and "hot blood" prevented the "tribes" from being agents.

Such conflicts were transposed onto the Moscow streets, as if they were redramatized there. In the winter of 1991, the Russian press seized upon an incident involving two Armenians and an Azeri taxi driver, in which the driver was killed in a dispute over fares. The whole affair reinforced Russian constructions of hot-tempered and violent Caucasians "killing each other," embroiled in endless, inescapable cycles of feuds among "clans" to even up monetary and "blood debts." Public transit also became a site of terrorist threat from "blacks." In summer 1996, bomb blasts in the Moscow Metro killed several people. The state responded to the second blast by unveiling "harsh measures" against criminals, including beefed-up visa regulations. After the third bomb, Moscow mayor Luzhkov pledged to "sweep out homeless and guest workers"[9] along with beggars. These people were to be identified according to what the mayor called their *vneshnij vid* (outward appearance).[10] A computer-generated composite image of the alleged bomber, with generic "southern" features, was posted on every tram and bus.

The weekend after that third blast, six thousand people were arrested for visa and *propiska* (residence permit) violations, mainly Asians, Africans, and people from the Caucasus, several such incidents being shown on television. Well before this incident, non-Russians had found it difficult to acquire Moscow residence permits. In earlier years, this had meant, for instance, that one could not obtain the *vizitka*, the card one had to show to state shop cashiers during the acute shortages of the late 1980s and early 1990s. The card limited purchases to registered Muscovites.[11] During that period, I often saw cashiers ask people with dark complexions or hair to show the card but hand a "Russian" their receipt straight away without even asking. In the winter of 1991, I too had no visitka, but I have a pale face and was *never* asked to show it. Such cards are no longer in use, although the internal passport regime remains in effect as of 2000.

Black Faces, Black Markets

Thus is enacted a grammar of surfaces. To trace the paradigms of that grammar, I need to sketch briefly categories of "race" in Russia, as their connections to other categories have been changing over the last few decades. "Race" is often left out of accounts of social hierarchy in late-twentieth-century Russia. In the early 1990s, Western journalists picked up the phrase "currency apartheid" to label the division of new, upscale commercial space into "ruble sides" and "dollar sides" (see Lemon 1998). However, they neglected more literal forms of racialized distinction that channeled market relations and colored discourse about market changes.

Racialized categories first came to my attention as significant to Romani daily life in Russia in 1990. I had been riding the Moscow Metro with a Romani man, the husband of a Romani ethnographer. People were shooting us hostile looks, and when I asked him why, he replied, "Because you are white and I am black." I was surprised, learning that the term "black" cut in a different place along the spectrum of racial categories than it would in American English. "Blackness" is everywhere culturally constructed; in Russia, "black" *(chjernyj)* refers very broadly to a whole range of people, including those whom North Americans would probably describe as "olive-skinned," with dark eyes and hair, *tjemnyj* (dark) or *smuglyj* (swarthy) may substitute. His wife later denied her husband's rationale, stating that racism did not exist in the Soviet Union: "Racism is something you have in America." This was several years after glasnost had begun, but she, a scholar at the Academy of Sciences, still echoed official Soviet discourses that had for so long depicted racism, colonialism, and ethnic nationalism as the sicknesses of capitalist countries alone. Indeed, Soviet affirmative action policies *had* improved life chances and social status for some Roma, and she had good personal reasons for investing in those discourses.

Other post-Soviet scholars, in conversation with me, argued that "race" was not a salient social category for understanding either the Soviet Union or the post-Soviet territories because the relevant terms in public discourse were not "race" but *natsional'nost'* (nationality/ethnicity) or *narodnost'* (ethnicity/peoplehood). Indeed, titles in 1990s Russian ethnology on conflict in the Caucasus or Central Asia read: "National and Interethnic Situation in X" and "Social tension and Internationality Conflict in Y."[12] However, one wonders whether "racialized" criteria informed local discourses about these conflicts. In 1994, a Russian scholar objected to me that the term "race" imposed a foreign category upon Russian social life. From the perspective of historical particularity, his point is well taken.[13] It is not my intention to transpose specific histories of slavery and repression from the American continents to Eurasia; the point is simply that Soviets, like most everyone else, did rely, in both daily life and in the execution of policy, on external signs (physical or not) to infer internal, biological or inherited essences and to explain behavior, culture, and social position. Most of my consultants, in everyday conversation, linked what they called a "black" complexion to a naturalized identity.

However firmly the Soviet state declared itself against racism, it purged neither racial discrimination nor racial categories.[14] And what official discourse minimized, literary genres hardly checked, as Slezkine remarks of 1930s–50s fictional representations of the North: "Now the fatherly 'teasing twinkle' had given way to the pristine color of the sky or the sea, which suggested the purity of the Russians' intentions and perhaps hinted at their racial superiority" (1994: 324). Numerous racialized terms circulated well before the 1990s, terms never totally eclipsed by categories such as "natsional'nost'." Racialized terms were used both to describe complexion and to index underlying character in Russian writing since at least the nineteenth century.[15] Collections of explicitly racial slurs recorded decades earlier belie attempts to trace them either as originating only with the post-Soviet period, or as bubbling up after long repression. Roback's (1979) dictionary of ethnic slurs gives pejoratives deploying "black," referring to both color and social category, recorded just after World War II, as do dictionaries of prison slang spoken in the 1960s (Rossi 1992). Terms such as *chjernozhopyje* (black asses) entered popular speech from such prison lexicons decades ago.[16]

Post-Soviets in the 1990s used racial discourses in nonuniform ways. The extremist press appealed to genetic and cultural purity, connecting race to Russian nationalism: "The highest goal of the government must be to preserve that racial nucleus which alone can create culture, beauty and all the highest values" (Russian National Union 1995). Terms such as "nation" were made to do the work of racial categories, as in this 1995 statement by the Russian National Union: "There are even people who . . . rush to mix with the Jewish nationality and expect all kinds of beneficial results. A man and wife who are both Russian and happen to want healthy, racially whole children are automatically labeled fascists" (1995:1). Others, such as the Eurasianists, argued for a historically unique, hybrid, racial *blend* of Asians with Slavs, one that would stand against the uniform hegemony of the West. Even across such a continuum, discourses of blood and kind had great currency in both Soviet and post-Soviet Russia.

In the 1990s, as before, the adjective "chernyj" (black) was sometimes a slur. Terms such as *litsa kavkazskoj natsional'nosti* (persons of Caucasian nationality, though there was no administrative label "Caucasian nationality") euphemized it, as did colloquial near slurs, such as *juzhnyje* (southerners). The Russian for "persons" *(litsa)* also means "faces," specifically human faces. Another term, *morda,* is used for animal faces and appears in unmistakable insults such as *zhidovskaja morda* (Kike mug) or *tsyganskaja morda* (Gypsy mug). But there existed no construction "litsa of Russian nationality"; it was reserved for non-Russians, as were the animal terms. Officialese thus hovered semantically close to slur, resonating with morda.

Such semantic description does not explain how the force of racialized terms and identities shifted during the 1990s, reweighted with reference to new cultural concerns and political agendas.[17] For instance, Russian constructions of Asians were always multiple (depicted less often as passive-aggressive inscrutables, as in the United States, but as fierce and rapacious Mongols and Tatars, as in Tarkovskij's 1966 film *Andre Rubljov*) but, more important, these images were connected to political and social interests; for instance, in the early 1990s, the Japanese were framed in terms of the debate over the Kuril Islands; the Korean diaspora within Russia, in terms of recent efforts to buy land in the Urals; the Siberian nomads, as inhabitants of lands rich in timber, coal, oil, and diamonds.

Commerce long had been pictured as the province of non-Russians (see Rieber 1982), Gypsies and Jews especially. Soviet-era theatrical representations had not severed such connections: in a 1950s Romani Theater script, a character mocking both literacy campaigns for minorities in general and "Gypsies" as mercenary in particular, claims that "the Gypsy alphabet begins with the letters *Ah-Be-Vy-Ge-Da: vygoda!*" The letters of this Soviet "Gypsy alphabet" are in fact the same as those beginning the Russian alphabet (ABVGD . . .), but when sounded out they spell the Russian word for "profit."

Racialized groups were seen metonymicly, in connection to material interests or possessions; such tropes are no doubt at work in depictions of ethnic "mafias" as networks of financial corruption. Of course, not all Soviet mafias were seen as ethnic: the Russian *nomenklatura* were often called "mafia," and there was the "Russian mafia." Soviets for decades had evoked "mafia" to account for nearly any injustice in distribution, and since distribution was such an existential problem, "mafia" links were a major ontological trope for Soviet social life. But as Western reportage replaced standard tales of Soviet bread lines with articles about mafia and corruption, both Russian and foreign commentary focused on identifying the "organized criminal groups" who were "infiltrating" government or hindering the "free market."

In fact, however, network-based strategies of attaining goods and privileges were widespread. So was petty theft from state property or em-
ployers. Illicit markets had been well documented for decades.[18] All this was
normalized; "Everybody lives this way" being a common refrain in daily
conversation. But networks in which *everyone* was implicated could not be
isolated and purged. Ethnic "clans," however, *could* be detached as visible
ciphers for the corruption of everyone else. Such associations of racialized
groups with crooked exchange practices are not peculiar to the former
Soviet bloc but have been played out there in specific ways, which have
changed at the fall of socialism.

This is not to say that the fall of socialism unraveled former networks;
toppling statues of Lenin in fits of iconoclastic vandalism did not change
the nervous procedures of commerce overnight. In Russia, privatization
rendered fluid some properties, such as real estate, that previously had been
fixed (see Condee 1995), but the arrival of the market did not erase most
people's experience of the bazaar. Most impressive was not that commerce
was entirely new but that it was displaced from its accustomed, out-of-
the-way venues. Exchanges became suddenly more *visible* in more central
places. Hawkers with card tables occupied every corner of every well-
trafficked street, behind stands and inside small kiosks, at every stop of the
Metro, both above ground inside the station and down in the tunneled
transfer walkways (see Lemon 2000). Though private trade restrictions
loosened and penalties for speculation ended,[19] bazaar trade, between
strangers in street crowds or kiosks, was still "scary" and "dangerous," and
fear of noise, distractions, false scales, and counterfeits remained.

The crowded markets were not new appearances of the invisible hand—
they had been there all along, only at the edges of town, cropping up most
visibly in times of crisis and shortage.[20] Younger people may have found
glamour in commerce, consumption, and everything foreign; this was system change, the end of a three-generation cycle of history. But for older
post-Soviets in the early 1990s, crowds hawking rationed wares at inflated
prices evoked the Great Patriotic War (World War II). In the early winter
of 1991, just before the Soviet breakup, and just as "democratic" and "free
market" reforms were promised, food was scarcer than the year before. No
bread was sold in the shops; there were sugar-ration coupons but no
sugar—"It's as bad as during the blockade, as bad as during the war." What
the American press wrote of as "free market reforms," these older people

experienced as a familiar response to crisis and disorder. To them, those markets offered not opportunity but the tedious and demeaning necessity to "scrape"—they linked visible street trade, not the socialist system, with shortage, stigma, and threatening enemies.[21]

Many Russians used race to account for the new market enemies. Even moderates layered economic discourses with moral statements linking race to nation to territory, painting impoverished Russians as inhabiting a vast country rich in natural resources, tapped by foreigners and the mafia. Extreme nationalists went farther, citing the lines of non-Russian peddlers with card tables in the park next to the first Moscow MacDonald's, across from Pushkin's monument, as "desecrating" this emblem of the Russian nation,"[22] forgetting that Pushkin's grandfather had been Abyssinian and that Pushkin had been a symbol for Soviet internationalism.

By the late 1980s, traders from Georgia, Armenia, and other republics, who long had been prominent at the official produce markets, *were* expanding their trade to include foreign cigarettes, liquor, cosmetics, and clothing. In the 1990s Russians became just as active in informal street trade—and had better access to the newly formed commodity exchanges in the capital and were better positioned to take over official stores and set up joint ventures. But non-Russian non-Muscovites had nowhere to set up shop but in the streets. Ironically, even while some "blacks" in the capital were excluded from certain exchange spheres and were relegated to the street, mercenary images were firmly embedded in public stereotypes of such peoples. Now trade was pinned to "blacks" because it was the only setting in which Russians saw them (Lemon 1995). Thus, in the 1990s, Muscovites were asserting with confidence that goods circulated through foreign, "black" hands. It was these people who were visibly distinct at the newly multiplied street bazaars, with oranges and leather coats for sale.

Because "blacks" seemed so visible just when trade itself had become more visible, it would be tempting to argue that change to a free market inevitably entailed a backlash of exclusionism and racial essentialism. Similar arguments have been made for other historical periods seen as "transitional." Historian Michael O'Malley (1994), for instance, argues that, during the American Reconstruction period, new market freedoms led society to reify and ossify racial categories. O'Malley, like many others, characterizes the free market as an unpredictable, agentless force; with anonymous cash crossing and muddying social boundaries, society must compensate by firming social categories, almost as if by reflex. But as Boas reminds us, different causes may have similar effects (19). Arguments that lay the blame for racial or ethnic hostility at the doorstep of the free market disregard similar phenomena in other kinds of economic systems.

Verdery (1993), in contrast, argues that fetishizing ethnic difference in Eastern Europe is neither new with the market transition nor undergoing a resurgence after having "lain dormant" — state socialism itself reproduced ethnic boundaries. To compete for resources, Romanian intellectuals had to evoke "national" values. Meanwhile, in an "economy of shortage," people relied on personal networks to avoid queues, and "when goods were short, they went to members of one's own group" since sharpening ethnic boundaries "expels competitors" (1993:176, 182). Likewise, in Russia, practical and discursive links between race and exchange did not spring fully formed from perestroika. They had roots in Soviet nationalities' policies and in informal trade practices going back decades, even to anti-Semitism from the last century.[23] It had been commonplace to describe Soviet underground trade networks as "run by" Jews, Armenians, or other non-Russians. The émigré Soviet lawyer Konstantin Simis, for instance, in a memoir about "corruption" in the USSR (1982:147), does sympathize with the non-Russians excluded from any employment but commerce, yet describes "family clans" and "tentacular sales networks." Other scholars on the USSR have argued not only that state socialist economies hardened social and ethnic boundaries but that nationalities policy likewise entrenched "ethnic particularism" (Slezkine 1994b). I am thus skeptical about whether any one type of modernist economic system has been more likely than another to entail that social categories become more rigid, racialized, or hierarchical.

As Verdery remarks, socialist exchange firmed up ethnic boundaries. All the same, in the 1990s, racialized surfaces and essences were related to social practices and public settings in new ways.

Dark Eyes and Gypsy Artifice

1990s discourses about the market met racial discourses at their intersection with an ontological problem related to the opposition between art and byt: the problem of distinguishing authentic persons and genuine motivations. Actually, since at least the late 1960s, a trope of hidden, authentic ethnicity had been surfacing in popular films, as the various incarnations of

Budulaj dealt with in various TV and film versions of *Tsygan;* this theme multiplied in the 1990s, as in *Luna Park* (1992), *To See Paris and Die* (1993), and *Shirly-Myrly* (1995). The device: a character is not "pure" Russian, and that fact is hidden by parents or foster parents, then revealed through telltale behavior. The 1995 slapstick farce *Shirly-Myrly* takes the motif to absurd limits. The hero, a criminal, doubles and triples into long-lost twins, then triplets, ad infinitum, discovering in turn that he is half-Jewish, half-Gypsy (revealed by his instinctive musical success), then half-African. . . .

Race poses the problem of authenticity because its signs are slippery; ostensibly essential, race is not always so clearly marked. For instance, in the countries of the former USSR, many Caucasians, Tatars — and Roma — are no darker in complexion than are some Russians. Moreover, other things besides physical features could index race. Of Gypsies, it was said that "trading is in their blood," that "stealing horses is in their blood," that metal working is "in their blood," just as "talent," especially in music or dancing, was said to lie "in the blood," passed along through the generations.[24] This Russian phrase, "in the blood," was not simply a metaphoric extension from a notion of ingrained habit; "national" practices were seen as innate. Witness how one retired Russian judge transposed an opinion, which I had usually heard expressed by means of blood tropes, into a scientific, genetic register: "It's in their genes. . . . do they understand their place in society? God found them useful, so they have a right to live. But their life is difficult, and their genes make them unable to work" (interview 1992).

Often such "national traits," less immediately visible than hair color or complexion — those said to lie *v krovi* ("in the blood") — had to be detected, unmasked. Communist-era Gypsy films and stage productions underwrote the trope of race as something under the skin, to be uncovered via signs of talent or other signs. In the Moscow Romani Theater adaptation of *Gypsy,* Budulaj searches for his family after the war. He stays at a collective farm and meets a boy who turns out to be his son. The boy's adoptive mother conceals his "true" identity and claims that a Tatar grandfather gave him his "swarthy face." Yet the boy betrays his blood when he learns "Gypsy dance" from visiting Gypsy youths — for he picks up the steps instantly, instinctively. His father thereby recognizes his own flesh just as immediately. The proof was in the performance.

Cash was another outward sign of the presumably internal mercenary proclivities of "blacks"[25] — the Gypsy woman whose long hair, like that of her literary Caucasian sisters, drips with coins that jingle on her chest. The image is extended to other minorities, as in this 1970s account of a Siberian shamaness: "There is fire in her black eyes; her braids tremble on her breast with a tinkling of coins, her gestures are energetic and imperious" (quoted in Slezkine 1994a:356). As a racial metonym, the motif of jewelry was used not only by Soviet novelists, but even by journalists, as in the following 1930s newspaper description of a Moscow Gypsy schoolroom: "Outwardly, the little Gypsies differ only slightly from Russian children. Only their dark, swarthy faces give them away. That, and [that] some still wear their glittering earrings and bracelets; dark, superstitious family life does not let the little Gypsies from its clutches. There, in the families, the children are made to wash floors, burdened with backbreaking work, prevented from attending school and doctors' checkups — and from removing their jewelry" (Goricha 1931).

At the time of this article's publication, Roma were being encouraged to study in Romani. However, they were expected to shed certain other distinguishing practices. Songs and dances were permissible, but gold jewelry indexed *both* a capitalist materialism and ethnic clinging to clan life and cultural backwardness. Armenians, Uzbeks, and Russian peasants alike were stereotyped by gold teeth. There is nothing particularly Russian about depicting coins as cleaving to uncivilized, oriental flesh; Simmel claimed it was "Eastern" to wear money on the body because, "in the Orient, all wealth is conditional upon the fact that the owner is able to flee with it" (Simmel 1991:329). Jewels and money melt into "dark, swarthy faces" as if all flow together in the blood. "Racial" and "bourgeois" identities, both seen as transgressive, were marked by overlapping signs.

Gypsies, unlike other "blacks" who were thought to rely on simple chicanery, were believed to *enchant* cash to themselves.[26] Crime journalists described the talents of Gypsy fortune-tellers in extracting money in physical terms: they have the "ability to read subtle changes of pulse rate, eye dilation, lid flickers, sweat, etc.," which indicated an emotional "readiness to believe" on the part of the victim.[27] In late Soviet films and stories, Gypsy dancing compels drunken aristocrats or foreigners to throw away rubles (or dollars!), just as in nineteenth-century literature, Gypsy song impelled Russian nobles to shower beautiful Gypsy singers with money.[28] The descriptions of Gypsies' bodily movements suggest that they are made of a substance resonating with, and thus attracting, money.

Conversely, when 1990s media claimed that Gypsies had become wealthy at the expense of society, it invoked the mysticism of Gypsy theatricality, song, and hypnotic power by naming their "dark eyes," as in this article titled "Gypsies Wander in Volvos: Their Way of Life as a Mirror on Our Economy":

> Mikhail Sergeevich [Gorbachev] perhaps made the greatest gift to the Gypsy people with his anti-alcohol legislation. Crowds of the thirsty in every city and backwoods were drawn to their Gypsy brothers: in Moscow, for instance, to the train stations, in Malojaroslav, to the railroad bridge. Here you could buy your favorite forbidden drink from these *possessors of dark eyes* at any time of the day or night. If you will, this was when the capital of several [Gypsy] families crawled into the first million. (*Rossiskaja Gazeta,* June 2, 1995; emphasis added)

The line "possessors of dark eyes" alludes to that most popular of Gypsy romances in Russia, "Dark Eyes" ("Ochi Chernye"), a song exalting dangerous, sensual magnetism (though to some it has the flavor of kitsch):

> Ochi chjernyje, ochi strastnyje,
> ochi zhguchije i prekrasnyje!
> Kak bojus' ja vas,
> kak ljublju ja vas!
>
> [Dark eyes, passionate eyes,
> eyes burning and marvelous!
> How I fear you,
> How I love you!]

The phrase itself alludes to Russian poetry about Gypsies since the nineteenth century.[29] In both the original song text and in everyday references to it, the erotic, even sinister force in the hypnotic black gaze springs from its power to create illusions, to mislead, to influence. "Do you know what dark eyes mean?" said one Russian trying to dissuade me from talking to Gypsies. "They mean that such people have sway over others — they have more *ekstra sens* [ESP]." Especially on the public stage of the bazaar, Gypsies were seen as supernatural masters of deceit. As one young Russian man (himself employed in buying secondhand gold on the streets), told our video crew, "Gypsies make you hand over money without even realizing it — it's like they hypnotize you" (Lemon and Nakamura 1994, videotape transcript). Tass reported in 1998: "Lvov Police are searching for Gypsy women who have hypnotized a 16-year old Ukrainian girl into giving them a gold crucifix and 9,000 grivnjas. . . . The girl, identified only as Kristina, cannot help the investigation much: she said a dark-complexioned Gypsy woman had looked into her eyes and kept saying something" [Itar-Tass, August 13, 1998]. To discern Gypsy trickery in "dark eyes" locates concern with misleading surfaces at its intersection with widespread anxiety about social and economic change.

This anxiety was partly fed by theatrical models that described a social world in which people must read through appearances and rely on manuals and advice books to detect swindlers and cheats. The historian Jean-Christophe Agnew (1986) argues that market transformations in sixteenth-century England generated a "crisis of representation" (97), in which people no longer knew how to represent "one's motives and one's relations" (x).[30] The market and the theater were special sites of crisis because they shared "conditions of belief and accountability" that set them apart from the rest of everyday life, reflecting each in the other. The theater "thematized representation and misrepresentation as the pivotal problems of its drama. For the first time, perhaps, theater made the . . . 'idea of the play' its cardinal concern and . . . [thus] invoked the same problematic of exchange — the same questions of authenticity, accountability and intentionality — at issue in the 'idea of the market'" (11–12). Echoing O'Malley (1994), Agnew argues that authority thus had to legitimize itself by clarifying social identities and boundaries, they had to "to 'purify' the terms of social relations . . . to name the cause of social anxieties" (xx).

While we may continue to doubt, given the arguments outlined in the previous section, whether any particular type of economic system, or "transition" from one certain type to another, demands a particular kind of shift in social identities, early post-Soviet Russia certainly experienced crises of representation. However, these were not utterly new crises but picked up where Soviet crises had left off (unmasking enemies of the people, detecting fictive marriage proposals, etc.), finding *new points of articulation* with understandings of shifting market relations and social hierarchies.

Swaths of post-Soviet literature and film dealt with the problems of sincerity and authenticity. The early 1990s saw a proliferation of advice books on how to avoid swindles and detect counterfeits, how to project a trust-worthy demeanor (or emulate one, à la Dale Carnegie). There were psychology books on how to read physiognomic clues (e.g., *What Is in His Subconscious? Twelve Lessons in the Psychotechnology of Penetrating an Interlocutor's Subconscious* [Panasjuk 1996]). Post-Soviets often spoke about fears of being cheated and looking for visible signs. During that time, product labels multiplied (dozens of vodka brands by 1997), as did the sorts of circulating currencies, foreign and domestic. People worried about whether the contents of pretty new bottles or boxes "matched the label," while TV and print media circulated advice about how to discern counterfeit products and bills. Anything might be counterfeit. Vodka had to be checked for poison or dilution. Foreign goods were particularly suspect, and foreign currencies had to be inspected carefully (see Lemon 1998).

Like the surfaces of labels or currencies, the human face could reflect trickery in market warfare. The blame for fraudulent labels sometimes even was transposed directly onto black faces, as when, in February 1996, Russian police raided a plant manufacturing bogus vodka and the "black" Armenian suspects were lined up against the wall as the camera slowly lingered on each non-Russian face. Here cameras amplified the structures of visibility by which Soviets "knew" race, anchoring the backgrounds against which race could be performed.

Performing Blood, Mistaking Race

Though Russians had not actually abstained from exchange in the Soviet past, some liked to believe that they had. But many had not stood exposed and visible as they made their deals, had not made them on the public streets. When they began to do so, it was as if they had transgressed accustomed, public roles to become these characters pointed out on train platforms by Russian grandmothers. Intellectual Russians who undertook trade in the 1990s described themselves as becoming "black." More than one Russian intellectual told me with regret, sorry he had to stoop to commerce, "We are all becoming Gypsies."

Still, Russians could claim to turn the tables on Gypsies without danger of becoming one. One young Muscovite, himself an active black market dealer in antique books and Stalinist medals, recounted to me in 1991:

I have no Gypsy acquaintances, I avoid them. They can swindle you. They used to fill cigarette boxes with paper and sell them after they had sealed them expertly. They sold shoe polish as mascara. But once my mother herself fooled a Gypsy. She was studying on a park bench, when the Gypsy came up and said, "I can tell you are going to pass your exam." She put the money from telling this fortune in her pocket and then, as she turned to do another reading, my mother plucked the money from her pocket. The people around saw this, and more and more came up to have their fortunes told. When she finally checked her pocket, where she expected to find piles of money there was none, as my mother had been giving it all back to the clients. (Interview from field notes 1991)

The wily Russian out-Gypsies the Gypsy—all the while remaining true to Russian networks and loyalties, "giving it all back to the clients," presumably innocent Russians.[31]

Roma, however, despite a reputation for masking, had little choice about the ways in which they actually were misrecognized. This was apparent when one Romani performer, Olga Demeter, described how she had escaped misplaced anti-Semitism on public transit. Here was a proof-by-performance echoing Budulaj's epiphanous recognition of his son:

Discrimination—there isn't any of that. Haven't I told you yet how it saved me that I am a Gypsy? I am on the bus, and a drunk, a Russian, was hovering near me. He said, "Huh, look here! Kikes! Jews! We should just kill them all!" and he came up closer—he held his hand over me. And I look at him and I say [she illustrates with a shoulder shimmy], "I'm a Gypsy!" He fell on his knees then and started to sing the song, "Dark eyes" and I answered him, "Passionate eyes!" And the bus stopped, and I ran away! (Interview from field notes 1993)

In the telling, she denies "discrimination" and any social asymmetries entailed by being seen as Gypsy. To the contrary, "dark eyes" (or at least their evocation) were useful—even though those very same features had led to her being misrecognized as another stigmatized minority.

Many Roma did not contest that external traits and internal talents were signs of racial or genealogical authenticity. Whether professional performers or not, they had profoundly internalized that dance talent and musicality—the dances themselves—were "in the blood." This seemed self-evident when so many children of famous singers had followed their parents into the profession. Many Roma, however, also spoke of blackness as distinguishing a "true Gypsy." While some emphasized that "we, too, have people with green eyes or pale skin," others teased paler Roma, calling them gazhje (non-Roma); one auburn-haired, teenage Lovari girl dyed her hair black for a time, so that unfamiliar Roma would not take her for a gazhji.

However, in the eyes of many Roma, applause for inherited talent, for "Gypsy art," could not always compensate for social barriers entailed by being "black" on the street or bazaar. Some were much more cynical about the troubles entailed by "being black," especially if they had not made a career on the stage. One Kelderari welder noted to me in 1991 that, once Russians identified him as "black," they expected a whole array of transgressions or economic crimes, so that he could not even purchase the things he needed: "All Russians care about is whether you're black or white. And if you're black you are obviously a speculator. Say I need to buy a lot of linoleum [points to the new house he is building, then at the ruined linoleum of his current house], say I need thirty sheets! They look at me and think for sure I'm just going to resell it, maybe they don't even give it to me" (interview 1991). "We are *negry*,"[32] he told me. "We are treated like a second class here, like your blacks in America." Here, certainly, *was* an importation of a foreign racial category, but one imported by Roma, and although grounded in images of a distant society, its foreign reference did not negate its local salience.[33]

By indexing *foreign* "blackness," Roma could shift their own place within local racial hierarchies, along the gradient of "civilizedness." And this was easier for them to do than to claim, "We are becoming Russian." Younger Roma especially were enthralled by the music and dress of the African Americans they saw on MTV, their fascination paralleling general Soviet attraction to U.S. pop culture. They traced affinity with American blacks not in terms of defeat or of being "second-class," but in terms of an "attitude" they claimed to detect in the movements of American rap and jazz musicians, an attitude they said rendered them "like us." They extended the logic to equate "blackness" with America ("The Statue of Liberty—isn't that where Michael Jackson dances in the video?"). Since America was culturally positioned by many post-Soviets as "better than Russia" (materially better off, more civilized), the youth could reverse the local valence of

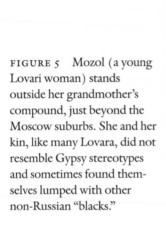

FIGURE 5   Mozol (a young Lovari woman) stands outside her grandmother's compound, just beyond the Moscow suburbs. She and her kin, like many Lovara, did not resemble Gypsy stereotypes and sometimes found themselves lumped with other non-Russian "blacks."

blackness and thus of Gypsiness: Roma, if more like American blacks (and thus more like Americans), must be "better" than Russians, all the more for being "black."

But convincing other post-Soviets of this logic was quite hopeless. In a romantic mood, a Russian might agree that Roma are "like American negry" for their ability to "musically improvise," but in daily life, Gypsies were but another example of clannish, local "blacks." These were not Americans performing on TV but "black" beggars of the bazaar. Gypsies were instead lumped together with "southerners" as "hot-blooded," with Jews as "mercenary," with Siberian tribes as "small peoples," "close to nature."[34] Roma had internalized some of this lumping and appropriated it when describing affinity between themselves and other Soviet "blacks." As one middle-aged Romani woman, a part-time marketer, told me: "Armenians know how to make money, like us, while Russians are too foolish."

Russians often mistook Roma for other blacks, and vice versa; sometimes they mistook refugees and beggars (for instance, from Central Asia) for Gypsies.[35] They could hardly see the difference between Lovara Roma and

Armenians. Russians' misrecognition became especially salient to Roma in the months after the 1991 coup attempt, just after the incident when two Armenians had killed an Azeri taxi driver. For some time after the event, Russian cabdrivers refused to pick up males who looked like "southerners" or "blacks." Because some Roma, such as Lovara, besides being "swarthy," do not dress in the fashion of filmic or literary Gypsies but instead in contemporary European designs (men in rayon baggy pants, women in long pencil skirts), Russians confused them with Armenians or Georgians. Taxi drivers would not pick up Lovara, either. As one teenage girl from a well-to-do merchant Romani family astutely noted, Russians depended not only on physical features but on markers like dress to classify "blacks." "You," she said as she fingered my foreign, silk shirt, "could be black, too, especially if they saw you with *us.*" As for the incident itself, she recounted the following:

> Since the Azeri thing, taxi drivers don't want to take blacks. You can stand for an hour, no one will stop. If you dress well — not like Russians — it means you are "black." Once me and my cousins were going home at midnight. We finally got a car — used our best Gypsy accent, "We are Gypsies!" and reassured him, "Gypsies always pay!" It was boring in the cab, so our brothers started joking, "You stupid Russian, we're really Georgians, we're fooling you!" "Get out of my cab!" He left us right there, and we stood for an hour! Those girls cursed their brothers! (Interview from field notes 1991)

The Romani teenagers found themselves, in this situation, less despised than another minority. It was to their advantage to perform themselves not as non-Roma (such as Georgians) but as Gypsies. But to do this, to avoid being mistaken for the wrong kind of "blacks," they had to "pass" as Gypsies in the manner non-Roma imagined them.

Gypsies are described with great regularity as masters of strategic masquerading. However, this time they had little alternative to such a performative strategy — the taxi drivers were mistaking their identity in the first place. Features ostensibly marking racial *and* market "blackness" (skin, clothes, cash, language) were in fact slippery; they umbrellaed numerous social "kinds" and indexed changing cultural and social hierarchies. Roma thus were used to being both misread and misrepresented.

At issue is who defines what "black" means. Roma performed racialized categories in more multivalent ways than did the media, taxi-drivers, or Russian neighbors. They could treat "blackness" ironically to reappropriate it. A Lovar writes his name in his Soviet passport, in Romani, as *Melalo Kalo* (Dirty Black) — "black" but in a language that no Russian bureaucrat would understand. Or, blackness could be rendered positive even if romanticized. At the Romani Sunday school, the children (themselves of varying complexions) were encouraged to draw dark-faced Gypsy girls, the teacher remarking of two pictures, "Of course the dark one [is better]. Again why? Because here we have a *clear type*."

"Blackness" being so broad and contextually dependent made it a "shifter": like a personal pronoun, it pointed to *relations* among "us" and "them" more than it referenced a stable group. Roma could choose to define themselves as "black" among other blacks, widening the inclusive indexicality of the term, to share being lumped together, as "us." This is how the Lovari girl mentioned earlier continued her narrative:

> Once we couldn't get a cab at all, so we took the Metro. We saw how all the gazhje were reading, and my cousin started saying, "What are they writing? What are they writing?" They thought he was crazy. All the other black people, Armenians and such, were smiling; they knew. "What are they writing about us blacks, eh?" One old lady said, "They are writing that we need to kill you all, that you are robbing us, and we are becoming poor." Then another black said, "We should kill you." My brother laughed and he said, "No, no, you don't have to kill her — this is a good, fat, Russian woman." We laughed so hard, we had to get off the train there!

"What are they writing about us blacks?" The question less requested information than it referred to a relationship to the majority that "we blacks" shared in that place at that time. It both indexed and performed their common experience of being lumped, marked, and described. Speaking directly of being shut out by print expressed how all the blacks on the train experienced an unimagined, anticommunity as non-Russians. I reverse Anderson's formulation of "Imagined Communities" (1983) because, in this case, certain citizens only watched while other citizens consumed print media. This exclusion was cemented not by inability to read (contrary to stereotypes of the illiterate Gypsy, many Roma in Russia can read, some in several languages), but lack of control over representation of (and in) public places. To joke about being written about and read about on public transport indexed other public exclusions and misrecognitions, whether in politics or on the streets. Those misrecognitions are mediated by ideologies about theatricality dividing street from stage, the sorts of places Gypsies supposedly inhabit, and concerns about counterfeit in both byt and art.

· 3 ·

"What Is Your Nation?"
Performing Romani Distinctions

In the 1990s Soviets often claimed that Gypsy beggars they saw on the streets were "actually Gypsy barons" who, by night, returned to extravagant houses to change clothes: "Tsygan jest' tsygan" (A Gypsy is a Gypsy). Although Romani "beggars" and "barons" were in fact different people, Roma lacked control over media infrastructures and so were unable to display self-representations of Romani diversity. In this representational void, many non-Romani investigators see themselves as penetrating a hidden social world, pulling back a curtain of false stereotypes to reveal the variety of the "real Gypsies."[1] But these unveilings sometimes reproduce the veil, if only because the model of a curtained proscenium divides observers and actors into two realms of "reality." The two realms continue to be imagined as maximally different. For instance, against the cliché of Pushkin's free-loving Zemfira, some declare that Gypsies "in fact" follow very "strict tribal laws" (Druts and Gessler 1990). But even when "tribal law" trumps Zemfira's volja, Gypies are nevertheless framed as traditionally antimodern, inherently rebellious against rational law and order. The category "tribal law" thrusts "wild Gypsies" into eternal "clan" conflicts each identically and internally motivated by "custom," like cell division.

Chaos or Caste? Ethnographic Accounts of Social Order

The resort to "tribal law" to explain Romani culture and difference is ahistorical, for differences and conflicts among Roma have had multiple causes, many not "internal." Therefore, explaining Romani culture and history should be a matter not of lifting a stage curtain or penetrating the backstage mystery of the proscenium but of tracing Romani practices and relations and discourse about them more broadly. When Roma themselves speak of differences among groups, they, too, refer to differences in "strict" customary law, but they also perform those differences by invoking pan-European discourses about "civilization," even when calling upon local memory to do so.

Throughout Europe, disunity is ascribed to Gypsies as if they were not only outside "society" but were incapable of being "social" even amongst themselves, as if they were most alike in being disunited. Liegeois (1994: 261) remarks, "After all, Gypsy social organization does not, as a rule, predispose them to a system based on association or federation: segmentation does not easily take to unity," though later he adds that "it is far from rare for 'outsiders' to provoke or exacerbate antagonisms and differences of opinion between different Gypsy organizations" (268). Journalists and policy makers rarely take Romani activism seriously and claim that political organization is impossible because Roma are predisposed to infighting. Romani difference is perceived as unruly; at a small 1996 Prague conference that gathered Roma from several different countries, an Organization for Security and Cooperation in Europe (OSCE) representative asked (in English) that the Roma present inform her about their problems—but warned that the OSCE had had its fill of conflicting reports and admonished them to first "agree among themselves" on "what Roma want." They treated real differences arising from varied local conditions as internal disagreements, rather than as problems that state policies produce differently, such that Roma across state borders are left with different issues to resolve.

For instance, Roma are situated within Russia differently from in other Eastern European countries; they are, in general, better off economically but more marginal politically (a situation that has reversed since the 1920s and 1930s, when Soviet Roma were more politically active than anywhere else in the world). These differences result more from policy and long-term social interactions than from inherent differences in "custom" among Roma in various countries. In Hungary and Slovakia, many Roma started working in state factories after World War II but became rapidly and massively unemployed in the late 1980s as factories shut down or foreign firms bought andretooled them.[2] In Soviet Russia, in contrast, few Roma were ever proletarianized, and the fall of the socialist state thus affected them less suddenly and sweepingly. In the 1990s in Hungary, the Czech Republic, Slovakia, and Macedonia, Roma sat in administrative positions, while in

Russia there are no Roma in public office, no Romani political parties, and only a few cultural organizations. On the other hand, Soviet Roma had nominal status there as a "national minority" after 1925, meaning that they could enter "tsygan" on the line for "nationality" (natsional'nost') on internal passports. Stalin distinguished between "nations" and "national minorities." "Nations" were to possess four characteristics in common (language, culture/worldview, territory, and economy) while "national minorities," more flexibly, need not possess all of these. Both could use the label "nationality." Most other socialist states denied Roma either status; Yugoslavia was the first to upgrade Roma to "nationality" status in 1981.[3] In Central and Southeast Europe, Roma are the largest and most visible minorities, living in compact settlements and ghettos. Their presence is easier to ignore in Russia, where Roma are more dispersed over vaster spaces. Although in numbers they are stronger than several other non-Russian "nationalities,"[4] Soviet Roma lacked both the territory and the administrative structures that had allowed certain other minorities to be heard, whether in the 1920s and 1930s, when Soviet policies regarding national minorities were being drafted and national republics were being formed, or in the 1980s and 1990s, when Soviet structures were disintegrating. In the 1990s, Roma had more of a voice in Eastern and Central Europe.

Yet Roma are described persistently as divided by their *own* Tower of Babel. In 1995, a Russian-speaking correspondent for Radio Free Europe in Prague attempted to interview me. His first question began: "Gypsies are a mysterious people, speaking so many different dialects that it is impossible for them to understand one another." There certainly *are* cultural, occupational, religious, and dialectal differences among Romani groups. However, landed nation-states encompass just as much linguistic diversity.[5] Romani linguistic diversity differs namely in that nation states control infrastructures, such as media and education, that establish a standard, while diasporic Roma do not. The Czech Romologist and linguist Milena Hubschmannova recognizes a parallel in the way political disunities among the non-Roma, the gazhje, are treated more leniently than those among Roma: "The fully understandable disunity in the political Romani movement reveals lines of very specific distinction within the Romani collectivity. As the group-distinction lines are different from those in the Gadzho society, and are more visible, 'Romani disunity' again is the target of misunderstanding and scornful criticism from the side of Gadzhos who are themselves disunited, but in a different way" (1993:35).

Reacting against widespread images of chaotic Gypsy social disorganization, United States anthropologists who wrote about Roma since the 1960s turned to structural explanations, citing Mary Douglas, but having resonance with Evans-Pritchard and Lévi-Strauss. The anthropologist Anne Sutherland (1986b) complained that the literature on Gypsies "gives the reader an impression of confusion, an absence of meaningful social units, and a lack of social ordering altogether." This perception motivated the structural-functionalism of her own ethnography, which followed Miller (1968 and 1975) in outlining a causal relation between pollution beliefs and social divisions, both among Roma and between Roma and the gazhje. Sutherland and Miller worked with Roma on the Pacific coast who speak a dialect among those that scholars call Vlax Romani (so-called because it developed in Wallachia and Moldova). Vlax-speaking Roma emigrated to Western Europe, Russia, and the Americas in the nineteenth century (some in fact via Russia). Not all Roma speak Vlax, but they are a majority in North America, and they are numerous also in Russia, although Roma speaking a dialect called Russka or Xeladytka have been there longer.

In the literature on Vlax Roma in America, pollution rules became the main focus. Those described included the following: women's skirts should not touch men or food, spoons or dishes that fall to the ground should be thrown away, separate towels should be used for the upper and lower body, and so on. Vlax Roma do not always agree about which transgressions pollute: but generally they involve sexuality, the lower body, outer body, and non-Roma. Breaking such purity rules could entail becoming unclean or outcast (*magerdo* in Lovari; *maggrime, pekelime* in Kelderari). Transgressions also can include abuse, adultery, breach of contract, or commensality with a person already declared magerdo. A system of pollution rules based on cultural binaries (pollution/purity) supposedly generated ordered, segmentary Romani social structures,[6] mainly because "purity" signaled higher status (Sutherland 1986b:260). "As in Hindu India, [Romani] rank is conceptualized in terms of the purity and singularity of kind" (Miller 1994:89).

But many have appealed to these same rules, these "strict tribal laws," to identify and interpret what they see as a "clannish" discord generated from within. However, while categories of purity/pollution may well have Indic connections, scholars and media often argue that social mechanisms dividing Roma were transported *whole* from India—where the caste system is typically described as duplicating itself through purity rules, rather than through politics. Hubschmannova (1993) writes that "endogamy is only one manifestation of the *jati* (caste) distance which . . . regulates relations of contacts between various *jatis* (castes) and *upjatis* (subcastes) of Roma. Here we come to another sort of distinction, the jat-distinction, which is typical of traditional India. Each sub-ethnic group of the Roma falls into various *upjatis* which stand to each other in a hierarchical order. The marker of the hierarchy is the consumed food" (38).

However, purity rules do not *explain* Romani social status in Europe, nor do they account for present-day Romani differences and understandings of those differences. The Indic elements in the Romani dialects and languages are hardly contested.[7] The connection to India has fascinated philologists since the eighteenth century, when a Hungarian theology student at Leiden some time after 1760 overheard visiting Indian students discussing Sanskrit and recognized similarities to the Romani he had learned from Roma in Gyor.[8] Romologists mainly concur that people speaking proto-Romani (probably Prakrits that merged later) left northwest India around 1000 A.D.[9]

In the United States, this knowledge remains esoteric, though it became more well known in the 1990s when Western journalists took interest in East-European Roma after the fall of socialist states. In contrast, under Soviet rule, the media often christened Roma "children of India." In East Europe the link to India has been well enough known to be deployed as a weapon, as when skinheads dubbed Roma "Asian parasites."[10] Everywhere, Indic origins often have been reduced from historical narrative to a source of stereotypes about India projected onto Roma. Many continue to claim that Roma were born into a low-caste position in India analogous to their current impoverished situation in Europe. Tropes of Gypsies as genetically isolated untouchables circulate widely and in high places—witness the title of a United Nations High Commissioner for Refugees (UNHCR) Report, "The Untouchables: A Survey of the Roma People of Central and Eastern Europe" (Braham 1993). Two Russian folklorists, writing for a Moscow daily, *The Independent,* cite a 1930s Soviet ethnographer: "A. P. Barranikov, a Russian scholar, believed that Gypsies' permissive views on theft [excusing theft from non-Gypsies, outsiders] must have survived

FIGURE 6   A lesson at the Romani Sunday school in Moscow in 1992. A student writes on the blackboard in Russka (Xeladytka) Romani, using Latin letters, as one of the teachers, L. N. Cherenkov, looks on. The chairs in the foreground have been placed upside down following the close of the regular school week.

since the time they left India. Indeed, the Indian caste 'Dom,' which many scholars think is related to Gypsies, shares the same attitude" (Druts and Gessler 1993). The Dom, however, are not a "caste" at all but a "conglomerate of tribes" (Fraser 1992a:25). But such details hardly disturb evocations of caste to explain the Romani political present.

It is only a short step in logic from characterizing Roma as a European "subcaste" to viewing this as a key structuring principle, recursively preventing the "Gypsy kinds" from uniting. As one of the teachers at the Moscow Romani Sunday school (a Russian) sketched it, "Between and below the castes were the Dom. The ancestors of the Gypsies in India danced and sang, worked with metal and marketed. They wandered and were low caste. . . . the survivals of the castes are the [various] Romani occupations. Just as each caste in India has a prescribed dress, food, Gypsies are that way too" (Romani Sunday school, field notes 1992).

While Romani and Indian scholars have argued that the ancestors of Roma were probably of many, mixed castes (see introduction), they did not intend to argue that these remained frozen in time. Their arguments depart from those of Roma who attribute *current* differences among Roma to "caste" and blame caste for Romani political disunity and fatalism. In an interview with the Czech press, Romani politician Ladislav Goral explained conflicts among Romani groups in the republic thus: "Between us there are castes. Why do you think that in the Czech Republic there are 53 Romani societies and 3 or 4 political parties? Why won't the Horvaths work together with the Gorals! It has been a good thousand years since the Roma left India . . . but such is caste hatred. We can never be united" (*Jirku* 1995). However, caste in India is not as immutable as European observers have portrayed it; before influences such as the British colonial census, caste was more easily overridden by other social identities, and caste always had been vulnerable to political interests (Dirks 1992). If "castes" even *within* India have been unstable, then why should Romani social structures and occupations in Europe be primordial?

Using a term like "caste" to explain socioeconomic positions and hierarchies in Europe suppresses ways in which more recent events and institutions have unfolded, from enslavement in the Carpathians and the European Porraimos (lit. "the devouring," the Romani Holocaust), to the Moscow Romani Theater and socialist affirmative action. The task at hand is to see differences among Roma without fetishizing them as generated by "strict tribal law." Indeed, Hancock and Acton criticize non-Romani scholars who portray Gypsies as a monolithic whole, specifically by attributing Vlax pollution rules to all Roma, such that "the reader might well conclude that all Gypsies everywhere adhere to the same beliefs and practices, that the Romani interpretation of purity and pollution is universal" (Acton 1979; Hancock 1989:43).

State Policies and Romani Distinctions

Befuddled by difference across diaspora, most accounts of the Romani past paint complexity as mystery, hidden behind a veil:

> The history of this people is full of riddles and confusions, and is surrounded by an aura of secrecy created by the Gypsies themselves. Their contradictory legends about their own origins are reflected in the multitude of names for the tribes, accumulating up to the 19th cen-

tury. They were called gipsy (England), Ziguener (Germany), boge-
miens (France), farao nepek (Hungary), gitanos (Spain). . . . they
call themselves romano, romali, romnitshel (gypsy people), sinte,
sinde (from the shores of India?)[11] or kali (black).

This account, from the introductory paragraphs of Shcherbakova's *Gypsy
Musical Performance in Russia* (1984:1), treats history as if Roma purposely
covered their own tracks through time. It assumes that particular biographies and specific, local events cannot be sifted out of various streams cut by
diasporic history, that history can be drawn only from a single fountain
of origin.

In their attempts to clarify this "multitude of names," Soviet scholars
drew on logics of authenticity based in origins. Phrases such as "question-
able nationality" in 1920s Soviet census takers' correspondence, in reference
to unexpected "mixed" groups (see Hirsch 1997:263), foregrounded a concern to make unambiguous distinctions. Like Soviet ethnographers, scholars of Roma followed Soviet nationalities policies to sketch segmentary,
branching, and unitary identities. From the 1930s on, the trunk of "world
culture" had to subsume each "nation" (*natsija*), which in turn subsumed
smaller branches: stateless "nationalities" (*natsional'nosti*) and landed (*narodnosti*), "national minorities" (*nationalnyje menshinstva*), which subsumed "ethnic groups" (*etnosy, narodnosti, etnicheskije gruppy*) and "small
ethnic groups" (*malyje narodnosti*), which in turn swallowed "tribes"
(*plemena*) and "families" (*klany, semji*).[12] Some of these terms are polysemic (*natsional'nost', narodnost'*). By the 1960s, when nationalities policies
had finished the swing from Leninist particularism (*korenizatsija*) to late
Stalinist merging of the peoples (*sblizhenije*) and greater de facto Russification, begun in the 1930s, all of these categories were generalized as levels of
"ethnos" and "subethnos" (see Cheboksarov 1967).

The application of taxonomic models to Romani social structures is not
unique to Soviet social science of course.[13] Sutherland (1967), following
Yoor's autobiographical account of Vlax Romani nomads before and during World War II, outlined four Vlax Romani categories or *natsiji* (*rasa*
being the Lovari term), a term she glossed as "nations or tribes" (10).
These four included the Lovara, Machvaja, Kalderasha, and Churara. Each
natsija subdivided into omnilineal and patrilineal descent categories each
called a *vitsa* (*tsera* being the Lovari term), and these in turn branched into

extended *familija*. Finally, there were more loosely structured residence-affiliation groups called *kumpanija*.

But once we start to compare ways various scholars have constructed Romani taxonomies with ways various Roma do so, questions of perspective emerge. Mainly scholars use the term "Vlax," for instance, to describe Roma who lived for several centuries in Wallachia, Moldova, and Transylvania, and who speak dialects having a significant Hungarian and/or Romanian lexical element. While Vlax-Romani-speaking groups in Central Europe and non-Vlax use the term "Olah" ("Vlax"), Lovara and Kelderara in Russia do not call themselves "Vlax Roma,"[14] which to them signifies instead a small group of Roma who call themselves "Vlaxurja" but speak a non-Vlax dialect (nonetheless not too distant from Vlax).

Among Vlax, the tangles seem just as complex. North American scholars limit the Vlax groups to a set of four and rank them by status, but Eastern Europeans name many others: Ventsel' (1964:11) lists Laeshi, Lingurari, and Vlashi in Moldova and Ukraine alone, while across Europe, there are Mashara, Poxtanara, Chergarija, and so on. Even when clusters of natsiji in different places have the same names, their relations differ and are contested. Sutherland (again following Yoors) describes American Vlax Roma as agreeing about relative natsija status, Machvaja being the highest and Churara the lowest. However, in Russia, many Roma ranked Machvaja (along with non-Vlax Beash) as the "lowest" and poorest, and did not agree on the rankings of the others. The tenor and type of natsija relations also differed. Kelderara and Machvaja intermarried much more rarely in Russia than in North America; in Russia it is more usual that Kelderara instead marry non-Vlax Russka Roma, or Vlax Lovara. In Poland, where Lovara and Kelderara were repatriated from Russia after World War II, these two groups even more commonly intermarried. Thus, a natsija's name may have transnational salience — but that salience will have different local weights.

Scholars also have described smaller-scale Romani social structures and their terminologies variously at different points of the diaspora. The Polish scholar Kaminskii, for instance, does not define "rasa" and "natsija" as different dialect terms, as does Sutherland, but glosses "rasa" as the category that includes all Roma in general. According to him, a *tsera* (Slavic, "tent") is not a descent category, not a synonym for "vitsa," but is a "household," and he gives the word "tabor" (Slavic, "camp") instead of *"kumpanija"* for residence groups (1987:332–334). These usages are closer to those employed by Roma in Russia.

There, as throughout the region, the issue is complicated by bilingualism and by the mutual influence of Romani dialects. In the USSR, the homophonic Russian term "natsija" ("nation") usually entailed a state or territory (as opposed to a "natsional'nost'" or "narodnost'")," although Soviets often slipped into more broad usage, even substituting it for "narod" (people/folk). Many Roma used both the Russian and Romani senses of "natsija" to refer to all Roma. Although many non-Vlax were aware of the narrower Vlax sense of "natsija" (subcategory of Vlax), usually only Vlax used it thus. Still, Vlax speakers themselves often labeled non-Vlax groups "natsiji." Lovara also used "natsija" (instead of "rasa") to refer to what Kelderara called "vitsa." Thus the question, posed in Lovari, *"Che tji natsija?"* (What is your nation?) could evoke answers varying from, *"Rom sym"* (I am a Rom), to *"Lovar sym,"* (I am a Lovar), to *"Me Koshchureshkinja sym"* (I belong to the Koshchureschi lineage).

Just as one categorical name could encompass a range of kinds of sets of people, conversely, different ethnonyms could refer to the same set. Roma who have lived in northern Russia for centuries call themselves Russka Roma, Xeladytka, or even Poljachi (Poles) but are called Romungri by Lovara, who lump them together with another group long settled in southern Russia who call themselves Servi. The name "Romungri" originates from when Lovara lived in Hungarian territories, where they met settled Roma who seemed more "like" Hungarians to them—thus the name "Rom + Ungri." As Lovara came to other countries, they applied this name to Roma already living there; it became dissociated from Hungary and came to mean something like "assimilated Roma," or "gazhje-like Roma."[15] The Russka, in turn, called the Lovara "Katolikurja," stressing religious difference, or sometimes lumped Lovara with Kelderara and other Roma from the Transcaucasus as "Hungarian Gypsies." Kaminskii similarly reports the Xeladytka as a branch of Polska Roma (1980:263, 268) while, across the border in Russia, Xeladytka are considered Russka Roma, though "closely related" to the Polska. These names' shifting reference can confuse some Roma themselves.

Scholars insist on general taxonomies that are actually local. But the gap between vantages of a non-Romani scholar and a Romani person is only one such possible. My consultants, even within the same family, mapped kin relations, for instance, in differing ways. Lovari children might order lists of relatives according to spatial referents ("those from Moscow, those from Kharkov, those from Kiev") or according to gender ("the girls, the boys, and the aunties"), while older persons would immediately organize them in terms of descent. People map relational structures differently depending both on "where" they are located and on what *other* categories they find relevant (see Schneider 1968). Ordering "larger" Romani social categories is perhaps even more complex; no single, organic, segmentary Romani social structure exists; thus there can be no single way to name social relationships or categories. This does not mean that there are no Romani social orders or structures. It does mean that Romani rifts and affiliations have multiple historical causes — they are not the result of a single, internal principle (such as pollution rules or "tribal law") that generated an ordered fission.

With this in mind, we can consider what has often been a missing point of triangulation: how have specific state policies and players affected differences among Romani diaspora communities? To compare, in Africa, Southhall (1970) argues, so-called tribal alliances (and names) were historical and political creations, and Comaroff (1987) has detailed ways economic and social hierarchies produce what looks like "segmentary ethnicity." Mandel (1990) likewise detaches ethnicity from assumptions about stable relations between groups in Europe.[16] Rather than assuming the integrity of ethnic groups, as if they merely maintain shifting borders (cf. Barth 1969), groups recoalesce according to different criteria in different places and under different political conditions. "Ethnicity" may not even be the determining principle. Most of all, relations between groups are not dyadic, but mediated by relations with state institutions.

Some recent ethnography (Stewart 1997) has discussed how state policies produced difference between Roma and non-Roma. Less has been done to examine how states have similarly influenced difference among Roma.[17] For instance, Czechoslovak resettlements of Roma from Slovak to Sudetan lands after World War II, and then state "dispersal and transfer" schemes in the 1960s, disrupted Romani kin ties. Later, the 1993 Czech citizenship law de facto excluded most of those resettled Roma and their children and compelled them to distance themselves from Roma considered even more "foreign," such as the Olah (Vlax). Or consider how, in the early 1990s, the Hungarian state offered small sums of money to any Rom who entered local elections — the effect being that too many individuals ran at once for any single candidate to garner enough votes.

Distinctions among Roma in Russia likewise have triangulated with both ideologies of social and racial distinction and with policies that defined Roma, both channeling them into and excluding them from certain professions and places. While popular Soviet representations divided Gypsies into "settled, civilized *artisty*" versus "wild swindlers and travelers," Soviet scholars simultaneously drew branching trees according to differences in dialect and occupation (they considered factors such as religion or nomadism secondary, not determining of identity). Some Roma themselves appealed to these criteria, at least in Soviet times; Olga Demeter-Charskaya, a retired performer, writes in her autobiography that paternal grandparents "by profession were named Kelderara" (1997:7) and that "every dialect of Gypsies had its own profession" (66). It would be difficult to say whether such categories were prerevolutionary, Romani, or purely Soviet; they are hardly an imposition of Marxist ideology binding labor to identity, as the name "Kelderara" derives from the Romanian "tinsmiths" and probably goes back to the time of Vlax slavery there.

Most Soviet Kelderara have remained metal workers, while in the Americas they have expanded their professions. Kelderara in Russia worked in state-sponsored metal-working collectives, which did well in the 1960s but hit financial trouble by the 1990s, when the agricultural collectives they had relied on for work foundered. All across Russia, the positions of other Romani groups have similarly shifted with policy shifts. Some Roma were experienced traders before 1991 but lived a shadow life as "speculators" of Latvian lipstick and touched-up state-issue scarves. When restrictions on commerce were eased in the late 1980s, they no longer faced prison sentences for "parasitism" and could travel to Greece or China for more lucrative goods. In contrast, urban Romani performers in state ensembles by the late 1980s could find work in hard currency restaurants or could emigrate. All these shifts in possibility and position, because they affected different groups differently, likewise affected their relations with each other.

Many introductions to works on Roma begin by acknowledging past state atrocities, but few have sustained historical inquiry to examine *how* interaction with dominant European majorities and state policies has influenced the *terms* of difference among Roma. Moreover, this interaction exceeds forms of blatant oppression, but also includes more potentially neutral and everyday governmentality performed through institutions of education or media, through which hegemonic categories take up residence in minority consciousness (Appiah 1992; Nandy 1983). Soviet categories of "civilization" and "wealth" are thus as important to understanding Romani difference as is "pollution." The goal then, in the remainder of this chapter, is not to map a perfect tree of kinds and connections, but to comprehend how Romani natsiji are performatively produced even where they cross broader, structured discourses and practices of social and material distinction (see Bourdieu 1984).

Knowing "Sa le Rom"

The Soviet triad for delimiting Romani identity (origin, dialect, and occupation) did not exhaust salient axes for Roma themselves. For instance, regional ties could override dialect. Families could switch occupations. Groups speaking differing dialects might work together. Official Soviet descriptions hardly mentioned religion as marking identity, for policy discouraged certain forms of ritual life, yet Orthodox Russka Roma took ritual differences between themselves and Xoroxane seriously (Muslim Roma from Crimea); one recounted anxiety about being invited to a Muslim Romani funeral, where she feared reprisal were she to cross herself.

This variety among criteria is one reason why, in Romani discourse, it was not so clear where Romani groups began or ended. One Romani group might see another as closely related, while that group might merely allow that they shared space under a pan-Romani umbrella. People often remarked "But Roma and'e Rossija!" (There are many Roma in Russia), but they did not agree upon a taxonomy of relations and difference. Still, being able to identify other Roma as different from or like "our Roma," and knowing "sa le Rom"[18] (all the Roma) was an important way to discursively perform being Romani. Most non-Roma absolutely could not articulate such distinctions at all, never mind in fine degrees.

One Lovar stressed to me that if "you want to know Roma you need to know about all the families," quizzing my knowledge of various genealogies. He held that only a Rom who could map all the Romani groups and lineages could have rights to leadership, to *represent* Roma. However, not all Roma were equally concerned with knowing so much about other

Roma. As one retired performer living in central Moscow put it: "I'm not much interested in the various tribes. I only know if I know them or not. Ours or not ours." Some individuals sketched minute webs of relations among Romani groups throughout Russia, even Europe, while their close relatives might know little about what other Roma were like, even in the same city. Much of this knowledge depended on degree of interaction; in one Kelderari village, for instance, the men had business dealings with other Vlax Roma living nearby, while some of the women played in an ensemble with *non*-Vlax from the next village. Women there would compare Vlax and non-Vlax pollution rules, while men would explain Vlax dialectal differences: "*Well,* the Lovara, their language is like ours, Kotlja-ritska [Kelderari], and theirs, Lovaritska are *almost identical. A couple of* words, *a couple* [differ]. They, *for instance,* say 'mesjali' for 'table,' and we say 'skafidi.' . . . *For instance,* they say 'vorbin' for 'talk' and we say 'den duma.' . . . *Well, thus* we can speak, *for instance,* with Lovara in Romani" (Lemon and Nakamura 1994, videotape transcript; italics mark switch from Romani into Russian).

The Kelderara women (in this village) would assert that they knew no Lovara: "I never get out much, I never approach other Roma, I'm afraid of them, they have a custom of stealing brides." Mundane interactions with other Roma affected the importance ascribed to likenesses and differences, but they did not determine all the criteria selected to signify difference. Axes of criteria were also underwritten by official and broadly public Soviet categories, such as "level of civilization," measured in terms of gendered deportment and ritual (such as bride stealing), material well-being, technical ability, type of etiquette, education, and even fashion sense. "Level of civilization" thus reinforced Romani ideas about pollution, while it also borrowed from literature and the stage. Even when Romani discourse about difference did focus on ritual pollution, it resonated with pan-Soviet and pan-European ethnic and racial ideologies. So also did the practices themselves, since their performance depended on metadiscourse about them. So-called tribal law is, then, unavoidably reflexive.

Performers and Intellectuals: Authenticity and Diaspora

Theatrical and musical performance were directly implicated in catego-ries delimiting the "civilized"; the line that split "wild Gypsies" from "civilized *artisty*" wound through the social organization of stage practices. To advance the argument in its crudest form: among Roma, Russka (or Xeladytka) were the most active on the stage. Not only did they thus participate most in producing images of Gypsies, they also had the closest, most continuous (and perhaps most ambivalent) relations with the state.

Russka/Xeladytka have lived in northern Russia, the Baltics, and eastern Poland since the sixteenth century. The name "Xeladytka" derives from regional Romani dialect for "police" (*xalado*) and "Russia" (*xeladytko rig* [police side]) and perhaps alludes to partitions of Poland that split Romani kin on the borders of each state.[19] However, in 1997, a Russka intellectual from Tver' (living in Moscow), Anna-Ganga Batalova, asserted that the term had been attached to Russka Roma after the Revolution because so many of them were thought to be Bolshevik activists (personal communication 1997); upon first hearing it decades ago, she took it as a slur. Some Xeladytka Roma in Moscow prefer to call themselves Russka Roma, while others prefer Xeladytka (Valdemar Kalinin, personal communication).

By the early decades of the twentieth century, most Russka had settled, though many others still traveled seasonally in the summer months, renting village houses or squatting in empty city shops in the winter. When traveling in the warm months, they used carts (not the covered wagons of Western Europe), over which they unfurled tents in the evening, either sewn themselves or of army issue, and in which they carried dishes, feather beds, mirrors, icons, and even a chair or two (Andronikova 1970:4).[20] At that time, the main occupations for men were horse trading and veterinary work, and women traded. Starting in the late 1920s, it was mostly Russka — and mostly those Russka who long had been settled — who worked in factories or joined collective farms. In the 1990s, many of the descendants of these people consider themselves assimilated, working for wages, and living in urban apartments, decorating them as Russians do, save for posters and memorabilia signifying a Gypsy identity — calendars with horses on them, guitars, drawings of stylized Gypsy women, and colored scarves.

However, Russka Roma were always most famous as entertainers, though only a minority were thus employed. In 1774, Count Aleksej Grigor'evich Orlov established the first Gypsy choir, assembled from his Romani serfs settled near Moscow (see Rom-Lebedev 1990:45; Bobri 1961; Druts and Gessler 1991:203). In Russia, most Roma were serfs of the crown, not enslaved, as in Wallachia and Moldova. This meant they carried a tax burden but were not necessarily bonded to an estate, though some were.[21] According to some sources, Count Orlov brought Roma from Moldova to his estate at Pushkino (Scherbakova 1984:9), but other researchers contradict such claims (Druts and Gessler 1990:203), since the Romani members of that first choir all bore Russian names and patronyms: "Gypsy choirs existed only among the Russian Gypsies" (202). That choir was liberated from serfdom in 1807, decades before 1861 general emancipation, and gained the right to settle in Moscow proper (Demeter and Cherenkov 1987:40; Shcherbakova 1984:10).

Moscow was otherwise forbidden territory to Roma. A decree by Empress Elizabeth in 1759 forbade Roma to enter the Russian capital in St. Petersburg (German:26) and, soon after, Moscow was closed to them as well, as it was to most Jews under the Pale of Settlement. Though repealed in 1917, this zone of exclusions was reinstated and enforced throughout the Soviet regime for Roma considered unassimilated or "foreign," along with convicts and exiles after Stalin's purges. Policy thus already distinguished Russka Roma performers from other Roma.

At the turn of the century, many choral Russka aspired to enter the highest circles of Russian society, drinking tea, educating their children, and keeping up with aristocratic dress styles. The first stars of the Moscow Romani Theater, indeed several entire "dynasties" of them, sprang from such Russka choral families. And it was the Russka performers who, in the 1920s and 1930s, made up the core of intellectuals who established Romani schools, journals, and the Moscow Romani Theater, people such as Aleksandr German, Ivan Rom-Lebedev, N. A. Pankov, and A. Taranov.

Performers and activists, especially as time went by, also included some Servi Roma. As in Russia, in southern Ukraine and occupied Moldova many Roma had been classified as serfs of the crown, and the tsars assigned proportionally fewer Roma to specific estates than they did other serfs. In these areas, most Roma had been settled even longer, some at least two hundred years earlier than had most Russka farther north. Some settlements had their own "atamans" (commander; originally from "Cossack chieftain," later applied more generally to appointed heads), and often occupied the edges of towns and cities, in quarters dubbed "Gypsy Burg" or "Gypsy Street."[22] The Soviet ethnographer Barranikov, countering a then current stereotype, reports in 1931 that "the cottages of the settled Gypsies in Ukraine are just as clean as the Ukrainian homes; the Gypsy women wash the walls with the same furor as the Ukrainian women do" (51). Many Servi were successful merchants.

Later, in the twentieth century, Servi came to work at the Moscow Romani Theater, even though the dialect most used on stage was the Xeladytka spoken by most prerevolutionary choral singers. Nikolai Slichenko, one of the foremost male vocalists in the USSR, Romani or otherwise, and artistic director of the Moscow Romani Theater, is a Servo Rom. His family has been prominent at the theater since the 1960s. Another prominent family of performers and intellectuals, the Demeters, consider themselves "mixed" Servi and Vlax by descent and are connected to the Slichenkos by godparentage.

Most intellectuals and performers are of these groups, though by far the greater number of Servi and Russka are not performers. These intellectuals and performers were more likely than other Roma to be concerned about origins and authentic ethnicity. For instance, they were more likely to argue that Romani groups who seemed to retain linguistic and cultural features closest to those found now in India were the most "genuine," the most purely Romani. These are concerns they share with Romani intellectuals throughout Eastern Europe, who quarry "strata of folk culture" to articulate a unified identity (Szuhay 1995) and unify those strata by connecting them to India.

Non-Roma sometimes belittle intellectual Roma for such pursuits, assuming that education voids their contact with other Roma; such people are depicted as alienated (from custom or "tribal law"), deracinated, or rejected by "the people."[23] Fonseca (1995:8), for instance, tells us that Polish Roma declared the Romani poet Papusha *magerdo* because she wrote poetry, as if all Roma believe that writing defiles Romani culture. Fonseca claims that there is no native verb in Romani for "to write," although, for the record, there are several such words in Romani, some of them even Sanskritic (see Hancock 1996:120–122), but at any rate, *most* languages have borrowed such words. Fonseca also asserts that authentic Romani songs are "distillations of collective experience" from which it is "impossible to tell the origin or era," whereas Papusha's poems expressed a "tension between loyalty to lore and the individual's slightly guilty attempt to map out his or her own experience" (5). However, as we will soon see, nonintellectual Roma in fact *do* sing and compose songs with personalized, local, and temporal grounding. Did Polish Roma then reject Papusha because she was an intellectual, because she wrote, or did *some* Roma in Poland reject her because she published *under the auspices of a particular state,* furthered particular policies, was loyal to particular sectors of gazhje and not others?[24] A photograph of Papusha in her middle years surrounded by her paternal kin (Ficowski 1964:287) would imply that she certainly remained in favor with some Roma. Are these Roma likewise to be dismissed as "inauthentic"?

Certainly the interests of Romani intellectuals, like those of any intellectuals, differ from the interests of other Roma—but why are Romani intellectuals dismissed as culturally "inauthentic"? This dismissal obscures understanding of political motivation. In the last few decades, Romani intellectuals have realized that being perceived as a diaspora adds more weight to political claims than being a "national minority" (see Clifford 1994). A diaspora needs a "homeland," so to trace Romani language and culture to a single, unified place and time—to India one thousand years ago—is to validate Roma as a single people, an authentic diaspora.[25] Romani intellectuals know that to have international credibility, they must conform to conventions of national unity held by many, from Stalin to the United Nations.[26] Rather than deconstructing essentialist categories, Romani intellectuals and activists have worked with them. Crafting a unified Indic identity is all the more significant because so many states have defined "Gypsiness" as a "lifestyle," lumping Roma together with Travelers, as in England or France, or with the generally impoverished, as in Hungary (see Acton 1974 and 1979; Hancock 1985). Hancock (1991) writes that "Gypsies" were historically "denied even physical distinctness," accused of using dyes to make themselves dark, or of merely being dirty. Throughout most of Europe, it was only in the early 1990s that Romani groups received status as "national minorities" with access to state funding—only in the former USSR had they had such nominal status since the 1920s.[27] It is in this context that Romani intellectuals in Eastern Europe insist that Roma are a *distinct* "nationality," "ethnic group," or "transnational minority."

Yet, sometimes Romani intellectuals skim close to the very racial ideologies that threaten them, to focus on India in ways that elide specific and more recent political and social constraints. I observed such an instance in Moscow at the Romani Sunday school. By the 1990s, everyone, from minority Roma to majority Russians, was beginning linguistic and cultural revivals, linking cultural and political self-determination to language use and education; in this context the Romani school had opened. Instruction was in Russian, since many of these children barely knew Romani. There were classes *on* Romani — on the Russka dialect spoken on stage. There were usually no Vlax-speaking children; one who had attended dropped out after a few sessions of hearing that he conjugated verbs "differently, not the way we are learning here."

Besides language, the school taught folk songs and history. The teachers stressed the ancient Indic moment of that history, often to the exclusion of other places or events. One afternoon, one of the teachers (himself Romani) energetically chalked on the blackboard the contemporary Hindi word *guru* (which he glossed as "sacred") and the Romani *guruvni* ("cow"). He then turned to the children and explained, in Russian, that "some Gypsies in Africa *still* refuse to eat cows. So you *see* the connection to India."

Language *does* offer the best available evidence for Indic origins of Roma, and arguments concerning the paths and timing of Romani migrations *do* find their best evidence in dated changes in lexical items and grammar (Fraser 1992a; Hancock 1999).[28] And many Romani words do show continuity in semantic domain over time, such as Sanskrit *trishula* (Siva's trident) into Romani *trushul* (crucifix) (Hancock 1998b). However, the teacher did not mention well-established, but less exciting, Indic lexemes such as "bread" (*manro*), "water" (*paj*), or "nose" (*nakh*). Instead, he linked "guru" to "guruvni" (from *guruv* ["bull"] + -*ni* animate feminine), which is not connected with the development of Romani from an Indic source. The lecturer wanted to fix dramatically the continuity of connection between practices and lexicons over time, both to prove that such words connect far-flung arms of diaspora to a homeland and to differentiate Romani from non-Romani languages and cultures.

This sort of move has had precedents in European philology. Ideologies linking language purity to cultural identity, widespread since the late eighteenth century, propelled some non-Romani philologists to puff up Romani vocabulary lists with Sanskrit or Hindi words, or replace lexical items having obscure Indic etymologies with words having better known ones.[29] In 1990s Moscow, I likewise heard pseudo-Indic etymology extended to the *Russian* exonym for "Gypsy," tsygan, that *tsy*- derived from a Sanskrit verb for "to steal," and that "-*gan*" was the river Ganges.

Less historically troubling (though politically problematic to some Roma), some Romani intellectuals argue for replenishing standard Romani lexicons with "Hindi and international words" (Kochanowski 1982, 1995). More troubling, however, is the possibility of excluding certain dialects and dialect forms as less Romani than others and of basing that exclusion on Indicness. The Polish linguist Pobozniak writes, "A Gypsy term is being usually accepted for genuine when an Old Indian equivalent is found" (Pobozniak 1964:63).[30] Pobozniak introduces his list of Indic words (70) by claiming that "Indian words belong to the basic vocabulary and refer to everyday life" and are closest to the "self." While separating layers of lexicon (tricky because of multiple borrowings) does help reconstruct migration paths (see also Hancock 1995b), defining Indic terms as "core," and thus closer to an essential self, rests on ideology more than on linguistic practice.[31] Does prior really mean most central? Can we assume "central" terms across cultures? That is, it may seem obvious to consider "father" a core term — but what about communities in which the more salient kin relation turns out to be "mother's brother." Moreover, Pobozniak's list of Iranian-borrowed terms are clustered as subordinate to the Indic list but include plenty of terms that also could be described as "everyday," such as "friend," or "neck," as well as a term often isolated by scholars as a "key term" in Romani culture: *baxt* ("grace," "good fortune").

Language standards that isolate a single origin are by no means unusual (consider French language policies). However, many of the words that permeate Romani daily life are not considered "core," because not Indic.[32] If one were to classify "key words" according to frequency and force of actual use, rather than according to origin, plenty of Russian words and roots would qualify. Roma in Russia utter the words *kommunisturja* (Russian *kommunist* plus Vlax foreign-marked plural ending *-urja*) or *xristos* quite often. But these would not be considered among the central terms — they would be ranked among those local terms that divide the diaspora. Indeed, borrowed words are *not* considered to spoil the *English* language, but instead manifest "qualities of liberality, decency and freedom. . . . the English language, like the English people, is always ready to offer hospitality to all peaceful foreigners — words or human beings, that land or settle on her coasts" (Crowley 1989:77). Romani, with no physical homeland from which to offer linguistic hospitality, is often said not only to "borrow" words but to "steal" them (St. John 1853:141).[33] Still, not all language standards are grounded in ideologies of linguistic purity.

In the UNESCO Sunday school class, the Romani intellectual had mirrored such discourses when linking lexicon directly to place of origin. But not all Romani intellectuals drew authority from India, even when they wanted to forge cultural unity across diaspora. While visiting Roma in Kiev, I met Servi intellectuals (earning livings variously as gardeners, musicians, and merchants) who assiduously collected books and pamphlets proving the linguistic link to India. They were working with an acquaintance, a Kelderar-Servi, to publish an international journal in Romani for which they had all written articles. In his office, they debated the dialect in which to publish the journal and what to name it. Their acquaintance wanted to name it *Romani Lumja (Romani World),* but the Servi resisted: "lumja" was a Kelderari word from Romanian, and they asserted that the Russka and Servi majority in Russia and Ukraine would not understand it. The other countered that "lumja" would be the best choice because Kelderara are the most widely dispersed Roma throughout the world, and thus the paper would ultimately reach farther. They retorted, "This word does not even come from Sanskrit!" The Kelderar-Servo, however, contended that a linguistic standard should not gravitate around Indicness in any case, that language choices should follow the thickest centrifugal outlines of diasporic dispersal.

Just as appeal to diaspora could override Indic languages as ideal model, so too could broadly shared notions about civilized propriety. This was so especially when the topic was not lexicon, but pragmatics. Certain uses of language were said to divide the "wild" from the "civilized" Gypsies. For instance, I asked various Roma about formulaic uses of the Indic verb *xal* (eat),[34] typically used by Vlax Roma more than by others. It can express affect, such as affection: *"Xav lako muj!"* (I eat her face!). *"Xav t'o kar!"* (I eat your penis!) is also seen as an affectionate joke, used only with small children, who are seen as not yet having sexuality, as clean. It can also give voice to real or mock annoyance or anger: *"Te xal tut e rak!"* (May cancer eat you!), *"Me xav tut!"* (I'll get you!). It also serves duty as an evidential, to stake a claim to adamant honesty: *"Te xal ma, te merav!"* (Let it eat me, may I die, i.e., "I swear!").

Roma spoke about these phrases in very different ways. A Kelderari woman characterized most usages of "xal" as "jokes." While she qualified the phrases as utterable only to an equal or a subordinate "unless you were really very angry," she was not the least embarrassed to speak metapragmatically *about* their social use. In contrast, Lev Cherenkov, Russian linguist of many Romani dialects, once noted to me over the telephone that "our Roma" (meaning Russka performers in the city) were embarrassed by such phrases and would not utter them. Pausing carefully, and avoiding direct reported speech, he linked such phrases to "caste": "Well, you know the Indian taboo about accepting food [pause]. A Brahman may give to a lower caste, but not the other way around [pause]. It is perhaps also a case of sympathy [pause]. Well, not exactly cannibalism [pause]. In Russian it would sound rude" (interview from field notes 1992).

Several Russka performers expressed similar embarrassment or exoticizing fascination with the phrases, as used by "real Gypsies." Use of "xal," while potentially authenticating some Roma as closer to India, seemed also to mark them as wilder, capable of strange acts, less worthy of civilized emulation—such phrases, though marked as Indic in the extreme, thus could not become examples of "standard."

India was a multiply weighted sign, one that worked differently for various Roma. Stewart (1997) informs that in Hungary, ordinary Roma do not favor the "stories of immigration by a pre-existing, primordial Gypsy population favored by nationalist Gypsy intellectuals," but in Russia *most* Roma are fascinated by India. All Soviets knew more about the link than did citizens of other states, largely because of friendly Soviet diplomacy toward India since the 1960s. State media had depicted Roma as a sort of diplomatic conduit to that country. The Moscow Romani Theater staged plays dramatizing the Romani exodus from India, notably *My — Tsygane (We Are Gypsies)* and *Latcho,* and in the early 1980s the company traveled to Punjab. In India, a Chandigarh scholar, Rishi, not only edits the journal *Roma* and has authored a Romani-Punjabi dictionary but also has written a book on Russian and Indian cultural affinity and a translation into Hindi of Pushkin's *Gypsies.* This *Druzhba narodov* triangle, Russia-Roma-India, was well publicized.

Given this broader circulation of images, pedestrian Romani interest in India differed from that of the intellectuals, though in kind, not in fact. In some ways, images of India were *more* present in their daily lives: Keldelara and Lovara adorned bedroom walls with posters of Indian movie stars, collected Indian videos, and dressed up in saris for photographs, perhaps leaning against a birch tree or the family car. However, unlike intellectuals,

FIGURE 7   Gafa (a Kelderari woman) poses in a sari in front of indoor murals depicting Russian birch trees. She, like many Romani women in Russia, collected saris, as well as Bombay videos and posters of Indian film stars.

they did *not* mark a car as impure or untraditional; the car *and* sari converged into a commendable, enviable image of Romaniness. But like intellectuals, other Roma also evoked India in political ways — if not as a point of pure origins to bond the diaspora, then as an Archimedean point from which to criticize the current regime. As one Kelderari welder stated to me in 1992, after enumerating the burdens of the new "presidential" taxes: "Why doesn't India take us back and set us up a homeland? There is talk going around the camp, 'Life is hard,' but just ask, what was there in Brezhnev's time? And how do Gypsies live now? It was good that Khrushchev punished those who did not work, everything was cheaper. . . . it would have been better if the [1991] coup had been won — they would have given us lower prices, not like now" (interview 1992). Note, however, that the speaker orients even reference to faraway India *within*, not outside, political concerns about prices, pasts, and created "homelands," discourses familiar to most Soviets.

"Something Not Quite Right": Stage
Standards and the Local Authentic

Romani characterizations of difference are not manifestations of tribalism but ongoing engagements with European and Soviet discourses about "civilizedness"; there is something very Russian, very Soviet, and very European about how Roma talk about "*sa le Rom.*" They also are grounded not in "clan" conflicts, but in political ones, and in relations to the state and its agents.

In the 1990s, the Romani intelligentsia still admired the old activists. Vlax sometimes called them (in Russian) *kegebisty* (KGB-ists), not because they had forsaken Romani culture by pursuing art or politics in general but because of concrete conflicts that were described as betrayals. For instance, some Lovara hinted that *certain* performers or intellectuals could not be trusted — still, they socialized with the families of certain others. To understand Vlax conflicts with non-Vlax, especially performers, in the 1990s, we need to consider their differing social and political positions in Russia over time.

Vlax Roma entered Ukraine from the south, and Russia from the west, via Poland, in the last half of the nineteenth century (Barranikov 1931a). Many had been enslaved in Wallachia and Moldova until abolition there in the mid-1800s (Fraser 1992c; Hancock 1987). At about that time, Vlax Roma dispersed throughout Europe and its colonies, emigrating to the Americas, South Africa, and Europe. In this century, there have been several smaller Vlax migrations into Russia, fleeing Eastern Europe before and during each of the world wars (some were repatriated to Poland in the 1950s [see Kaminskii 1980:267–273]). Thousands of other Vlax were deported from Romania and Hungary after World War II to camps in Siberia.[35] Some Lovara moved to Russia from Hungary after the 1956 uprising there (Lev N. Cherenkov, personal communication 1997). Until the late 1950s and 1960s, some Vlax continued to travel until either forcibly settled or subsidized to do so with Khrushchev's 1956 "Gypsy" decree.[36] With a five-year labor sentence for resisters, it was "the only law in the history of the Soviet Union to define a crime in terms of the activity of an ethnically marked group."[37] A few families still travel seasonally in Siberia, but since Russians often confuse Roma with refugees or itinerants (see Humphrey

1993), many journalistic sightings of "Gypsy camps" around Soviet train stations must be taken skeptically.

Historians and ethnographers identify Lovara as having "formed ethnic solidarity" in Hungarian-speaking parts of Transylvania, before moving gradually into central Hungary (see Pobozniak 1964). They arrived in Russia later than other Vlax, at the turn of the century and just before World War I, and appeared in Moscow only in the 1920s (Demeter and Cherenkov 1987:43). Some Lovara came directly from Hungary, but others fled Poland to Russia just before World War I, having already left Hungary for Poland a generation or so before.[38]

When Lovara first arrived, they mainly sold small goods; some of the women told fortunes, and the men traded horses. Their ethnonym in fact derives from the Hungarian *lo* ("horse"), but having developed a reputation for wealth, many Lovara claim an etymological link to Romani *lové* (money). The word "lové" passed into slang across Eastern Europe and Russia, and is one of the few words non-Roma in Russia recognize as Romani. Pobozniak (1964:19) notes that the Nazis were aware of folk etymology and, taking it at face value, cited it to justify Gypsy extermination. By the 1930s, the state classified Lovara trading as criminal speculation and nationalized their horses.[39] Some Lovara joined industrial cooperatives with other Roma, but the state's police apparatus, the People's Commissariat for Internal Affairs (NKVD, which later became the KGB) dissolved most of these in the 1930s. A few worked in mining; the papers photographed twice the grandfather of one Moscow family as a model Gypsy worker — once on a parade horse, and once under a beam in the mine where he later died. None of his descendants, however, have consented to work in a state industrial enterprise, and it is rare to find Lovara working in bureaucratic institutions, as Russka and Servi more often do.

Some Lovara were given houses in the 1930s, though most had to move again during World War II because of evacuations and resettlements. Older Lovara remember traveling again in wagons until the late 1950s. While intellectuals dwell upon the cultural destruction of settling after 1956, Lovara (and other Roma) fully remember the cruelty of soldiers and the problems they had attaining passes, identification papers, and permits, but in the 1990s say that they prefer living in houses and clearly are proud of them. After settling, they continued to buy and sell, using family ties in

FIGURE 8 Lovari family
photos from the 1920s and
1930s. The man in the upper
photos is the grandfather
featured in newspapers as a
model Gypsy proletarian,
the "first Gypsy miner."

other cities and making short train trips to supply goods that were locally in shortage. Some spent years in jail for selling lipstick, some got into trading more illicit contraband, some prospered. Their black market activities hardly differed from those of many other Soviets — but besides trade, they had little other livelihood, no workplace perks or elaborate *blat* connections. Since the mid-1980s, many Lovara prospered with the relaxation of border restrictions and marketing laws. By the 1990s, most Lovara were living in the outlying suburbs of large cities such as Moscow, St. Petersburg, Kiev, and Kharkov. About one hundred Lovara households are scattered throughout Moscow's suburbs, a dozen more or so in city apartments. In the early 1990s, some were still in the process of moving from Ukraine to escape radiation from the Chernobyl nuclear accident, settling around kin nearer the capital in Russia.

There are few Vlax Roma at the Romani Theater, and few Vlax intellectuals in Russia. Lovara rarely work as performers in Russia (whereas in Hungary they are more prominent both on stage and in academics). A few Lovara men worked as back-up guitarists in ensembles organized by Russka singers, though two had ensembles of their own. Vera Iljinskii, a retired Russka dancer, complained that in the early 1970s "they began to let those Lovara in" (interview, 1992), while Lovara disclaim their involvement: "With us, the guys go to the Romani Theater sometimes, but just to get a work certificate, so that if the police stop them, they can prove that they work." The myths (and the true tales) of Romani singers who had married gazhje fed gossip about adultery backstage at the Romani theater. Lovara in Moscow thus kept their older daughters away from the stage and the handful of women who did perform were talked about as prostitutes. The criticisms cited media and literary legends of *tsyganshchina* and *razgul* (abandon) that lingered around Gypsy dance just as they did Romani tradition. Still, most Moscow Lovara have been to the Romani Theater, have seen Gypsy films and television shows, owned and circulated audio and video cassettes of famous ensembles, and could sing the Russka-dialect songs that Gypsy films made famous.[40] Russka, recall, was the dialect of Romani briefly standardized in the 1920s, published mainly only in the 1930s, and used only in snippets in the 1990s to represent "Gypsy language" on stage. Collections of "Gypsy folk songs" concentrate mostly on Russka. All Vlax performers have had to learn it; Olga Demeter-Charskaya, though the child of a Kelderari father and Servi mother, nevertheless wrote many of her songs in Russka (1997: appendix).

Though most performers were Russka or Servi, not all Russka or Servi, by any means, were performers. But just as many Soviets conflated categories of performer and Gypsy, Lovara similarly often lumped together "the performers" and "the Romungri." Some Lovara associated all Romungri with performers because their dialect had dominated what little Romani was spoken on stage or in film since the 1930s. Because of state backing and censorship of Romani theater and film, Lovara saw the Russka (or Xeladytka) dialect, like Romungri themselves, not only as Russified, but as having become part of the "system." Though some Lovara spoke somewhat proficiently in Xeladytka, they rarely used it; speaking it entailed admitting that Xeladytka reigned. The following illustrates how some Lovara negotiated linguistic relations with Russka in Russka.

In 1993, two Russka women were waiting for a twenty-year-old Lovari woman, Mozol, to return home, whiling away the time by silently watching a movie on television with her husband and me. They had come to purchase one of the household's older televisions. When Mozol arrived, she chatted with them in Russian, save for throwing in a few words in Russka, mostly lexical items that she could handily modify from Lovari by using Xeladytka phonology: *javen* (come on) instead of Lovari *aven*, *gadzhjo* instead of *gazhjo*. She also uttered Xeladytka expressions widely known from films, such as *Poliles?* (Do you catch it?) instead of Vlax forms *Dikhes?* (Do you see?) or *Xatjares?* (Understand?). The visitors did not reciprocate by speaking Lovari, and when they had left, Mozol sighed and crossed herself in mock exorcism, as if expressing relief that she had expended so much energy to pronounce words of an intrusive Romani in her own house. In this case, speaking Xeladytka Romani had been *almost* as unwelcome and tiresome as speaking Russian.

More specifically, Lovara, more than other Roma, were especially critical of Romungri *artisturja* (Russian *artist* plus Vlax plural suffix -*urja*). Lovara often said that performers, by playing to the gazhje, had become like them, that their fame was unjustly earned, that it was Lovara who had better preserved Romani language and customs. Lovara were certainly among the least socially integrated Roma in Russia, even though others claimed that they had "lost their culture" because they possessed "European" and "modern" clothing and furniture. However, while some children of Lovara attended school, they spoke almost exclusively Romani at home. In a video interview in 1993, I recorded several Lovara discussing the difference between performers and Lovara. The speakers were the matriarch of the house, Draga (D), the middle-aged brother of her daughter-in-law, Shikorro (S), and an elderly male relative, Fedja (F):

F: *No* mek von, *da* von *otlicha*jlin.
[*OK,* let them, *yeah,* sure they *differ.*]
S: *Da no* //
[*Yes but* //]
F: Romane san!
[They are Romani!]
S: //Dikhes, sar keren butji, *no govorja otkrovenno,* Romano Rom//
[//See, [it's] how they work, *but speaking frankly,* a Romano Rom//]
F: *Nu* so? Khelen, gilaben.
[*Well,* what? They sing, they dance.]
S: *Da, no* von *otnosh*in-pe sar gazhje, *xotja* naj ande lende kasave *tsyganshchina.*

[*Yeah, but* they *relate* like the gazhje, *though* they don't have in them any of that *tysganshchina.*]

F: Romanipe zhjanen.

[They know Romaniness.]

D: Lende aba si zakonurja Romane, *no* but si lende aba gazhjikane.

[They have Romani laws, *but* they already have a lot of gazhje laws/traditions.]

S: Naj lende kasave *dostoinstva* sar ingerel *obshchestvennyj* Rom, dikhes?

[They already don't have those *qualities* that a Rom *of society* maintains, see?]

F: Ame *proshche* sam!

[We are *simpler*!]

S: Ame *priderzhivalin traditsija,* zakonurja, sa Romane //

[We *keep* the *traditions,* laws, all Romane //]

F: Romane!

[Romane!]

S: Pativ, *ugoshchenije,* aj kadale artistura, lende *chto-to* //

[//The "patjiv," the *hospitality,* but those performers, with them *something* //]

D: Sar e gazhje.

[Like the gazhje.]

S: // *Chto-to ni to.*

[//*Something* [is] *not quite right.*]

(Lemon and Nakamura 1994, videotape transcript; italics mark Russian)

Diplomatically, the Lovara elders allowed performers some Romaniness ("Their laws are still Romani"), not classifying them with gazhje, but as "like" them, as less traditional, lacking understanding of values like *patjiv* (respect, hospitality; see Appendix C).

All the same, the talk about tradition links to broader discourses about Soviet modernity that they, too, partially shared with the gazhje and the performers. These links are especially visible at code-switches, where the speakers use Russian lexemes or Romanized Russian roots. Switches to Russian included phrases keying seriousness and sincerity ("speaking frankly"), terms describing social relations ("differ," "relate," "society"), and those connoting degrees of cultural or social authenticity ("tradition," "hold to," "tsyganshchina," "something not quite right"). Although Romani equivalents exist they were not deployed alone, but only alongside the Russian.[41] Why these categories, and why were they expressed in Russian? The answer has less to do with the "content" of the code, but with sensibility of register: Soviet-era media had familiarized Russian terms like "tradition" and "tsyganshchina," and moreover had publicized particular ways of linking them to categories of performance and authenticity. Roma, like everyone else, knew such phrases' pragmatic force; when they faced a camera, they had already learned that such registers were appropriate in public representation.

Notice also that the elder Lovara described the performers vaguely. It proved difficult for them to hit on what, concretely, made them different from Lovara, aside from "what kind of work they do," a statement that followed from a question about "performers" and that resonated with regional practices of dividing Roma by profession and dialect simultaneously. In the end, Shikorro claims not to be able to fully illustrate; it is an inchoate "quality," something "not quite right." In fact, Lovara, not required to analyze particulars of speech and gesture professionally in order to portray them, usually spoke more vaguely about whether performers' staged depictions of Gypsy life were authentic or not than performers did; often, when I asked about various plays and films, they did not detail why they were "not right." They criticized the stage not as inauthentic in form, but as a social arena commanded by other, distant Roma (see Ginsberg 1994).

Lovara did not pose the question "Is he *authentic?*" but "Is he *ours?*" That is, in the dialogue above, "relate" and "quality" do not refer to the ability to display "typical" Romani manners but instead to the propensity to fulfill acts that reproduce Romani relations. For Moscow Lovara, identification was *not* a matter of performing "Gypsy" movements or words that signified authentic "Indicness," or real "wildness."

When one young Moscow Lovari woman, Mozol, did use Russian "*nastojashchij*" (authentic) to comment on differences among Romani groups, it was not to categorize them as types (i.e., "wild" vs. "civilized," etc.), but to index familiar local memories and relationships. I had shown her lyrics from a collection of Romani songs printed in Russia.[42] Even though the book listed some as Lovari, she claimed (in Russian) the words were not right: "*Ne nasha*" (Not ours). Mozol continued, "Give me a pen, I'll give you an *authentic* Lovaritsko song!" She explained that she was writing down a song that in-laws sang for their new *bori* at a wedding. "*This is how the guys [shave] sing it*," she said, pointing out the innovation to the song made by adolescents in her circle, writing out the Romani in Cyrillic (here only that first line transliterated as she wrote it):

> Ando Kosmos tut andem, me abjav kote kerdem, Na, na, ne, ne, ne.
> [To the Kosmos I took you, and made a wedding there]

What she wanted me to notice was that the *shjave* had cleverly inserted the name of the hotel Kosmos into the wedding lyrics. The Kosmos Hotel was the largest Soviet-built hotel in Moscow, erected across from the entrance to VDNX (the Exhibit of National Economic Achievements). Moscow Roma considered it a prestigious place to hold a wedding dinner. The most recent, most extravagant wedding—one that had attracted four hundred guests, including Swedish Lovara (on the bride's side)—had been held the previous year in the Kosmos. The name of the hotel had been placed into the song to particularize it, to make it "ours." It evoked familiar memory to those who had been there, and mention of the place also indexed those forms of consumption that marked high status for Lovara. Although a folklorist might deem the song polluted by imagery of urban architecture, it was *fully* authentic to her.

Indifferent to ideal borders, she instead treated the joint recitation of specific, shared memories as more important to a performance of solidarity. I had attended that August 1991 wedding before meeting her, and when I told her I had been there, we compared notes—who had sat by whom, the fact that the bride was from Sweden, the ages of the bride and groom, their height (the groom had been shorter), and their relative physical attractiveness. I was not always so included in such conversations, but she and her kin relished such discussions of details. "Remember this?" "Did you see that face he made?" Such co-narrative worked, performatively, to authenticate people as "the same." It is not only *what* one does that makes one "us," but with whom one does it and with whom one remembers it—although such performances could not alone make just *anyone* always "really Lovara."[43] Still, the greater detail one could discuss about familiar individuals, about their deeds and foibles, the more one might be described as already "us." Family and natsija inclusion in practice were also performed and tautological—those who are Lovara are Lovara because they are us, and anything *we* do is potentially Lovari.

Consumption and the Soviet State in Romani Distinctions

One might assume that Lovara would maintain a wider social rift between themselves and performers than they would between themselves and other Vlax, such as Kelderara. Vlax dialects are more formally similar, after all. As it turns out, many Lovara in Moscow (though not all Lovara in the country) distanced themselves from Kelderara more sharply than they did even from Romungri. If dialectal differences, segmentary clan principles, and "tribal laws" really were to blame for Romani disunity and perceived Babel, this would not have been the case: Roma would have affiliated with those who shared lexicons and rituals. Instead, more important were specific memories and performed loyalties, occupational opportunities and relations to the state, and stereotypic discourses circulating about Gypsies on stage and in the media.

Although Lovara learned about other groups at the same time as they learned about their own, they did not learn about them in the same ways. Understandings of "us" were based almost entirely on everyday interactions and performances of memory, but ideas about "those other Roma" drew also from more distant sources, filtered through various media. This was true both of what Lovara knew of Russka, who had greater access to media, and what they knew of Kelderara, who had much less, though more than Lovara had.

Speakers of Kelderari are the most widely distributed Roma in the world. Their villages are likewise distributed widely throughout the former Soviet Union; even distant Kelderari settlements in Russia are connected by marriage and kin ties (though they have few such bonds across the border, unlike Lovara). Kelderara were among the first Vlax to appear in Russia in the nineteenth century, stirring a sensation by their Carpathian dress, the men with big, wide-brimmed black hats and large, silver jacket buttons, and the women with long, coin-woven braids and multicolored skirts. It is they who, with their full, pleated, patterned skirts, scarves, and braids, are the most visible and exotic to Russians as "real Gypsies."

Visibly unassimilated, they were excluded from residence in major cities, under tsarist, Soviet, and post-Soviet regulations, kept outside a one-hundred-kilometer radius.[44] In the 1990s, such regulations affected Kelderara most of all, since their distinctive dress continued to make them easier to single out than other Roma. In central Russia, their settlements are concentrated along railway stations, usually outside the one-hundred-kilometer radius from Moscow, near towns such as Tver', Penza, and Tula. Some Kelderara have managed to rent apartments closer to city limits; and near metropoli farther east, such as Perm or Ekaterinburg, they live outside the city, but not as far.

Kelderari men in Russia, almost without exception, work with metals. When they first came to Russia, they repaired kettles and vessels, but in recent decades they have taken up welding, repairing agricultural storage containers and bakery equipment, and dealing in scrap metal. Such enterprises remained modestly lucrative under socialism, because Soviet industrialization did not overwhelm small-scale repair to nearly the degree that it did in the United States and Western Europe. Especially when Kelderara could establish steady relations with local collective farm leaders, work was steady. Though Kelderara formed state-licensed cooperatives, work teams (often brothers or cousins) still had to actively seek commissions from the collectives, bringing home metal canisters and parts to work over in plots between houses. When they pulled in enough work, they could hire local Russians. In the 1980s, they were free to form cooperatives, and by the 1990s, those well located near surviving collectives still did well, but some were losing commissions as collective farms floundered. Throughout, Kelderari women either traded or read palms at bazaars or train stations, usually working in groups of three or more with small children.

Lovara did concede that Kelderara were "more like us" in dialect and culture, but in the Moscow region they never socialized with Kelderara, as they more often did with Romungri, even performers, who were sometime business partners and who invited Lovara to weddings or baptisms. For despite all their criticism, Lovara were sometimes nevertheless drawn to and impressed by the influence and cachet that urban performers wielded. In contrast, Moscow Lovara, youth especially, would avoid the Kelderara they saw on the streets, and it was rare for them to have business ties or for Lovara to be invited to a Kelderari function and vice versa. In the countryside, things were different, and closer to Ukraine one could find villages where Lovara and Kelderara had intermarried — but this was not the case in the capital.

Many Lovara in Moscow (as opposed to in the countryside, and especially of the younger generations) learned most of what they knew about

Kelderara custom via the media, rather than from interaction. They were in fact as familiar with such "ethnographic" depictions of custom as were any Soviets. In the winter of 1992, sitting in a warm, well-stocked kitchen, several Lovara listened while (the yet unmarried) Mozol read aloud from a newspaper article written by a Russian journalist and published in a popular Russian weekly (*Argumenty i Fakty* 1992, no. 7). The article was titled "The Gypsy Pays Gold for His Wife," but when Mozol came to the segment on bride-price, she interrupted herself to interject: "This is only about the Kelderara — only *they* have bride-price. *Our* weddings are free!" Those gathered laughed at the journalist's account of Kelderara "throwing away pots dirtied by women's skirts," while a younger cousin who had never heard of this practice before exclaimed in shock, in Russian, "Like primitives!"

The Lovara were miffed to have been passed over yet again by the journalists, overlooked by the ethnographers in favor of other Roma. The Lovara (as did many people) considered the Soviet media an organ of the state. Since the early 1970s, those Roma writing most often for the press included a family of Kelderara-Servi who publicly emphasized the Vlax strands of their genealogy. Perhaps they had been privileged by the state because they could serve as an example to even the most "backward" Kelderara, or perhaps their visibility was an accident of talent and fate. At any rate, in the media, Kelderara customs had come to stand for all of "Gypsy culture." Sometimes journalists took up Lovari "criminality" as a topic, but not Lovari "culture." Mozol wrapped up her reading with the remark: "They always write about Kelderara because they work within the system — but we are *firmennyje* — we were the first to make markets in Russia, to bring in good stuff from abroad. Then the gazhje started to do it, too" (interview from field notes 1992).

This Russian word "firmennye" (from "firm," as in "company") is significant in how Mozol positioned Lovara, and it has several senses. First, it can be translated as "foreign-made," especially when applied to goods with labels from a well-known designer or factory in one of the "capitalist countries." It also refers to goods produced in the second economy: "house brands," "our own make," or "private label." A homemade recipe is *nasha firmennaja bljuda* (our own house special). It is thus one of the many words that can translate the English "private," supposedly lacking in the Russian language. In Mozol's use, it signified independence from state production and distribution to thus illustrate the difference between Lovara, who work for themselves, and Kelderara, who work "in the system" that supplied collective farms and who have visible representatives "in the system," in media. As Mozol saw it, state contracts supported metal-working Kelderara, Romungri factory workers, and performers in their livelihoods — but not merchant Lovara, who were instead triply marked as "capitalists," as "parasitic," and as "foreigners."

Moscow Lovara were indeed more prosperous than many Russians and in Russia were the wealthiest of Roma. The large rooms of the wealthier houses were lushly decorated with oriental carpets, paintings of the Madonna and saints, and icons, both real and imitation, some commissioned from a Romani painter in Moscow. In a high corner in a back room, several icons might group in corners resembling Russian *ikonostasy* (icon stands), but with photographs of relatives intermingled. The usual Russian tea sets stood along counters and walls — except that some Lovara had a dozen instead of two or three. They also had indoor plumbing, unlike many rural and even suburban Soviets, and large bathrooms with raised tile baths. Large, artificial plants in shiny, white plastic urns and multiple sets of china were favorite decorations. Side closets held stacks of white feather beds and pillows, covered by a lace curtain — these supplemented beds (the fancier ones had canopies) and couches for extra guests. Still, the overall effect was less cluttered than that of many Russian homes, with no stockpiles of items in short supply, less bric-à-brac, and none of the dust that bric-à-brac collects. The most striking thing about Lovari homes was their spartan, pristine cleanliness, with floors meant for walking barefoot (Russians insist on slippers).

Such displays of material affluence aroused suspicion among both Russians and many urban Roma — even poorer Romani visitors from farther south or east sometimes remarked that such Lovara "live like Russians." But Lovari domestic comfort was bought with the combined labor of entire extended families at the bazaars. Trade in cars was a lucrative but dangerous and infrequent job left to the men, often financed by women, who amassed capital buying and selling domestic scarves, vodka, chocolate, lipstick from the Baltics, shirts from Turkey or Vietnam, and angora sweaters from China. The state had heavily restricted commerce of this kind until the early 1990s. Lovara women had been highly visible as street hawkers (as had

Romungri and other Roma). The long hours they spent standing in bazaars or pedestrian underpasses did little to refute their reputation in Communist Russia as "unable to work." Their effort was invisible to Russian neighbors, market labor being suspect as "speculation."

One former stage performer (one of the rare Servi-Kelderari performers) compared Lovara to Kelderara unfavorably, and, nodding to their ostensible lack of traditional "law," labeled Lovara wealth as wicked:

> L: Their riches are not honorable riches, like our Kelderara. They don't like us, we don't like them. Among them nowadays are a lot of drug addicts, among the Lovara. Thieves, bedlam, they live somehow not by our laws. . . . Very rich — the Lovara are the richest people. It's hard to say how Lovara are now considered Gypsies, it's hard to say. They don't keep any kind of law, they dress ultramodish, [have] the most expensive things, live really richly. They have mansions with luxurious furniture. The whole wedding, they do it without Gypsy traditions. Nothing Gypsy there. It's for aristocrats — when it isn't really an aristocrat, but they put on airs as if they were aristocrats. They are underground — you know what they do — but they make as if they were nobles or aristocrats. (Recorded interview 1991)

"Unmasking" was a key term in Soviet denouncement genres, intended to uncover false identities and conspiracies (see Fitzpatrick 1994); here the performer unmasks Lovara, saying that they "pose" as "aristocrats." In Soviet discourses, accusations of "false" social climbing were often grounded on signs of improper accumulation (Dunham 1976); this performer thus mobilized a very Soviet mode of accusation to demarcate differences among Roma. Moreover, she aligned her words within the discourses of her profession: she spoke "as" a Kelderari, but "like" a performer, concerned with the *forms* of authenticity.

In attributing sinister meaning to particular forms of consumption in a Soviet manner, note that the performer also voiced a broader, European, romantic ideal of "true" Gypsies as possessionless wanderers. She had traveled throughout Eastern Europe and had been impressed, particularly in Romania, to see how impoverished the Roma were who lived there, and credited this to explain how "purely" they spoke Romani. She explicitly equated cultural purity with poverty, a lack of things to consume.

Lovara on the other hand expressed no stigma against forms of conspicuous consumption, though they in turn projected mercenary motives onto
Kelderara:

> G: They are more — a lower natsija, understand?
> S: The Kelderara, yes, yes. They act, see. It's dirty in their houses. No
> culture really. Their kids are dirty, the *house* is dirty.
> F: Though even among them there are *some who* //
> S: There are, there are, even among the Kelderara there are //
> F: //*all kinds.*
> S: // [They are] *calculating.* Two, three families are better, live well,
> there are some like that. . . . A Kelderari comes over, comes to your
> house, you make him patjiv, understand what I say "patjiv," — a table,
> right? And he says to you, "Buddy, give me money //
> F: "Give me money, money!"
> S: // give me money and then I'll make you patjiv." Like I'm supposed
> to give you money, and then you make me respects.
> F: "I'll make you patjiv," how about that!
> S: But it isn't *proper*, it isn't *right*. You come to me, I make you respect,
> [then] I come to you . . . there are more patjivale [respectable]
> Kelderara, I swear, there are. But those are exceptions.
> (Videotape 1993; italics mark Russian; some terms left in original
> Romani)

"I give you patjiv" (*Dav tuke patjiv*) in both Lovari and Kelderari glosses as
"I lay out hospitality for you" or "I pay respects to you."[45] The implication is
that money cancels out proper ritual hospitality and true relations, a view
that echoes Soviet ethnographies and media that condemned practices such
as bride-price and godparentage as venal.[46] The characterization of the
Kelderara as exploitive and mercenary thus echoes the ways that Soviets described all Gypsies, "blacks," and foreigners from the "capitalist countries."

Lovara often cited the bit of 1990s historical revisionism that said the
Bolsheviks had stolen from the rich because they "wanted everyone to be
alike," when they recounted memory of specific confiscations of family
property and gold from Roma. Some Lovara believed that, somehow, Kelderara had escaped these confiscations and still hoarded their gold, refusing
to spend it on "decent" clothes and cars.[47] The Kelderara appreciation of
money in itself was seen as unsophisticated, as if they were primitive con-

sumers of cash. Once, when a Lovari grandmother displayed the dollars and deutsche marks she had been gathering for several years, her daughter interjected, implying that hard currency was more advanced, "See, Alaina, you asked why the Kelderara love gold — but my mother loves *dollars* more!"[48] In Lovari eyes, miserly greed engendered Kelderara material primitivity; they did not show proper *patjiv* but had bride-price. Moreover, it seemed to Lovara the state overlooked all this, in return for their becoming part of "the system."

Nevertheless, Lovara narrative sometimes depicted Kelderara as uncomfortably close. The following song figures this tension again in terms of problematic consumption and its power to transform social categories — through a metaphoric reference to eating that in fact recalls how other Roma linked *xal* to "caste," though not in the same way. A four-year-old Lovari girl composed these lines in 1992, set to a well-known tune. Over the next months, Lovari families around Moscow quickly picked up the lines and sang them over and again, and soon even relatives visiting from other cities knew them:

> O nano Kolja
> pel Pepsi cola
> xal gamburgari
> kerdjel Kelderari.
>
> [O Uncle Kolja
> drinks Pepsi Cola,
> eats a hamburger,
> turns into [or feigns] a Kelderari.]

There were multiple levels to the song's appeal. First, the images of Pepsi and a hamburger represented prestigious commodities, commodities that stood all across Russia for wealth and the then fashionable, "civilized" West. By design the newly built first McDonald's in Moscow (then still the only one) evoked cosmopolitanism, having a Paris room, a China room, a Malibu room, and so on. Lovara who lived near Moscow would occasionally make the trip to that McDonald's, bringing French fries home, along with plastic cups to display on knickknack shelves, as did many Soviets. The more light-hearted butt of the joke was not Uncle Kolja, but any "uncivilized" Kelderar, who supposedly does not know a hamburger from a shashlik.

But this McDonald's also happened to have become one of the most visible new sites not only of imported food but of street peddling and of begging by the non-Romani speaking Moldovanura (Beash), who, along with a handful of Machjaja who begged outside Red Square, were the most visible Gypsies in the capital, especially to foreign tourists. These were the "Gypsy bands" about whom the Moscow American embassy had posted warnings. Some of these people were among the hundreds of seasonal traders, beggars, and workers who began to come up from Moldova and Romania since the late 1970s. In the summer, they would camp in parks near the Moscow Kiev train station. Some continued as seasonal migrants; others by the 1990s tried to settle in makeshift shacks along the southern suburban train lines, lacking all comforts but rudimentary electricity. Although they were a tiny minority among all the Roma in Russia, by the mid-1990s these people were the most conspicuous Gypsies on Moscow streets. Most other Roma called them Moldovanurja, and some considered them hardly Romani at all.

Because of this hawking and begging, places like McDonalds had become an easy target for xenophobic writing in the early 1990s extremist press. The precarious situation of non-Russians in the capital was visibly manifest on that public square, performed in the interactions of people selling, eating, and begging. If Lovara wanted to eat a hamburger at McDonald's, they had to walk past these Moldovanurja beggars and confront their own simultaneous disdain for them as people, and affinity with their situation.

> They don't speak Romani, the ones at McDonald's. . . . But once, we saw a girl there begging, she looked just like Violetta [the speaker's deceased niece] and we felt so sorry for her that we gave her a 2,000-ruble bill [then about three dollars]. But we kept asking, "Kon tu?" ["Who are you?" Romani] but she wouldn't answer. . . . but they have gold, and big houses in Moldova. And you should see how clean their bedding is at the train station. (Field notes 1993)

Lovara, like many Russians, thus repeated the myth that Gypsy beggars are actually wealthy. But their accounts of meeting such beggars also foregrounded the tension between their hopes for becoming civilized Roma and their fears of losing everything for being labeled as "Wild Gypsies."

In the song, the elevation of status that should accompany the consumption of prestigious hamburgers does not happen: Uncle Kolja becomes (or

playacts) not a rich American in the Malibu beach mural, but a poor Kelderar, closer to Moldovanurja than Lovara. The hamburger joke was potentially bitter: Lovara were politically marginal, and their current material
well-being was precarious because, should neighbors turn against them,
local police would do nothing. Lovara could lose everything they had, be
reduced to the poverty they saw in Kelderara, just as they had during the
confiscations of the Revolution and the last world war. Their "civilizedness," insofar as it rested on property, was contingent.

"Our Laws and Theirs": Civilization, Gender, and Pollution

Lovara repeatedly described Kelderara, in Russian, as "primitive," or
"lower," and characterized Kelderara gendered practices as dangerous and
primitive: "Their laws are more strict." In 1991, I had been invited to
a Kelderari wedding a few hours from Moscow and had asked a Lovara woman whether she and her brother might accompany me — she had
laughed outright, explaining, "You know how Russia is lower than America? Well that is how Kelderara are to us," and warned me not to go alone —
"Look out, those Kelderari men might steal you!" Her warning evoked
nineteenth-century literature, Soviet ethnography, and film in which bride-
stealing betrayed the "wildness" of subject peoples. (For the record, in
Russia it is Lovara, not Kelderara, who practice elopement.)

Referring to their success at trading and their relative wealth, Lovara
considered themselves the most "civilized" and "cultured" among Roma.
They described this as signaled by the ways they had accomplished a whole
range of things — they had mastered Euro-Soviet etiquette and technologies of hygiene; they had accumulated electronic goods and fashionable
clothing; they had a certain sophistication in gendered relations. Indeed,
even while Soviet official culture stigmatized some forms of wealth, despite
years of Soviet socialism, many signs of civilizedness in the 1990s were
material, even for the Russian intelligentsia. Significantly, Lovara often
described "traditional" adherence to purity in ways that overlapped with
the appearance of "wealth." Still, certain Roma perceived others as relatively
"more strict" about purity although also unenviably poor and "uncivilized."

Lovara did not see practices marked "civilized" as contradicting Romaniness or as signaling cultural loss. Lovara considered themselves both authentically Romani *and* "civilized." Indeed, their patronage of restaurants,

use of cordless telephones, dental floss, cars, and houses did not hinder Lovara from socializing exclusively within a large network of Romani families[49] or from speaking almost exclusively Romani at home. In outward appearance, Lovara women resembled neither the Gypsy fortune-teller nor Carmen; they could be invisible to Russians as Gypsies. In the early 1990s, they did not wear "national/ethnic dress" but chiffon-sleeved blouses or angora sweaters with long, straight, narrow skirts of dark linen or rayon, cut with a graceful slit in back. Younger Lovara prized foreign designer fashions, such as Armani and Versace. The sexy allure of imported women's styles passed muster as long as they remained modest, covering the legs; imported clothing could project *both* "traditional" feminine modesty and a family's wealth and level of "civilizedness."

But when Lovara described *other* Roma, they replicated "European" oppositions of "civilized" modernity to "tradition," the ones by which Russia faced "the West" and Gypsies faced the Russians. For instance, Lovara grudgingly respected Kelderara for maintaining certain "strict" traditions, but they also criticized them because, for instance, they did not "tuck their shirts in properly" or "match colors like civilized people." One young Lovar, a ten-year-old boy, to demonstrate Kelderari lack of sartorial refinement, pulled his sweater collar askew, yanked his pants half down and mussed his hair: "They dress badly—it's all the same to them, they like everything." His little sister laughed and added her own wordless commentary by tugging at her belt and dancing. "They dance badly," he added, and demonstrated formless shaking.

While these are obvious distortions, the visible markings to which these children referred index broader cultural ideologies of civilizedness. Kelderari women did dress in long, pleated, patterned skirts in two layers, the second layer an apron covering the front.[50] To non-Roma, these most resembled the "real Gypsy skirts" of stage and film. Kelderara themselves remarked on the difference between their dress and Lovara dress, embedding their judgments also in a discourse about the relative "strictness" of tradition. Here, taped in 1993, unmarried Gafa (G) and her bori (brother's wife) Lena (L) explain to me (A):

> G: The Lovara, they don't wear braids, they just put a scarf there on their hair just any old way, right? And their skirts, [their] *skirts are cut different //*

FIGURE 9   Lena and an in-law wearing braids. When Kelderari women marry, their hair is braided on each side in plaits that join under the ear. Braids, according to some Kelderara, were a mark of moral distinction.

> L: They wear ones like you do [referring to A].
> G: // *without pleats or folds, and without the apron part.*
> A: And what kind of rules do they have? Do they have laws [traditions]?
> G: I don't know their laws [pause]. I haven't seen them.
> L: *They have laws like we do, they have laws. Also like we have. But we have stricter laws than they do, just different. Ours are stricter.*
> (Audiotape interview; italics mark Russian)

As one Kelderari man later claimed to the camera: "Their women, they wear short skirts, that's how they stand out, that they are Lovara. Because, look, ours can't wear them. If they did — pow!" (Lemon and Nakamura 1994, videotape transcript). Lovara women, in fact, wore long skirts to cover their legs just as carefully as Kelderara women did, but Kelderara did not perceive this care.

Lovara, for their part, agreed that Kelderara were "stricter" about female dress and pollution rules. At the same time, they saw the pleated and layered Kelderari skirts as signs of primitivity. As Lovara were aware, for Kelderara, the danger of skirts lies in feminine pollution. Lovara knew that Kelderari women were not to let their skirts touch men's bodies, nor to wash skirts together with men's clothes, nor to walk on a floor above a man's head — such actions would "pollute" him. A Kelderari woman should not pass in front of a man without warning him to turn his head first, and icons were veiled with lace curtains to protect them from the touch of her skirts. Here, an elderly Lovari speaker, Draga, describes the strictness of Kelderari pollution rules by imitating them, performing them for the camera:

> *What, is he filming?* This is how the Kelderara pass in front of the man. They get up. [To grandson whom she uses as model "man"] You, sit there, just sit there — and they gather their skirts to themselves like this, see. They pass by him, they pass like this, and say to him, "Stand up, so I can pass there." Well, what else? This *rug* is defiled [pointing to rug on floor]. It's defiled because the women walk over it, understand? And that's why they can't *hang* that *rug* on the wall. (Lemon and Nakamura 1994, videotape transcript; italics mark Russian)

Although Lovara described Kelderara as more extreme in this regard, they too had concerns about pollution. Like most Vlax, they too called arbitration councils (*krisi*) that could declare *magerdo* to ostracize the offenders. Like Kelderara, they generally associated *mageripe* (pollution) with sexuality, lower bodies, the floor, and so on (but also with "microbes"), but they did not see women's *clothing* as particularly more polluting than these other things.

On the other hand, Lovara sometimes criticized performers as not strict *enough,* disapproving of the stage convention where female dancers "cascade"[51] skirts above the waist. Lovara called such dancing *lazhjaveski* (shameful), because the skirts rise above the dancer's head, showing her legs. But skirts did not condense concerns about pollution exactly as they did for Kelderara. When Lovara explained why their women wore long skirts, they spoke less about mageripe, and more about shame, *lazhjav.* They viewed the Kelderari emphasis on pollution, especially gendered pollution, as primitive, echoing the Soviet assimilative drive to emancipate Central Asian and Caucasus women from patriarchal custom, particularly to phase out veils and clothing that restricted visibility or movement (see Massell 1974).

In fact, both these Lovara and official Soviet discourses seem to be embedded in pan-European rankings of shame and pollution as steps along the road to the evolution of self-consciousness. In numerous religious, philosophical, and ethnographic writings, fear of pollution has been depicted as "primitive"; next comes shame before a collective; then finally, evolution of feeling to individualized guilt.[52] This social evolutionary ranking, incidentally, rests on yet another proscenium trope dividing the visible from the hidden. Within this theatrical ontology, pollution beliefs are represented as limited to physical "surfaces," while shame presupposes a veiling of inner transgression from an external, social collective. Finally, guilt marks the appearance of a second proscenium layer within, where a divided self both observes and hides from itself. As we shall see in the next chapter, there are echoes in the projection of a lack of reflexive consciousness — onto "castes" seen as motivated by "shame" or "pollution" — in descriptions of "wild Gypsies" as people unable to "make a frame," unable to separate "art" from "life."

· 4 ·

The Gypsy Stage, Socialism, and Authenticity

Early in my fieldwork, a Rom who had worked at the Moscow Romani Theater explained the difference between himself and "more traditional" Roma thus: "They are wild and do not know the difference between art and life; they do not know how to make a frame."[1] Performers certainly did learn to "make frames" in ways that other Roma did not, stage performance being their livelihood, but still, the allegation was exaggerated. Nonetheless, this sort of statement points to ways stage practices and discourse about them in Russia have divided Roma there. Besides being sites for projecting Gypsy volja and "dark eyes," stage performances, media images *and their production* both forged new social ties and fractured old ones. Romani performers, more than other Roma, expressed intense anxiety about these social ties and fractures and framed that anxiety within a discourse about authenticity, about whether their theatrical work violated natural cultural identity, about whether the proscenium truly set them apart from other Roma.

Authenticity Complex

This chapter investigates the practices and policies that have both subsidized and limited Gypsy stage performance, doing so through archival sources and ethnographic description. After tracing archival accounts of the establishment of and theatrical practices at the Romani Theater and relating them to Soviet nationalities policies, it turns to an ethnographic account of two 1990s film shoots (a documentary and a feature film). In both textual administrative records of decisions made in and about the Theater, and in oral discussions that wove through film production, Russians and Roma declared theatricality alternately "transcendent" and "out of touch" and called performers simultaneously "natural" and "alienated." For some, these oppositions constituted poles of a "paradox"; for instance, one might describe the very same Romani singer who transcended everyday reality through song as "paradoxically" caught up in modernistic practices that deracinated him. Unraveling how such "paradoxes" have been authorized through performance practices over time illuminates the processes by which Gypsies are racialized.

Among Roma in Russia, Romani performers and intelligentsia speak most about the "loss" of Gypsy tradition; they repeat that "real Gypsies" are disappearing, the caravans gone. As one Romani film consultant (for non-Romani directors) averred, urban life had ruined them: "We, by virtue of our alienation from the camp, from the people — we have lived apart from them for twenty-five years — already we have stopped, by virtue of our own intellectual culturedness and education, we have stopped wearing our national dress. Because we have already turned out, well, very civilized. . . . it was not a decision: time did it. Civilization did it. A very wise person once told me that civilization is the end of culture" (interview 1992). Yet, the fact that most of the famous Gypsy choirs had been urban did not stop performers from appealing to "Gypsy art" to position *themselves* as authentic, when they could recast it in antimodern terms: "Gypsies don't read music, but sing naturally."

Still, modernity threatened to taint Gypsy art. As the elderly Russka dancer, Zina Ilinskaja,[2] put it in a home interview conducted by the choirmaster of the Romani Theater, "Why have all the Gypsy songs been distorted? They've started to sing by reading notes! But really, back then, Gypsies never read music. . . . with literacy, Gypsy art disappears" (recorded interview 1992). But a regression from urbane, tsarist civility into primitivism *also* degrades Gypsy art: Zina Ilinskaja's sister, Vera, places the death of talent during the New Economic Policy of the 1920s, when she was still an infant. "Before the Revolution," dance movements had been subtle, every movement "just a hint at dance. . . . the torso was straight, upright, reserved." One could "put a glass of water on the dancer's head and it wouldn't spill." Gypsy choir costumes had been elegant and aristocratic, in monochrome black or white with a diamond brooch, "none of those multicolored shawls."[3] With the New Economic Policy, the audience changed, the public becoming cruder, less "cultured"; Ilinskaja traced further degradation from the 1930s on: dancers waved their skirts above the knee ("God

FIGURE 10   Roma perform outdoors in 1991 in a Moscow suburb. The girl in the foreground executes a move called *kaskad*, swirling her skirts as she steps (revealing more of her leg than many other Roma would approve).

forbid [before then] her legs would show!"), danced barefoot, began to shimmy with no restraint. By the 1990s, according to some older performers there was no finesse and dancers were vulgar: "They tear their hair, God save us!" Zina repeated, "They imitate each other and dance exactly the same." "It's all become more primitive," agreed the Romani choirmaster interviewing them.[4]

Since at least the 1960s, the prerevolutionary past had figured in many Soviets' memories as a source of cultural authenticity; by the 1990s such double-edged nostalgia was fully public.[5] But models of authentic Gypsy art could be found in Stalinist era stars, as well. Many asserted that 1990s songstresses could barely imitate those of the 1930s, that their art (like their urban lives) was no longer "genuine." The socialist past thus alternated in memory with the tsarist one as a source of both the false and the authentic. Indeed, the first post-Soviet film produced by Roma, *The Sinful Apostles of Love* (1995), anchors authentic Romani experience not to prerevolutionary times, but to the Soviet era, to the patriotic years of World War II: "The

War. Having invited the Gypsies to a celebration, the fascists set up a firing squad, shooting it on film," reads the film blurb.[6]

Urban Romani performers opposed and combined "culture" and "art" with "civilization" and "modernity" in ways familiar to most Soviets, at times rejecting parts of those hegemonic categories only to reproduce their terms (see Appiah 1992; Nandy 1983). In addition to working through those widespread discourses about authenticity and modernity, Romani performers and intellectuals had also to confront ideologies about theatricality that problematized their "Gypsy" identity in particular ways. Mainstream theater in Russia since the 1930s, as elsewhere, was framed as separate from the rest of everyday social life (byt); this being the Russia of both Stanislavskiian and social realism (I leave aside for now avant-garde frame-breaking from Pirandello to the performers in New York City's "Squat Theater"), theater was often set apart from byt as less "real" but more *convincing*.

The problem of authenticity was thus complicated for Romani performers, more so than for actors in mainstream Russian theaters. If audiences and actors usually make a "basic conceptual distinction" between a fictive character and a real performer (Goffman 1986:128), at least when the actor is "offstage," such expectations about role separation did not apply to Romani performers — Gypsies were to play themselves, *as Gypsies,* and to continue to do so after curtainfall. A Gypsy character was to be played by a Gypsy person, and the more "real" the actor's origins (if he could claim he was "born in a Gypsy camp" [Slichenko 1984]), the more authentic his characters. Senior actors at the Theater indeed insisted to me that "all the Gypsy parts are played by Roma; we have only a few Russians in the company."[7] Romani performers thus were held to a dramatic unity of character both on- and offstage that ordinary actors, not expected to play themselves, were not. It was as though the proscenium at the Romani Theater should not have bordered an ordinary stage, but a window penetrating into "real Gypsy life" — and since it was judged not to do so, it came to be seen as mere "kitsch." The final twist, for actual performers, was that the conventions of the stage, its daily practices, supposedly adulterated and degraded performers' cultural authenticity; it was as if they had become ersatz Gypsies in real life.

In the face of such authoritative contradictions, Romani actors were understandably anxious about identity. Whether or not life onstage had diluted their genuine Gypsiness, their *concern* with authenticity *was* linked to their occupational practice as ethnicized actors, their anxieties connected to the Sovietized habits of a profession that demanded analyzing and displaying ideal identities. They had to be able to distinguish "real Gypsies" and to judge the proper portrayal of one. They would dissect, in great detail, how non-Romani (even Romani) actors failed in this. They took pains to ensure that I, the foreign researcher, understood that various actors who have played Budulaj on stage, screen, and TV were not Romani. How could one tell? Budulaj does not move the right way, he snaps his fingers in the wrong direction, he uses Romani words in the wrong situations. They reported encounters with "real" Gypsies at railway stations and bazaars: one actress described a trader who had clacked her fists together from the cold, calling out to potential customers in a thick "Gypsy accent." The actress had appropriated the gesture and imitated the accent, as stage bits to refine the authenticity of her character. In fact, since the early 1930s, as an antidote to potential stage artificiality, Romani Theater actors went on field trips to camps and collectives where, in addition to proselytizing and recruiting new singers, dancers, and actors from among the *tabornyje* (camp) Gypsies, they educated themselves about "life on wheels." They collected "authentic" folkdances and songs, examples "from camp life" to incorporate into plays.[8]

Authenticity anxiety was a discursive practice distinguishing performers from other Roma, the concern even apparent to some non-Roma. In 1993, in a video interview at the Romani Sunday school, the choirmaster of the Romani Theater and leader of Gilorri, Vladislav Demeter (D), described in psychoanalytic terms his personal identity "complex" in response to my question, "Who do you consider yourself to be?" He and Russian linguist of Romani, Lev Cherenkov (L), face the camera together:

> D: I am, of course, a Gypsy! You know, the thing is, this is one of my complexes //
> L: And *my* complex, too!
> D: I have suffered it since childhood. When I am in the midst of Gypsies, I feel a sort of //
> L: Sometimes it can be uncomfortable!
> D // Like being on alert.

L: Yes, yes! And sometimes the other way around, right?

D: First of all, in comparison with Gypsies who lead a traditional way of life, there is the ethnic milieu of the intelligentsia — artists, scholars, writers, and so on — that is, ours. And then there are those Gypsies spread all over the country, who live a traditional life. When we meet them, I personally — I immediately suffer a complex. I don't know the language as well — I speak in Gypsy with them, but they can tell I have trouble in a few places. I feel uncomfortable then. . . . Maybe there are some customs necessary to observe. I know them theoretically, I could write an article about them, I can talk about them on television, but when I am socializing, I might leave something out.

(Lemon and Nakamura 1994, videotape transcript)

Over the twenty-minute interview that included this segment, both men edged ever closer to the camera, shifting footing slightly, each smoothly stepping a bit ahead of the other to claim each turn. And while the Russian deferred to the Rom as the real expert, he left his own identity ambiguous. Both speakers qualify "complex" (a term that probably began to circulate in the USSR in the late 1960s, though Western psychoanalysis was still officially censored) with *singular* possessives, as if an identity "complex" were *individual* and inalienable, and thus more familiar to Romani intellectuals than to other Roma. When the Romani performer announces his own complex, his Russian interlocutor chimes in to claim one as well: "and *my* complex, too!" But the two complexes are pragmatically different. Although the choirmaster's "complex" frames an account about fear of diluted ethnicity, from the perspective of a knowledgeable gazhjo, to possess such a "complex" signals authentic understanding of the "paradoxes" in Romani intellectual life. Still, for both, focus on the authenticity complex confuses understanding of any gap between people who publicly portray culture and those who "really live" it.

The Romani Theater Elite and the Word of Lenin

The anxiety that intellectuals felt over any gap between themselves and other Roma was reinforced by ideologies about performance and by transpositions of the dramaturgic models into social life. But anxiety was also buttressed by Roma's memory of the Romani Theater's role in state assim-

ilation policies. The Moscow Romani Theater had been intended to transform Gypsies from wild parasites into civilized workers, and Romani actors
had actively proselytized the cause, spent much of their lives arguing that
the New Gypsy could work in a factory or become an academic, and publicly extolled the benefits of socialism, Romani success stories in medical
and scholarly careers. Settled and urban, no longer traveling or "close to
nature," performers were implicated in a socialist project that, by its last
decades, many Soviets saw as violating nature.

Some performers thus blamed the state and state-sponsored performance
for driving a wedge between themselves and "real" Roma. In describing the
forced settlement of 1956, a Russka Romani performer stressed how the
state, by privileging them, had removed them from a natural current of free
movement as surely as it had other Roma, though by different methods:
"Wherever they caught them, 'This is your home.' It was a concentration
camp, a reservation! Many families died, big ones, maybe forty people, six
or seven tents each. They were unaccustomed to labor, they were a free
people, caught fish and rode on further. But they set them up in wooden
barracks and set guards to watch them. The Theater never felt that—we
always had good hotels, were greeted with bread and salt and embraces,
given food and special ration coupons" (interview 1992).

But while in the 1990s some performers asserted that socialism had broken up Romani social ties and destroyed Romani culture and art, others
(sometimes the same people) insisted that the socialist state also had preserved them. And while some emphasized cruelty in socialist policies, such
as forced settlement laws, others remembered free education, clothing, and
subsidized housing that, in some cases, put Roma ahead of others.[9] Not all
were even ambivalent about a socialist past: that past had ensured their
personal success, made them "civilized."

Though at first well intentioned, both Soviet nationalities policy and
policy about performance divided Roma, in part by defining and reifying
"Gypsy professions." In 1931, at a meeting between the Narkompros committee on Nationalities, the Horsebreeders' Union (Konevodsojuz), and
the Moscow Soviet Executive Committee (Mosispolkom), a representative
of Konevodsoyuz asserted that, "by strength of Gypsies' natural inclination
towards horses, many of them could be made use of in work at the Konevodsojuz."[10] Theatrical images reinforced such suggestions at the policy
level; in the 1979 TV version of *Tsygan,* all the local, settled Gypsies are em-

FIGURE 11   Meeting of the Russka intelligentsia with Anatoly Lunacharsky in 1930 to establish the Moscow Romani Theater

ployed at the horsebreeding collective, except for Budulaj, who is a metal smith. Indeed, long traditions of typecasting nudged policy decisions on matters from forced settlement to the "liquidation" of targeted customs.[11]

The Moscow Romani Theater was supposed to encourage recalcitrant Roma to use their occupational talents for the state, and also to fight nasty stereotypes along the way. In 1930, the Russka intellectual (later playwright and actor) Ivan Rom-Lebedev appealed to the Commissar of Enlightenment, Anatoly Lunacharsky, with the argument that a theater for Gypsies would raise standards of living and proletarian participation via political literacy. He quotes Lunacharsky in his memoirs as having responded, "Gypsies?! Does this mean that the word of Lenin has reached even them?" (1990:165).[12] On October 4, 1930, the People's Commissariat of the Enlightenment (Narkompros) approved the Studio of the Indo-Romen Theater. The prefix "Indo-" was later dropped (Rom-Lebedev: 165), and the Romani Theater opened in January 1931 in the former Komissarzhevskoj Theater, later moving across from Stanislavskii's Moscow Art Theater. Officially, the Romani Theater was created both to "preserve a national culture"[13] and to "aid the assimilation, sedentarization, and education of nomadic peoples." The *Great Soviet Encyclopedia* of 1974 explicitly asserts that the "Romen" Theater was intended to facilitate policies such as the Order of the Supreme Soviet of 1926, which provided land to Gypsies wishing to settle and work. However, only *certain* forms of "national culture" were judged useful enough to preserve and depict favorably on stage.

In its early years, the theater was to "carry out agitation" among nomadic Roma. Rom-Lebedev recounts in his memoirs how groups of actors from the theater visited camps "as if passing by" and then "as if by way of an aside" led the conversation to themes of collective life (1990:192; see also Seton 1935:67). He describes Roma in the countryside as naively interpreting actors' messages, recounting that they thought Marx to be "a good man," thinking he must be a Rom, for in his picture "he had a Gypsy's beard" (164). The Romani Theater repertoire would remedy this naiveté with plays that urged Roma to become literate, to learn about socialism, to settle and join collectives.

Performance and policy had, however, been in dialectic relation well before the Revolution. That is, tsarist policies restricting Romani movement and occupations were the conditions that saw the rise of the Romani choirs — and a Romani elite. From the mid-eighteenth century, the tsars had imposed taxes on Roma and limited their livelihood, registering some as serfs. The tsars moreover restricted Roma from major and capital cities; in 1759, Empress Elizabeth forbade Gypsies to enter the capital in St. Petersburg (German 1930:26), a law repealed in 1917, but reapplied in practice later under the Soviets. The first Roma in Russia to legally transcend the tsarist settlement regulations had been musicians and choral singers, after Orlov's Gypsy choir was released as a special case from serfdom in 1812. Members of these Romani choral families set to learning aristocratic manners and sending their children to gymnasium, nurturing the beginnings of a Romani intelligentsia (Rom-Lebedev, passim). This fact that the Romani elite were performers significantly shaped Russian imperial and then Soviet perception of Gypsy "kinds" and Gypsy problems.

The socialist state, in contrast to the tsarist one, stopped neither at taxation nor at policies regulating movement and settlement;[14] in the early Soviet decades, Gypsy assimilation policy was quite aggressive. Roma were to assimilate "at the same pace" as other minorities. In the mid-1920s, the state classified Roma as a "national minority,"[15] devoting special departments to Romani affairs within the National Minorities Sector of the Ministry of Culture. For a few years, the state offered Roma free land without a wait. There were even tentative proposals to establish a Romani Autonomous Region, to be called Romanestan, though these proposals came to nothing. Some Roma enrolled in schools that taught subjects in Romani, while some had steady employment in urban collectives and cooperatives. Most of these programs lasted less than a decade and were liquidated entirely by 1938.[16]

The All-Russian Gypsy Union, established in 1925, oversaw early state initiatives to distribute land and to eliminate illiteracy among Gypsies, but it was especially short-lived. The Gypsy Union had twenty-three members, led by Andrej Semjonovich Taranov, a Russka graduate of a state school in the Urals, veteran of the civil war; its secretary was Rom-Lebedev (see Popov and Brils 1934; Druts and Gessler 1990). It was dissolved early in 1928, charged with mismanagement of funds and fraud (the Union was implicated when papers bearing an allegedly false "Gypsy Union" stamp turned up),[17] failing to open departments in the Soviet localities, and failing to settle nomadic Gypsies. The party and the NKVD took over its concerns. Still, the people who had led the Gypsy Union were not themselves purged but went on to head other Gypsy programs and remained in the forefront of the Gypsy "cadres." An educated, urban, Romani elite continued to rise.

Again, this elite had its beginnings in the Russka and Servi prerevolutionary choirs or wealthy merchant Romani families that managed to penetrate the big cities. It was Roma who had sung to aristocrats who most actively aligned themselves after the Revolution with the state, drawn to the early Leninist socialist commitment "national minorities" and to "national cultures." At least, Romani intellectuals depicted them that way decades later: "The movement toward cultural rebirth among the Gypsy people began in those first postrevolution years precisely in the milieu of the Moscow choral Gypsies. In that sphere appeared the first Komsomol cells, the first communists" (Demeter and Cherenkov 1987:45).

Indeed, there was plenty for the Romani intelligentsia to be excited about. By the end of the 1920s, Roma published for the first time in Romani — poetry, fiction, and translations. At least four schools opened to teach literacy in Romani. Before being dissolved, the All-Russian Gypsy Union managed to organize the creation of a Romani alphabet.[18]

According to interpretations during the twenties and thirties of Leninist nationalities policy ("Nationalist in Form, Socialist in Content"), national minorities were to become politically literate in socialism through the medium of their mother tongue. Political literacy, not literacy in Romani itself, drove themes and subjects. A Romani grammar taught the alphabet through a parable: a family starves because they subsist on the wife's fortune-telling, until they begin work in the factory. A moral lesson accompanies each letter: B is for *butji* (Romani, "work"): "Our work," "Masha works," "Our Romani women don't work but tell fortunes," "I want to work" (Dudarova and Pankov 1928). *Romani Zorja (Romani Dawn),* a journal erratically published in Romani between 1927 and 1930, followed by the monthly *Nevo Drom (New Road),* published in Romani from 1930 to 1932, were awash with articles explaining the five-year plan, how to work in collectives, how to be an atheist, how to live in a house, and why go to school.

The journals were shut down in 1932 for not exposing the "real concerns" of Roma, for not authentically reflecting "class struggle" between rich and poor Roma.[19] Nevertheless, hundreds of books and plays were published in Romani until 1937,[20] when the state terminated all publishing and most education in Romani.[21] By 1936, most Romani language schools were closed,[22] a move that was part of a larger reversal and move toward Russification. Arabic-script languages were Latinized and printed in the 1920s, then Cyrillicized and limited in the 1930s. Romani lost out along with other minority languages. Presses for all minorities lacking a republic were shut down. Druts and Gessler argue that the national presses that survived did so merely because they could be transferred from Moscow to a respective republic capital and that Romani simply fell through the cracks, having neither republic nor capital (1990:303). However, while the end of Romani printing and education may have been no more than a casualty to the swing in nationalities policy, the picture is complicated by the fact that the Romani Theater survived, even as other national theaters were closed.

After the first three years, the Theater switched from Romani-only plays to Russian, and the audience became increasingly Russians or Russian-speaking Soviets in need of entertainment, rather than Roma in need of political education. Still, the repertoire maintained a core of assimilation stories and amplified its claim to be preserving a culture.

These stories depicted Romani groups as divided by *choice* (of livelihood) and by "taste," both underplaying the linguistic differences favored by

FIGURE 12   Page from the Romani journal *Nevo Drom* (*New Road,* 1931, nos. 4–5). The journal ran some stories specifically for Roma, but many pages were taken up by translations of general propaganda from Russian into Xeladytka. This page tells of "ancient customs" that oppress women: the title above reads, "Women in the East," and the one below exhorts "Romani daughter-worker, write about your new life." Courtesy of the Lenin Library.

Romologists and avoiding any reference to rifts created or reproduced by policy. Instead, particular "traditions" metonymically indexed supposed class struggle among Gypsies. Such struggle was the theme of the Theater's first two didactic plays, *Life on Wheels* and *Between Two Fires,* both written in Romani by Romani playwrights, both driven by conflict between those who want to become Soviet workers and those who avoid jobs in collective farms and move in "clans," following the lead of a rigid, hot-tempered patriarch. The 1935 film *Poslednij Tabor (The Last Camp)* conformed to this formula. The film opens with water dripping through the canvas roof of a caravan onto the face of a crying baby. The big wooden wheels of the Gypsies' wagon are stuck in the mud—a Russian suddenly appears to help push. He understands a few words of Romani! He is the instructor for Gypsies sent from the capital to carry out assimilative work, and he convinces them to consider joining a nearby collective. But after the Romani heroine visits the collective and her father learns to cut wheat (in time to orchestra swells!), her family is driven from the camp by the wicked patriarch.

Two decades later, and three years after Khrushchev's 1956 decree had outlawed traveling, a play titled *Gorjachaja Krov' (Hot Blood)* opened, another tribute to the virtues of settled life. Romani playwright Ivan Khrustaljov cast the dramatic conflict between a nuclear Romani family settled on a horse-breeding collective (they resemble Russka) and a larger nomadic group with whom they used to travel (dressed much like Kelderara). The settled Gypsies, wholesome and hardworking, value *certain* traditions — songs and dances — but eschew practices considered repressive and uncivilized, especially arranged marriages or gender-segregated tables. The first act of *Hot Blood* begins when a Russian comes across a camp of nomadic Gypsies and tries to convince them to join the collective. They protest that they are already living "socialistically" — a word they mispronounce, revealing their lack of political literacy: "We are *sushul* people! In our camp we have *sushulizm!* We live like angels in heaven, we divide everything in half: he gets the piglet, I get the ears! [Aside] What have I said!?!"

The nomads, with irony, compare the party ideal to a Romani ideal of customary equal distribution. Indeed, many Vlax Romani communities *did* split earnings, a share going to those who could not work (see Demeter 1988:24).[23] Soviet scholarly and popular ethnographic genres described such practices as "Asian" and "primitive communistic," and the analogy here to "sushulizm" is supposed to jar, to seem crude — hence the mispronunciation, should any miss it. The Gypsy character, in her aside, subverts the egalitarian analogy, however, revealing "class" rifts within the camp and foreshadowing the group's unraveling.

The camp decides to visit the settled Roma. They joyfully reunite, toasting and singing — though they are confused at first about whether the women should sit apart from the men. The traveler patriarch reminds the settled father that they had betrothed their children years ago, "according to tribal law." The settled Roma protest; they do not want their daughter to live in a tent and learn to steal and tell fortunes, but the father finally submits to decide the matter by duel, according to "unwritten Gypsy law." As the duel begins, the Russian suddenly reappears, *deus ex machina;* these are modern times, he says, they should not solve conflicts with violence. The traveler warns him: "You don't know what Gypsies can do — we have hot blood." The Russian only replies with stories of Gypsy patriotism — a Gypsy man and woman, World War II partisans, sing to their deaths; another infiltrates fascist enemy lines to smuggle papers tucked in baby swaddling. The nomads remain cynical: "What kind of money did they fight for?" But the duel is averted, the nomad patriarch discredited and abandoned.

Even in 1997, several years after the official end of the socialist state, *Hot Blood* remained part of the Romani Theater's repertoire. And Russian writers in the 1990s continued to describe gendered practices, such as arranged marriages or Kelderari bride-price, as "patriarchal holdovers."[24] If prerevolutionary poets had accented "Gypsy freedom," Soviet writers and activists by contrast stressed saving Gypsies, *especially* women, from a captive life of custom — gendered divisions of labor, proscriptions about female dress, and pollution rules. "Custom" was seen to divide Gypsies from the good life and, as a crutch to "clan" and "caste," from each other. The rhetoric of "bringing wandering Gypsies to work and a settled life"[25] was couched in promises of a life free of the capricious rule of kin and patriarch. Such gendered Socialist "civilizing projects" paralleled, for instance, British colonial treatment of *Sati* (See Spivak 1988) and were, in some ways, continuous with tsarist imperial treatment of gender, except that the Soviet version described women in class terms as "exploited," especially in communities where "class" could not be found.

Stage productions pushed women to assimilate not only via examples in the scripts, but by example of the Romani Theater performers themselves, who were to teach and display the new ways. When dancers recruited "from the camps" resisted wearing pants to rehearsal, the director chided them, pointing to the more experienced choral songstresses and dancers; "You should be proud of being *artisty!*" (Rom-Lebedev 1990:171). Performers became "cadres," cultivated examples of how to "overcome" repressive Gypsy custom. Nonetheless, the same actresses who wore pants for Theater rehearsal donned elaborate, colored skirts for the stage. Skirts were never targeted for widespread phasing out; indeed, they gave Gypsies "national color."[26]

Such displays and similar cadre examples were lauded as successful until the 1990s and paralleled a heroic genre of rejecting "backward" custom. The Demeters, for instance, credit their Kelderari grandfather, Ishvan,[27] as the first to defy pollution rules; he refused to discard a fallen spoon as *maggrime,* saying, "Wash and give it to me."[28] However, such "successes" were limited. Most Vlax Roma took only selective part in assimilative programs, which more easily accommodated the already more Russified Russka and Servi Roma.

At their inception and even through the late 1980s, newspapers reported on the early Romani agricultural and industrial collectives in central and western Russia, Ukraine, and western Siberia as successful, destroyed only by World War II. But according to the archives, many were eliminated earlier.[29] Russian and Romani intellectuals did not publicly mention prewar failures and liquidations until after glasnost was well under way — until then, the fascist invaders were said to have destroyed the collectives. In fact, however, by the late 1930s, the NKVD had liquidated many Gypsy collectives and farms, the organization having taken over Gypsy collectivization and resettlements in 1936.[30] Some Roma in urban collectives were arrested well before that, and many Roma were resettled en masse in Siberia in 1937–38. In 1991, the choirmaster at the Romani Theater recalled resettlements of Vlax Roma in the years leading up to World War II: "They were taken away in freight cars — not even passenger cars. Then they were just dropped off without any supplies at all, and many died. They called it 'industrial espionage' or called us 'Hungarian spies.' Especially Lovara and Kelderara were victims" (Field notes 1991).[31]

Druts and Gessler argue that Gypsies should have adapted quickly to collectivization because "the idea of socialism in no way contradicts the internal social structure of Gypsy society" (1990:280). However, even long-standing practices of collective redistribution could not guarantee Soviet collectivization policy (for Roma or for anyone else). Often the central government assigned Roma land, listed them as collective members, sent them off to farms with no livestock, no supplies, and no instruction, and then forgot them. Or Roma were thrown into collectives together with Ukrainians or Tatars (Druts and Gessler 1990:293; *Pravda,* July 26, 1932). Those farms that did reasonably well were usually staffed by settled Russka and by Servi, rarely by nomadic Vlax. A few collectives in the Smolensk region and in the northern Caucasus thrived because two Romani officials in the nationalities department of the Central Committee kept in close contact with them (Druts and Gessler 1990:288) and were able to ameliorate supply problems and mediate communications with non-Romani state bureaucrats.

Other Soviets did not always take kindly to the distribution of social goods to Gypsies. After World War II, for instance, many Roma who had been evacuated and removed to Siberia returned to European Russia. Though most still were defacto excluded from settling within a hundred kilometers of cities such as Moscow and Kiev, some of those returning to smaller cities such as Kharkov or Tula received apartments, which angered Russian and Ukrainian majorities. But for the most part, after the war, the state ignored issues concerning Romani work and education, although the Romani Theater continued its rounds. Rom-Lebedev wrote to Stalin then, complaining that there had been no support for Gypsies since the end of the war, and that many had thus returned to nomadism,[32] especially Vlax Roma and Romani war refugees from Europe. In 1953, Nikolaj Aleksandrovich Pankov, Russka author and translator (son of the choral singer Valentina Efgrafovna Pankova), wrote to the Central Committee, complaining that, because of the war and then postwar "inertia," the state was neglecting Romani culture, especially in the provinces. Two years later he wrote again, to Khrushchev himself, on the "situation of the disorganized wandering tribes," and urged him to take measures to settle them (Druts and Gessler 1990:305). A Romani Theater choirmaster recalled that settlement this way: "The result of the 1956 law was great hunger. Soldiers with guns rounded up all the camps. They were made to shovel — but how could they? They did not know how. They were paid practically nothing — they did not know this kind of work — and they went hungry. The Theater received a letter from some of these, asking for help: "We are perishing. . . . " They had eaten some spoiled potatoes at that collective, and died of poisoning. A commission which included Rom-Lebedev was sent from the Theater" (interview 1991). I did not find results of this commission in the theater archives but do not doubt that many Roma viewed the Theater as a locus for mediation, a place where other Roma might be found who would intercede for them with the state. Of all the state programs initiated for Roma, only the Moscow Romani Theater remained. Indeed, intellectuals in the 1990s remembered it as "the only thing the Gypsies have left." It was then still the single most important institution from which Romani families found a foothold in Moscow artistic and intellectual social circles and could enter Soviet higher education.

The Romani Theater nevertheless did as much to inscribe difference among Roma as it did to organize or integrate them. The Romani Theater originally was intended to buttress assimilative nationalities policy with ideological work, and indeed the most long-standing changes that the Theater effected were on social relations, but not as planned. The Theater was an institution, a place where Roma strengthened some social networks, created others, and severed still others. With the Theater as a central node, the state nurtured there whole cadres of Romani elites — *dynastii* (dynasties) of performers and their children, and a handful of academics and professionals. "The Gypsy Theater gave birth to a national intelligentsia, whose first university it was" (Slichenko 1984).

Tsyganshchina

Various boards and commissions over the decades accused the Romani Theater of being "out of touch," "nonproletarian," "kitsch." To demonstrate its usefulness, the Romani Theater, like other Soviet theaters, gave a certain number of free performances each month to factory workers or hospital patients. For instance, after a tour stop in Tjumen in 1980, a Theater press release reads: "All local workers who go to Moscow are automatically signed up for a free visit to the Romani Theater. They will not only see plays but meet the troupe and tell us about how they live and how they get oil. We are also planning a stand in the Theater foyer that will recount the lives and work of this collective of many thousands of geologists" (*Sovjetskaja Kul'tura* 1980:3). But free shows for the workers never seemed to relieve performers' authenticity complexes. Nor did they lessen a spreading consensus that the Theater was in decline. Some traced the crisis back to the 1960s, when musicians and singers began to leave for independent ensembles, playing in restaurants for foreigners or wedding parties, or to emigrate to New York City. Some blame the move to the Theater's current home in the Sovjetskij Hotel, far from the center of Moscow where it had first been located, where "we could wave through the windows to the actors at the Moscow Art Theater" (interview 1991). Some accused those who had left of mercenary motives, of chasing hard currency. Those who left blamed nepotism and said that the Theater directors "were Stalinist" and gave only bit parts to those with "authentic talent" so that mediocre relatives and favorites could shine without competition. Indeed, by the early 1990s, when virtually no theaters in Moscow had sufficient funding to expand repertoires, performers who remained at the Romani Theater were accusing each other of not only having no authentic talent, but of not being Gypsy at all.

But the Theater all along was embroiled in authenticity politics. In the 1930s, alongside doing assimilation work (which later was seen to divide performers from the "real, wild, Gypsies"), it was supposed to displace other Gypsy ensembles then judged inauthentic and alienated from real folk culture. The battle against Gypsy "kitsch" was in fact well under way before the Theater was established. Gypsy music was associated with merchants and aristocracy, and when the Bolsheviks began to reorganize cultural institutions after the Revolution, Gypsy choirs kept a low profile. Some performers emigrated, to play in Paris or Berlin to émigré audiences. Soon, however, those who remained in Russia resurfaced and began playing in restaurants and even in state choirs, such as the Leningrad Ethnographic Gypsy Choir, founded in 1925 under Lengoestrad (Leningrad City Stage), or with the State Circus (Demeter 1997:35). In the restaurants, they played not to aristocrats, but to the newly wealthy NEP-men (new economic policy–men). But by the mid-1920s, many of these performers were perceived as a threat to "authentic" Gypsy folk art, and the Soviet state began resolutely to weed out Gypsy ensembles, to eradicate "tsyganshchina."[33]

The word has several meanings. First, "tsyganshchina" indexes a milieu of vice, the restaurant atmosphere surrounding Gypsy musical performances, a smoky haze of "bourgeois decadence" populated by wealthy patrons who showered money and gifts upon female Gypsy singers. In the restaurants, female singers with accompanists were sometimes commissioned for small parties in chambers separate from the restaurant hall; from a Russian perspective, the singers' morality was suspect (see Gilliat-Smith 1922:62). Roma counter these slurs with recollections that singers were always surrounded by family, by the choir, and that they did not keep the proceeds from *chambres séparées* performances.[34] Regardless of such details, Soviet musicologist Shteinpress characterized this sort of restaurant performance as a degradation, a vulgar popularization of the Romani choirs once kept by aristocrats, however exploitive they might have been. "Tsyganshchina," second, more vaguely described inauthentic Gypsy art. As director of the Romani Theater, Nikolaj Slichenko asserted in 1984 (pre-glasnost) regarding his institution's achievements: "The true folk art of Gypsies long remained unknown. Until the 1920s, variety theaters, restaurants, and cabarets presented the extravagantly exotic charms of Gypsy songs and dances, a pseudo-art called tsyganshchina. This was a slur on the authenticity of Gypsy art and a major threat to its survival." Third, "tsyganshchina" or "pseudo-tsyganshchina" described the practices of Russians who dressed in Gypsy costume, performing "Gypsy songs" (see Rom-Lebedev 1990:68; Shteinpress 1934:44). There were several such popular performers, nearly all women, before the Revolution, and there have been several more since.[35] Finally, performers in the 1990s sometimes used "tsyganshchina" to label any Gypsy performance that smacked of *xaltura* (hack-work) — a term once used to attack "bourgeois" art but which in the 1990s did not ring so politically.

The Soviet ethnographer Barranikov argued in 1931 that Gypsy dance had been corrupted by city culture and Gypsy ensembles. He singled out the inappropriate popularity of what he saw as a decontextualized "Gypsy" dance move — a rapid shoulder shimmy performed by women: "This ancient dance element, brought from India . . . [thus] loses its aesthetic value and serves to satisfy the baser instincts" (1931:66). "Real" Gypsy folk songs and dances performed for the right purposes, by the right people, and in the right milieu needed aggressive "preservation."[36]

In the battle against tsyganshchina, the state encouraged "authentic" Gypsy songs — but just which songs were authentic had yet to be established. The approach was often not as contextual or pragmatic as Barranikov's and entailed merely blacklisting certain works, mainly songs belonging to the genre of "Russian romances" which the choirs had made their own. There was no central authority to approve lists of censored and approved Gypsy songs until the Romani Theater was founded in 1931. Even then there remained, for a short time, contestation, couched mostly in terms of style. In 1934 some Roma argued at meetings within the Theater that there was, in fact, "no special Gypsy singing voice" after all. "People are just used to hearing that [style] in restaurants," argued one Rom, who said he had traveled the country and "heard nothing of the kind" in the camps.[37] But non-Romani experts, such as an instructor from the State Theatrical Union, seemed to prevail in defining what would be presented on stage as authentically Gypsy. He suggested in 1934 that the actors find a vocal teacher who would "develop vocal training in accordance with that national color, with that national sound, which is laid into your national character. . . . if they give you European training, [on European] principles it will deform you. In the best case you would end up with a European, ill-cultured voice."[38] The authentic Gypsy voice was thus racialized — its textures could not be changed without incurring disfiguring damage. The idea that whatever Roma did might be considered authentically Gypsy was never discussed outside these early Theater meetings.

The Roma involved in those debates had in fact been recruited as soldiers in the battle against tsyganshchina. Even though the choir singers had once catered to aristocrats, most were not blamed for having produced elitist art. Rather, they were absolved for having been themselves exploited in its production, as when Shteinpress attacked the popularity of "Gypsy romances" as an expression of "Russian chauvinism" (1934: passim). Despite the attack on tsyganshchina, the social ties that performers had had with Russian aristocracy and merchants did not entail their doom; they could represent members of an "oppressed nation."[39] That they had been exploited was one of the arguments the Romani intelligentsia made to the head of Narkompros (People's Commissariat of Enlightenment), Anatolii Lunacharskii, when they first petitioned him to establish the Romani Theater.

Though its directors and producers were to be non-Roma, the Theater had been the idea of literate Roma, the same Roma who had worked in the 1920s literacy campaigns, setting up cultural centers and schools (Rom-Lebedev 1990:165). The lead roles were to be filled by selected former choral artists. What was transformed was not the personnel but the old choral settings and repertoire; costumes were altered to reflect "real Gypsy camp life," and ball gowns, lace shawls, and tiaras were replaced by multicolored skirts and earrings. At the same time, the principles of vocal projection and other techniques of professional staging were hardly changed. Thus, prerevolutionary choral stars such as Ljalja Chjernaja (Ljalja Black), Marina Cherkasova, and Maria Skvortsova became the uncontested stars of the Romani Theater; they already knew how to behave on the stage. Looking back, Rom-Lebedev rationalized the choice of Ljalja as "best for the matter at hand." Staging the first play at the Romani Theater, the head director asked the troupe who to cast in the lead; " 'Ljalja Chjernaja,' we all said as one" (Rom-Lebedev 1990:176). Stars such as Ljalja Chjernaja were sometimes described as "only one quarter Gypsy" (Druts and Gessler 1990:260),[40] yet such luminaries were rarely singled out as inauthentic for having diluted "blood" — a few drops in her case were apparently potent enough.

So when and how did accusations of performers' inauthenticity begin to figure? Doubts about the authentic social composition of the Theater then followed a less explicitly racialized tack. In 1933, Ivan Petrovich Tokmakov,[41] a Rom and instructor in the Central Committee's Nationalities Division on Work among Gypsies, was manager of the Romani Theater. In a protocol to the Moscow Executive Committee "on the state of the actors' cadres" he reported that "in its work, the Theater has not endeavored to attract proletarian [Romani] actors from workers' artels and collectives. I hear constantly about the Theater's achievements, manifested in its attraction of a number of actors from one collective farm, and of one candidate to the Party, but all the same, the troupe is contaminated by alien elements."[42]

The protocol contradicts more public official histories of the Romani Theater that claimed great success in recruiting Roma from the rural, poor, or nomadic Gypsies. Failed recruitment echoed likewise in attacks on the Theater's communicative competence and relevance. Already by 1934, it began to seem that the Theater could not reach the very people it was both to portray and recruit. Part of the problem was perceived to be linguistic code differences. The "Romanian and Hungarian" (Kelderari and Lovari) Vlax dialects spoken by the nomads most targeted for assimilation were thought too difficult for the actors, who mostly spoke Russka (Xeladytka) or Servi. Thus the performers were caught between communicative ideals: they were both to educate "non-European" Roma and to develop a stage Romani that would satisfy European literary conventions. Actors themselves complained that there was no standard stage Romani, that backstage there were "too many dialects," and that actors were always correcting each other's speech: "Where is the authority who would come and say, 'Here you need to speak this way, and there that way,' and not otherwise. But now we don't have that [authority], and so on stage a kind of tower of Babel is built. . . . that is why [even other] Gypsies understand us poorly."[43]

For the first three years, the Theater performed in Russka Romani, but by late 1934, it no longer produced entire plays in *any* dialect of Romani— only lyrics remained Romani.[44] Into the 1990s, texts in Romani appear only as untranslated songs or short snippets of "understood" interaction studded throughout the production. To non-Roma, the words mean little; embedded within a play, they represent merely a public "secret code" in a spectacle about exotic people speaking a foreign tongue. By 1934, Narkompros and the Romani Theater managers had decided that, since the Theater was not reaching those Roma who needed political education, then at least other Soviets would be entertained. By the mid-1930s, Soviet art was to be transparent, to reflect "socialist reality," which for the Romani Theater in practice meant being intelligible to majority Russians. Didactic plays were left in the repertoire, translated into Russian. But spectacle began to regain precedence over messages of radical change in everyday Gypsy life.

Although the Theater had been established to combat both negative and romantic stereotypes and "decadent bourgeois" tsyganshchina, now plays such as *Karmen* (adapted from Bizet's *Carmen*) were added to the repertoire — but not without argument. Before its scheduled opening as the first play of the 1934 season, the Romani party activists Ivan Tokmakov and Nikolaj Pankov condemned *Karmen* at a meeting of the Gypsy Section of the Moscow Executive Committee: "The Romani Theater has lost touch with the Gypsy masses. It is working on the play *Karmen,* which was long ago condemned by public opinion, since it gives nothing useful to the Gypsy masses. . . . the theater is making its actors into variety performers and not Soviet actors."[45]

In defense of adding *Karmen,* M. I. Goldblatt, then director of the theater, justified the play as a "work of classical dramaturgy," arguing that these scripts would give Romani Theater actors a chance to prove their ability in genres besides those narrowly defined as "national." "We can do more than just dance and sing — we can also speak."[46] But to Tokmakov and Pankov, vehicles such as *Karmen* projected mere images of Gypsy culture through a kind of minstrelsy, without examining social realities. Pankov expressed additional concern that both policy and performance develop without being diverted into tracks worn down by popular images propagated by people who were "out of touch."

Such accusations of inauthenticity were *couched* in terms of social alienation. Nevertheless, authenticity was *identified* via form and style: the right sort of "nationalist form" was the *visible* proof of honest "socialist content." Other signs betrayed masking. In his memoirs, Pankov describes the Russians first involved in constructing the Romani alphabet. The cultural work of the Gypsy Union in the 1920s, he says, had attracted "all kinds" of non-Romani people, from real Russian scholars to tsyganshchina imitators:

> [Ivanov] collected rare books on the Ilinskaja bazaar, was drawn to ethnography and archeology, and named himself a professor without having a department. In his apartment one could see iron lattice-work that had once decorated some little house out in Zamoskvorechie, and a statue of an angel from some liquidated little church. Sometimes he organized wild, strange "ethnographic" concerts as if they were Yakut weddings with shamans, who (and quite successfully it seems) were depicted by the talented Gypsy singer Sofia Lebedeva. . . . yet some-

how he managed to attract a few real scholars to come to the aid of the Gypsy Union with their knowledge. (Quoted in Druts and Gessler 1990:293–294)

This Ivanov, being a person who "used [acquaintances] like trumps in a card game" (294), managed to set up a conference for Gypsiologists in 1926, though he soon dropped out of sight, an irresponsible pseudo-intellectual. Pankov then introduces into his memoirs the Russian responsible for Gypsy letters, Professor M. V. Sergiejevskij, a future dean of Moscow University, quite differently. On his way to visit the professor, Pankov frets that he might again see

> The furniture of some kind of old-regime doctor, with wild and strange collections and a peculiar interior. But everything was otherwise. The host greeted us simply and from the heart. In his office were the usual surroundings, and on the table lay a heap of Moldovan newspapers, the books of Miklosich and Pott, and thick journals from the 60s and 70s on the Gypsy language or folklore, with the pages marked. . . . he did not limit himself to office work and reworking materials. Despite all his other duties . . . he found time to go everywhere personally — to the Gypsy school, to the Gypsy cooperative, to the club, to the theater, to the camp — in order to see the life of Gypsies in all its various forms. (Quoted in ibid.:295)

Contrasting the two Russians, form (books, angels) signals mental and moral seriousness or their lack. One man collects prerevolutionary religious kitsch and engages Gypsy performers to impersonate shamans, while the other keeps the authoritative volumes of Miklosich and Pott (the nineteenth-century linguists who surveyed Romani dialects to draw their paths of migration). Soviet linguistics, in the 1920s and 1930s, had additionally an aura of a hard social science, which ethnography then did not.[47] The contrast between the armchair, curio-collecting, self-named ethnologist, and the hearty, sincere fieldworker echoes and reverses romantic formulas for authenticity that oppose art to "daily life." Thus a "genuine" Romani script was constructed from knowledge of "real life," "scientifically based."

The alphabet's authenticity was unmarred, in this account, for being attributed to a Russian, not a Romani scholar. Plays likewise did not need to be composed by or even for Roma; Romani authors no longer filled the repertoire, though they did not disappear. The Theater became "internationalist." In 1935, with none of the controversy that had erupted over *Karmen,* it offered an adaptation of Pushkin's *Gypsies* alongside a piece by Romani playwright Aleksandr Germano, *Gypsy Fortune.* Administrators described the two plays as striking a "balance in the repertory politics," with a "classic" and a "play written by a Gypsy." The year 1937 would mark the state-organized Pushkin Jubilee; preparations began well in advance, and the Theater would contribute with this staging. The Germano play on the other hand was to be a propaganda work, a comedy, "in which a former wanderer, illiterate and superstitious, is completely reborn through work." The play was to be a step on "the path toward finding positive Gypsy images."[48] Yet, over time, it was the former type of romantic, Pushkinian script that would define key tropes of authenticity.

How have Romani performers represented their own part in enacting state policies and in reproducing ideologies of the authentic on stage? Rom-Lebedev, one of the theater's playwrights, was born into a well-known choir family and gives one such view in his memoirs. His mother was a Russian who married a Russka Rom, then found her calling singing in her husband's Gypsy choir; his family spoke mostly Russian at home, and he learned Romani only in adolescence. After the civil war, Rom-Lebedev aligned himself with the Bolsheviks as a Romani *intelligent* to battle "archaic" Gypsy customs, and became a leading Romani activist, writer, and performer. But he begins his 1990 memoir with an impression from his pre-Revolution childhood: "A cardboard Gypsy hung over my bed — in a green hat, black jacket, blue, wide baggy trousers, in boots. A sack hung over his shoulder, from which peered some frightened little children's heads. If you pulled on the long thread that let out from the Gypsy's back, he waved his arms and legs. Every evening before sleeping, I looked at him for a long time, and tugging the string, made him dance. Because he submitted to me and obediently danced, I was not afraid of him" (Rom-Lebedev 1990:11).

This is an odd montage of two stereotypes: the dancing Gypsy and the Gypsy who steals children. Rom-Lebedev claims to have felt no fear of the thief when he pulled the string. But the string might be interpreted as recalling historical realities, namely, that the earliest Romani choirs had been composed of serfs, made to sing on command. Soviet literacy materials for Roma in the 1930s indeed asserted that Romani serfs had been "traded *kak negrov*" (like negroes) and that "if the Gypsies didn't come when called to entertain, they were beaten or killed." A children's book by one Romani *aktivist* depicts Count Orlov, not as he was remembered in the 1990s — as inspired to create the first choir out of love for music — but as a despot, trading Gypsy slaves "like negroes," picking out the pretty ones who could sing, exchanging the others for dogs or pigs, breaking up families, and killing those who refused to entertain (Pankova 1934). Later Soviet accounts glossed over Romani serfdom in Russia and slavery in Moldova; instead, people who had few occupational choices save to perform once again were depicted as embodying volja and embodying it best when performing. Like other "national minorities" under socialism, Gypsies were categorized and tamed through performance.[49] They sang and danced on demand; for many this was their job and the highest possible expression of their ethnic, "cultural" being. Rom-Lebedev does not mention Romani slavery but he probably knew of it from the literacy materials; the puppet could point to a gap in late Soviet official memory.

In their own work, Rom-Lebedev and other Romani intellectuals tried to create "new, positive" Gypsy heroes for the stage — yet these heroes, like the puppet, continued to dance on demand. From the 1930s on, images of the Gypsy partisan countered crude representations of thievery but nonetheless shared the stage with the fiery lovers in musical versions of Gorky's *Makar Chudra* or Lorca's *Blood Wedding*. In Soviet discourse, only their reactions as musical beings marked the Gypsies' experiences as unique among the Soviet peoples. Rom-Lebedev himself described Romani reaction to policy with whimsical, musical touches of romance: "One by one, in pairs, and then in groups . . . the long awaited inhabitants of the 'choral republic' finally began to visit [the Gypsy club]" (Rom-Lebedev 1990:160). Onstage, the Nazis eugenic treatment of Gypsies was later muted; the war was a tragedy for *all* the Soviet peoples. Meanwhile, in Ukraine, Belorussia, and the Baltics, occupying armies had apprehended and killed Roma, throwing them into mass graves along with Jews (see Druts and Gessler 1990; Crowe 1995). Nonetheless, many Roma were not aware that Gypsies had been special targets for extermination until long after, even if they knew Jews had been: one elderly Xoroxane woman told me in 1992 that she had had to "hide from the fascists, because [she looked] like a Jew." The Romani Theater was on tour in 1941, and when the USSR entered the war it stayed on tour, giving free concerts to soldiers and hospital patients.[50] But most

FIGURE 13   A postcard commemorating the sixtieth anniversary of the Romani Theater in 1991. Courtesy of Moscow Romani Theater.

Roma were not specially evacuated from Moscow as many performers were. The experiences of Gypsy victims were later distinguished from those of other peoples only via images of Gypsy musical talent. Druts and Gessler write that "Gypsies tell a story" recounting that when Nazis prepared to shoot a camp of Gypsies in Belorussia, the women begged for mercy but, gaining none, began to sing in front of the guns and died singing (1991). Even Budulaj, a decorated veteran of the Great Patriotic War (World War II), tap dances and broods from under thick, dark eyebrows, remaining always a "typical Gypsy." Roma thus become part of larger historical narratives only via performance.

Since the late 1980s, Romani groups in the Czech Republic, Hungary, Slovakia, Macedonia, all parts of the former Soviet bloc, have begun to use theatrical forms in socially embedded ways Pankov would have approved—for instance, producing TV documentaries about Romani Holocaust victims. They are also staging translations of Shakespeare into Romani (rather than adapting Bizet into Russian). The Moscow Romani Theater, on the other hand, in the 1990s still continued to stress entertaining non-Roma,

and rarely directly addressed the politics of representation as did its counterparts in Eastern Europe. Instead, Romani performers in 1990s Russia
only obliquely spoke to those models of theatricality and ideologies of
authenticity that so crucially affected their lives.

Directors: Producing and Performing Authority

In 1990s Russia, strong romanticizing conventions of Gypsy representation endured. Producers and directors could reproduce these conventions
easily because they relied on bits of action or decoration that could be
inserted into performance — for instance, occasional Romani words (*"Ekh,
duj, trin!"* [One, two, three!] *"Romale!"* [Hey, Roma!]), multicolored
dance costumes, particular dance moves. Because they were familiar, end-
lessly reiterated, they lent verisimilitude and added credible force to the
celluloid surfaces on which "Gypsies" lived fictional lives. One instance of
such reiteration that I encountered involved images of birds deployed as
icons for volja. In the summer of 1993, in a small city northeast of Moscow,
Midori Nakamura and I spent several days in a television studio editing
T'an Baxtale!, a video documentary about Roma that we had codirected.
Much of the first day passed debating with the studio director. We wanted
to begin with a shot of a Lovari boy in a synthetic parka playing soccer in
the snow; by framing the documentary with these shots, we hoped to
unsettle particular local stereotypes from the start, to at least stress images
valued by Moscow Lovara. The studio director, unnerved by this, wanted
us instead to "fix" Gypsy identity right away in a more familiarly Russian
mode. As we fast-forwarded through some video material, a shot of birds
circling blue sky around a golden church cupola caught his eye: "Birds!
Free like Gypsies! *That* is how you should begin!" His idea converged precisely with those genres we hoped the documentary would reveal and unravel: we imposed our own conventions, of course, but hoped at least for
new juxtaposition.

No Roma were present to argue with either him or us — and had there
been, they might have agreed with him, yielding as much to his authority as
a television expert as to that of a familiar canon. We were foreigners, but
he was in our employ, and we controlled production choices, pulled the
strings. The shot was indeed very beautiful and, after all, some Roma themselves cite the metaphoric link between birds and Gypsies in Russian poetry

from Pushkin on.[51] It is thus not only non-Roma who enforce representational and performance conventions: I have seen Russian backup musicians instruct Roma to "change the tempo" or to hold a note longer because "it's more Gypsy that way," but I have also heard Roma tell each other to step more briskly, clap faster, be more "really Gypsy" in ways recalling Romani Theater styles, not only during rehearsals, but at home.

Stereotypes continue to exist not only because they are embedded in intertextual webs, but because people iterate them from structured, shifting social positions. To show how this works in real time, I move now from archives and oral histories of the Romani Theater to ethnography of 1990s documentary and feature film production.[52] One of the virtues of focusing on production rather than on finished plays or films is that, during a rehearsal or a shoot, it is easier to see *how* performances are not merely citations of text, not merely enactments of a script; they are woven in and of social relations.

The social relations under examination here are those enacted between performers and directors. Like authors, directors deal with texts, but the agency and authority of most mainstream directors contrast with that of an author in important ways. Here I must take issue with Bakhtin, who contrasts literary to dramatic dialogue. He argues that most authors strive to control their characters' actions and voices — to speak through them in a monologue that only appears to deploy many voices. He thus admired Dostoevsky's unusual ability to create real polyphony, to develop characters who seemed truly free to speak and act without the author knowing what they would say or do next (1984).[53] The precondition for polyphony in the text, Bakhtin argues, was Dostoevsky's refusal to map characters' fates from beginning to end, as if he placed himself into the same stream of time with them. Bakhtin did not believe that such polyphony existed in drama, which he described as "almost always constructed out of represented, objectified discourses" (1984:188), meaning that speech was described from outside, as a typological feature. To be polyphonic, dialogic speech would have to be rendered as experienced by the characters. But Bakhtin did not take into consideration real-time directorial struggles to orchestrate an ensemble of living actors. For even in the most cartoonish or allegorical of stage dialogues, the director's ventrilocution is mediated by many human agencies besides his own.

Directors work not with words and paper, but with casts of real people who have their own ideas about their lines, their scripts, and their blocking. But at the same time most professional directors in Russia (as elsewhere) have been trained to see their job as "realizing a theatrical production according to a single, coherent vision," as both a Romani Theater director and a student in the directing program adjunct to the Moscow Art Theater described it to me. While there were directors in Russia with more Brechtian approaches to mise-en-scène (alienation effects, divergent readings built into staging, etc.), such people did not work at the Moscow Romani Theater; the Theater staged mainly fantastical and romantic musicals. There, as in mainstream theaters, actors were expected to fulfill the director's vision, to animate his reading of the script.

For professional Romani performers in Russia, such relations of authority backstage or on the set were compounded not only by general occupational concerns about wages or reputation but also by ethnic hierarchies. Romani actors usually worked under non-Romani directors, for although early playwrights for the Moscow Romani Theater had been Romani, the directors were not. Even in its early days, most were sent from the Moscow Art Theater, to "bring the minority performers into the realm of world culture" by teaching them Stanislavskiian and other European stage methods and conventions. In tones alternating between anti-Semitism and a sense of a shared fate, Romani actors in the 1990s sometimes claimed that "most of our directors have been Jews."[54] Although the head of the Moscow Romani Theater was a Servi Rom (Nikolaj Slichenko), most of the acting directors of individual productions in the Theater were non-Romani. Filmmakers shooting "Gypsy themes" likewise remain almost exclusively Russians or foreigners, though they employ Roma as consultants.[55]

I now take up two production processes in which participants performed social relations and distinctions. The first was the making of a short documentary segment at a Kelderari village for a Moscow television station. The second was the making of a feature film by a Russian director who employed professional Romani actors.

Rehearsing Reality

In the autumn of 1991, I went to a Kelderari settlement with the crew of a Moscow television show and the Romani consultant they had engaged for the trip. Their responses to the encounter recalled the remarks of the Romani intellectual who had claimed that "wild" Roma did not know how to frame art as separate from life. The TV crew were not particularly pleased to include an American, even after their Romani consultant had introduced me as a "specialist on Gypsies" and had spoken Romani to me to validate my intrusion. We came to the village by van; an old Russian man passing by on a bicycle had pointed us back down the dirt road after we had driven right past. The television star claimed that he had recognized it the first time, pointing out a row of clothes laid out to dry along a wooden fence, pronouncing them "real Gypsy skirts."

The Kelderari settlement was separated from the Russian parts of the village by a road and by fences on the Russian side. Unlike the Russian dachas with the individual gates, theirs stood unfenced, surrounded instead by stacks of metal and rows of canisters, sheds, and welding areas. About sixteen houses ranged up the street, each one with one or two stories of white concrete brick, save for a few accent bricks arranged in geometric patterns and painted in bright primary colors. New houses were being built. After pulling up next to a house constructed with these patterns of colored brick, the crew waited beside the van while the Romani consultant, a relative of the villagers on her grandfather's side, and I went ahead.

We walked down the middle of a wide dirt lane between the houses, and to the children approaching to see who had come she called out a Romani greeting, "*T'an baxtale!*" (Grace/fortune be with you!). Their blunt response, "*So bikines?*" (What are you selling?), dismayed her. "Look at what is happening to our people now in this country,"[56] she mumbled under her breath to me, her lament echoing a common one claiming the moral decline of the country into commercialism. She thus also distanced herself momentarily from the "byt" of her relatives by adding to me that she was *not* a merchant Gypsy, not a beggar, but a performer, an *artistka*. What she offered her kin were not goods for sale but social and cultural capital.

With the aim of recruiting villagers for the documentary, the Romani consultant began to "audition" the children, clapping her hands to the music from their cassette recorder and marveling that they had picked up "Gypsy stage" (*tsyganskaja estrada*) dance steps from TV, in addition to "our own" Kelderari tap-dance steps. The village indeed had its own amateur ensemble, which had played once, years ago, at the Moscow Romani Theater and had once traveled to Germany. She made promises, told the children how she wanted to take them to France to perform.

FIGURE 14   A cameraman for Moscow television takes sightings in a Kelderari village. He and the director were disappointed to find interiors that they thought looked too much "like anywhere else."

Once they had obtained permission via the consultant, the TV crew began canvassing the village, setting up light meters and microphones, and taking them down again. Most of this took place outdoors: the crew did not want to tape indoors; they did not find the decor sufficiently exotic to intrigue Russian audiences, who they assumed would not want to see Gypsies living in ordinary houses rather than in "traditional" tents or wagons. Like most such houses in Russian villages, theirs lacked indoor plumbing and potable water (the women drew drinking water from a well across the road in the Russian part of the settlement),[57] though they were heated with steam radiators, and the whole settlement shared two telephones. But all the houses had electricity, a refrigerator, stove, and television, and some had a VCR. Such fixtures severely disappointed the television emissaries, as evidencing loss of authenticity. They wanted to associate Gypsies with wide open space, Russian *prostor*.[58] For their part, the Kelderara did their best to draw the crew's attention indoors.

Like Russian houses in the country, Kelderari houses had no hallways (each room opened into others farther back), but unlike some Russian homes, these had intermediate rooms between the street and the interior living areas, where Russian hired workers could sit to eat after work, discouraged from penetrating beyond. While many Russians might be dissuaded from entering the Kelderara *wanted* to welcome the prestigious Russian TV star and his crew deeper inside—they were delighted with the idea of showing their homes on television. But the mundane Soviet-made shelved hutches with glass doors, the bits of Czech crystal and St. Petersburg china, the collections of American beer cans, the rows of family photographs, arrangements of knickknacks, and painted wall decorations—all documenting local memories and attachments—went mostly unnoticed.

In one of the small houses, with cameras turned off, the Russian television star began his own "auditions." He explained in some detail what he was looking for—something melancholy, a sad song to "signify the disappearance of traditions," or a classic Gypsy romance. A Kelderari man took up a guitar, but it was a six-string, and the television star chided him, "How can you lose the tradition of the seven-string guitar," not realizing that Kelderara came to Russia from Romania, where the seven-string guitar was never played by anyone, having become a musical totem only for the mostly Russka Roma of the Russian choirs, and that only since the nineteenth century. The Romani man humbly mumbled agreement that his was "not a very good" guitar. Next, it turned out that they did not know any nostalgic romances, and that the best they could offer was a song in Romani set to the tune of "Hotel California." The television host at last took the guitar into his own hands and demonstrated, "something like this," as he sang a slow romance. One of the Kelderari men then remembered a slow jazz tune in Romani, one that in fact did recount the end of traveling, but the film crew only made faces at the style: "Too modern."

"Listen, we only play lively songs, dance tunes, on the accordion," they finally told the Russians, commanding the young, unmarried girls to display their dance steps. For the occasion, the girls used the door frame between the two main rooms as a make-shift proscenium, rather than dancing in the room, pushing each other out into the director's view one by one. They made precise tap steps on precariously high heels, laughing when they lost their nerve before the famous guests and running back behind the door. Calling for the women to dance like this was something that Kelderari men in Russia might have done at any celebration—dancing for adults and potential husbands at Easter, at weddings, and so on, was spoken of as a duty. There was often even a similar atmosphere of evaluation, not so unlike this audition, when visiting Roma would size up a young girl as a potential *bori*. Only this time, the girls were being looked over not by potential in-laws, but by strangers from the realm of television and by a relative from the famous Moscow Romani Theater.

"All right, I see you can only play merry tunes. . . . Well, that's what it will have to be then." The director then suggested that the Roma build a bonfire for the camera outside on the street, around which they would dance. They objected with understated diplomacy: "But it is cold on the street—why don't we stay in and drink tea? Bonfires are for summer." He shook his head, so they shrugged and went to gather wood. Once the fire was lit and the sun had set, the television star described how he wanted the women to dance. He exhorted the men to stay out of camera range, for they were dressed in jeans and T-shirts; unlike the women with their long skirts, scarves, and braids, the men were "not interesting." The women were to dance all in a bunch near the fire, so that the cameraman could crouch at their feet, and get tumultuous shots of multicolored skirts and moving feet. "This isn't going to work," an older woman standing near me quietly mumbled in Romani, objecting to this aesthetic, "They should dance one by one, so we can see how well they do it, but like this they are crowded and get in each other's way!"

But they continued dancing as told. At only one point during that day did any Kelderara break the frames established by the film crew. The only interview conducted indoors involved the oldest woman in the village, who was asked to sit on the floor "like in a camp," rather than on her sofa, which was cut off by the shot. The television host sat cross-legged on the floor beside her. To the crew's consternation and irritation, she continually tried to direct the attention of the interviewer to objects and people over by the sofa and her knickknack cabinet, outside the shot frame so carefully established by lights and microphones. In all, however, the Kelderara adjusted to the video crew's conventions of framing.

On visiting the village a week later by myself, I was surprised that the Kelderara did not criticize how they had been filmed, especially given how often many Roma criticize gazhje who "don't understand Romani ways." In the coming months, what eventually offended them was, rather, that the segment was never televised, as promised. I pressed, "But what about the campfire in the street, and the women dancing all at once?" While they agreed that these things were all "wrong," it was no more than to be expected from outsiders. It was only much later that a few villagers would express annoyance at frequent visits from curious, Russian folklorists and other film crews: "*My kto — Chukchi?*" ("Who are we, Chukchi?" [a northeastern Siberian people often featured in pop ethnography and in ethnic jokes]). But for the present, they focused on the thrill of a visit by a famous man.

It seems then that the production, the process of filming, had indexed profoundly different framing of social "reality" for each side. The director had framed their performances as if separate from lived social relations in space and among people, while his crew's camera shots were to represent penetration "into" an unknown world. But for the Kelderara, the presence of the camera pointed "outward" to a world of renown and to chains of social capital reaching back to Moscow.

In fact, though they located them differently, Kelderara themselves shared and valued some of the same forms of stereotypic representation valued by the crew. Some families had commissioned local Russian artists to paint elaborate murals: Jesus with Moses, birch trees on a brilliant blue lake, and an Indian woman in a sari departed from the usual images, but murals of Gypsies in flowing sleeves playing violins in meadows did not. This is not to say that the TV crew would have reached a final realm of authenticity, of "nonperformance," by filming indoors, but that they neglected the ways Kelderara themselves divided and mingled what they saw as reality and representation, the ways they did frame "art and life."

Their urban relative, the consultant, explained to me a few days after the shoot that the television star, "as an artist," wanted to make the shoot "beautiful," and that she understood his motivations. Her support of this director contrasted with other instances when she had vehemently condemned dilettante filmmakers; directors with whom she had collaborated who had "got everything wrong," to whom she had threatened that she would quit because of "shameful inaccuracies" in their screenplays. Her most lurid example was the case of a French woman writing a screenplay about a teenage Gypsy girl who asks a boy to elope. She argued with this woman, saying that no real Romani girl would suggest such a shameful

FIGURE 15   One of the Kelderari interiors that the TV crew avoided filming, a year later. A young man stands with his (Russka) bride from a neighboring village in front of a china collection and below a display of family photos. They had married some months earlier, but she put on her wedding clothes for the camera.

thing, and especially no Kelderari girl. In the case of the Kelderari village shoot, however, she agreed with how the "beautiful" underwrote conventional representations. Complexity (here as hints of "modernity") had to be veiled. "Who wants to see that Gypsies have china collections and live in houses like everyone else?" Indeed, she considered the china cabinets a sign of cultural decay. She wanted to go to Romania to make a film, for she had heard that Roma living there were extremely poor, living the "real" life of Gypsies.

Her subject position in thus speaking may have been shaped by past interactions attempting to amass financial resources to make her own feature film about Gypsies after the Revolution. She had written a screenplay and was elaborating it with customs and phrases culled during field trips to *tabornyje tsygane* (camp Gypsies) and from the recollections of her Kelderari grandfather (not those of her Servi and other grandparents). For that historical screenplay, she regarded representations that evoked a memory of Romani life more "genuine" than the ways most Roma actually lived. She was also willing though to tolerate that the documentary crew had masked current material life — as long as they foregrounded remembered tradition as the "real" reality.

The Black Pearl

Paradoxically, the "true Gypsy" is primitive and poor and needs no furniture, but is also draped in jewelry and coins, and full of schemes to swindle people. These contradictory depictions, as expressions of broader concerns about assimilation and authenticity, were especially salient in 1990s productions. I had long wanted to observe rehearsals at the Romani Theater, to see how directors and actors negotiated such contradictions, but this had not been possible because no new plays had been added to the repertoire and so no rehearsals were needed. A general theatrical crisis at that time, a lack of financing, meant that few post-Soviet theaters overhauled their repertoires for years. The repertoire was stagnant; the first new play to appear in the 1990s opened in 1996, titled *The Gypsy Countess*. It was a musical comedy set in an "authentic," presocialist past and accompanied not by Soviet-era compositions but by music imported from the Spanish pop-folk group, Gipsy Kings.

In the summer of 1992, however, I did observe a Russian film director shoot a film that employed actors from the Romani Theater. The screenplay echoed Romani Theater scripts while also playing upon the widespread sentiment that the Theater's urbanized actors had lost touch with authentic "Gypsiness." On the set as well, interpretations of the Romani Theater's civilizing project and of the effect of that project on its actors played themselves out in social interactions among director, crew, and actors.

The director attributed his drive to make the film to becoming intrigued by what he saw as a contradiction between "modernity" and "Gypsy culture." He based his concern about this "contradiction" on his commitment to realism, and presented himself as someone who "respected Gypsy ways." He *was* more inquisitive about Romani practices than was usual among Russians I knew — he had made a point, for instance, of learning several words in Romani and had scripted a few of them into the text. Thus, in production, unlike many other directors, he did *not* rely only on the conventional horses, campfires, and twirling, multicolored skirts. Nor did he purge "civilized" cars, designer clothes, or restaurants from the script, but instead deployed them on the set. However, he did so to stress another form of "primitivity," manifest in what he called the "paradox of Modern Gypsies." This paradox was, in fact, also a metaphor for his vision of 1990s social and economic change in Russia:

> They just want to preserve their traditions. They also want to become civilized, but that is impossible. They try to do this [in the film] by opening a restaurant, but it falls apart; they are not capable of organizing. Just like the Romani Theater, it all falls apart from within, *not* because of external forces. . . . No, it had to fall apart. Gypsy culture is limited, theater is not their affair, their affair is to attract audiences to restaurants. . . . This film . . . is also a metaphor of the changes in our country: we are now allowed to pursue business, but we don't know how either. These people are unable to organize — the clans know only how to fight. They cannot run a business or think about tomorrow . . . but then, neither can we. (Interview from field notes, 1992)

The director asserted that Roma are unable to organize either themselves or social institutions, and hinted that in his film they therefore stood for something else, specifically, chaotic and changing economic conditions in Russia. "Uncivilized" people, former nomads, perfectly symbolized the instability of the future during "transition." He claimed also that they were too disorganized to run a theater, and were made instead for restaurant singing (even though the Romani Theater *had* survived more than sixty years). He thus reversed the terms of the 1920s battles against tavern tsyganshchina; the director found authenticating to his "real Gypsies" precisely what the Bolsheviks once banned as ersatz. This reasoning followed the early 1990s fashion of reevaluating prerevolutionary practices as more genuine than those of the present; Gypsy restaurants were, in his film, ciphers for such nostalgia.

The film tentatively was titled *The Black Pearl,* the last word of the title resonating with the family name of a well-known Romani dynasty of performers (the Zhemchuzhnyje, "Pearls") and the adjective being a not-so-subtle racial marker. Its hero is a young Romani boy who wants to marry a girl from a wealthy restaurant-owning "clan" but is unable to pay brideprice for her. They try to elope, but when her brothers catch them, he kills one of them and is imprisoned. After his release, he opens his own restaurant, employing his "clansmen" as entertainers, but, plagued by debts to a

FIGURE 16 A ciga-
rette break on the set
of the *Black Pearl*.
This door represents
the back door of a
restaurant, from
which the hero was
to elope with his
beloved, played by
the Servi actress on
the left. The mus-
tached man, center, is
the director.

Russian mafioso and conflicts with his kinsmen, the restaurant collapses,
and the Gypsy entrepreneur fails to win his bride.

The entire screenplay was an allegory refracting anxiety about value, and
in particular about money, after the fall of socialism. The clan conflicts
gravitated around money (the bride-price, the debts), as did relations with
non-Roma (as in scenes where audiences paid hard currency to restaurant
musicians). This thematic focus was clear even in directions to code-switch.
The director ordered the actors when to switch from Russian to Romani,
even which words to speak (though mere "Gypsy language" usually suf-
ficed). He would issue these directions through a battery-powered megaphone "*Govorite* Romanes!" ("*Speak* in Romani!" [italics marks Russian]),
especially, as he put it, "where the action is understood." The reference of
these "unintelligible" words usually counted less than their function indexing authentic, exotic foreignness. But a few cases dovetailed more closely
with the director's aims. Besides the word "gazhjo" (non-Rom), "lové"
(money) was the word the director, through his megaphone, ordered the
actors to utter in Romani most often — often as the single Romani word in a
Russian sentence. In fact, it was one of the few words that he used consistently in stage directions: "*Pokazhi* lové *na fone beloj rubashki!*" ("*Show the*
money *against the background of the white shirt!*"). The value of money in
relation to other social values was certainly a painful issue in 1992, when
erratic inflation had reduced rubles to nothing, and when everyone sus-

pected everyone else of money lust. These formal details — from the film title to use of code-switching — seemed to ratify projecting such suspicion onto "blacks" and foreigners.

In parallel decisions, the director projected conflict *among* Gypsies where fault lines among Roma did not exist, warping their descriptions of social difference to fit his narrative. During the shoot, he thus displaced the pragmatic sense of Romani practices and the metadiscourses about them, as understood by the Romani actors whom the film both employed and ostensibly portrayed. That is, this displacement distorted what practices or metadiscourses usually indexed about social relations. For instance, in one scene, a Romani woman appears on a balcony, wearing mauve tights with a green T-shirt and a man's fedora. Her husband emerges and chases her inside to a dressing room, threatening to flog her with his guitar. In the next shot, inside the dressing room, he chastises her in Romani: "Don't show people your legs! People are looking!" She responds in Russian, as she dons a skirt over her head to cover her legs: "Don't you tell me! There are women who go around in long skirts and yet cheat on their husbands, but I am faithful to you!" A few members of the film crew of Russians, looking on, maintained to me that the character had violated a "strict custom" among "patriarchal Gypsy clans."

The issue of whether women should wear pants, depending on which Roma one talks to, could evoke a range of concerns about morality and pollution (for instance, for Kelderara, to have an actress don a skirt over her head would make matters worse, since skirts pollute heads and should be stepped through instead). Of course, these concerns are *not* universal throughout the Romani diaspora: in Prague or Budapest, most urban, *non-Vlax* Romani women wear pants in public. This variation locates pants as a focus for controversy about authenticity and difference. In fact, the first question a Vlax-Romani woman whom I met in 1995 in Budapest asked me was, "Do the Roma in America wear skirts or pants?" But these discourses, salient as they are, were miscited in the film.

The idea for the scene, the director said, was generated in a dispute between the Romani actresses and the Russian costume designer; according to him, the very authenticity of the scene lay in the fact of this "impromptu" discovery. The costumer had wanted the women to wear colorful lycra tights on-screen because they *did* wear them to rehearsals but they resisted. She complained, "They didn't want to show that. They said,

'That's not allowed for Gypsy women!' But look at them, they themselves are all in tights! What a contradiction!" The women, for their part, fretted that "stricter," more "traditional" Roma might see the film and criticize them. The costumer read this desire as simple hypocrisy (for the record, *some* women in "stricter" groups likewise sometimes wear pants at home or when they do not anticipate "being seen."). The director, inspired by the dispute with the costumer, decided to incorporate an argument about pants into the script. But while Romani women performers often do wear pants, and while dressing actresses in them could add visual verisimilitude to the film, by staging a conflict over pants *between married performers,* he both distorted the social relations among actors and displaced the broader cultural politics of pants among Romani groups. That is, the fact that other (namely Vlax) Roma criticize urban performers on the grounds of "immodest" dress was transposed into a marital conflict between actors, people who were actually long accustomed to women wearing pants. Rom-Lebedev's description of training Romani Theater recruits in the 1930s to take pride in wearing pants during rehearsal echoes here — except that applause for newly acquired, civilized flexibility has given way to conflict over "lost" tradition. The director had taken up what had been an emblem of oppressive, gendered traditions to socialist theater workers decades earlier, and reversed the arrows to trope a different kind of authenticity.

While the actors sensed something "off" about the scene, they did not have a strong position from which to argue to change it, perhaps because the scene *visually* resembled aspects of daily experience. The practices of transposing words and things from the sphere of "life" to that of "art," to achieve verisimilitude in pragmatically distorted ways, accustomed performers to become likelier to see *themselves* as inauthentic rather than the production. Though the director conferred with a few selected consultants, and Romani actors made occasional suggestions (this was, after all, a film about a Romani musical ensemble), he rarely heeded their observations. One non-Romani actor (one of the few who often plays Romani characters at the Romani Theater) protested, for instance, a scene in which the clan patriarch sets a bride-price that the hero cannot afford: "What is this?! Everyone knows that the kind of Roma who own restaurants don't have bride-price traditions?!" He was right: in Russia, mainly Kelderara pay bride-price, but the director ignored him.

Rather than challenging the director's interpretations — and authority —

in the moment of production, actors transposed tensions over authenticity and representation into struggles over work time and discipline. In such interactions, it was the director who was revealed as not recognizing the divisions the performers drew between art and byt. One afternoon, during an outdoor shoot, the cast slaughtered and roasted a black lamb over a fire. The Russian crew watched from about thirty meters away — the slaughter and its consumption made the actors seem more authentic in their eyes, "wild," as they put it to me. The director, however, scolded the actors for "sitting around and eating all day." The actors challenged his attempt to discipline them outside the working-day performance frame: "Are you saying a person cannot even eat lunch?" At the end of the same day, while the director informed them of the next day's schedule, this exchange took place:

> Actor: Ivan Ivanovich [not his real name], do you respect Gypsies and our ways?
> Director: Of course I do, I love Gypsies, or else I wouldn't be here.
> Actor: Well then, you must eat some of our shashlik!
> (Field notes 1992)

The director declined to eat. Of course, shashlik (a kind of shish kebab) is considered in Russia to be a Caucasian and Central Asian dish; the Romani actors called it "ours" not because it was a "Gypsy" dish, but because Roma had cooked it. It was thus the focus of an inclusive circle drawn by ideal hospitality, which, many Roma insisted, "one must not refuse." By forcing the director to reveal that he did *not* respect "Gypsy hospitality," the actors momentarily placed him as an outsider, a person who refuses hospitality, establishing themselves as the real cultural authorities on Romani life. For his part, the director interpreted their words and actions as reaffirming his notion that Gypsies were incapable of discipline and organization — traits that, recall, provided the foundation for his "paradox of Gypsy modernity." But the paradox was only a paradox when he defined where art, where performance, began and ended.

Roma often expect gaps in understanding between non-Roma and themselves. Romani performers in Russia had for decades become used to simplify their words for audiences. Of that brief window of time when Romani was used on stage, Rom-Lebedev writes in his memoirs that the Theater's first production had been a complete failure to communicate with the audience: "*'Romale shunen'te tume man!'*" (Romale, listen to me!) I vainly called out in someone else's voice. . . . there were no Gypsies, and there was no one to understand" (174). Rom-Lebedev describes his own voice falling into an empty space of no response, rendering it foreign even to himself.[59] The audience, however, satisfied with the musical interludes, left unaware of any disjuncture of codes or of incomprehension that to Rom-Lebedev permeated — and became — the meaning of that performance.

Decades later, Romani performers would tell me they had "two kinds" of songs, those for the gazhje and those "for ourselves," sung "more genuinely" at home. In some ways, this was a very Soviet distinction; they idealized the home as a shelter from the political; the home was the site of the real, unstaged, unofficial, even antistate, as when one retired singer recounted their at-home linguistic subversion of musical commissions from the party. "Even in those fearful times my father . . . was not afraid to make up different [Romani] words to the melody: 'We [Gypsies] eat, drink, sing songs, and remember God'" (Demeter 1997:68).

We should keep in mind, at the same time, that successful Soviet Roma were more likely to speak about needing a private space for songs than were Roma less involved with the state because they were professionals in the business of "Gypsy" representation. Some thus drew a metaphoric proscenium where the state ended and "home" began — one overlapping the line where gazhje space ended and Romani space began. But was there always a perceived boundary between real life and the stage, between audience and performer, between public and home, Roma and non-Roma? Or was it just that, wherever certain kinds of social relations and ideologies intersected, an imagined proscenium materialized? State policy, market relations, and ordinary conversations certainly assumed boundaries modeled on a theatrical partition — their participants all the while denying that performance had anything to do with producing social distinctions.

· 5 ·

The Hidden Nail:
Memory, Loyalty, and Models of Revelation

In preceding chapters I have detailed how memory of state involvement in performance has complicated relations not only between Roma and non-Roma, but among Roma. For many Roma in Russia, memory and understanding of current loyalties were deeply tangled. But from a non-Romani point of view, the ways that models of theatricality intersected images of genuine Gypsies (as unpacked in preceding chapters), entailed that Gypsies were suspect of possessing the capacity for neither memory nor loyalty. In this chapter, I investigate narrative memories and archival texts explicitly concerned with transgressions of loyalty — and implicitly with ontological distinctions between revelation and concealment, with tropes of theatricality. I deal first with a Soviet archive (a record of criminal prosecution of Roma that included both ethnographic and biographic reports) and then locate Romani readings of that text in relation to biographic and religious narrative, and to everyday concerns in the 1990s. These intertextual and pragmatic readings hopefully will counteract ways in which historical memory and religious faith (and thus all deeply felt social loyalties that many experience as based upon them) have been posited as antithetical to authentic Gypsy character.

Veiling Recollection

In those rare official histories that mention, or even dedicate themselves to Roma, theatrical and musical deeds override all others. Theatricality, though empowering in some ways, hinders recountings of Romani history at other levels of detail: Gypsy performance veils Romani memory. Underwriting this absence are tropes of Gypsy timelessness, themselves supported by images of natural Gypsy freedom and improvisational talents (see Trumpener 1991). It is as if "having" a history would cramp Gypsy volja: "Unlike other groups we can feel vaguely romantic about — the Celts, the nomads, the American Indians — the Gypsies have, it seems, a particular aversion to remembering their collective history, as if that too were an inconvenient brake on their freedom to live day by day" (Kobak 1995). The Polish scholar Slawomir Kapralski (1997: 12) similarly claims that Roma do not memorialize the Porraimos (Holocaust) because they allegedly lack consistent funerary rites, and instead manifest an "attitude to death," in their taboo on speaking of the dead, that entails ignoring the past to render an "identity created in the framework of culture, not of history." Western journalism has made much of such speculations, as if "culture" impedes memory:

> What ultimately distinguishes the Sho'ah from the Porraimos is not what happened to Jews and Gypsies under Nazism . . . but rather how the two cultures have responded after the fact. . . . [As an oral culture] Gypsy memory remains within the confines of the community: for most Roma, monuments, museums, and miniseries about their history have little relevance. Indeed, Fonseca notes, the act of forgetting the Holocaust (not out of negligence but as a form of defiance) is the more meaningful response for many Gypsies. (Shandler 1997:93–94)

However, public Romani monuments are lacking not out of some cultural aversion to recollection or out of deficient religious motivation but because Roma have only rare access to the media technologies that broadcast memory and mourning and do not control the architectural boards and educational systems that display and reproduce them, that perform them. Moreover, the socialist states of East Europe, where most Romani survivors lived on after the war, censured war memorials that singled out any ethnic category as having suffered in particular. The problem then is not that Roma deny history, but that no infrastructure magnifies their memories as broadly collective, as constituting as "imagined community" (Anderson, 1983).

For the record, in the early part of the twentieth century, Roma did attend dedications to monuments to emancipation in Romania (Haley 1934:184), and in the late part of the century they did hold vigils in Chicago to commemorate Porraimos victims. Meanwhile, the rest of the world pays little notice to oral histories of Romani concentration camp experiences published in the 1990s in the Czech Republic, documentaries on wartime survivors produced by Roma for postsocialist Hungarian TV, Karl Stojka's paintings depicting camp life, and the wartime memoirs of Mateo Maximoff (1946). It is as if these accounts produced by literate Roma were not properly representative of Gypsy pasts at all, for Roma who *do* publicly perform memories in writing, speech, painting, or video often are dismissed as ethnically inauthentic, even insincere.

For instance, almost by way of apology, the Russian painter Nikolaj Bessonov prefaces Olga Demeter's autobiography by characterizing its historical relevance as narrow: "'Big history' enters the pages of her book only when it immediately touches Gypsy interests. Of course, this manifests not only the author's personal qualities, but an age-old foundation or, as it's called these days, mentality. That which is strange to a politicized, autochthonous people is completely natural to Gypsies, living for centuries with no homeland" (1997:5). But are Romani autobiographies really more self-interested than anyone else's? Conversely, why should it be judged strange that Romani personal stories weave through broader ones, that Romani sons could be born, same as Russian ones, "the year they launched Gagarin into the cosmos."

Gypsies have been stripped of meaningful memory in outsider accounts just as have other "peoples without history": history belongs to those who produced "civilization." Most accounts dismiss the historical particulars of Romani diaspora because without the frame of a unifying state, those details *seem* contradictory. If Roma in Poland are Catholic, while many Roma in Bulgaria are Muslim, how can Roma have a "history" of religion, or have a capacity for faith at all? If Roma everywhere do not share consistent funerary rites or other rituals, perhaps not only do they lack memory, not only do they lack a coherent historical narrative, but perhaps they have no attachment to anything. Such arguments treat particularities in diverse contexts as clear signs of theatricality, of performance in its sense of protean dissimulation.[1]

We do not need to discard performance, or discount the biographies of elite musicians in order to rehabilitate other Roma as historical agents, or even as ordinary folk with selective memories. Instead, we first need to understand how official historical accounts position Gypsy social life through ideologies of theatricality and dramaturgic models of the proscenium.

Condemning Culture: Revelation, Betrayal, and the Proscenium

This chapter juxtaposes two separate accounts of the biography of a Romani man, to trace differing understandings of loyalty, of ways in which "betrayal" is assumed to underlie motivations, themselves read as hidden or revealed, or not. The first account, generated by Soviet state prosecutors as part of a criminal case in the early 1930s, builds its argument through tropes of penetration of masks that conceal social action, that action diluted to "mere" performance. The second, told by the man's descendants, assumed that concealment was motivated by loyalty and faith. Since the state's investigating committee chose the sites of penetration, it could frame interactions as if under a proscenium separating the visible from the invisible; it could represent its own interpretations of motivations as "revelation." Indeed, the courts and prosecutors chose sites of observation and framed evidence in ways that placed Roma into situations where it seemed they had to betray *someone;* multiple social obligations thus were read as tangles of calculated deceit. Doubts of Gypsy sincerity were not unique to these reports, which drew strength from contemporary pan-Soviet discourses about unmasking (Fitzpatrick 1994) and broader pan-European ones about theatricality and trust. Nevertheless, assumptions about Gypsy social structure and culture mediated their particular force in these accounts.

The two biographies were positioned differently as different sorts of memory; one was embedded in a larger, 1930s criminal case against eighteen Roma and is preserved in state archives, and one was passed orally among Lovari family members up to the 1990s. The official, archival account described motivations within a single moment of transgression and framed that moment with ontological divisions of the social world into discrete spaces onstage and offstage. By contrast, the family accounts placed their hero's motivations within a longer durée of events and a wide web of social relations, grounded less in discrete divisions but in religious and everyday knowledge. They did not conceptualize pertinent social boundaries in terms of penetration and masking, but in terms of shifting points of access and exclusion. Moscow Lovara had many times related versions of this family history to me before we videotaped this one in winter 1993:

> Our grandfather . . . came from Poland. He had his own land there. He had his own servants. He kept servants, he kept horses, even he kept them. He rode in a carriage. He was most honored among Roma. . . . My father was arrested in the year '38. . . . The authorities took him from Vanode, because another Rom betrayed him, gave him into their hands. And they took many Roma. And they were lost there. And they were sent to [the labor camp at] Kolyma. And most never came back. (Lemon and Nakamura 1994, videotape transcript)

Later that summer, while searching for material about Soviet Gypsy policy in the Central State Archives (TSGARF), I came upon a file of documents recounting the criminal indictment of eighteen Vlax-Romani men in 1932—the last name on the list of the accused belonged to the man described by the Lovari woman above as "arrested in '38" (late-Soviet media barrage about 1938 mass purges had probably influenced her to recall that later year). I will call him Janosh.[2]

The criminal case capped a long criminal investigation, one that resembled an ethnographic investigation and one in which elite Roma collaborated. In the 1920s and 1930s, Romani party members took on roles of researchers and "ethnographers." Thus, while at that time Romani Theater performers were visiting rural Roma to observe "camp life" and to glean authentic gestures for use as stage bits, socialist Romani activists paid less friendly, more surreptitious visits to the camps to report on "class struggle" within them. One such activist wrote in a report to the Central Committee that he had penetrated a "sordid warren" of camps near Moscow ruled by "Gypsy kulaks." These kulaks "with all their strength" prevented poorer Gypsies from joining the *kolxozy* by telling "false stories" about abuses and by reminding them of "the Gypsy law: 'Russians with the Russians. Gypsies with the Gypsies,' a law fortified by capitalism." The credibility of such accusations of lying may themselves be dubious, since, in the same archives, other reports tell of Gypsies starving on many collectives.[3]

The account of the criminal proceedings followed a similar arc of blame. Its centerpiece had been a failed Gypsy artel (workers' brigade) called the Romanian Foreigner, its members being Vlax Roma only recently immigrated to Russia from Romania, Hungary, and Serbia. Druts and Gessler

(1990:292) remark briefly on the case, speculating that the artel had been dissolved and its members sent to the camps because its "bizarre name [was] clearly out of tune with the times." Indeed, if all diasporic minorities within the USSR were suspect, "foreign" Gypsies were doubly so,[4] but still, the accusations and evidence were complexly argued in terms that hovered around but exceeded simple xenophobia. The accused were tried together as coconspirators, as was common to Soviet trials at the time, and faced a veritable bouquet of charges from economic sabotage and conspiracy to taking bribes. The case against Janosh was subsumed within the case against the leaders of several Moscow Gypsy artels: the Romanian Foreigner, the Red TransBaikal, the Serbo-Romanian. Janosh had unwittingly catalyzed all the arrests when he revealed to the leaders of one of the artels, two Kelderara brothers, that Romani activists had been building incriminating files on them. Janosh alone, howevver, was charged with revealing state information.

The damning files contained reports not merely about economic misdoings, but also about social ties and cultural activities, and umbrella condemnation of certain Romani cultural practices strengthened the individual charges. "Culture" was on trial, this time not as inauthentic art (tsyganshchina, for instance) but as illegitimate byt, the "traditional" but corrupt habits of "everyday life." Official 1930s Soviet discourse routinely defined certain categories of "custom" as both collective shortcomings, and as traceable individual culpability. In the north, individual shamans would be blamed for purposely reproducing backwardness: "According to Stalin, every evil had to be socially defined, personalized and then, by one method or another, neutralized" (Slezkine 1992:62). The 1930s juridical process against the Roma similarly rested upon an ideology of deliberate cultural constructivism;[5] culture was to be changed consciously once its devices had been unmasked. The Revolution was to have proved that no tradition, no social hierarchy, was essential, and that eliminating certain kinds of custom was not only possible but was an individual and collective moral obligation.

Practices of Armenians, Chukchi, and Russian peasants alike were targeted, and some were criminalized, defined by law as "Crimes that Constitute Survivals of Tribalism."[6] Slezkine notes that the most prominent crimes on the list (blood feud, bridewealth, and polygamy) were those that the lawmakers considered to create inequality (1992). To the state's battle against material class or gendered exploitation I would add its campaign against "hidden" customs, and customs of concealing, not because they hid things, but relations, because they obscured loyalties other than to the state. Nothing was to be veiled or concealed from the state, be it a woman's face or a fictive kin tie (on veils in particular, see Massell 1974). In the 1930s, criminal motives, painted as anti-Soviet and antimodern, were assumed to lurk "behind" the scenes of hidden religious practices. And decades later, Soviet ethnography still described the "family and its dark corners" as the preserve of Islamic religious survivals (Snesarov 1973:226), in language suggesting that suspicion of what went unseen within the family outran suspicion of any particular religious practice. Often the concerns about invisibility and revelation were, however, expressed in the archives only implicitly.

In the 1932 case against the Roma, witnesses explicitly pointed to material exploitation and social inequality as motivating the charges. However, in the records, the ways in which witnesses framed evidence — and especially the ways in which they used formal rhetorical features such as poetic parallelisms — imply a preoccupation not with economics, but with visibility and the well-worn, double face of performance.

The All-Russian Gypsy Union had been dissolved only a few years before, but at that time accusations of inefficiency had nearly eclipsed any of conspiracy, concealment, or corruption.[7] In the 1932 files on the Vlax artels, however, descriptions of accounting irregularities and crooked trade practices abounded. Moreover, they echoed tropes of the covert: foreign Gypsy artels and collectives were hiding profits, hiding foreign hard currency or gold. They did not buy raw materials from government sources such as Metximprom (Metal and Chemical Industries) but "somehow . . . who knows where or from whom, they freely spent their means . . . and kept no formal accounts."[8]

As the case progressed, the testimonial record condemning hidden custom (and customs of concealment) began to overwhelm the initial round of explicit protest against financial misdeeds and "exploitation." The consideration of evidence moved from signs of bad bookkeeping to ethnographic-style accounts of secretive "tribal law." The witnesses, for instance, took pains to detail social behavior, in order to show that corruption reproduced "Gypsy tradition." In characterizing this corruption, they depicted the arrested artel leaders as circulating within hidden social networks and as communicating with one another in incomprehensible ways.

They spotted such veils to communication not only between elite Gypsies and the Soviet state, and between elite and other Gypsies, but among all the Gypsy masses, as if the elites purposely wanted to divide them. Otherwise Gypsies should have been drawn to socialism naturally, as members of oppressed nationalities. The opening paragraphs of the case report laud state resolutions to settle nomadic Roma and claims that the rank and file were responding enthusiastically:[9]

> A range of measures taken by the Soviet government . . . regarding work among backward Gypsies to attract them to a settled, working life met with lively response from among the Gypsy masses. In recent years, traveling, foreign Gypsies — apparently immigrants from the Danube countries who appeared on our territory during the imperial wars — have thronged to Moscow from all ends of the USSR. By 1930–31, nineteen cooperative workshops for tinning boilers, cauldrons, and various vessels were organized in Moscow.[10]

This introduction stresses benefits for "foreign Gypsies." However, it was mostly the long-settled Russka (or Xeladytka) and Servi Roma, not the "foreign," nomadic Vlax, who had turned to the state measures, working on collective farms and in artels since the 1920s. Educated Russka administered the Gypsy clubs in the cities. The larger urban cooperatives, such as Tsygximprom (Gypsy Chemical Manufacturing) and Tsygpishchprom (Gypsy Food Production), tried to recruit Vlax but hired most workers from the Russka. The Romani masses were thus already being divided in practice through application of policy, not singlehandedly by Vlax artel leaders. The omission is especially telling because, during the court proceedings, the accused were exclusively Vlax Roma, while the witnesses were mainly Russka and Servi intellectuals, performers, and activists. Lines were drawn thus not between all Roma and the state, but between some Roma against other Roma with (and as) the state.

To be sure, however, Soviet policy and procedure defined *how* the lines were drawn. The state is absent in the rare accounts of Romani history published in Russia. Such histories describe discord among Roma as arising from "caste" or dialect difference itself, or, as in Soviet assimilation tales, from a conscious decision to assimilate or rebel. The complex triangulated relationships among Roma, Russians, and state institutions are collapsed and dismissed rather than being investigated in order to understand why and how some Roma resisted development, others welcomed it, and still others did both. Indeed, in the 1930s "foreign Gypsies" were not flocking to join the programs. And it was those few who *did* join who were later blamed for the hesitancy of the rest.

Roma who joined the state as collective laborers were supposed to undergo a social transformation, an accelerated progress through the social stages, as the archive continues:

> Settling foreign Gypsies according to profession[11] (as smiths, copper workers, tinsmiths), to form cooperatives and artels, undoubtedly would change their way of life and relations of production. This was sure to affect class divisions . . . between rich and poor Gypsies. However, the even greater cultural backwardness of the Gypsy masses, bound together by many years of patriarchal custom and the hegemony of elder wealthy and literate Gypsies, helped the Gypsy kulaks to grasp artel leadership for themselves, to subsidize them with their own funds, and under the guise of employers to exploit the work of others.[12]

But the Romanian Foreigner artel did not generate a new social structure; Vlax Roma had long worked in artel-like groups. Indeed, Kelderari division of labor should have posed little problem to reform; Nadezhda G. Demeter, in her 1988 candidate of science dissertation on Kelderara, describes Kelderari work partnerships (*vortache*) as communal, with proceeds split evenly, and implies that "Gypsies were the first communists."[13] Surely over time, simply forming artels could change Vlax productive and social relations very little — work groups continued to draw kin together as members, for instance.

Since social structure did not appear to change quickly enough, as far as certain parties in the state were concerned, the patriarchs, motivated by individual financial gain, must have sabotaged social and cultural transformation:

> All of these measures for improvement . . . struck against stubborn and diverse resistance among the Gypsies, coerced by the chiefs, kulaks, and princelings who understood that to raise the Gypsies' cultural level and attract them to socialist building would unavoidably draw the masses away from the old patriarchal customs and caste distinc-

tions of which the rich Gypsies made use. The tribal chiefs and prince-lings had built their own personal prosperity by variously exploiting the main, poor Gypsy masses.[14]

Anti-Sovietism thus is depicted first as a betrayal of all Gypsies, "caste" against "caste." The language is similar to what is found in any 1930s description of transgression against the state. The word "caste," for in-stance, was typically used to describe tsars and nobles (see Ushakov's 1930 dictionary) — but here, describing Gypsies, "caste" also evokes an Indic past, projecting a functional hierarchy upon Romani groups.

Allegations of abuse of patriarchal caste and custom resound through texts contemporaneous with the case, such as the film *The Last Gypsy Camp* (1935). In it, the "Gypsy baron" uses "unwritten Gypsy law" as a tool to suck labor and wealth from rank-and-file Gypsies. In a key scene, the "baron" (a term applied by Russians to those they assume to be Gypsy leaders) has just driven another Gypsy (both played by Russian actors) away from the camp because the latter wanted to join a collective farm. The intertitles announce in a curly white font: "According to ancient, unwritten gypsy law, a man could only leave the gypsy camp if he returned his horse to the *baron,* and could only take with him what he could pull himself on his cart" (*Poslednij Tabor* 1935). The assumption is that "barons" held absolute authority over both property and custom, that authority in the camps was stable and caste-like, and that it was easy to determine who held power.[15] "Castes," like "tribal" and "unwritten" law, render authority and status im-mune to reflection and contestation, they make exploitation automatic. And to describe Romani inequalities as regulated by "unwritten law" both highlighted their assumed primitivity and embedded Gypsies in a world without real law.

Soviet programs for "bringing Gypsies to literacy" centered around "po-litical literacy," aimed to convert them to a world of civilized, hygienic, and efficient Soviet laws. Having mastered letters, sensible Roma would give up "unwritten laws." Such was the course of events in the Romani Theater's *Gypsy Fortune,* "a prosaic comedy about a Gypsy, a former traveler, illiterate and superstitious, who is completely reborn through work and becomes a cultural builder."

In Russian and Soviet stereotypy, from European literature to journalis-tic travelogues, illiteracy remains the expected "authentic" Gypsy condition.[16] Perhaps this illuminates why, although caste, custom, and "unwritten law" were blamed for exploitation, the court witnesses nevertheless ascribed the same evils to Gypsy literacy—the state had similarly equivocated about "bourgeois specialists" among other peoples, but not to the point of finding mere literacy suspicious (see essays in Fitzpatrick 1978). One of the witnesses, himself highly literate, an editor of the Romani-language journal *Nevo Drom (A New Road)*, testified: "These persons, sufficiently literate and knowing Russian well, gradually spread their influence amongst all the foreign Gypsies in the city of Moscow."[17] The "Gypsy kulaks," portrayed as opposing efforts to raise the "cultural level" by convincing Roma to keep their children out of school, possessed the very abilities that the state purported to encourage among the Romani masses—only in the kulaks' hands, the skills were suspect. In their case, literacy only increased alienation from the real sentiments of the poor, illiterate Gypsy masses, and allowed the strong to strengthen secret ties among themselves. For all the early drives to "liquidate illiteracy," an educated Gypsy remained an enigma, another "paradox" of Gypsy modernity.

That "unwritten Gypsy law" in fact did not proceed as portrayed in film or in the case records was particularly evident in the witnesses' own descriptions of the "Gypsy court," or *kris* (*krisi* in Lovari, *krisa,* pl.), the Vlax arbitration council. The witnesses denounced the kris as a survival reproduced through the willful greed of a few elite men: the "so-called Gypsy court was composed of the tribal chiefs, now the rich Gypsy kulak leaders of the artels," whose decisions were "obligatory and incontestable."[18] However, a few paragraphs later, one witness subverts this view with a rather detailed description of a particular kris. At this kris, participants had formed loose groups in corners of the Gypsy club where the proceedings were being held, "each expressing its own opinion about one or another matter." Only after long discussion and argument did the judges finally have their hearing to decide the issue.[19] Such socially collaborative discursive practices hardly support the argument that kris judges acted as despotic individuals.

Indeed, as Vlax Romani consultants described them to me in the 1990s, a kris involves days of discussion in which, ideally, any male person may speak ("off-stage" women take part in ongoing moral discussions, and during intervals even instruct male relatives about what to say). Judges are not permanent but are selected on a case-by-case basis, and either party may refuse to participate in the kris if they do not agree upon the choice. Judges also must defer to social consensus,[20] because the only sanction if defendants default on paying restitution is social ostracism, the guilty declared *magerde,* unclean or outcast.[21]

What perhaps most disturbed the witnesses for the state was not that the ostensibly despotic judgments of individual Gypsy "kulaks" imposed inequality, when even their own testimony about kris procedure too obviously contradicted this. Perhaps more threatening was the fact that an arena of "law" existed that was invisible to the state.[22] Even kris sentences were concealed from the state — punishment was invisible, one had to have social knowledge of who was outcast and who respected the declaration: "Thanks to the existence of such courts, a series of crimes, committed by Gypsies amongst themselves were not passed on for inquiry . . . to the [state] organs . . . and were hidden."[23]

The "apprehension that chaos would ensue if any single group of participants were recognized as having autonomous rule-making powers" (Sarat and Berkowits 1994) is not peculiar to Soviet law, being common to most modern states. But though insistence upon a unified law code and distrust for difference may not be peculiarly socialist, the tropes of theatricality that framed the accounts took a Soviet form, historically common to many depictions then of transgression, and especially to those of Gypsies.

In the USSR, "unmasking" (of former kulaks or false Bolsheviks or insincere lovers) was an official (and popular) concern even into the 1990s. The people forging the state through rounds of dislocations and purges were especially concerned with purity of origin and (in)authenticity. Such imagery was not peculiar to descriptions of Roma; but, unmasking discourses intersected attributions of craftiness to non-Russians, and especially to Roma, in particular, racialized ways.

Witnesses "unmasked" the Romanian Foreigner artel as run by elites "linked amongst themselves by kinship ties," who conspired against both the state and the mass of Gypsydom. Vlax social organization, regardless of ways their organization of labor was also said to resemble idealized early communism, was read as conspiracy. That is, social ties were seen not as complex, historically co-constructed networks of mutual reciprocity but as webs woven by scheming individuals. Tropes delineating this individualist ontology of conspiracy ring especially clearly in a witness's description of Lovar Janosh as a performer par excellence, introduced in the archives thus:

> At that time, a certain Gypsy, Janosh, worked as a public instructor in the National Minorities Section of the Moscow Soviet. As it later turned out, he was an alien element who had *pushed his way into* the party, the son of a wealthy Gypsy, former Polish landlord. Pursuing a *two-faced politics* Janosh, on the one hand, tried variously *to show himself* in the Moscow Soviet as an active, civic-minded person, a Natsmen ["national minority"]. On the other hand, he maintained close ties with the Mixaj brothers to whom he leaked the complaints gathered on them. . . . *A clever man,* Janosh had somehow quickly *managed to creep into* a position at an electric factory, where he *got himself elected* as a party candidate. . . . *cleverly,* he *set himself up* as public instructor in the Natsmensektor of the Moscow Soviet. *Janosh carried out a Janus-faced politics:* on the one hand, he acknowledged that various frauds had been carried out by kulaks in Gypsy artels who held the main Gypsy masses under their influence, and that Gypsy courts existed under the leadership of the Mixaj brothers. . . . On the other hand, he kept close ties with these very same persons, sensing that to quarrel with them would not be profitable given his past, about which talk had already begun among the Gypsies.[24] (Emphasis added)

At this point in the text, poetic repetitions stress Janosh's qualities as a double-dealer. He is "two-faced," "Janus-faced," and has "cleverly" maneuvered, he is an actor on the stage of politics, a person who could consciously "show himself" and "set himself up as" one kind of person in order to infiltrate, "push his way into," or "creep into" the party, all the while keeping "close ties" with the wrong sort of Roma. Janosh was thus depicted not merely as an unmasked former landowner or patriarch, but as cynically untrue even to the Gypsy ties that he maintained so carefully behind the scenes, as if back there were yet another proscenium dividing him from the other Gypsies.

Denying Faith

According to one witness, Janosh was bribed to discontinue collecting files;[25] as evidence, the witness offered that the Mixaj brothers, several days after being told about the files, were seen at the baptism of Janosh's child, one of them acting as godfather. The incident was interpreted with the presupposition that patronage and exchange nullify sincere affect. The accusation must also be understood in relation to the ways the Soviet state sanctioned religious practice. Romani baptism was discouraged, not just because it ritualized religious ideas counter to socialist ideology, but also because it ratified fictive kinship bonds. The state intended Gypsies to forge one common identity — actual and particular affiliations that Roma created themselves (whether based on lineage, marriage, or baptism) threatened the unity of that identity.[26]

At work was the doubt that Gypsies might practice baptism for reasons that were not mercenary. Theatrical models underwrote such doubts about Gypsy faith, which, like memory, has often been dismissed, as here by a Soviet Romani author and performer:

> The Gypsies' many centuries of wandering about Asia and Europe affected not only their language, their songs, but also their religious beliefs. . . . The wandering Gypsy tribes, secretive, swarthy, telling auguries and speaking an unknown language, were subject to expulsion . . . as if linked to "unholy forces." Wandering from country to country, taught by experience, the Gypsies began to adopt the religions of whatever people they were among at the given moment. "What is your faith?" they asked the Gypsy. "Which one do you need?" answered the Gypsy. (Rom-Lebedev 1990:80)

The Soviet Romologist Barranikov (1931:62) uses the same punch line ("Which one do you need?"), though he attributes it to Ukrainians speaking about Gypsies, not to Roma themselves.[27] Barranikov does so en route to claiming that Gypsy religiosity is mercenary, writing that when they ask gazhje to be godparents, Gypsies invite "six to a dozen pairs of godparents, often christening the children five or ten times" (62). Daranes, drawing from a Fraserian hodgepodge of sources, remarks on a "proverbial indifference of Gypsies to religion" (201) and echoes Barranikov (quoting Kogalnitchan 1837): "In Moldavia and Wallachia they have their children baptized by the Orthodox priests — but not from religious motives: it is done for the irresistible argument of Don Basilio, for the sake of the money they receive from the godfather or godmother."[28] In the West, Werner Cohn is among those who claim that Gypsies "will often feign Christian commitment and patriotism" (1973:66). Such remarks often appeal to archival documents reporting that Roma, when they entered Europe in the fifteenth century, asked for papal protection letters. The assumption is that they pretended to be Christian refugees, regardless of there being no way of knowing whether they were in fact more opportunistically motivated than other such pilgrims and refugees.[29] And though the papal protections lasted only a few years and covered only a handful of Romani bands, they continue to be cited as if they produced centuries to follow of supposed Gypsy religious deception.

Because Roma *are* variously Muslim, Catholic, Orthodox, and Protestant, it is often assumed that they cynically adopt only the "outer forms" of faith (Clebert 1967:170). Acton (1998), however, gives counterexamples of strong attachment to different creeds even within Romani communities; for example, he writes of a Muslim Romani woman who marries into a Romanian Romani Orthodox family but remains committed to Islam, despite in-law pressure. Not much is written on Romani devotion, which is dismissed as inconsistent, and Acton calls for attention to how "social and political implications of organized religion affect the collective position and strategy of Romani peoples as they do that of other communities" (1998:1).[30]

Under a state that negatively sanctioned religious practice, Soviet Gypsies were *lauded* for their "indifference to religion" (Rom-Lebedev 1990:81) (although this would work against them in other arenas). However, in their recollections of Soviet rule, most of my Romani consultants described commitment to their faith, be it Islam or Orthodoxy, even in the face of general pressure to recant. Decades-old family photographs affirmed that baptisms and priests' blessings at funerals had been ongoing — ritual practice and religious identity did not disappear under *gazhjikane* pressures to convert to atheism. Orthodox Russka in the 1990s, for instance, emphasized differences among themselves, "Catholic" Lovara, and Muslim Roma. Roma, moreover, cited religiosity as what most set them *apart* from the Communist gazhje. Lovara attended church only a few times a year — but they pointed out that that was more than did most gazhje. They saw the *gazhje* as uncommitted, observing that few Russian children were baptized, while *all* Lovari children were, throughout Soviet years. And despite problematic interactions with church authority (for instance, one Lovari boy recounted in 1992 that at the most recent baptism, the priest had rejected their suggested name as "not Orthodox"[31]), church blessings were not taken as optional.

Nevertheless, to the majority of writers, when a Muslim Rom prays to Allah his words never count as sincere because another Rom may pray to Christ. Variation over the diaspora is projected onto evaluations of local practice. Just as Russians believe Gypsy beggars change into expensive clothes at the end of a workday, they similarly imagine that a Christian Gypsy today was yesterday playacting a Muslim. Similar accusations are rarely applied to other peoples; when a Siberian peasant takes a sick child to a priest *and* a shaman, this is *syncretic* — if a Gypsy does the same, it is deceit. And though Russians have historically converted from Orthodoxy to atheism and back again, Russian character is hardly maligned as spiritually dishonest; history is to blame.[32] Religious change among *Russians* indexes historical movement; religious variation among *Gypsies* evidences collective lack of sincerity, a lack that is figured in ways paralleling those that describe Gypsies' supposed indifference to historical memory.

In 1993, I attended Russian Orthodox Easter with a Lovari woman. She was taking a basket of food for the priest to bless — three of everything ("God loves threes," her daughter had recited in Russian as she packed the basket). We burned candles at the icons after she had pressed skillfully through a crowd at the vestibule candle vendors ("Gypsies don't stand in line," she joked, riffing on state privileges that allowed veterans or certain high-status persons to jump queue). The pushiness of the crowd recalled to me the Metro. There were police inside and outside the church. "Why?" I asked her. She looked around apprehensively, and I noticed again the curious, drunken teenagers pointing at crosses, asking what they were. "So people don't laugh," she said. "It is sinful to laugh here, and these Russians might laugh." She recalled later, on the way home, that under the Communists, youth had been encouraged to drink and disrupt Easter nights. In 1993, this was no longer officially condoned, but by inertia drunken youths still milled about.[33] The Lovari woman, by opposing her own piety to Russian hooligan irony, in a limited sense aligned herself with the police who cordoned the church — with agents of a new, postsocialist Russian state, one that encouraged the religious revival of Russian Orthodoxy (though not all other religions). Such a momentary alliance would seem duplicitous only if we disregard her accounts of her and her family's past and present, and instead assume a proscenium: one that sets the limits of public space, dividing all Roma from all non-Roma.

Lovari Memory and the Hidden Nail

It would have been useful to juxtapose a Lovari account of Janosh's trial to the state archives, but once he was arrested, his relatives never saw him again, and none were present at the proceedings. Thus not only can I not unravel what "actually" happened, but I also cannot truly contrast divergent views of a single event. If the activities of many Roma were invisible to the state, the workings of the state were invisible to Roma, and to just about everyone else, though in differing degrees.[34] But degrees of knowledge and transparency index constructed boundaries of social space. And, conversely, the places where the visible and invisible are framed as such are precisely sites to look for ways performance models inform — or don't inform — categories of persons.

What I can do then is compare the archives to other versions of the biography, other explanations of its subject's motivations, as they relate to still other formulaic family narratives about morality. The first person who told me about the arrest of Janosh, in the autumn of 1991, was his grandson Anton, who then lived in a large Ukrainian city and rarely came to Moscow. He had arrived at his mother's house in the Moscow suburbs for the three-year gathering (*pomina*)[35] in memory of his brother, whose oil portrait hung in the widow's bedroom, framed by the white eyelet curtains of her canopy bed. The widow and all her children still lived with her departed husband's mother. Moscow Lovara spoke of second marriages as sinful; a widow should continue to remember and to "love only one husband" even after his death, her loyalty cleaving to his kin, for she was expected to stay with her in-laws if there were children. Breaches of such forged loyalties were not forgiven quickly (youthful elopement from a parental home was taken much more lightly). This social arrangement respected memory of what his past had created; at least it was more often described in terms of *memory* than in terms of *patriliny*.

When I visited that morning, the widow and Anton just had returned from the cemetery. She introduced me to him as "the Gypsy correspondent from America," for though I had explained many times that I was "an ethnographer," she remained impressed by the fact that she had first taken note of me during a press conference on Roma at the Palace of the Soviets earlier that fall. Her presence in the Palace of Soviets had been unusual for a Romani woman; she had been given access only because her young children sang in Gilorri to entertain the delegates there — performance had been her pass into a gazhjikani ruling space.

Convinced that an American met at the Palace of Soviets, at a meeting on behalf of Roma, was a worthy interlocutor, Anton put aside the thick journal he was reading (a recent issue devoted to a biography of Stalin) and pressed me to retrieve notebook and pen to record details of his family history. Dressed in an immaculately pressed gray suit and silk print tie, Anton paced the large, carpeted kitchen. He began his account with his great grandfather, the wealthy Lovar who once "had an estate and servants" in Poland. He had been dispossessed sometime "around 1914," after which his two sons came to Russia. The story was a mythic charter, the family's claim to high status among Roma. Lovara have often spoken of themselves as a "Gypsy aristocracy," in Russia and in other parts of Europe (Pobozniak 1964:19; cf. Yoors 1987:132 and passim), but, according to Anton, it was about time the world recognized not only the Lovari natsija, but also his family within it. "You want to know about Roma? Then you have to know all the families," said Anton. "This family is of the highest line, our surname was purchased.[36] Go to Poland and look it all up. Discover that it is all true, and find the papers that document ownership of that estate. Then you can show the world that there were Gypsies who lived in high-class style. We are civilized. All the Gypsies know, they will tell you, [our name] is the highest" (interview 1991).

Anton's invocation of landed property and wealth to prove a high "level of civilization" was not uncommon in post-Soviet Russia. Lovara were not alone in striving to acquire what they saw as the material signs of civilizedness. His account resonated with those of Russka performers who traced kin ties to Russian aristocracy, recalled royal invitations, rich clothing, and jewels. Even the carriage was a familiar detail, one mentioned by the Russka performer Vera Iljinskaja (interview 1992); seeing her father riding by in a fine carriage, Russians would exclaim, "They say the owner is a Gypsy!" Rediscovering (or claiming to have rediscovered) lineage, landed ties, and anti-Bolshevik affiliations was all the rage in 1990s Russia. What is more, earlier Soviet discourses had not condemned all consumption unequivocally. There had been no lack of officially approved film or literary representation of material extravagance, even if that extravagance was sometimes cast as immoral. Properly intended consumption in fact strongly marked culturedness *(kul'turnost')* throughout the Soviet period. Soviet ideology actually encouraged material consumption, especially of productive goods (dacha and gardening supplies) or communal pleasures (champagne, sports, films). Even individual pleasures (dresses, wristwatches, lipstick) were acceptable as long as their purpose was mere pleasure, aesthetic or material. However, wielding goods *as symbolic capital,* as masks to attain social capital, was branded immoral and inauthentic consumption. To use wealth to craft a counterfeit surface, to pass as a higher or alien social identity, was problematic (see Dunham 1976).

Certain forms of consumption were more likely to draw censure than others — and the right sorts of displayed wealth indicated proper sorts of people. As we already have seen, to most Russians an "authentic Gypsy" could be either poor and ragged or covered in gold decorations — but this authentic Gypsy wealth had to be mobile, consumed immediately. But a Gypsy with property? Even after socialism this seems suspicious to non-Roma. The irony is that, even though Gypsy wealth is seen as mobile, and Gypsies themselves as rootless, even the wealthiest Roma are more limited than most other people in the kinds of border they can cross, be it into Moscow or over to Germany because of the ways citizenship is defined. Many Roma, however, saw no contradiction between property and authenticity.

Many Lovara near Moscow had prospered in gray market trading on the bazaar, more than had Kelderara at metalworking, and rivaling some performers. For this, some other Roma censured them. But to Moscow Lovara, a Mercedes, a Chinese carpet, even cash were not treasures to be hoarded by individual misers (or social climbers), for Lovari men or women could earn neither status nor prestige without spending generously on gifts or on collective celebrations. Wealth could only be collective. Its main purpose was not to enable movement into gazhje spheres or to pay for emigration — but to keep people together, *and' jekh than* (in one place). Wealth embodied *baxt* (luck, grace, fortune) for the entire extended family. As Anton described it then, his grandfather's owning property in Poland did not undermine his Romaniness, did not alienate him as a "Gypsy kulak," but rendered the *entire* family "aristocrats" among Roma.

While the biography was thus a charter, some versions of it also testified to troubled, shifting relations with the state. Over the next year and a half, the pivotal details as I heard them varied little, always tracing a narrative of unstable fates — wealth followed by dispossession, successful Communist promotion, then arrest. The grandfather had left Poland for Russia after his property had been confiscated just around or after World War I. Then, a decade after the 1917 Revolution, when Romani performers and intelligentsia were beginning to establish collectives, clubs, and Romani-language journals, one of these sons went to work in the Moscow City Soviet, another at the NKVD headquarters at Lubjanka. Then both were "unmasked as White Army officers" and "shot in 1937 or 1938," as Anton told it.

Nearly two years after Anton had first told me the story, I copied down sections from the archive by hand and took them to his brother's widow. Anton had been hoping, when he told me about his family's past, that I could go to Poland to find archives documenting their family's past ownership of an estate. What I did find in Moscow archives confirmed his story, but in another way. Though a criminal case, it validated claims to former glory; there, in the description of Janosh, was written admission of a "civilized," land-owning aristocratic past. And of course, in the 1990s being seen as anti-Bolshevik was itself not a bad thing.

When I brought handwritten copies of the archive to the family and read them, the family focused on certain details and not others. I reproduce part of that day from my field notes, to show how everyday activities and conversations framed those readings:

> Entering Robinta's house through the doorway, hung with two layers of gauze against the insects, and leaving my shoes outside, I find Robinta on the leatherette sofa, in a new leopard-print dress. But Bibi (Auntie) Draga is not home.
>
> "What do you want her for?"
>
> "To ask her about the old days, about the 30s."
>
> "She is in the hospital. Her stomach hurts — must be the [atmospheric] pressure."
>
> Machonka [Robinta's youngest daughter], however, is healthy again and busy in the yard hitting the boys with an oversized, inflatable hammer embossed with a pale green Sprite logo. I wait with Robinta for Mozol [Robinta's oldest daughter], and we watch a TV show about fetal surgery. When Mozol comes back from visiting the hospital she

sets to work in the kitchen . . . making soup, laughing, "I don't know how to cook!" She has me test for salt. I decide to risk telling her about the archive, and she asks me to read what I have.

By this time, Dunja [Robinta's sister] is there too, waiting for one of the young men to come drive them to the marketplace to sell scarves, and after a few sentences she catches on and has me start over, exclaiming her amazement: "Eat my blood!" Robinta overhears, "What is it, what is that? Tell us!" They have me read and repeat the bits about their relative, and especially the names of those who betrayed him. They want to know more about Janosh's fate, . . . "But don't tell Auntie Draga for a while."

"Why?"

"Well — it will be more interesting for her then, when we know. . . . If we could find out at least where they buried him, or if they just cremated him."

The women decide not to go to trade after all. Rain adds to the entropy, but we all drive to Dunja's house. "Is the fat one home?" Mozol's husband, who drives Mozol and me, inquires about Dunja's mother as we pull into the alley behind the courtyard. She is home. After 3 days with her brother for his birthday, she is worn out and cranky, and when a small granddaughter spills nail polish remover on the floor, and the smell of acetone fills the room, she grabs her own braids and violently shakes her head with them: "Arggh!"

[So] we don't dare tell her about the archive until much later — when it is quieter and some visiting relatives had all gone. She had me sit by her and read. . . . She had me repeat the parts on the Polish land . . . and [then]: "Yes, yes, he worked in the Moscow Soviet. They were Chekists. But they captured them, shot them. He had quit that job and gone back to traveling again for three months. And they caught him in the post office, they sent him a telegram and took him on his way. And his sons they took too. And he was in jail too. . . . Ten kilograms of gold they took from them!"

As is apparent in these notes, the new information from the archives was not shared with everyone immediately. Time passed, people waited for the appropriate moment, the appropriate place to discuss and evaluate the text and what actions it might implicate.

Some in the family suggested filing for reparations and began to talk about what the state had taken from them in numerous confiscations — a common theme in postsocialist Russia. In the weeks to come, they were obsessed not only by the fate of Janosh, but by other memories of loss and of lost family wealth ("ten kilograms of gold they took").[37] Hoping to build a case, they sent me on various archival errands over the next few weeks. However, Janosh's "personal files" were not located in the Central State Archives, to which I had access as a foreign scholar, but in the KGB archives, and only kin could authorize or acquire the necessary passes and stamps to read "personal files" there. They soon dropped the idea of reparations rather than brave those portals; papers, passes, and officials all marked limits to possible action, as they saw it. While they might have received them, they had no confidence in being able to do so. The hesitation to enter a state archive seemed connected to experience of exclusion from other gazhjikane spaces. That Janosh had once worked *at* such a place, in the Moscow Soviet, had only been possible during the brief convergence in the 1930s of an affirmative-action-style policy with the short-lived departments dealing with Roma.

Thus, while the archival accounts portrayed Janosh as corrupt and insincere, his descendants saw him as displaying unusual ability — he had succeeded, he had stepped into high gazhjikane spheres. As I first read the archives aloud to them, I hesitated over pejoratives such as "alien element," and qualified them as "Soviet propaganda" but they brushed aside my obvious explanations. Not paying heed to explicit archival discourse about exploitation, they honed in approvingly on the implicit themes, signaled for instance by the poetic repetition of terms describing Janosh's "cleverness." He, Odysseus-like, maneuvered many seas. At first glance, this might seem no more than a self-exoticizing internalization of the stereotype of Gypsies as performers, maskers, and tricksters. Certainly, some of my consultants claimed "cleverness" and the ability "to lie" as symbolic capital — "There is no such thing as an honest Gypsy." But the repetition of such generalizations even by Roma does not make them true. And it would be misleading to stop there, to explain a favorable reaction to archival characterizations of Janosh as a spontaneous celebration of masking.

To clarify, I introduce a religious narrative that is familiar to Moscow Lovara. I do this both because they reframed archival details in ways that recalled this other tale and because it, like the archives, traces tangles of loyalty, sincerity, and transgression. Versions of this tale are often included in popular books about Gypsies, in introductory sections on "origins," often interpreted in ways that "explain" Gypsy marginality. In contrast, I limit interpretation to the social situations in which Moscow Lovara performed it. I had actually already read a different version first, one published by Russian Gypsiologists Druts and Gessler (1990:8–9).

Two Roman soldiers were sent to procure four large nails to crucify Christ. On the way, however, they squandered half the money on drink, only then remembering their commission. They found two smiths, who each declined to forge the nails, one because the fee was too low, the other because he learned for whom the nails were intended. The soldiers beat them both, but they could not return to their commander and admit failure, as only half their purse remained. They set out for the edge of town to find a Gypsy smith. He agreed to the low price and was undeterred by the nails' purpose. But when he tried to cool the last nail, the metal kept glowing red hot: in panic he took up his possessions and fled with his family. The hot nail pursued him wherever they went: "This is why," the story goes, "Gypsies keep moving."[38]

Of course, there is no factual basis to the tale, for Roma were nowhere near Jerusalem at that time, having left northern India only a thousand years later. In such versions, a just-so story explains wandering, nomadism, a relict like the elephant's trunk, an inherited and indelible brand of past sin. Indeed, several scholars have noted the parallel with imagery about Jews, also implicated by some Christians in the death of Christ (see Kenrick and Puxon 1972; Hancock 1987).

Many Roma are familiar with versions of this tale but position it in pragmatically different ways. During my 1991 conversation with Anton about his grandfather, he pointedly asked me what I made of the tale he referred to as "How they say a Gypsy forged and stole the nails for the crucifixion." His version, moreover, "explained" not nomadism, but criminality, by aligning the Rom differently, not against Christ, but with him. Anton's affinal niece Rufa, who spent her days caring for her grandmother and learning English from Euro-MTV, told me this version in even more detail, in reference not to family history but to everyday masking. We had been discussing whether it could be moral to hide one's "national" identity; I had just told her that, feeling unsafe in the bazaar on the way to her house, I had denied being an American. That reminded Rufa of the story:

When the Jews wanted to crucify Christ, they went to a Rom, and they made him make five nails.[39] But this Rom knew they would nail the fifth one through God's forehead, so he hid it in his hair. And when the soldiers came back, he said he had lost it, he said he didn't know where it was. They didn't believe him, but he wouldn't give them the nail. They couldn't put that nail through Christ's forehead, and so he didn't die completely. And he was able to rise up. And the Rom put a fly on his forehead, so the soldiers would think it was a nail there. And so the Rom saved his life. And so Christ told him, I will forgive the sin if your descendants steal or lie. (Interview from field notes 1992)

This time, the Gypsy smith does *not* agree to forge the nail, as he does in the Russian version, but instead hides it, "steals" it. Folklorists and police who knew this second version like to claim that it "functions" to justify Romani crime; they assume that all Roma believe it literally. But Anton, for one, having mentioned the version, had denounced it: "Somebody made it up so they could just pray afterward and then go do it again." Rufa, for another, spoke of herself as "unable to steal," even though she knew and could recite the tale. The story did not "work" for her, even though she, too, claimed that Roma "use" it cynically to vindicate stealing. However, such general, "functional" explanations forestall more historically particular discussion of the tale's possible indexical meanings.[40]

First we need to examine the category of "criminality" as one potentially delimited by ascribed social identity rather than by activity. The glamorous Gypsy thief saturates public culture, from Russian poetry to Soviet stage. There are Roma who steal, but the extent to which Soviets believe in the thief lacks statistical support. More importantly, Roma are held differently accountable than are majority Russians for similar transgressions. A Russian judge I spoke to in 1992 acknowledged this and asserted that, if a Russian takes chocolate from the factory where he works, "it's not called stealing, but 'carrying away.' Why do Gypsies steal?" he mused. "Because they have no jobs from which to carry" (interview 1992). Majority post-Soviets justified their own pilfering ("everyone does it") by blaming the structures of power; after all, they say, the Bolshevik government had founded itself on stealing, and now the 1990s privatizers were doing it again. Most Soviets classified Gypsy theft, however, as a transgression against society itself, not one against the state or its "imposed" structures.

Roma were not well positioned to debate the structural conditions under which the majority defined not only theft, but Gypsy practices, and Gypsies themselves, as criminal. Roma even acquiesced to those definitions, at least in part. In 1996, I had pressed one of the Lovari girls to elaborate on recent problems with the police, because human rights organizations were trying to collect information about police violations. She replied that she did not want to stir up trouble because "we are all criminals." Whether she had internalized this definition or was quoting it ironically, thus indexing a footing from which she was impotent to say otherwise, was not clear to me then.

This is *not* to say that the "subaltern cannot speak" (see Spivak 1988), for Roma did articulate social contradictions and structural inequalities at times in more straightforward, explicit ways.[41] The nail tale, however, is not among these more transparent such articulations. Dense and formulaic, it was instead better suited for polysemic reiterations, performances that would implicitly evoke other narratives.

The story of a *hidden* nail, as Moscow Lovara told it in the 1990s, makes better sense if we see it not as a representation of criminal acts, but as an indexical map. In the contexts of its post-Soviet tellings, it indexed relations with powerful non-Roma (the state) who considered Romani practices (such as the kris) transgressive, making their concealment necessary.[42] The nail's association with historical relations in which it was necessary to conceal identity could be more forceful for Roma in the USSR than for Roma elsewhere. The state, for instance, repressed many expressions of Christianity, and Lovara, who saw themselves as devout, spoke of their faith as something to be hidden. Objects like icons (used during a kris to swear truth and loyalty) hung, unseen by casual visitors, alongside portraits of kin in inner rooms.[43] Crucifixes, given to children by godparents, were hidden under clothing, especially if made of gold, as Soviet law restricted its ownership. Romani parents spoke of the authority that banned religion as *Russian:* "Do what you like with your Russian children, but these are ours." As they spoke of it, *Roma* had kept faith, while Russians wore crucifixes and attended church in the 1990s because it "came in fashion." Religious signs, then, like the nail, functioned to index both Romaniness and the ways it had to be hidden.

The nail story exonerates transgressions of concealment as preferable over crimes of violence or betrayal. In the Lovari version, the Gypsy smith

FIGURE 17   Rufa (a young Lovari girl) stands before icons hung next to a portrait of a deceased cousin. Her family, like that of many Roma, placed such images together, nestled into a well-protected corner of the house. Memories of specific kin and talk about religion framed performance of self and of Romaniness much more than did images of Gypsies from stage or film.

does not *agree* to forge the nail, as he does in the Russian version, but is *coerced* to do so by Roman authorities. In the usual literal reading, Christ's promise excuses Gypsy theft and deceit in the present and future. However, an indexical reading points to social, relational tensions, tensions obvious to Moscow Lovara but not to other post-Soviets. The story draws an analogy between Christ's position vis-à-vis the state and that of the Romani smith; both are first subject to state power but then transcend or transgress that power (Christ is resurrected; the smith does not give up the nail). To the smith a choice is posed: to give the nail into the hands of the soldiers, or to betray Christ. Ideally relations among Roma, following the indexical arrows, should resemble the relation of the Romani smith to Christ; they must not betray one another—"*Te na del and'e vast*" (Do not give into [their] hands). The story does not so much permit theft as it interdicts betrayal. Christ's forgiveness ratifies not "crime," but extreme solutions to crises of multiple loyalties, while attributing those crises to structures of authority. Similarly, if I might return finally to the Lovari hearing of the archives, the approval of Janos celebrated that he had not betrayed Roma. He had honored baptismal ties—even the state had remarked so. He had shown respect for ongoing networks of exchange and obligation; he had made patjiv.[44]

This is all the ideal, of course. But the nail was all the more a powerful symbolic condensation precisely *because* everyday moral dilemmas, including ongoing social ties of obligation with non-Roma, constantly challenged the ideal of Romani unity. The archives likewise threatened such ideal ethics, recalling that Rom *had* betrayed Rom, albeit Roma from different, at that time more socially distant, natsii. Indeed, the family had been anxious to avoid potential disagreements over how to share possible reparations and this may be one reason why they did not immediately circulate the knowledge of the archives.

Certainly hearing about how the state had set Roma against each other in the courts could be distressing. And it seems that the case I discovered was not the only one (in fact, a 1980s episode of *Budulaj* sets Roma against each other in a kolkhoz people's court). Performers also had recalled to me that they had been made to choose between loyalty to the state or to other Roma, placed on public stages and tested there. As Olga Demeter remembered:

> One time was on *concert tour* with my husband. And in this one town they were *trying* a Romani woman. And they summoned me to court, *"We heard that you know a lot of Gypsy dialects, come help translate."* But look—*what a situation!* I got there and all the people were gathering. Well, the judge asked, *"Where were you on this night and at this time?"* I know that the Romni understands everything, *of course,* but I ask her:
> "Daughter, what should I tell the gazhje?"
> And she, "To . . . in their face!"
> *She insults them, so I had to make something up,* I say, *"She doesn't know, she doesn't remember."* And my husband sits there, hardly keeping from laughing, he never let me go anywhere alone, and the Roma gathered there yelled at me, "Don't you reveal that we understand the gazhje! You betray us and we kill you!" You see?! (Interview from field notes 1993; italics mark Russian)

It would be superficial to claim that the performer had "chosen" one side over the other. In this case, there was no off-limits "backstage" where she could be tested as real or counterfeit—the real resided in *both* the visible performance for the court and the "hidden" social relations with the Roma. Nevertheless, the state had set up a stage, and those present accordingly mistrusted those across its proscenium; even though the singer spoke Romani, the other Roma were wary of her because they met her *in court*. The state had claimed to expose inauthentic exploiters, to unite the Gypsy masses, but instead it often set Roma against each other in very visible, public ways — whether in a theater or in a court.

· 6 ·

"Roma" and "Gazhje":
Shifting Terms

As if from another planet, they were completely indifferent to the everyday concerns of civilized earthlings. Disdaining the "constraint of the suffocating cities" [a quote from Pushkin] scorning peasant work, they became suspect.

— T. Shcherbakova, *Gypsy Musical Performance in Russia*

These remarks open Shcherbakova's 1984 monograph on Gypsy music. Like most accounts of Gypsies, it begins by insisting upon their disdain for "society." And like Shcherbakova, many writers, scholars, and journalists from Pushkin to Pravda, from Mérimée to CNN, have insisted that Gypsy pride *causes* their political, social, and economic marginality (cf. Barany 1994). Some even argue that all Romani culture, from pollution rules to occupational choices, is based on estrangement from the gazhje, as did one tsarist encyclopedia of imperial peoples: "Strong attachment to their own tribe and alienation from all other peoples makes up, one might say, the root of all Gypsy life. In this tribalism are also subsumed the particularities of Gypsy byt" (*Zhivopisnyj Albom* 1880:231).

Such claims are, however, insupportable. It is merely a truism that all social groups make self-other distinctions of some kind, and many of those most successful at maintaining them can hardly be labeled "marginal," be they Soviet nomenklatura or U.S. country clubs. In fact, those Roma who are *most* marginal are *least* invested in distancing themselves from gazhje — it is the gazhje who build literal walls to exclude *them*. In regions where they live in urban ghettos, are barred from nightclubs, restaurants, and swimming pools (as in the Czech Republic and parts of Slovakia), some Roma express *shame* about being "Gypsy" and avoid speaking Romani with their children (Weinerova 1994; Guy 1998:37). It is not those Roma who most explicitly disdain non-Roma or describe gazhje as "polluted."

Culture of Alienation? "The World Divided into Two Parts"

Many Roma in the diaspora, especially Vlax Roma, know the maxim *"Rom Romensa, gazhjo gazhjensa."* In Russia, scholars of Romani and Roma gloss this to mean "A Rom is with the Roma — a gazhjo with the gazhje." In the United States, Ian Hancock gives another possible reading: "[Act like] a Rom with Roma, a gazhjo with the gazhje" (personal communication 1999). In either case, the binary pair "Roma/gazhje" is a discursive landmark. But even key semantic oppositions do not simply reflect social categories so much as *ideologies about* them, or rather about assumed links among culture, social categories, and language (see Cameron 1990; Hill and Mannheim 1992). Such semantic oppositions do not reproduce themselves; it takes effort to articulate them. And while "gazhje" may roll off the tongue many times a day in opposition to "Roma," such utterances alone do not perform marginality. They are forceful not in themselves, but as they are located in relation to institutions, ideologies, and practices.

The first part of this chapter thus unravels popular and social science arguments depicting Gypsies as separate from society. The next part takes up interactions in which Roma *did* perform difference from the gazhje — but in ways that dovetailed with Soviet, Russian, and pan-European modernist ideologies. Finally, the chapter unpacks interactions in which and discursive practices through which Roma aligned themselves *with* various sorts of gazhje. All of these locate performances of distinction in relation to particular social positions or institutions.

Here, code-switches between Russian and Romani, and discursive shifts among topics, genres, footings and voices are especially key — as are ideologies *about* such shifting. Ideologies about shifting illuminate what is at stake when people disagree about what constitutes a code or a linguistic border. One person's code-mixing is another's pure speech. What is at stake when people contest whether certain kinds of switching or shifting undermine a speaker's authenticity or sincerity? Many post-Soviets (including some Roma) speak about certain kinds of switches as if they marked social "types" or behaviors as sincere or devious. Certain sorts of shifting seem inappropriate to certain social "types." For instance, many post-Soviets, in the media and in conversation, asserted that if Gypsies shift from statements expressing Gypsy identity to gestures of Russian nationalism that it is a mask. It is as if Gypsies were innately adept at face-changing, naturally (*and* culturally) protean and shifty. We might unhinge such notions were we to forgo interpreting discursive shifts as bipolar movements "front- and backstage," with one code being assigned to each "side," and instead to read them as grounded in a locus of multiple social relations and commitments.

Many European authors, Western anthropologists, and Roma as well have concentrated their accounts around ways Roma distinguish themselves from non-Roma, by means ranging from structural-functional and historical to romantic. For Pushkin, Gypsies romantically troped resistance to the state and to the cold, market encounters in the city. At the end of *Tsygany,* when the camp abandons the non-Gypsy Aleko, Pushkin's old Gypsy lays out their difference thus: "You were not born for a wild fate, you crave *volja* for yourself alone" (Pushkin 1956:55). Here Pushkin distinguishes Gypsy volja from *individual,* rational liberty. Gypsy *volja* thus preexists the laws against which Aleko struggles, preceding any state and its authority. Some social science, too, defines Gypsy culture as anarchic, but unlike *volja,* in opposition to forms of authority. The anthropologist Miriam Lee Kaprow (1982:419) describes the Cale Gypsies who have lived in Spain for several centuries, characterizing Gypsy social "disorganization" as almost strategic: "Given the Gypsies' characteristic pattern of intragroup conflict and the way that this conflict is an integral part of their system of communication" (419) they "maintain a cultural pattern that supports their resisting both assimilation and the Spanish state."[1]

Writing in the 1970s, the anthropologist Anne Sutherland also stresses resistance to gazhje authority. Sutherland conducted fieldwork with Vlax-Romani speakers whom she met via California welfare system workers, and unavoidably perhaps, the welfare office being the contact point, the ethnography details cases of welfare fraud (and fortune-telling scams) as examples of interactions between Roma and non-Roma. Roma appear as a "closed group" who react to questions with hostile and evasive means, including "feigning imbecility." But are such reactions directed toward all gazhje, even to all gazhje authority, or are they reactions to specific kinds of gazhje aligned with specific sites and institutions of authority?

Sutherland acknowledges the effects of historical repressions ("centuries of experience in avoiding the prying questions of curious outsiders" [21]); still, often explanations of Romani relations to gazhje hinge less on that history than on binary structures, particularly divisions of pollution and purity that are seen to functionally determine the internal segmentation of group and kinship categories. It is as if boundaries between Roma and gazhje are likewise maintained by, and generated from, these binaries. Not only that, but Romani culture would not be Romani without them, for Roma, "Do not ignore the gazhje world, but regulate contact with it and place the quality of that contact within a fairly rigid moral system. . . . This moral system, *romanija,* which is based on divisions determined by degree of purity, is the key to their uniqueness" (287). Sutherland wrote her ethnography at a time when Mary Douglas's *Purity and Danger,* along with other structuralist works, dominated much of cultural anthropology. Although Douglas never intended to argue that the relation of purity/pollution rules to social boundaries was unique to any particular culture, many Western anthropologists writing about Roma took them up as key to Gypsy culture. Their work has been adopted by other Western writers, some of whom have, for instance, lifted descriptions of Vlax-Romani categories in the United States to insert into generalizations about, often non-Vlax, groups in Eastern Europe (see, for instance, Barany 1992; Fonseca 1995).

Some such structuralist texts have since circulated to Eastern Europe, and similar ones have been generated and mobilized there, by both non-Romani and Romani intellectuals.[2] For instance, in a 1993 video interview with me, Vladislav Demeter and Lev Cherenkov elaborated on "the most important words" for Roma. They immediately took up the question as "linked with Gypsy consciousness itself," voicing the ideology that language and its structures unmediatedly manifest culture. Speaking about Romani culture was a profession for both; recall that Cherenkov (a Russian) was a well-respected linguist of Romani and that Demeter (a Rom) was a Romani choir director. But note that, in this excerpt, the linguist (L) does not take charge of linguistic definitions, but defers to the native speaker — though he interjects phrases that (D) takes up:

D: The question itself is very interesting. It is of course linked with the very Gypsy consciousness, the way Gypsies view themselves. I think that here most important, in its historical specificity, is [their] aloofness, rejection of everything //

L: Agreed!

D: // and the other is [their] closedness, guardedness from the rest of the world.

L: Self-protection!

D: Self-protection. Yes, at the same time, of course, without that world it would be impossible to live //

L: Precisely!

D: // [without] concourse on some kind of minimal, most primitive level, not allowing for discourse between souls and so on. . . . uh, it seems to me that the most important word for Gypsies is the word "Rom."

L: Absolutely!

D: "Rom" and then "non-Gypsy," with that everything is said.

L: The world is divided into two halves!

The men next run through a nesting hierarchy of key terms: "God," "father," "mother," "sons," "woman/wife," where they digress onto a metapragmatic theme, that is, they discuss the (in)appropriateness of uttering the word "wife" in gentlemen's company.[3] Then, they end this discussion of terms by returning to the Roma/gazhje opposition:

L: "Rom" and naturally like the antigod to that conception, the antithesis —

D: Ahhhhhhh, yes, yes, yes, yes, yes, yes, yes!

L: "Gazhjo."

D: "Gazhjo."

L: The world is divided into two parts //

D: "Gypsy" and "non-Gypsy."

L: Yes, "Gypsy" and "non-Gypsy."

D: "Gypsy," that is "Rom," "gazhjo," that is "non-Gypsy."

The two men finish each other's sentences; they agree to define the terms as a basic binary. By framing their entire list of terms with "Gypsy and non-Gypsy," they formally and rhetorically authorize claims that semantic oppositions among lexical items embody a border between Roma and everyone else. They index this border throughout by using mainly Russian and switching to Romani only when giving key terms, although several terms, such as "God" and "father," remain in Russian, as did the formula uttered before mentioning a "wife," which would have been *t'as baxtalo* ("bless you," "good fortune to you").

The words constitute a taxonomy that ostensibly mirrors splits in social structure, as if the semantic order transparently mapped all important social classifications. The men begin by basing Gypsy self-consciousness on aloofness from the world, ranking first in importance the term "Rom" and all that is Romani. Second comes the divine, and third, patriarchy (*"shjavo,* son, not so much daughter") with its gendered separations (the tabooed "my wife").[4] They give both first *and* last place to the opposition between Roma and gazhje, even repeating the formula "the world is divided into two," as if for Romani culture this were its most highly recursive and generative level. They dismiss contact with the rest of the world as "concourse on the most primitive, limited level."

That they dismiss this contact as limited and crude deserves attention, for it bears the mark of broader ideologies that characterize relations between Gypsy and gazhjo as based on absolute difference and mistrust, and thus rationalize social distance between Roma and gazhje as if created by Gypsy trickery. "Minimal" and "primitive" refer not to "uncivilized" encounters, but to a sort of flatness leveled by a proscenium. Indeed, the Romani heroes of narratives in this vein express their sophistication by only *pretending to be* less sophisticated than gazhje, more out of touch with civilization than they really are, as one Romani performer recounted:

> *Well* there are a lot of stories like that—*for instance,* one Rom was working, with steel. *But* the gazhjo couldn't pay him, because it was under the table—they didn't have the papers. And the Rom comes, and talks and talks, to turn the head of that gazhjo. *But* the gazhjo said, *"Go there, to that other boss, he'll pay."* And he, "But please, couldn't you please call him on that gramofon." *He knew full well that it was "telefon"* and not *"gramofon,"* but that's how he said it. And *then,* "But how does he look—like you? Does he also have a thingie like this?" And pulls on his tie, as if he doesn't know what it is! (Interview from field notes, 1992; italics mark switch into Russian from Romani)

Most Roma are bilingual, and here the performer figures a Rom as insincere when misusing Russian words for modern implements, taking at more than face value another Romani maxim: "Romani for truth, gazhjikani for lies." Yet even a trickster hero has to partake of the world, to know its ways in order to turn them on their head. But when the division between Roma and gazhje is seen as absolute, communion with the world is only at the surface, "on the most limited level."

The differences *are* important in Romani life, but the challenge is to connect discourses about them to social relations and practices in ways that do not place agency performing them wholly "backstage" or "within" Romani culture. British anthropologist Michael Stewart is one scholar who has made such connections (1997), taking into account histories of Hungarian state policy. For instance, rather than explaining Romani pollution rules as tools or mechanisms that maintain Barthian ethnic borders, or treating them as vestiges from India without examining their current political significance, Stewart anchors pollution practices to recent experiences within an economy that defined Romani labor as worthless and Romani bodies as trash; he thus links particular ideas about difference from the gazhje to local conditions of poverty and to socialist assimilation policy.

Romani linguist Ian Hancock (1991) similarly cites histories of slavery in Wallachia and Moldova and of genocide during World War II to explain why many Roma avoid gazhje, especially authorities. He argues that the Indic diaspora, on reaching Europe after several centuries in Anatolia and Greece, split into ever smaller groups to be less vulnerable to persecution as they moved farther west. The result, he argues, was perpetual marginality as a thinly spread minority; *these conditions* motivated distinctions between Roma and gazhje, which are

> kept up by cultural behavior and by verbal reinforcement. . . . Non-Gypsies and non-Gypsy cultures are seen as threatening to *Romanipe* ("Gypsiness") and to be avoided. Opportunities are taken to point out to children unsanitary or disrespectful non-Gypsy behavior whenever examples occur, e.g., on TV. . . . In the Romani language, the words for man, boy, woman and girl differ depending on whether they refer to a Gypsy or a non-Gypsy. . . . in the absence of a political homeland, and with the population so widely spread around the globe, it is the sense of "us and them" and everything which rationalizes it, which has served as the principal cohesive factor; in a sense, *Romanipe* may be seen as the Gypsies' transportable homeland. (1991:254–55)

Thus while Hancock notes that linguistic categories mark key distinctions,[5] he attributes agency to the political conditions of diaspora, not to the terms for "gazhje" or to categories of pollution.

"Gazhje" as Shifting Category

Paying heed to particular historical and political relations elucidates how Roma characterize gazhje in variable ways. Even the association of gazhje with the state depends on histories of policy regarding Roma. In Macedonia, for instance, Roma are a stronger political presence than elsewhere, especially since World War II, and there, rather than avoiding gazhje institutions, Roma run in elections and organize radio stations: they are another minority among many minorities.[6] Within Russia, not all gazhje are seen as all alike: there are Russian gazhje, Armenian gazhje, foreign gazhje (who break down into French designers, black American singers, and so on). Sometimes only Russians, being the local majority, counted as "gazhje." Was Jesus a gazhjo? Such questions could puzzle: "Yes, but no." One addresses or speaks about gazhje bureaucrats differently than one does long-term gazhje neighbors, and local strangers differently than faraway strangers.

The way in which a particular gazhjo or gazhji was classified was not always stable, either. How Roma referred to me in the third person, for instance, changed; some wavered between *rakli* or *amari amerikanka* (our American girl), "rakli" being a term for unmarried female non-Roma, which can be uttered with a bitter intonation (suggesting a "hick" or "slut") or with a neutral one. Some younger people, if they knew me, spoke about me with the diminutive *rakljori*, a term often used for young Romani girls, or addressed me as *phej* (sister) or *shjej* (daughter), terms that index solidarity. But those who thought I might be Russian or who just did not like my face were more likely to name me a gazhji or rakli, and to do so in excluding ways: *"Dikh, sar beshel e rakli"* (Look how the rakli is sitting!). Terms for non-Roma thus cannot be charted onto "kinds of people" in a one-to-one, referential way—rather, like other shifters (such as pronouns or certain kin terms), they too index contingent social configurations.

Finally, Roma identify *with* some gazhje against other gazhje—"We are like your *negry.*" American blacks may be "gazhje," yet they are removed from post-Soviet politics, distant from Russian gazhje, and thus other attractive models for crafting alternate selves. The appeal of things American was common to many young Soviets and post-Soviets, it was "antiestablishment" in a popular way,[7] but Roma, themselves defined as "foreigners," claimed a different relation to this foreignness."[8] Thus, not all forms of "gazhjeness" were kept "out." If all gazhje are not alike, classed on the opposite side of a binary, then ways of thinking about and interacting with the gazhje *must* intersect broader sorts of categories and practice, such as "civilizedness."

Although sometimes contrast between Roma and gazhje is structured rigidly, it is not always so. Observations about the malleability of binaries and borders are not new to poststructuralist anthropology and have been especially key to rethinking language use (Hymes 1974), literary models (Derrida 1988), race (Gilroy 1993), gender polarities (Strathern 1980), or performative intersections of gender and language practice (Hall and Bucholtz 1995). Particularly relevant for Russia and East Europe are recent essays by anthropologists Susan Gal (1995) and Caroline Humphrey (1994) who both demonstrate that under socialism lines between the powerful and the weak, between "us and them" were not always so clear-cut as people claim in explicit discourses about identity and power.[9]

I do not mean to argue that all social boundaries are porous or malleable — most Roma in Russia do not associate often or freely with gazhje, nor often drastically shift social alliances and loyalties. The point is less ambitious; many Roma regard, for instance, their own patriotic gestures as sincere, as not contradicting being Romani. The incidents described below are thus interactions in which Roma did perform distinction from gazhje, symbolically valuing themselves as superior, but in ways that also demonstrate intense involvement in "the concerns of civilized earthlings." And again, salient as the performed oppositions may be in the moment, they do not *cause* Romani marginality, nor are they always forms of resistance.

Gazhje at the Threshold

The first example exemplifies a moment of self-presentation — a performance by Lovara for the video camera during 1993. In the several generations they have lived in Russia, Lovara have had minimal and temporary involvements with state institutions, with its factories, or with the Romani Theater. There were not, as yet, Lovara public intellectuals in Russia as there were in Hungary, for instance (such as television host Agnes Darocsi, educated as a sociologist). Lovara were mostly traders throughout this century, and thus they knew best spaces on the streets and inside their homes; they knew their way around Moscow's restaurants and cinemas, but they rarely walked the corridors of bureaucracies, in buildings that required passes. This did not entail zero involvement with gazhje; they spoke to customers, trading partners, neighbors, and house cleaners (well-to-do Lovara recruited maids from the neighborhood,[10] who vacuumed, scrubbed, ironed clothes, and took out garbage), waiters, police, and the occasional doctor (who still makes house calls in Russia—Lovara who were both settled *and* registered were entitled to health service). Some children attended school; others had neighbor Russian playmates. Thus, Lovara were "marginal" from Russian society in some ways but not in others.

Lovara were less anxious than performers about ethnic authenticity; according to them, *Lovara* had preserved Romanipe. Some Lovara occasionally did say, with tones of regret, "We are becoming civilized," but crises of authenticity were not a dominant conversational theme even with outsiders, as they were for the performers and intellectuals. All the same, when faced with the video camera on this occasion, the Lovara worked to perform and display an exemplary model of Romaniness and to delimit ideal borders of their social world. Unlike the Kelderara in the village that was so often visited by documentary film crews, or the urban performers who spoke (or sang) about themselves for the mass media, Lovara had had little press attention; their homes and dress did not seem exotic enough to document—perhaps "invisible" differences such as language use, hospitality and exchange practices, and kin networks (precisely those of such interest to 1930s criminal prosecutors!) did not film as well. They were keen for a bit of the spotlight and wanted to represent Lovara and their own family well to the scholars, students, and especially potential Romani viewers across the ocean, whom they assumed were all more well-to-do than Roma in Russia.

When we turned on a video camera in 1993, my Lovara consultants behaved differently than they had both before and after the shoot. Social configurations and footings shifted: voices usually audible to me became inaudible to the camera, and vice versa. The people who had been my closest companions—young women such as Rufa or Mozol—disappeared into the background, replaced by the eldest women and their middle-aged sons or daughters, who for the two weeks of filming became the camera's main interlocutors. These elders directed the performances of others; they urged children to dance or prompted young sons-in-law to elaborate particular kinds of kin relations.

Besides Lovari standards about who should participate in depictions of the family, more widespread theatrical and filmic conventions were at work. As experienced television viewers, they were accustomed to both Soviet and European ethnographic documentaries with narrative voice-over and assumed that future viewers would want to see this kind of framing of their actions and words as if abstracted to represent "pure" culture. However, they suggested ways to represent this abstraction differently than had the Russian TV crew who visited the Kelderara, who had avoided filming indoor furniture because this would suggest that Gypsies lived like "anyone else." To the contrary, the Lovara were pleased to display microwaves and televisions that the Russian crew would certainly have hidden. One young boy proudly recounted how his mother had brought home refrigerator magnets from a trip to New York City. These items, though purchased abroad in gazhje shops, detracted from Romanipe no more than did other high-tech possessions.[11] Material wealth did not signify the decay of authentic Romani culture, just as exhibiting wealth did not function merely to showcase symbolic or social capital. Wealth afforded concrete means to keep kin together *and' jekh than,* and demonstrating wealth signaled readiness to offer patjiv (hospitality) and sustenance to kin and guests.

Other sorts of hybrid images, however, were more problematic and required more engineering and reframing. These were moments during shooting when difference was stressed between Roma and local, low-status gazhje. In one shot, a Romani woman stands just in front of an internal archway to an anteroom for the front door. She announces to the camera that her brother is about to enter the house "to greet America." His entrance, however, is nearly spoiled when a Russian neighbor boy first darts inside the front door to fetch his mother (the gazhji house cleaner). He does not belong in the scene; without looking at him the Romani woman deftly but gently pushes the boy behind the archway and out of camera view before he reaches the sitting room. The Russian boy, though accustomed to sliding unnoticed into the house every day, was cropped out of the ideal picture. His entrance violated an *aesthetic* of separation; how to explain a gazhjo who, in actuality, blends into the rhythm of the household?

Like most Russian houses outside Moscow, Lovari households usually are surrounded by high walls or fences that shield the house from view. To enter, one first passes through an iron gate, which is locked at night. Next, one passes through a courtyard, and then a small, airy porch screened by lengths of gauze, a breezy place for grandmother to smoke or nap.[12] The door into the first anteroom of the house is left open in the summer. From the anteroom, an archway opens into a large sitting room, open in the middle with couches along the walls and Chinese carpets on the floors. Unlike Russian homes, Lovari rooms were spacious, clutter-free, with furniture pushed against the edges of walls, leaving space in the middle for tables during holidays.[13] This domestic realm was "Romani" and to be recognized as belonging inside, one had to navigate the threshold in a *familiar* manner. Roma on formal visits might stand for a moment inside the archway of an anteroom doorway and call out *"T'an baxtale!"* ("Be fortunate/blessed!") by way of hello. More frequent visitors, such as relatives already in residence for a few days or close kin, just walked inside, without any greeting and without knocking—as did regular servants.[14] Many Roma in the countryside, like villagers in general, do not lock their doors during the day when they are at home. Before I adjusted to this, the bori once caught me about to knock and chastised, "Just go in—*police knock!*" But infrequent Russians (handymen, trading partners, etc.) would stand awkwardly at the gate or outside the external doorway, not knowing whether to move into the intermediate anteroom spaces, broadcasting their own awareness of being an outsider. Other gazhje became familiar with crossing those thresholds (the maid and her children), though they did not all become integrated into social life or conversations in the house.

Crossing thresholds is often a moment far from the liminal (cf. Turner 1987:25) or the inchoate; often precisely such moments demand the most strict declarations of identity. At some thresholds—doorways just as state borders—identity must be verified, whether engraved in a passport, on the face, or in bodily demeanor. All is not in flux—there are recognized ways to cross (see Frake 1975).

"Look at How the Gazhje . . ."

Usually, when Lovara interacted with non-Roma, rather than ignoring or hiding their presence, as happened before the camera, they positioned gazhje as loci of discursive attention. They sometimes did so with a phrase like: "*Dikh sar e gazhje* . . ." (Look at how the gazhje . . ."). The directive "*dikh/dikhen*" (imperative sing./pl.) oriented coparticipants to focus on a topic, and it aligned social affinity and cued proper footing, the positions participants should take to each other and to what was being said.[15] "*Dikh e gazhjen!*" anchored Romani participants within a space surrounded or infringed upon by gazhje. "Dikh" could index with neutral affect, such as mild curiosity ("Mama, dikh the red stockings on the gazhji"), but more often would key a statement to follow as critical ("Dikh, those Russian girls are ugly, don't you think?"). As Bakhtin tells us, a word takes on the echoes of its remembered utterances, and it did seem that some Roma used "dikh" so often in pointing to gazhje that, given the presence of gazhje, it alone could cue participants to attend to gazhje, without the word "gazhje" even being spoken.

"Dikh" offered numerous deictic possibilities; I heard at least one person use "dikh" to both key a shift into an ironic interpretive frame and to index non-Romani difference. A usage of "dikh" in this mode occurred at the twelfth birthday party of a Lovari boy, held at the home of his extended family, a two-house compound near a suburb of Moscow. It was warm, and several younger, unmarried adolescents and I congregated in the courtyard in white plastic chairs around a plastic table that shaded us with a white plastic umbrella, drinking Pepsi. The party drew guests from Ukraine and even Sweden, the Swedish Romani relatives being much wealthier and the Ukrainian in-laws a good deal poorer than the Moscow Lovara. A visiting Lovar from Sweden, a boy about thirteen years old, was entertaining us, manically lighting cigarettes and mimicking the nervous gestures of some movie character. Before the party, a Russian neighbor had been cleaning and arranging tables; now she sat alone in a chair by the side of the house, several yards away, waiting to be given another task. Glancing at her, the boy stopped his mimetic performance and said, having already stopped looking at the maid, but vaguely gesturing in her direction:

Dikhen — muri gazhji, muri romni, chi phenel khanchi.
[Look — my wife, my wife, she doesn't say nothing.]

To understand that he was shifting to ironic commentary on the present, one needs to know that he was quoting from a Lovari song:

Kutkar avel o vonato.
Opre beshel muri gazhji,
Sar voj beshel, kade rovel
Nich na phenel, so voj kamel.

[The train comes from there.
In it sits my gazhji,
how she sits and she cries,
not saying nothing that she wants.][16]

As other Vlax Rom had explained to me about a year earlier, in *this* song "gazhji" happens not to signify a non-Romani woman, but a *Romani wife;* Vlax-Romani husbands sometimes use the word "gazhji" as a term of endearment (less often, wives use "gazhjo" similarly). The tone of the song is affectionate and melancholic; the lyrics pity a wife among strangers. But by reframing the opening lines with "dikh" and looking at the maid, the boy brought "gazhji" to bear on the present situation, evacuating empathy and warmth from it and shifting the word's sense from metaphoric to literal. That the Russian really did "say nothing" pragmatically transformed the line from lament to humor. All this was possible not only by means of "dikh," but because "gazhji" is labile and polysemic — "gazhji" *can* signify an "insider," too.

The shift also drew attention to a gazhji's incomprehension, to perform her difference. Gazhje usually do not know the simplest words in Romani, though they sometimes haughtily described Romani languages as having no more than elementary vocabulary or as mere "secret jargons."[17] Of course, since Romani is neither taught in Russian schools nor broadcast, and only rarely printed, much misunderstanding is hardly a ruse that Roma create; the possibility of being misread is one that structures most encounters with gazhje. Non-Roma are often completely unaware, however, that there is something that they do not understand. For instance, some claim knowing a few words to be equal to "knowing Gypsy language." In 1992, I went with a group of young Lovara to a restaurant across the highway from their house at the outskirts of one of Moscow's "suburban" cities. The young men had to haggle with the waitress before she would deign to serve us; in the 1990s, restaurants in Russia were still not places for casual culinary enjoyment. Entering a dining hall, invisible from the street and curtained with scalloped drapes, often required a bribe or affiliation with the regulars or what they called a local "mafia." The Lovara had rented that hall a few times in the past for small celebrations, but were not part of "the mafia" of businessmen and small traders gathered there that day.

The Romani brothers began talking to one of the Russians, who was very drunk, about a car the Russian claimed to be selling. The car salesman sat down at our table, and asked who we were, by which he meant he wanted to know our "national" identity. The Roma answered by asking him whether he knew the "Gypsy language" — using the word "tsyganskij," not "Romani," since they figured the Russian would hardly recognize the latter term. "Of course I do," he said, and drunkenly began to toss the word "lové" (money) into sentences, as a sort of emblematic code-switch.[18] That such a seedy Russian claimed to know Romani was initially disconcerting, but his actual performance soon confirmed that his knowledge of the language beyond this single word was shallow. It was the only one he knew — it had entered Russian slang (recall its emblematic use by the director of *The Black Pearl*) but had retained an etymology as a "Gypsy word."[19] On leaving, the Lovara remarked, "Russians! Really the dimmest of all the peoples!," the phrase "All the peoples," echoing Soviet formulas.

Roma were used to the way other Soviets belittled their language by reducing it to bits of slang and remembered phrases from movies and the Romani Theater. In 1991, a Moscow restaurant opened called Romale, the plural vocative being another of the Romani words that Soviets knew from films. This restaurant was in fact run by a well-known family of performers, not by gazhje. A Lovari woman, after passing on to me rumors about misdoings at the restaurant, criticized the menu, which listed a dish called *shjavale* (vocative plural for sons/kids). "'Shjavale'—that means 'Ladies and gentlemen' [English]. How can they do that! It's *people!*" By her description, the language of the menu did not include the Romani words for things like "potato." I remarked that Russians do not know any words in Romani anyway, besides "*Romale! Shjavale!*" She acutely quipped, riffing on the menu's pragmatic indelicacy: "Yes, like I know 'excuse me' [in English]! I'll have one 'excuse me,' please."

Besides not comprehending Romani language, gazhje did not know the *zakonurja Romane* (Romani traditions or Romani laws).[20] Lovara viewed Russians as morally lax — which would surprise those non-Roma who eulogize female Gypsy volja.[21] The Lovari image of Russian immorality was no simple inversion, however: Russians saw Gypsy women as *lacking* shame entirely, while Roma described Russians as *ignorant* of appropriate shame and of proper gendered conduct.[22] Lovara pointed to how Russian men and women sit mixed together at celebrations, a practice censured by Vlax Roma who assert that it is shameful even for Romani spouses to touch in public. They avoided such displays of affection, and there were no public wedding kisses. Russian wedding guests punctuate the feast with the Russian word *"Gor'ko! Gor'ko!"* (Bitter! Bitter!),[23] a demand that the bride and groom kiss. At a 1993 Romani wedding, young male Lovara cried *"Gor'ko!"* to the bride and groom, laughing at the absurd impossibility of their request, and mocking Russian custom.

Gazhje ignorance of *appropriate* shame signaled their dissolute character as did their romantic efforts to cast off all shame. One house cleaner, an alcoholic neighbor, was remembered by a Lovari girl as especially *dili* (crazy) because she tried to imitate what she saw as Gypsy "passion." She and her brother recalled giving the neighbor shots of vodka and then urging her to dance. She would fling her skirt as she fancied "Gypsy stage dancers" did, emulating the kaskad and showing her legs: "We told her she danced like a black, like Michael Jackson, like us Gypsies, and she did it even more," mocking her via the very theatrical forms that typecast Gypsies. Believing she was approximating Gypsy sensuality, she only shamed herself, displaying that she lacked not only morals but sense.

Simply drawing attention to ignorance was one way Roma could try to reposition themselves at the top of a social and moral hierarchy, but even on home territory it took symbolic effort. One such instance involved a Russian neighbor at another birthday party in 1993. She sat on a sofa, blinking awkwardly, neither understanding what was being said in Romani nor responding to indirect cues in Russian for her to leave, such as, "So when are you coming back next time?" One of the Lovari girls sitting next to her picked up a bit of bread that had fallen on the floor, and was thus polluted, winked at me, and then offered it to the neighbor girl, who ate it, to her delighted disgust. *"Dikh, e rakli xal les!"* ("Look, the rakli is eating it!"), she said, switching into Romani. Ridiculing ignorance of such a transgression both proved and performed that gazhji's ignorance.

That the girls set up this performance of incomprehension and difference could be interpreted as creating a sense of autonomy from gazhje—in a world where Roma are in fact far from autonomous.[24] Some interpretations of similar Romani performances end there, linking present-day discourses about pollution to ancient India, or reiterating how pollution rules create binary self-other distinctions. However, in observing a gazhji pollute herself, the Lovari girl had winked at a second gazhji—at the American (me). Again, not all gazhje are always treated alike. Performing difference from any particular gazhjo or gazhji could entail aligning with other gazhje. Consider another instance: in 1991, several Lovara youth and I were on the way to a wedding at the immense concrete, Soviet hotel, the Kosmos (the same hotel made locally famous in song, recall). We were standing at the curb trying to hail a car, when an elderly Russian woman approached, wanting to know how they groomed such beautiful hair. "I want my grandchildren to have such hair, but nothing works, what do you use to make your hair so beautiful?" With a straight face, the youngest brother replied in Russian, switching into English on the crucial word:

> Rom: Do you know that new shampoo, 'Shampoo *Fuck*'? It's really good.
> Russian: No, no, I don't know about it.
> (Italics mark shift into English)

At this switch into English, his sisters' restrained smiles twitched, breaking into laughter as the Russian woman turned away. Uttering that word in this context had, first of all, invoked a difference between Moscow Lovari and Muscovite Russian ideologies about the propriety of swearing. Unlike urbane Russians (especially women) and also unlike Romani intellectuals, Moscow Lovara (among same-age or gender cohorts, at least) did not consider use of profanity to mar a speaker's virtue. But on another level, the joke, and the reshuffling of social hierarchy it fleetingly seemed to accomplish, hinged on incomprehension. Speakers perform social relations by anchoring their interactions to broader cultural schema and rankings of value—even as they negotiate those rankings through talk.[25] Yet social relations emerge even when participants do not realize which rankings matter how to their interlocutors. In this case, the youth had had no intention to jointly calibrate social worth with the Russian; she was instead an "object interlocutor," a "dummy" in both senses of the term. Again, however, not all gazhje in this interaction were excluded or rendered objects: for months after the teenagers recalled the incident triumphantly whenever they saw me, referring to it as "*Shampun* Fuck" ("Do you remember 'Shampoo Fuck'?"). Perhaps the original choice of an English word, with its cachet from imported American films, had been calculated to include "the American girl" with them against a Russian babushka.

Although it is important to consider discursive binaries of exclusion and inclusion, more complex understandings of social life and even of identity should include that which is *not* marked as exotic. The totality of daily life, though webbed through by discourses about difference and authenticity is only incompletely, partially structured by them. Roma do not live *between* "two worlds" but *in* one world of many overlapping spaces. Roma thus may find particular boundaries more transgressable than others, allowing one to recognize affinity with people or practices that, at certain times, belong to the "other side." Roma, individually and collectively, may even highly regard idioms or practices marked as gazhjikane, recruit those idioms to reimagine themselves, even to criticize Romani culture. And even the most explicit statements about difference are in fact grounded in discourses and practices that have provenance far beyond the social realms in which those lines seem (to those who experience them as well as to many others) to be drawn.

A key source of such discourses for Roma was the media, for Roma were surrounded by Russian public culture. They knew the classics of Soviet film and had seen the screen adaptation of Bulgakov's *Heart of the Dog* as many times as anyone. They watched *Irony of Fate,* a film broadcast on television on New Year's Eve every year, and recited its plot as well as anyone else. They knew the pop videos of Alla Pugacheva — although the youth then preferred the rap star Bogdan Titomir, whom they called a "Tatar" and considered "black." They also cited Russian proverbs such as, "When it thunders, *then* the Russian crosses himself," acting them out as "the Russian." Lovara kept boxes of family photographs taken against the background of Russian landmarks such as the Kremlin or Saint Basil's Cathedral, the beach in the Crimea, Gorky Park. Russian birch trees framed studio portraits in which Romani girls posed in saris.

Soviet Civilization

> We must not fall for the sentimental notion that the "people" have held onto an indigenous national tradition, that only the educated bourgeoisie are "children of two worlds."
> — Anthony Appiah, *In My Father's House*

It is usually not Roma who find "hybridity" problematic, but non-Roma, who see it as shifty, as an attempt to "pass." But acts of *shifting* between codes or cultural repertoires need not reveal shifty character; shifting is a basic condition of all social interaction and relations, which are always multiple. What follows is my account of an expression of explicit alliance with "civilized" gazhje, articulated by the "educated bourgeoisie," though as we will see, they are not alone. Olga Demeter belongs to a lineage of urban performers and intelligentsia, whose founder, Ishvan, had put their family on the path to "civilization" by discarding pollution practices. In the 1990s Olga lived with her sister, also a veteran dancer, in a two-room apartment in the center of Moscow, on the ground floor — a good thing, since Olga taught tap dance to Russians and to the aspiring children of Romani performers. Olga agreed to tell me, in Romani, her views of history and "folklore" if I agreed to pay for dance lessons. Their apartment resembled many Moscow apartments, memorabilia on the tables and knickknacks lined up inside glass cabinets. The only difference was the number of photographs, records, albums, and books devoted to Gypsy music and folklore and to the family. An entire wall was devoted to a family tree: large portraits of the grandfather and grandmother in old Gypsy attire commanded the top of the wall, ever smaller photographs descending from them. Olga kept a pointer stick propped against the wall to point out their genealogical relationships to visiting journalists. Although proud of being Romani, and especially of being a performer, she was also self-consciously Russified and spoke Romani with a Russian accent. In 1993, for a video interview, I asked her how the gazhje lived. She answered in Romani:

> O: How do the gazhje live? The gazhje work in a factory, in the factories they work. They pay them wages — before they paid very little, now they pay a little bit more. Their life mostly goes [on] in factories, of course. We have in Russia many theaters, movies and theaters we have, [and] we have Romani associations here.
> N: The Romani Theater!
> O: The Romani Theater, we have.
> (Video recording 1993)

The topic shift from gazhje occupations and institutions to Romani ones makes sense in terms of Olga's biographical trajectory in terms not of present-day contexts and structures, but of remembered ones. Olga had

worked briefly in a Soviet factory (Tsygpishchprom, "Gypsy Food Industries") gluing labels onto packets of tea in the late 1920s. The shift from the
topic "gazhje life" and its institutions to Romani associations parallels her
own progression from one state institutional site of employment to another. As Olga shifted from third person *"their* life" to first person *"we* have
in Russia," the pronoun "we" at first seems to include Russia and its citizens,
but then shifts to index a Romani minority. The fluidity of this shift seems
itself to index perception of the state as relatively beneficient.

This makes great sense given the value Olga ascribed to being "civilized."
Often, when I arrived at her apartment, as she would take my coat from my
hands to hang it on the rack, she would make me repeat the Kelderari
Romani for "coat" *(raxami),* as a sort of vocabulary test. From focusing on
the word she would shift to speaking about the coat itself—or rather, to its
place as a material prop for the polite threshold crossings expected of urban
people who freely enter and exit public buildings. For instance, even as she
uttered the Romani word, she would chastise me for not having sewn a
hook into the coat lining for hanging—in much the same way as matronly
Russian coat checkers in the archives and theaters chastised such foreigners
as myself who did not know any better, albeit Olga spoke in a gentler tone.
Coats *must* be checked at all public venues, ostensibly because, as one coat
check explained to me with some irritation, they are "not sanitary." Check-
ing the coat and showing the pass, the *propusk,* remains an obligatory ritual,
even after the post-Soviet shift in regime, upon entering any enclosed state
or public space—from swimming pools, to Houses of Culture, hotels, theaters, and archives. It was a ritual to which she—like many urban Roma—
was accustomed.

The practices surrounding this species of material item, the coat, also
anchored a narrative about the difference between Olga's family and other,
"wilder" Gypsies, and evidenced her family's level of civilizedness. She told
me about a "fiery, temperamental" Lovar who had come to work in the
Romani Theater and taken a Russian wife. One day, the wife had asked him
to help her to remove her coat, and he had flown into a rage, threatening to
kill her. Olga focused on differing understandings of etiquette: "To them, to
those men, it is very shameful to help a woman with her coat, or especially
to help someone with their shoes. Russians, they do it all the time. And in
our family, we are more civilized, and the men always help our women with
their coats. We live more like the gazhje" (field notes). Olga coded levels of

"civilization" according to gendered modes of deference and respect: gendered practices, recall, had been a principal target of Soviet assimilation policies. Note that both gendered and threshold practices evoke metacultural discourses about pollution that are Soviet as much as they are Romani.

Not all Roma characterized gazhje "civility" so wholeheartedly. In 1993, for the camera, I asked an elderly Lovari matriarch, Rubinta (R), and her daughter, Dunja (D), to speak about how one should behave around gazhje. Their joint answer turned upon the term "culture," with implications of internalized discipline that usually adhere to "civilizedness":

> A: Aj kana, kana trobul te *obshal*in gazhjensa *inogda zamechajesh'*
> [And when, when you have to *socialize* with gazhje *sometimes do you notice*]
> chto trobul te ingeres-pe *kak-to* //
> [*that* you have to behave *somehow* //]
> D: Te ingeres-pe maj *kul'turno?*
> [Carry yourself more *cultured?*]
> R: *Konechno!* Ingeres-pe maj *kul'turno* ingeres-tu!
> [*Of course!* You hold yourself, more *cultured* you behave!]
> D: Sar von, dikhes pe lende soske von pativales ingeren
> [As they, you look at them, how they hold themselves respectably,]
> aba vi tu ingeres sar von.
> [and already you act like they do.]
> A: Aj so i kodo "maj *kul'turno*"?
> [And what is that, "more *cultured*"?]
> R: *Nu,* maj feder.
> [*Well,* better.]
> D: Maj feder.
> [Better.]
> R: Maj feder ingeres-tu!
> [You act better!]
> D: *Nu* chi s-, na romanes, ingeres-tu sar won kaj rodin-pe.
> [*Well,* not h-, not the Romani way, you hold yourself like they expect.]
> Ingeres-tu sar e gazhji, kaj rodin-pe ando lenge, mashkar le gazhje
> [You act like a gazhji as they expect among them, when you are among gazhje]
> kana san, no rodis tu vi t'jekh tsirra te *priderzhival*is tu lengi *kul'tura.*

[you just expect also a little bit to *keep to* their *culture.*]
Aj kana vi sam mashkar le Rom, *tozhe* kasave *kul'turni* sam,
[And also when we are among Roma, we are *also* that kind of *cultured,*]
sar te phenav, *"kul'turni"* vej na *"kul'turni"*?
[how would I say it, *"cultured"* or not *"cultured"*?]
(Lemon and Nakamura 1994, video transcript; italics mark switch to Russian)

Again we see Lovara using Russian metacultural terms such as "cultured," and "uphold," and later in the interview they use still others. These were, moreover, the only Russian words introduced in Russian grammatical form, excluding emphatics or particles like "of course" and "well." Neither woman uttered many Romani metacultural terms, except for "Romanes," again perhaps because the camera framed the situation as one intended for a future public, and the Russian terms they may have learned were appropriate for such situations. They belonged to a mass-media register of metacultural talk. But more interesting is when, toward the end of the exchange, Dunja wavers over whether to apply the Russian term "culture" to social behavior among Roma, though hinting that *both* Russian *and* Romani etiquette required formal good behavior. When first pressed to define "more cultured," they define it as "better." Dunja then characterizes the behavioral or verbal shifts required in interactions with the gazhje as concessions; "better" means acceding to the standards of the gazhje, observing and doing "like they do." Yet, later, the force of "better" decreases to neutral difference, as Rubinta sums up, "With the gazhje you have other words." "Better" thus did not index full investment in hegemonic cultural values, but recognized that some situations demand control. Indeed, sometimes "better" could be "worse." Both Russians and Roma would concede that Western Europeans were more elegant than Soviets but could "spoil" hospitality with too many, too stiff "manners." Comparative talk about "better manners" and "culture" that valued the familiar and the simple over the "better" were part of a widespread Russo-Soviet discourse vis-à-vis Europe.

Gazhje Dreams and Dreaming the Gazhje: Hybrid Cultural Reflection

Sometimes, "gazhjikane" words or actions could be valued and repeated even within what would seem to be the most intimate of Romani realms. The question is, how were they connected to other modes of self-representation and of memory? In the early autumn of 1991, a Lovar died abruptly three days after a giant wedding at the Kosmos hotel. Within a day of his death, a few dozen relatives arrived at the family's home at the outskirts of Moscow, increasing the ranks of those already gathered for the wedding. They kept vigil for three days until the funeral. Following the burial, I returned to Moscow proper by suburban electric train. On the ninth day the first memorial service began, the *pomina* (the next would be in forty days, then others, once yearly). I returned for the *pomina:* more relatives had arrived whom I did not recognize. Throughout that morning, those newly arrived to the women's table ignored me, the gazhji; even though the matriarch of the house had taken care to speak Romani to me in front of them they took me for a Russian neighbor.

Only by late afternoon, when one of the younger women took a break from serving the men's table, did I venture to speak to anyone. I told her that the night before I had seen the deceased in a dream. Hearing me out, she went silent, and then called for everyone to listen, calling me a rakli, rather than by name, as she usually did, perhaps identifying me for those from out of town, or perhaps too shocked to avoid the term (earlier that week she had declared me "*not* a rakli"!): "*E rakli dikhlja les ando suno—shun!*" (The rakli saw him in a dream—listen!). For the first time that day, the mourners paid attention to the gazhji—several men even came to stand in the door to the next room to listen. I awkwardly recounted that in my dream I had seen the deceased loading large crates of matches into his car. He had turned to me and had said, smiling, that since there was a shortage of matches he hoped to make a profit. Upon hearing the dream, people began talking all at once, his wife and sister began exclaiming, "*Chjores! Chjores!*" (adv.: It's really bad! Really, really bad!). I ventured that he had been smiling after all, but they replied that this made matters even worse; their "rule" (as one of the girls explained to me later) for interpreting dreams or portents was to take their opposite, thus to dream something "good," omened something "bad." She explained further that they were most upset because they had buried him with cigarettes—but had forgotten to leave matches. He had been a heavy smoker. Besides the cup of tea and sliced black bread set beside him during vigil, they had placed still more food and a carton of Marlboros in his grave. Many Lovara (like many people in Russia, the Balkans, and Central Asia) considered such supplies necessary to pay funeral respects. It is also possible that my dream superimposed onto events something I had read and forgotten the year before: Demeter's dissertation on Kelderari custom describes the final act after a burial: lighting matches and throwing them behind one as one leaves the grave (Demeter 1988:107).

Before he had died, the man actually had traded electric irons, not matches, which had not been scarce then, though practically everything else in Moscow was (matches had been in short supply a year earlier). The dream nevertheless resembled scenes familiar to my listeners from daily life. Goods in short supply and semiillicit trade were moreover highly politicized, for such trade and discourse about it intersected racial and national ideologies.[26] Envious Russian neighbors saw Gypsies as having manipulated, even created shortages through illicit networks. Roma, though they valued the marketing profits they made and esteemed those who could accumulate them, realized that many Russians regarded visible street trade as miserly and sinister and marked the hawking of scarce goods a "Gypsy occupation." The image of the deceased loading his car for the bazaar — when described by a gazhji especially — thus resonated with vexed images of illicit economic activity described by other non-Roma, images linked to social marginality as we have now seen many times in preceding chapters.

I was a foreigner, new to these problems and only temporarily troubled by most of them, and that I was an outsider was not forgotten; I was told later that the family of the deceased had given special credence to my dream precisely *because* I was not Romani; that to reach kin, dead people sometimes sent messages specially through outsiders. Whether this could be generalized to all gazhje was never clear to me. Perhaps, the *kind of* gazhji they considered me to be most affected the force they attributed to the dream-telling. Roma in Russia often spoke of Americans as having connections and abilities different from and more "civilized" than those of a Russian gazhje. From Russians and Roma alike, my presence often evoked comparisons with an imagined world across the ocean — "Where is life better, here or there?" Like Russians, Roma often would claim that "here" life was "not normal" and would posit America or Europe as the standard of "normalcy." While the dream images of scarce goods were local, coming from me they called to mind difference with America, where "you have everything already on the shelves." They thus could be taken up by my listeners not only to reflect on the misfortune of this bereavement, but also to evoke pervading definitions of crisis and civilization in market terms.

Europeans associate Gypsies with fortune-telling and vague hypnotic powers. However, Roma whom I knew in Russia did not accord mystical significance to all dreams; some they even dismissed as "nonsensical." When attributing "truth" to a dream, as in the dream about the matches, they did so not out of absolute awe for dream worlds, but only when references framed in the dream-narration indexed in compelling ways the situational and social identities of the dream-teller and audience, or their symbolic and social capital. A very different situation from the one recounted above unfolded when a Kelderari woman told *her* dreams (which claimed allegiances to particular aspects of gazhjikani culture) to me in the earshot of her kin.

Gafa lived in the settlement near Tver that the Russian documentary film crew had visited in 1991. Her father, an elder there, was a self-proclaimed Communist who argued for the return of order in a "strong hand" like Stalin's. Since the 1960s, their settlement owed the success of its metal-working cooperatives to a mixture of state subsidies, legitimate contracts with collective farms, and benign state neglect of their more independent enterprises. Her father avowed that Soviet leaders had "liked Gypsies" but denied that Kelderara had "become like Russians"; unlike Olga's urban family, Gafa's did not claim "civilizedness" over other Roma.

The foibles of the gazhje were, at the same time, a less constant topic at this Kelderari village than they were among Moscow Lovara. In this village, the Kelderara lived close together, having their own sections through which gazhje rarely walked. They did not hire gazhje house cleaners, though they employed gazhje workers outdoors, to help weld and build, attracting them both by paying a little more than the state factories could and by giving them some board, although, as one Kelderari remarked: "They eat and drink here, but they only drink vodka, while we drink Napoleon amaretto!" (Lemon and Nakamura 1994). At the same time, these Kelderara were more involved in performing on stage for gazhje at local cultural centers than were most Lovara (or other Kelderara living closer to Moscow) at the Romani Theater.

Gafa, without classifying her*self* as "civilized," was fiercely loyal to Russian "high" culture and protested, with the intensity of any Russian Mos-

FIGURE 18 A man in the Kelderari village instructs a gazhjo worker (in welding suit) hired to help with a large commission.

cow intellectual, that it was unfair that the West claimed to generate "civilization" and that the state was misguided to allow so many imports in the 1990s: "We could be using our own inventions, but they think it cheaper to buy foreign." Gafa praised Russia and the beauty of its landscapes, its birch and pine forests, the mermaids (*rusalki*) in its rivers: "The way my mother always told stories about Russia—it seemed like a fairy tale. It is so beautiful, I don't understand why the foreigners don't want to live here." She immersed herself in practices and hobbies marked as "Russian": she had started winter seedlings in small boxes, and planted a flower garden with a small white fence around it, and wanted to build a Russian *banja,* or bathhouse, but her father would not allow it. She often mentioned wishing—if she could have lived any other life and been anyone else—that she had been born a Russian in tsarist times. "Russian culture" offered her material for fantasies of alternate selves—perhaps not so differently from the ways in which literary Gypsies offered material to Russians for nostalgic fantasies of recreating themselves through volja.

She wanted escape, "to fly away like the Phoenix women, where no one would see me." Thirty years old when I first met her, unmarried, she looked after her brothers' children in the daytime while their wives traded and told fortunes at nearby markets or train stations. Still, her social capital in the community was better than that of the young *borja,* who were usually taken from other villages, for she lived with her own brothers and parents rather than with "strangers." However, even at thirty, she was not allowed to leave the settlement without an escort of brothers, or at least a group of children; she complained that she could never "just go to the movies." She criticized the "strictness of our laws," which, she objected, "demean women," and was therefore glad that she had remained a "girl," because then, at least, rules proscribing married women's deportment, as laid out in a Kelderari-Vlax discourse of pollution, did not constrain her.

We spent our days trying to converse over the clamor of her charges and the shouted demands of her mother, sometimes by escaping outdoors, walking in nearby birch woods. Sometimes she told me about her dreams, which the children scoffed. While some Roma insisted to me that dreams carry omens, should be heeded, or that, for instance, dreaming children should not be wakened, it was apparent that listeners did not evaluate all dream narratives in the same way. In some cases dreams revealed deeper truths, but in others dreams were written off as misguided fantasy.

Gafa's listeners focused on and dismissed what they saw as overly personal insertion of individual and idiosyncratic dilemmas.[27] For instance, one afternoon, Gafa told me of a dream about St. Catherine, who, she said, had been too proud to marry until she underwent a conversion and became the bride of Jesus. In Russia, it was rare for a Kelderari woman not to marry, divorces also being rare. The fact that Gafa was unmarried was not a topic she liked to discuss openly; telling about the proud bride of Jesus was a less explicit way to lionize her own status. At least, this may have been the strategy her kin perceived, as her sisters-in-law rolled their eyes and made sarcastic comments.

Gafa herself commented on her own dreams in ways that suggested *she* saw them as illuminating relations to both divine and non-Romani worlds. At night she often stayed up reading an illustrated children's Bible or religious pamphlets. Gafa occasionally spoke of wishing she had been born into a "family of believers," for although her family celebrated Easter and baptisms, her father declared himself an atheist, and churchgoing was erratic. Thus her sources for religious images were books. She also anchored her accounts of dream images to relations, things, and events that were visible in her social world, about which she repeatedly spoke in waking life. I will elaborate some of these connections soon. My focus throughout is her discourse, not dreams themselves.[28]

When Gafa had finished the story about her dream of St. Catherine, she switched to talk about another dream, one that shared the religious theme. In that dream, she entered a beautiful house "with a huge staircase and pillars." An angel appeared who told her, "First the tourists will come, and then you will go out." Then Jesus entered with the Mother of God and blessed her. Gafa's brother was in fact building a new 2-story house, the plan of which was being then much discussed in the settlement—when I returned several years later, it had been built around a wooden, spiral staircase. The tourists were perhaps gazhje, curious visitors, like folklorists and the Moscow film crew. What about frightening dreams? I had pressed her then. "A man, he looked like Dobrynin, was trying to grab me when I went outside. I got away. Then I dreamed a second time that he wanted me to open the door. I went to the window, and he grabbed me and pulled me onto the sill. . . . I saw that there was no floor, only an abyss. I hit him and ran away. Then I dreamed again that his mother's voice said to me, 'Why do you drive my son away? He loves you.' Then he never came back again" (interview from field notes 1992).

One of the older children interrupted her then with a mocking, invented account of the dream teller's improbable wedding, describing flowers in her hair, a white dress, and the groom. The children went into fits of laughter. Offended, Gafa cut her story short. A potential mother-in-law and an abyss could be interpreted by some in psychoanalytic terms as speaking to the precariousness of her unmarried social status (or, given the relief she expressed at being able to ignore the gendered restrictions of a married woman, to fears of being taken in marriage). But rather than impose such a frame, it is perhaps less distorting to restrict analysis here to showing intertextual connections among her dream accounts and more broadly circulating texts. For instance, she described her frightening dream suitor, as someone who "looked like Dobrynin," the revolutionary hero, a famous *Russian*. Her memory of propaganda texts, biblical texts, and Kelderari gendered proscriptions all mingled together in her dream-tellings, themselves hybrid reflections on being Romani.

Her dream narratives also indexed community stories about tensions at village boundaries with the Russians. "Demons are always chasing me. . . .

I dreamed I was at the well, and I ran and ran away down those narrow alleys. I finally crossed the road [back toward home] and felt happy . . . and free. But he stood there and said, 'You haven't got rid of me!' They wanted to make me sin . . . make me steal, or lie, or love another woman's husband" (interview from field notes 1992). I asked her to elaborate what she meant by "sin," but she was again interrupted by teasing about an imaginary wedding. Her description of her trajectory in the dream up to that point traced familiar social boundaries. The alley in her dream-story had a counterpart in daily life that ran from the well across the road among Russian dachas to wind back to the Romani settlement. Each day, when she went to fetch water, Gafa traversed that path between high Russian fences, overlooked by windows of Russian dacha owners. The alley was a dangerous boundary, a place where Russian boys ambushed Kelderari boys, asking them, "Are you a Russian or not?" and beating them up no matter how they answered: if "no" for being Gypsy, if "yes" for "lying." Note that the demons who chased her down the narrow alley, and who wanted to "make her sin," came from the Russian side, leaving her in peace only when she reached the Romani side.

These descriptions of dream images recalled the threat of hostile neighbors, while others admitted the very possibility of a "Russian" suitor, in the form of Dobrynin. Meanwhile, when speaking about waking life, Gafa complained not about the alleys, but about the gendered rules that kept her from crossing those alleys alone. Her kin considered her a little crazy in her outspoken, critical reflexivity, though they never accused her of being un-Romani; she did not cross the wrong borders in "reality," she only spoke of wishing to transgress them, and in dream language or in talk about art. And in any case, accounts of maneuvering around non-Romani worlds exemplify common tensions of being Romani, as we saw in Janosh's case; Gafa was skilled in speaking and reading Russian, and her relatives respected this talent. When non-Romani strangers arrived from Moscow, they came to *her* father's house first; she, speaking disarmingly rapid and literate Russian (many Roma in Russia are at least technically literate in Russian; she was perhaps particularly bookish), had recorded stories with Russian folklorists and spent more time with such visitors than most of her other relatives — men or women. It was she who competently mediated with the Russian administrators at the House of Culture in town when the young people of the settlement's amateur musical ensemble performed there.

Over several years, I witnessed various situations in which Gafa shifted between Russian and Romani, and Gafa had significant things to say on the topic of shifting. For instance, once in 1993 I accompanied Gafa and the youth choir to the town's House of Culture. When in the settlement, Gafa usually spoke a mix of Romani and Russian to me, but, on the decades-old, stuttering, Hungarian-made bus on the way to town, she spoke only Romani to me and to the children, shielding me with her body from Russians in thick coats pressing by with baskets, and warning the children not to misbehave, "*Na keren! Xoljajlen e gazhje*" ("Don't do that—The gazhje are getting mad"). At the club, Gafa spent several minutes speaking with the organizers, in Russian, getting the key to the rehearsal room, and fetching long, red velvet dresses for the girls. In rehearsal, Gafa directed the children in Romani, but, at last irritated with the children's mischief, she threatened: "If you don't start listening to me now, we are going to do the whole rehearsal in Russian! I will count in Russian!"

But, despite making such threats, she was proud of her Russian. A few weeks after the House of Culture visit I asked her about Budulaj, the war hero from the 1970s TV serial. Several Romani performers in Moscow had insisted I make note of the fact that Budulaj was played by a gazhjo, a Moldovan actor, who used the wrong gestures, said things that no Rom would say. I expected a similar, even more detailed, response from Gafa, who after all belonged to a group of Roma whom the intellectuals considered to be most authentically Romani. However, what rang false to her about Budulaj was not inauthentic *Romani* but his poor *Russian* speech, which differed from her own:

> Naj, *no* vo, sar te phenav tuke, *mozhet byt'* si kadalo manush. Vo *prosto*
> [No *but* he, how to tell you, *maybe* there is such a man . . . he *simply*]
> kamel te kerel—*i daj poklon*—te kerel *istinno ot i do.*
> [wants—*all respects to him*—to do *sincerely from start to finish.*]
> *Iskusstvennyj* manush. Man *lichno* vo *razdrazhail* man, lehko divanos,
> [An *artificial* man. *Personally* he *gets on my nerves,* his speech,]
> sar vo, lehki *rech',* sar vo, phagavis, sar naj anda mashkar e Rrossija.
> [how he, his *speech,* how he, it breaks, like he's not in the middle of Russia.]
> Vi kana *ploxo* divinil—tu dikhes sar me diviniv rrossitsko? Mishto *i*
> *chisto,*

[And when he speaks so *badly* — see how I speak Russian? Well and *cleanly,*]
aj vo sar *innostrants*ura divinil, *nu* kodo *rasdrazha*il, no but!
[but he speaks like *foreigners, well* that *annoys* [me], but how!]
(Audiotape taped interview 1992, italics mark Russian)

Gafa did not believe that her authentic Romani identity needed to be grounded in clear-cut distinctions of language use — Roma speaking Romani, Russians speaking Russian. She accented this with poetic force, in fact, by echoing the very ideologies she denied — by code-switching into Russian to express semantic binaries. Gafa's shifts into Russian were thus *not* produced mechanically, by a "world divided into two parts," but track her reflective awareness of metacultural discourses about hybridity and authenticity.

Besides Russian evidentials and emphatics (such as "maybe," "simply," "personally"), the use of Russian clustered around the *very idea of social distinction.* "Purely," "sincerely," and "from start to finish" all evoke wholeness and unity, while her uses of "artificial" and "foreigner" index transgressions of social borders and integrity. Romani has equivalent lexical items (*vuzhes, chjachjes*) — however, the Russian terms had circulated broadly in the media, in discourses on nationhood, and Gafa, like any other Soviet, knew their force. Romani terms, with their different histories of use, would not have performed the same way. But Gafa's code-switching did not necessarily mean that she unambivalently inhabited exclusive, nationalist ideologies. She was critical of depictions of "sincerity" and uttered words like "cleanly" to mark distance from assumptions that Gypsies cannot speak Russian, cannot *be* Russian and also really Romani. Such reflections challenge Romani studies to acknowledge social interactions that do not frame and perform "difference."[29] What seems — to the media or the Russian bureaucrat — to be a paradox, a loss of culture, from the vantage of this Romani woman did not. Even in intercultural interactions that do frame difference, people remain grounded in specific social loyalties and familiar memories. These loyalties intersect a biography from many directions, but they are still *specific;* and because they are specific, actors may not construe them as paradoxical, or as split by a proscenium.

Gafa's shifts among speaking Russian, avoiding Russian, threatening to speak Russian, and then claiming perfect Russian were not tricks and only seem contradictory if we assume a theatrical model. For in each situation, each footing *was* "sincere" — but without trying, "from start to finish," to be always consistent. To achieve such consistency would in fact entail attempting to live like a Stanislavskiian system actor, aligning each scene's "units and objectives" to an overarching "Super Objective" (Stanislavskii 1936: passim). Perhaps frustration with such theatrical ontologies, as they hovered around such everyday shifts, motivated Gafa to declare once that she wished to become invisible, "to fly away like the Phoenix women, where no one would see me," to disappear from the stage of the world. Her sister-in-law, however, had responded to this utterance by saying, "Why would you want to do that? What good is living if no one can see you?"

· 7 ·

Conclusion: At Home in Russia

> In Gypsy tales the hero never lies but has the advantage of knowing
> how to make the orders he receives mean something different from
> what the master or the powerful thought they were telling him.
> — Michel de Certeau, *The Practice of Everyday Life*

The epigraph is taken from a footnote in a work that is not about Gypsies
but about everyday tactics of reappropriation, about structure and resistance to structure in the modern city. Here "Gypsy tales" (presumably tales
told about Gypsies, not by them), stand in not only for ranges of resistant
practice, but for the sort of marginal folk who seem to engage in them. For
DeCerteau they warrant only a passing footnote, but many post-Soviets in
the 1990s were much more explicit in describing Gypsies as temperamen-
tally ironic, as slippery by nature. While dissident intellectuals claimed that
their own use of irony marked their disengagement from hegemonic master
narratives (and their engagement with counternarratives), the irony that
Gypsies were imagined to employ all the time in fact overrode their agency.
Ironical Gypsies become a trope for resistance, but as if they have no choice
but to be insincere, to always be on stage.

Sincere Ironies: Diaspora and Dramaturgy

The dualities assumed to underlie resistance (e.g., powerful/repressed)
resonate with dramaturgic metaphors throughout Western social thought.
As the anthropologist Johannes Fabian asserts, "One of the connotations
from which performance should not be purified is that of just being performance, of putting on an act, of tricking and dissimulating. . . . the shuffle

and dance to which the oppressed have to resort . . . have been so many ways of surviving" (1990:20; see also Scott 1990). The scope of this resonance is important—it is not only Gypsies who are seen as tricksters.

But in the case of Gypsies, both imagined irony and the "shuffle and dance" of performance also intersect equally imaginary mappings of wandering. This representation of rootlessness codes Gypsy culture as itself shifty, across both physical and moral space. Individual Gypsies in turn are assumed to be innately liars, especially if they speak about matters that ideologically require "roots."

However, diaspora does not prevent "home" attachments to a place other than the place of "origin." Indeed, place matters to most Roma a great deal, especially a place near kin. The Vlax phrase for "together," *and' jekh than,* glosses literally as "in one place," just as does the Russian adverb *vmesto.* This semantic possibility may not encapsulate a "Romani worldview," but it would undermine any claim that a "Gypsy worldview" is altogether indifferent to place. Many Roma in Russia historically anchor kinship networks to localities, and in the late twentieth century understand those kin loyalties to be contained by national borders. Regardless of how other Europeans may see Gypsies as *randomly* scattered, Roma in Russia chart their families with *specific* reference to Russian towns and cities ("the Penza Kelderara," "the Tula Roma"). They also figure Russia as a moral center of gravity (American Roma "are not as hospitable as we are in Russia"). As one middle-aged Kelderari man said:

> We're Gypsies, right? It would be really difficult for us to go away somewhere. For any other nationality it's easier to leave, because they have fewer roots, fewer ties. But we Gypsies have ties all over the Union, relatives, nephews, uncles, aunts, and to go away somewhere means to tear ourselves away from everything. It's really hard, you see? . . . I couldn't live abroad, even in America or Germany. Because I am used to my country, I have to see my own people. A Russian for instance, he can live somewhere else—or like you live in the city, alone, with no relatives around. But we live the whole camp together. We have to associate with each other. (Lemon and Nakamura 1994, video transcript)

The Kelderari man not only emphasizes family connections, but plots them onto Russian or Soviet territory. The possibility of staying "and' jekh than" entails honoring state borders.

While many non-Roma might claim to detect a shift here from an "authentic" Gypsy voice, Roma may detect no such shift at all; in many ways interpellated as Soviet subjects, they do not perceive expressing Romani loyalties in terms of Russian or Soviet ones as problematic.

Diasporic tropes, dramaturgic metaphors, and the ideologies that buttress theatrical models intersect in powerful ways to pervade performances of social relations among Roma and other Soviets. Sometimes such intersections are clearest when performance frames leak or are broken. The conclusion thus unpacks social interactions in which certain discursive shifts and switches index what were read to be problematic contradictions of supposedly stable ranked identities, and in which all parties doubt the sincerity of the others. My account of these interactions takes up threads running throughout the book to draw together ways in which people perform social relations by pointing not only to immediate and "shared" context, but also to distant and remembered events and performances.

Performing Paranoia

Lipa, a Kelderari man, lived in the Ural mountains near Perm, twenty-four hours by train from Moscow and the Romani Theater. I met him only twice in 1993, in the company of Russians from Perm, *Permjaki,* who had offered to take me to visit Roma living on the outskirts of their city. I usually preferred to meet Roma through networks more familiar to them — this time we would descend without warning, in a blitzkrieg like party activists, journalists, or TV crew. The Permjaki, however, feared letting me go alone and drove me to the village. Yet, uncomfortable as they were with Roma, the interactions' very awkwardness illuminated how paranoia must be performed (see also Daniel and Knudson 1995).

The Permjaki drove me to the Kelderari village, parking their car at the end of a lane of houses. From the car, I explained our presence to young men standing in the lane until a young woman approached and suggested we go speak to the "old man." In a house further down, Lipa greeted us and ordered nieces and *borja* to prepare tea and snacks. My acquaintances from Perm sat up straight and stiff, glancing queasily about the room, ignoring my previous admonitions to eat anything offered.

Later, on the way back to the city the Permjaki dwelled upon visual impressions of dirt and "primitive" poverty. But what they recalled most vividly as signs of dissimulation were several shifts in code and topic that Lipa made when we had first sat down. Lipa had first informed me, in Romani, that some relatives of his had gone to America in 1924, and he had given me their names and his own address, in case I should ever meet them. Having said this, he switched to Russian, called himself a Muscovite, and turned to the Great Patriotic War (World War II). "I've lived all my life in Russia. I remember the war," he said, speaking in a generic aging, Soviet patriotic voice. Then Lipa continued, citing a familiar narrative, one popularized onstage and in literature (but often presented as folk memory circulated not through media, but alone by *tsyganskaja pochta* [Gypsy post]), one that hooked onto official histories via musicality: "Hitler shot more than one thousand of us, with the Jews. Threw them all into a hole, the kids on top, except for one beauty that the general wanted to marry. She cried and sang, but she wouldn't go with him, so they shot her." He praised Stalin because "he did not give his Gypsies away to Hitler!" and had preserved the Romani Theater when other minority theaters had been closed down.

On that drive back to Perm, the Russians interpreted Lipa's switch into Russian to declare his own Soviet patriotism and to witness the war as tactical, *theatrical* performances for their sake, a front for a "true" Gypsy identity. They speculated that just before switching he could have "said anything in Gypsy." Their mistrust was confirmed less by his having spoken "Gypsy" in the first place, as by the point at which he switched into Russian. Certainly, in Romani Lipa *had* recalled kin dispersed beyond the state's borders. However, Lipa's talk about those bonds did not cancel out a possibility that he experienced Soviet allegiance. A second interaction a few months later strengthens the case for this possibility, and illustrates the ideologies supporting models both of theatricality and of diaspora to which non-Roma (and some Roma as well) appealed to deny that possibility. That interaction again involved Lipa, his nephew, an American (myself), and two Russian musicians; it thus triangulated among several "national" frames and discursive footings and entailed more than one kind of shift — or seeming shift — problematic for the participants.

The second visit fell a month after the first. There had been a wedding the day before: over the first house of the settlement, a long, dark pink scarf hung from a pole, a symbol of the bride's patjiv ("honor," "respect," "hospitality," but in this context, "virginity"). When some Roma told the Russians what the scarf signified (it was an icon for the bride's blood), they were amazed and horrified — after all, the Soviet state had targeted such practices for eradication as backward and patriarchal. This time, the women who greeted us in the road let us know that Lipa was still drunk from three days' festivities, and warned that we "would not want to see him." Instead, a younger man, the father of the groom, approached and led us to his house, saying he wanted to show off his new bori, his son's new wife.

It turned out that Lipa was the father of the bride; he himself soon entered, indeed drunk. When he saw me, he began to abuse me for not having written to him. He took this postal silence as a sign that I had deceived him, and alleged that I had claimed to be a journalist, and that since no article had appeared in the local papers since my last visit, I had falsely masked as a journalist and was a foreign spy. I denied that I had ever professed journalism, and pointed out that I had not yet been back to America in order to post a letter from there. To save myself, I then remembered to convey him greetings from Kelderari relatives of his living near Tver', who had been happy a few weeks before to hear that I had met Lipa. At first, Lipa exclaimed and repeated each familiar name. In my enthusiasm, however, I went too far — I pulled out a kin chart, connections and names neatly penned for me by one of Lipa's nephews. Rather than being satisfied that I really knew a branch of his family, Lipa became more enraged: "She is collecting materials, making a map of the world to sell!" He ordered me to leave, not to return lest he kill me. But instead, his son-in-law, Piko, threw *him* out.

What had seemed innocent to Kelderara near Moscow, more certain in their location of my identity, to Lipa all too closely resembled the state's sinister modes of mapping and surveillance. Lipa's fear was not born of some generic, "cultural," antigazhje sentiment, it was historically tied to actions of Soviet and European states and to their treatment of diasporic and stateless minorities such as Roma and Jews. Lipa was old enough, and had then lived close enough to the Western front, to remember that before and during World War II, the German state had collected Romani genealogies. Lipa might have remembered Soviet deportations of minorities such as Ingush and Chechens. He recalled that the Soviet state had kept records of *everyone's,* not only minorities', kin relations, that work questionnaires had asked about parents' and grandparents' occupations, about relations abroad. Such connections were fraught and I had no right to make them visible.

Lipa also knew all too well the official routines intended to pin down such connections, by demanding papers that declared citizenship and origin, and had earlier told of experiences with their limiting and punitive consequences. He, like many Vlax Roma especially, had often been treated as foreign; especially since many Vlax had written "Hungarian" or "Moldovan" on the line for "nationality" on Soviet passports, rather than the stigmatized "Gypsy," and doing so had sometimes backfired, as when some were rounded up during World War II as "Hungarian spies." When Lipa returned to the house a second time, he shifted into the authoritative voice of a border guard, expressing suspicion in a mode similar to that which Soviet militia doubtless had used with him. When Lipa burst in and asked to see my documents, the tape recorder had been running (my friends from Perm had been asking Piko about "Gypsy customs" and listening to his *bori* play a new electric synthesizer. After Lipa and I made peace an hour later, he asked me to erase a different part of tape, but did not object to this section). Lipa asked, in Russian, for my name and passport number, and ordered me to write down my coordinates in Russian, not in English and not in Romani. (In this excerpt, L = Lipa, A = Alaina, P = Piko):

> L: Write it well, so I understand!
> A: In English?
> L: In Russian! . . . I am afraid now. . . . write me your apartment number and telephone — *if* you [really] live in Moscow.
> A: This one [address] is in America.
> P: [to Lipa] What do you need America for!?
> L: I need it, I need it! I will talk to America, I will pay half a million, and I will talk and verify this!
> P: Right! Sure you have that money!

Lipa insists on Russian over English. I had merely wanted to ensure that he had a version of the address that the U.S. postal system could read, for unlike Soviet postal workers, who know Latin letters, U.S. postal workers do not read Cyrillic. But my written switch from Russian to the language of America unnerved him. He did not consider writing such information in

Romani appropriate either but for different reasons: on my first visit, Lipa had given me a large photograph portrait of himself with his late wife and had asked me to write the message from him on the back, since he could only sign his name. I had begun in Romani, sounding it out, but he made me finish in Russian.

But although Soviet authorities, in Lipa's experience, spoke Russian, this did not mean that my attempted shifts from Russian into Romani could, by itself, create a protected space for Lipa. To the contrary (and despite a Vlax-Romani maxim, "Romani for truth, gazhjikani for lies") to Lipa an American stranger who switched between Russian and Romani was dangerously untrustworthy. But this mistrust was not driven by opposition of Roma to all gazhje; it found purchase in memories of particular interactions with (and media depictions of) Soviets, Russians, foreigners. Lipa explained the reasons for his distrust to his nephew, now son-in-law, Piko, first in Romani, but switching to Russian to drive home the point:

> L: A katar zhjanes so kerel e butji? K' xatjarel Romanes, *nu?*
> [And how do we know what work she does? That she knows Romani, *huh?*]
> P: *Nu* xatjarel, *nu* . . . ?
> [*Well,* she understands, *so* . . . ?]
> L: Aj sar avel *po-russkomu* [sic] *govorit'?!*
> [But then how did she come *to speak Russian!?*]
> P: [laughing] *Pochemu — ona kontraved!* Kutja-so!
> [*Why — she is a counterintelligence!* That is how!]
> (Italics mark Russian)

Social paranoias are often described as driven by binaries: us/them:sincere/false, and so on. But here a Rom aligns with Russia against America; the triangulation vexes such straightforward transpositions. Lipa voiced his paranoia not by contrasting Romani folklore to gazhje symbols, but by deploying historically Soviet xenophobia and speaking in Russian. Decades of negative sanctions had bred similar fears of association with foreigners among older Roma as they had among other Soviets. Though socially embedded in different ways, with different pragmatic valence, such fears were expressed in formally similar ways.

Yet the Permjaki, for their part, mistrusted Lipa's expressions of patriotic suspicion, precisely because they recognized these forms as their own. They credited neither his experiences nor his "right" to speak them: when Lipa alleged that I was composing a "map of the world" to sell in America, he had shouted, "We will not sell Russia!" My urban associates laughed about this on the second drive back to the city: "Our homeland, *our* homeland, what a patriot!" they repeated in the car, stressing what they saw as a comic use of the first-person plural possessive. Such lines were uttered by Russian pensioners in vegetable queues, with whom younger people might usually empathize even if they found such forms of Stalinist patriotism passé. But the Russians found it hilarious that such lines could be uttered by a Gypsy—for them, it was as though he had broken character.

But Lipa's citation of patriotic formulae may not have been masquerade—Soviet Russia had been his home, too. Such hybrid discursive practices honeycomb the former USSR, and so the possibility that Roma could sincerely appropriate Soviet and Russian nationalist discourses to articulate local experience should surprise no one. Yet, to the Russian visitors, to whom Lipa's biography was invisible, his words seemed hopelessly "out of context"; they saw them as strategic dissimulation "onstage." It was only behind the veil of "Gypsy custom" where they assumed authentic Gypsies to reside. What these particular Permjaki imagined to be genuine, however, was saturated by depictions of Gypsies (and of *chjernije*) from media and literature, from brief sightings on the markets — not by continuous interactions with Romani neighbors. Those Russians who maintained such interactions were few, and themselves were relatively marginal to economic, educational, and media infrastructures. Gypsy patriots may be depicted on stage and in old movies, but no "sensible" person would admit to believing in Budulaj in real life, besides a few drunken war veterans like Lipa (and the Russian pensioner who had burst through the proscenium at a Romani Theater Sunday matinee).

Lipa had been mocked even by his own nephew, who claimed that Lipa watched too much television. The nephew had gibed: "What, is she going to find all your nuclear rockets? Is she going to sell you for American dollars?" *His* irony drew attention not to the supposed duplicity of a Gypsy patriot, but to the drunken assumption that Gypsy patriotism could matter. It should have put him more firmly on discursive ground with young, dissident-admiring Russians from Perm than could Lipa's old-fashioned patriotic talk. However, his irony did little to realign the ways they read his words — on the way back to the city, the Russians dissected Piko's joking as likewise insincere "staged" for their benefit: whether Roma cynically mocked or earnestly declared patriotism, such topics did not belong to them. That realm of discourse could not include shifty players or nomads.

Closing Words

Such intersections of nationalist with theatrical ideologies in fact challenge the extent to which we might consider the Romani Theater to have been performative. Its plays did display and produce social relations, but they emerged in ways not intended. The Theater and Soviet representational practices produced neither friendship of the peoples nor belief in the new Gypsy patriotism. However, though discredited as "kitsch," its plays nonetheless foregrounded certain assumptions about what categories of person should speak in which sorts of ways, that is, they entrenched metapragmatic assumptions about what frames "international" communication.

But these assumptions and the communicative practices that they attend were not produced by theatrical performances alone. In the context of the regime change and market reforms of the 1990s, Lipa's words seemed even more out of place than they would have a decade earlier. After perestroika, Roma became more excluded than ever from public media discourse, especially from debates about border changes and citizenship. They were not only a distrusted, diasporic minority with untidy transborder links but were also thought too primitive to partake in such discussions, let alone know for whom to vote. Visible in the media as Gypsy performers, Roma were excluded from public debates that would frame the terms of their own citizenship.

While theatricality and display can be empowering, in post-Soviet Russia discourse *about* stage performance, whether deployed in social practice or to explain social practice, informed racialist criteria. It laid the ground for misrecognition, in fact limiting the ways Roma could represent themselves, because only those features that could be placed on either side of an imagined proscenium were accorded visibility, framed as authentically Gypsy. Anything else was labeled shifty. All the same, attention to everyday, conversational performances (even those that draw from theatrical displays or models) overturns the persistent conviction that Gypsies embody "rootlessness." Overturning *this* stereotype has theoretical implications beyond mere disenchantment, because it discourages letting any particular people stand as a trope *for* resistance. Without Gypsy "nomadism" as an emblematic limit case, we are forced to be wary of sweeping claims about diaspora as an experience of exile or movement, and to remember that even "rhizomatic" identities touch ground and ground memory in particular places (cf. Deleuze and Guatteri 1987:21, 23; see also Malkki 1997).

Any theory of social subjectivity, diasporic or not, must weave itself through intersections of real-time performances with ongoing relations and enduring discourses. For, even if "hot-blooded Gypsies" dance only in a fleeting present, performance does not compel Roma to forget to remember.

APPENDIX A   Roma and Other Tsygane in the
Commonwealth of Independent States

No census breaks down Gypsy population; this appendix orders them by rough estimation, most numerous first, according to Barranikov 1934; Demeter and Cherenkov 1987; Demeter and Demeter 1990:5–6. Self-ethnonym is given first in italics.

Servi   Ukrainian-Romani speakers, also known as Ukrainska Roma or southern Russian Gypsies

Russka (Xeladytka)   Baltic-Romani speakers, known as Russka Roma, northern Russian Gypsies or sometimes Polska Roma or Poljache

Kelderara,[a] *Lovara, Ungri, Machvaja*   All Vlax-Romani speaking, sometimes referred to in Russia as Hungarian Gypsies or foreign Gypsies

Vlaxurja   Speak a dialect that Cherenkov defines as belonging to Ukrainian Romani but close to Vlax-Romani (Demeter and Demeter 1990:6)

Xoroxaja and *other Balkan-Romani speaking groups*[b]   Xoroxaja are also known as Crimean Gypsies, or Muslim Roma (see Barranikov 1931b). Speakers of Balkan-Romani live in Moldova and southern Ukraine.

Beash (Boyash) and *Rudara*   Speakers of archaic Romanian, often called Moldovanurja by Vlax

Karpatska and *Bergitka*   Carpathian-Romani speakers, southwest and west Ukraine, sometimes lumped with Hungarian Roma[c]

Sinti   Germanic-Romani speakers, living mostly in central Russia

Lom, Bosha, and *Karachi of the Caucausus*   Lom speak a dialect descended from proto-Romani, but distinct from European Romani (see Hancock 1993; Papazjan 1901; Patkanoff 1908)

Ljuli of Central Asia   Speak Tadjik and Tadjik-based dialects (Nazarov 1982–83:7–9), perhaps only distantly related to Roma but lumped with them as tsygane in the Soviet census

   a Called Kalderash in North America and parts of western Europe. See glossary for an explanation of how Romani adjectival forms for ethnonyms are used in the text.

   b Cherenkov (cited in Demeter and Demeter 1990:5) and Ventsel (1964) include Ursara in this group, while Fraser (1995:226) includes them with Beash and Rudari as speakers of Romanian, not Romani.

   c Ventsel (1964) puts Ungrike Roma (Ungri) in this category, but Lovara in Moscow insist that Ungri and Lovara come more recently from Hungarian-speaking lands.

APPENDIX B   Dialect Differences

Romani is an Indo-Iranic language, hence its basic grammatical and lexical elements are from Sanskrit. There are at least ten Romani dialects in Russia, belonging to both Vlax and non-Vlax groups. Russka (or Xeladytka) is the dialect dominant at the Moscow Romani Theater and in media. A "northern Russian" Romani dialect, it is more closely related outside Russia to Balkan Romani (see Hancock n.d; Kochanowski 1982 and 1995) and northern Carpathian (see Hubschmannova and Sebkova 1991) than to Vlax. Russka has layers of Greek, Serbian, Romanian, Hungarian, German, and Polish vocabulary, but Vlax shows more Romanian and Hungarian influence. Below are differences that speakers of Lovari and Russka find salient or interesting when they talk about differences in the other groups' ways of speaking (differences between Lovari and Kelderari are given in the glossary [Appendix C] where applicable).

Lovari and Russka: Some Features Salient to Speakers in Russia

Lovari	Russka	Gloss
Phonological distinctions:		
gazhjo	gadzhjo	non-Rom
aven!	javen!	come!
shjavo	chjavo	son
phral	pshal	brother
dej	daj	mother
sar	syr	how
Lexical distinctions:		
ratjija	brvinta	vodka
trajo	dzhiiben	life
vorbiv	rakirav	I speak/say
sostar	palso	why/what for?
kaj	karik	to/to where
chi	na	negative indicative

Morphological distinctions:

— Most Romani plurals are formed with *-a* (masc. pl) / *-ja* (fem. pl.). Russian roots in Russka retain Russian plurals, while Lovari marks such foreign plurals with *-urja* (masc. pl.) / *-uri* (fem. pl.), or *-i*.

— Russka declines adjectives for case and gender. Lovari inflects only for gender.

— Russka present is formed like Vlax future, with *-a* suffix: *shunena* in Russka is "they listen" but in Lovari it is "they will listen."

— Russka adds Russian verbal prefixes to roots: cf. Russka **ros**phenel to Rus. **rass**kazyvaet "narrates," or **ot**phandel to Rus. **ot**kryvaet "opens, unbinds, uncovers." Russka **za**lelpe to Rus. **zanimaetsja,** "occupies oneself with."

— Russka calques syntax: cf. Russka *dzhjav pala rom* and Rus. **vyidu zamuzh,** "I marry," lit. "I go behind the man," to Lovari *meritiv-ma.*

Russka*

Babano: *Pshala* i phenja! Me Romano *chjavo.* Me chjororro syr i tuma. . . . i *palso* mange te xoxavav tumen? Oke **po**dykhen, *karik* **za**lydzhjine tumen tumare barvalju**ki.** Amen, *galjev,* umarn*a.* Parne *xelade* amen *na* zrakhen*a,* a tasaven*a.* Amenge trebi te u*dzhj*as ko **bol'sheviki.** J*one* kharn*a* sar*en* chjorerren i **za**marden manushen. J*one* kamen *vash* amenge la*chj*o *dzhiiben.* I ame *bange* te maraspe tagari*skire* manushentsa i pe*skire* barvalju*k*entsa. . . . Me *rakirava* tumenge, syr **roz**marde *jone* amaro saro **taboro** i **za**keldyn*e* amare gr*en*!

[Babano: Brothers and sisters! I am a Romano son. I am just a poor little man like you. . . . So why should I deceive you? Here, look where your kulaks have led you. They surely kill us. The White soldiers do not save us, but oppress [us]. We need to go over to the Bolsheviks. They call out to all the poor and persecuted people. They want a good life for us. And we must fight the Tsar's people and his own kulaks. . . . I say to you, how they trampled our entire camp and seized our horses!]

*From a 1932 script by Aleksandr German for the Romani Theater (following his transcription).

Russian prefixes, suffixes, and borrowed lexical items are boldface.

Other features distinguishing Russka from Vlax are italicized.

In the first line, "Me Romano chjavo" rather than "Me som Romano chjavo" is undoubtedly a calque on Russian, which does not use existential verbs for nominative predicates in the present tense.

APPENDIX C   Vlax-Lovari Romani Glossary

This glossary of the Lovari dialect of Romani is much more limited than already existing dictionaries and is meant only as a quick reference tool for readers who may not have time to look farther. I have limited it to terms that appear in the text, especially those shared with other Vlax dialects in Russia. The reader is referred to other texts for grammatical paradigms: for extensive treatment of Lovari grammar in Poland, see Pobozniak 1964. For Russka (Xeladytka) dialects, see Ventsel 1966 and Maxotin 1993. For Slovak and Carpathian dialects, see Hubschmannova and Sebkova 1991 and Romano Racs 1994. For Kelderari, see Demeter and Demeter 1990 and also Boretsky 1994. On Vlax, see Hancock 1995. See also Sampson 1968.

— Verbs are given in 3rd p. sing. present indicative (root + -*el*), as there is no infinitive standardized in Romani (Demeter and Demeter [1990] give 1st p. sing. [root + -*av*]).
— Adjectives are given with feminine -*i* ending (-*o* is masc., -*e* pl.) merely because it is already conventional to transpose "Romani" from *Romani shib* to generalize, as in "the Romani people." In the text, only adjectives and nouns describing people decline according to gender or number ("one Machvano man," "several Machvaja," "a Lovari girl"). Nominal forms are sometimes given (Lovar [sing. masc.], Lovarka [sing. fem.]). But note that in Kelderari, the -*ari* suffix is neither adjectival nor feminine (i.e., *Kelderari* = Kalderash male). For simplicity, the text uses adjectival "Kelderari" (rather than *Kelderashitska*) and "Lovari" (rather than Lova-ritska) to refer to people and dialects, unless quoting.

aba   (adv) Already, hardly
abjav   (n) Wedding (also *bijav*)
akana(k)   (adv) Now
ame   (1st p. pl. pronoun) We
amari/-o/-e   (1st p. pl. poss.) Our. "Amari shib" (our language)
anav   (n) Name
ande, and'   (adv) In. "And' jekh than," lit. in one place, together. "And'o kher" (in the house)
avel   (v) S/he comes
baxt   (n) Luck, happiness, fortune, grace. "Sar e baxt? So del tuke o Del

kodji e baxt." (What is luck/fortune? What God gives you, that is baxt.)

baxtali   (adj) Fortunate. "T'as baxtali, te trais jekh shel bersh tire shjavensa, phralensa, phejensa . . . t'aven tuke sastipe aj zor!" (May you be fortunate and live a hundred years with your children, your brothers, your sisters. . . . May you have health and strength!)

bersh   (n) Year

beshel   (v) S/he sits; resides; serves time. "Vo beshelas and'o temnitsa desh bersh, muro dad" (He sat in prison for ten years, my father [did])

bezexali   (adj) Wrong, sinful

bibi   (n) Aunt

bikinel   (v) S/he sells

bori   (n) Bride, daughter-in-law: female in-law in virilocal or patrilocal household. "Kotka trail muri mami, lako shjavesa, lengi borjasa" (Over there lives my grandmother, with her son, and with their bori)

butji   (n) Job, task; kerel butji (v) S/he works

but   (adj/adv) Much, many, for a long time

chjachjipe   (n) Truth

chjachjes   (adv) Truthfully, truly. "Chjachjes, te merel muri semji!" ("Truly [I speak], may my whole family die [if I am lying]!"); chjachji. (adj) true

chjor   (n) Thief; chjoro (adj) Poor

dad   (n) Father

dej   (n) Mother

o Del   (n) [The] God; Devla God (vocative). "Yoj, Devla, naj ma(nde) lové!" (Oh Lord, I have no money!)

del   (v) S/he gives away. "De man(ge) tsivara" (Give me a cigarette); "Von dine les and'e vast" (They betrayed him, gave him up)

dikhel   (v) S/he looks. "Me chi dikhav khanchi!" (I don't see anything!) "Dikh!" (imperative) (Look!)

dili   (adj) Crazy, eccentric. "Te na shun sar vo vorbil, vo dilo si, but vorbil, a sa crazy [Eng.], dikhes?" (Don't listen to how he talks, he's crazy, very crazy, you see?); stupid

diljavol   (v) S/he gets confused, stupid; loses head over (strongly likes). "Dikh, le gazhje sa diljaven sar voj khelel!" (Look, the gazhe are all losing their heads for how she dances!)

dji   (n) Stomach, heart, soul

djili   (n) Song. "Chjalel tu(t) kadji djili? Man chjalel, but kamav Michael Jackson." (Do you like this song? I like it, I really love Michael Jackson.) [cf. Keld. *gili*]

e, o   (masc./fem. sing. def. art.); le, 'l, 'e. (pl. def. art.)

gazhji   (n) Non-Romani woman; gazhjo (n) non-Romani man; gazhje (n pl.) non-Roma

grast   (n) Horse

iskiril   (v) S/he writes

jakha   (n pl.) Eyes

jilo   (n) Heart, especially as emotional seat

kadale/-a, kado-ja   (adj, deictic) this; kakale/-a these

kadja   (n) Thus

kana   (adv) When

kaj/ka'   (adv) Where, to where; (pron, anaphoric) whom, which

kathe/katka   (adv) Here [cf. Keld. *katse, kache*].

kodo/-ja   (adj) that; kodole/-a those

kothe   (adv) There. [cf. Keld. *kotse, koche*]

kerel   (v) S/he does, makes; renders, offers. "Ker maj lokes o televizoro" (Turn down the television), "Kerav lenge pativ" (I offer them respect/hospitality)

kerdjuvel   (v, causative reflexive) S/he makes self into, turns into, feigns (kerdjol [past])

krechjuno   (n) Christmas. "Pal Krechjuno zhjas ka'l restaurano?" (Are we going to a restaurant for Christmas?)

krisi   (n) Council, legal forum, tribunal [cf. Keld. *kris*]

khanchi   (n) Nothing

kher   (n) House. "Kasko sas o maj angluno kher?" (Whose was the first house?)

laki/-o/-e   (3rd p. fem. sing. pos.) Hers

lashji   (adj) Good

lazhjal   (v) S/he shows shame. "Xa! Xa, na lazhjes-tu!" (Eat! eat, don't be ashamed!)

lel   (v) S/he takes begins. "Vo lel te phenel mange jekh vorba" (He started to tell me something)

lengi/-o/-e   (3rd p. pl. pos.) Their(s)

leski/-o/-e   (3rd p. masc. sing. pos.) His [cf. Keld. *lehki/-o/-e*]

lil   (n) Letter, paper, document, passport

lokes   (adv) Quietly, carefully

Lovara   (pl. n), Lovar (sing. masc. n); Lovarka (sing. fem. n); Lovari/
    -o/-e (adj)

lové   (n) Money

maj   (adv/adj) More

mangel   (v) S/he asks for, wants

magerdo   (part.) Polluted, outcast [cf. Keld. *maggrime, pekelime*]

mageripe   (n) Pollution [cf. Keld. *maggrimos, pekelimos*]

mami   (n) Grandmother

manush   (n) Male person (Romani or non-Romani)

mashkar   (adv) Between

me   (1st p. pronoun sing.) I

melali   (adj) Physically dirty, muddy (but not polluted)

merel   (v) S/he dies, (1st p.) Te merav; expression of sincerity: "Te
    merav, maj but chi kamav" (I swear, I don't want any more); expres-
    sion of strong liking/impression: "Merav anda lende!" (I just love
    them/They kill me!)

muli   (adj) Dead; e muli/o mulo (n) A dead woman/man, ghost

muri/-o/-e   (1st p. sing. pos.) My, mine [cf. Keld. *murri/-o/-e*]

nano   (n) Uncle

nashti(k)   (adv) Impossible; not allowed

patjiv   (n) Respect, hospitality; honor; virginity

Patradji   (n) Easter

pel   (v) S/he drinks; smokes

pomina/pomana   (n) Memorial gathering for the dead (*pomina* likely a
    calque on Russian pominka)

purani   (adj pred. of a thing) Old. "And' e phurani vremja" (in the olden
    time)

pushel   (v) S/he asks

pushka   (n) Gun. "Den pushka le gazhje jekh jekhesa—so amenge lengi
    putscha?" (The Gazhje are just shooting each other, what do we need
    their [1991] putsch for?)

phej   (n) Sister; cousin [cf. Keld. vera]

phral   (n) Brother; cousin [cf. Keld. vero]

phuri   (adj pred. of a person) Old; e phuri/o phuro (n) old woman/
    man

phuril   (v) Open; tell openly, all about. "Me phuriv tuke akana sa am[ar]e zakonurja" (I tell you now all our traditions)

phuv   (n) Earth, (home)land

phenel   (v) S/he tells

raj   (n) Authority, boss, master

rakli   (n) Non-Romani girl; rakljori. (dimin) little non-Romani girl; little Romani girl [cf. Keld. *rakljorri*]

Rom   (n) Romani man; husband; (pl.) Romani people, "Kana mashkar le Rom sam" (When we are among Roma) [cf. Keld. *Rrom, Rromanes,* etc.]

Romanes   (adv) Romani way, style

Romni   (n) Romani woman; wife

Romungri   (adj) Russka or Ukrainska Roma (if uttered within former USSR)

Ruso   (n) Russian man [cf. Rus. *Russkij;* cf. Keld. *Rrusso*]

Rusijaka   (n) Russian woman [cf. Keld. *Rrusajka*]

semji   (n) Family (cf. Rus. *semja*)

sovel   (v) S/he sleeps

suno   (n) Dream. "Dikhel o suno" (He sees a dream [he dreams])

shoxa   (adv) Never

shunel   (v) S/he listens

shjav/shjavo   (n) son; child

shjej   (n) Daughter

shjib   (n) Language; tongue

te   (particle) marks imperative, "Te na ker!" (Don't do that!); conditional, "Te kames, me zhjav tusa" (If you want, I'll go with you); subjunctive, "Vorbi maj zorales, te shunav" (Talk louder, so that I can hear); optative/hortative, "Te merav" (May I die [if . . .])

terni   (adj) Young, youthful; le terne, "youthful ones," newlyweds. "T'aven le terne baxtale!" (May the newlyweds be happy/fortunate!)

ternimata   (n) Youth (collective pl.). "Si, si and'l ternimata akana kaj zhjal gramotni" (Among the youth today there are those who are literate)

tiri/tji, tiro/tjo, tire/tje   (2nd p. sing. pos.) Yours

tradel   (v) S/he goes by conveyance; sends

trajo   (n) Life

tsera   (n) Tent

tu, tume (2nd p. pronouns, sing. and pl.)

tumari/-o/-e   (2nd p. pl. pos.) Yours

than   (n) Place; bed

them   (n) Country, land

thuli   (adj) Fat; e thuli/o thulo (n) fat woman/man

vov, voj, von   (3rd p. pronouns) He, she, they

vorba   (n) Word

vorbil   (v) S/he speaks; converses [cf. Keld. *del duma*]

xal   (v) S/he eats; xal-pes (reflexive), lit. "he eats himself," to argue, yell

xoxajmata   (n) Lies, fibs

xoxavel   (v) S/he lies; jokes

zakono   (n) Law, tradition

zhjal   (v) S/he goes by foot. "Zhja avri!" (Get out! = I don't believe you!)

zhjanel   (v) S/he knows

zhjuvli   (n) Woman (neutral as to Romani or Gazhjikani)

NOTES

Archives

GARF Gosudarstvennyj Arxiv Rossijskogo Federatsija (State Archive of the Russian Federation) (formerly TSGAOR — Central State Archive of the October Revolution)

TSGALI Tsentral'nyj Gosudarstvennyj Arxiv Literatury i Iskusstva (Central State Archive of Literature and the Arts)

RTSXIDNI Rossijskij Tsentr Xranenija i Izuchenija Dokumentov Nedavnej Istorii (Russian Center for Deposit and Study of Documents for Recent History (formerly the pre-1953 Party Archives)

Introduction

1 The 1966 novel (Kalinin 1991) betrays its non-Romani authorship in several places where it attempts to deploy Romani names and terms. For instance, one of the female characters is named Sheloro: the -*oro* diminutive suffix in Romani is masculine, -*ori* would be feminine.

2 In Russia, Gypsy beggars are in fact a minority among beggars in general (and a tiny minority among Gypsies), but because they are marked as ethnically different they are more visible.

3 In 1926 there were officially 61,299 people classified as Gypsies in the USSR, 40,943 of them in Russia (Barranikov 1931). In 1939 Goskomstat recorded 88,200 in the USSR; in 1959 132,014, with 72,000 in Russia. In 1970 there were 175,335 Gypsies in the USSR, 97,955 of them in Russia. In 1979 there were 209,157 in the USSR, 121,000 in Russia. In the last Soviet census of 1989 there were 262,015 counted in the USSR, 152,939 in Russia (Goskomstat, USSR). Unofficial counts double these figures, which seems reasonable, depending on whether census takers went by documents, self-ascription, or ascription by others (no Roma I knew wrote "tsygan" on their papers, but instead, "moldovan," "ukrainka," etc.).

4 Descriptions of World War II in terms of Jewish suffering was likewise muted. But many Jews left the region after the war and could voice memory by publishing accounts elsewhere, while most Romani survivors remained in Eastern Europe.

5 I also distinguish "Gypsiologists" from "Romologists." By the former I mean folklorists, scholars, or romantic hobbyists who focus on traveling groups who may or may not be Romani speakers. By Romologist, I mean someone who studies specifically Romani culture, language, or history.

6 I use the term "Transition" with caveats; it may be teleological (if not arrogant) to assume that changes occurring after 1989 and 1991 should have entailed a

247

particular transformation from one kind of society to another. However, the term "Transition" remains salient to post-Soviets who were using it.

7 The Soviet-Romani ethnographer Demeter (1988:6) strongly criticizes this tendency.

8 "Xeladytka" is both the feminine and the plural adjectival form in that dialect, "xeladytko" the masculine.

9 First suggested by Brockhaus in an 1844 letter to Pott cited in Hancock 1995:26. Brockhaus assumed the contemporary sense of *Dom* as "very low caste" to extend into the past, but Kenrick points to an earlier, more general sense: "person," or "man" (cited in Hancock 1995:19).

10 Other Persian records recount various captures of Indian prisoners in the ninth century. Arab writers mention migrations of Jats into Syria at that same time. These accounts may be connected to the Ljuli and Domari populations in Central Asia, but probably not to European Roma (see Hancock 1995a:20).

11 Hancock (1999:7) notes that military vocabulary in Romani is Indic, whereas metalworking and agricultural vocabularies are not. On Indic grammar in Romani, see Friedman 1991 and Hamp 1990.

12 See Marushiakova and Popov 1997. See also Hancock 1995b; Rishi 1976; and cf. Fraser 1992b.

13 See Guy (1998:28–29), who states that most Roma in Austro-Hungarian territories such as Slovakia had been settled since the fourteenth and fifteenth centuries. "In any case, most Roma appear to have been settled by the time of Maria Theresa, and the 1893 census showed less than 2 percent of Slovakia's 36,000 Roma to be in any way nomadic—and this at a time when nearly a quarter of all Slovaks were emigrating to the United States!"

14 Since Romani was classified as an Indo-Aryan language, Roma themselves were thought to represent descendants of the true Aryans. Himmler even suggested that a few "pure" Roma be kept alive in a compound for anthropological study. However, this suggestion was dismissed as "hare-brained" (Hancock 1996:47), and it was soon decided that all Roma were "mixed" in varying degrees (Kenrick and Puxon 1972:59). Still, Dr. Robert Ritter was funded by the German state from 1937 to 1944 to conduct genealogical and anthropological research on Roma and Jews (Müller-Hill 1988:57; Alt and Folts 1996:20; Tyrnauer 1989).

15 For these reasons I do not include genealogies. Only people I knew for several years drew kin diagrams for me; others were suspicious even of questions about kin. Tracing genealogies to a common point may well be how new Roma acquaintances place one another upon first meeting (*"Kaski san?"* "Whose are you?" or if said to a male, *"Kasko san?"*) —but one has to already know connections to be trusted with more.

16 See, for instance, Grant 1995.

17 Olga Demeter refers to herself and is known by this name, however. She published her autobiography as Demeter-Charskaja.

18 See, in fact, Stanislavskii's first chapters of *An Actor Prepares,* which gently

mock a fictional beginning actor's attempts to rehearse the part of "the Moor," Othello, by grimacing in the mirror and applying blackface (1983:1–30).

19 The affinal kin-term does not shift (i.e., from "bride" to "sister-in-law"), depending on speaker; different affines use *bori* to refer to a single person (my son's *bori* is also my *bori*), as with Russian nevestka.

20 For official versions translated into English on the Romani Theater's evacuation tour during the war, see Radzinsky 1945, and Bogomazov 1945.

21 Neither Lovara nor several other Romani groups in Russia practice bride-price, as do the Kelderara, but Lovara parents do prefer arranged marriage alliances. Thus, while Kelderara parents may sometimes pressure sons to elope to save on bride-price, this would not be the motivating logic in a Lovari elopement.

22 For accounts of American and British stereotypes of Gypsies in mass media, Ian Hancock 1987 and Silverman, in press.

23 1990s anthropology saw several calls for greater rigor in describing resistance: Abu-Lughod (1990) argues against "romanticizing resistance," Ortner (1995) pleads for more ethnographic subtlety in studies of power, and Humphrey (1994) calls for unraveling sharp divisions between the powerful and powerless. Gal (1995:412), critical of James Scott's (1990:29) assertion that the oppressed cover true feelings in order to survive, reminds us that the powerful also must pretend, restrain, and mask behavior and speech, *must perform,* to validate their power. On a more formal level, Hymes (1974) decades ago opposed Chomsky's separation of linguistic "performance" from "competence," which "reduces 'competence' to knowledge of grammar, 'performance' to behavior, and 'creativity' to novelty" (121), and which characterized performance as "largely an imperfect falling away" (131) from the ideal structures of grammar. According to Hymes, performance partakes of the familiar and the formulaic, not only of the subversive or "anti-structural" (see also Bauman 1977).

24 On linguistic shifts and shifters, see Jakobson 1957; Friedrich 1966; and Silverstein 1976.

25 On shifting frame and "footing," see Goffman 1974 and 1981. A "frame" is metacommunicative; that is, it tells participants what kind of interaction to expect (playful, serious, threatening, etc.). A "footing" is the attitude or position that a participant takes vis-à-vis other participants in the interaction, or to other aspects of the event.

26 Distinctions between code-switches and borrowings are slippery; some scholars focus on how participants identify the limits of codes, and others resist the distinction entirely (see Urciuoli 1995:528–530). Linguists' mappings and classifications of a code often differ from speakers'—they see syncretism and "purity" in different places.

27 Similar angst about "cultural loss" is noted throughout the ethnography of cultural nostalgia, invention, and revivalism (see Handler and Linnekin 1984; Herzfeld 1987; Clifford 1988; Lutz and Collins 1993; Ivy 1995; Myers 1994; Conklin 1997).

1 Pushkin, *The Gyspies,* and Russian Imperial Nostalgia

1 Original Russian: "*Potomu chto tam mnogo radosti. Tam vsegda veselje. Tam ochen' xorosho.*"

2 The "capacity of the Negro" to write literature was similarly denied. On ways that this denial relates to Herderian and Humboldtian links between race, nation, and language, see Appiah 1992:52.

3 See Bauman 1993 on disclaimers, and strategies by which speakers shift into and out of taking responsibility for narrative performance.

4 See, for instance, Sinjavskij's biting *Walks with Pushkin,* 1975.

5 Dostoevsky's "*Rech o Pushkine,*" delivered on 8 June 1880 in Moscow, was first printed in *Dnevnik Pisatelja,* August, 1880. In a printed preface to the speech, Dostoevsky made four points, the first being that "through the images of Aleko and Onegin, Pushkin shows the rift between the intelligentsia and the people, as well as its groundlessness, showing that the intelligentsia must unite with the people" (summarized in Grishin 1974).

6 Dostoevsky 1984. See also Mirsky 1958:270 for praise of Pushkin's alleged "pan-humanity, which is the gift of understanding all peoples and civilizations."

7 For an account of the choirs' effect on at least one foreign visitor, see Liszt 1926.

8 See, for instance, Lermontov's 1829 "The Gypsy Girl." Baratynskij published a similarly influenced poem of the same name (at first titled "The Concubine") in 1831. Rachmaninoff based his 1893 one-act operetta, *Aleko,* entirely on *Tsygany.*

9 See Rom-Lebedev 1990; Druts and Gessler 1985: passim; and the memoirs of Grigor'jev (1988) and Blok (1927).

10 Russians likewise have been painted as promiscuous by Western European observers (see Vowles 1993). On the construction of the "oriental" male as "hot-blooded southerner" with an "undifferentiated sex drive" see Said 1978:311–315.

11 Note the analogous 1990s Disney film liaisons between Pocahontas, Esmeralda, and various white male saviors (thanks to Ian Hancock for the connection).

12 See also Layton 1994 on the ambivalent romance of Russian poets for the Caucasus, and on the ways in which Russian poetry expressed a wish to become Chechen, to transform the self into a conquered people. See also Taussig 1993.

13 On Gypsy imitators and hobbyists in the United States, see Hancock 1976.

14 Tolstoy's representations of non-Russians differ from Pushkin's or Lermontov's. Though in their own way prone to orientalize, his accounts of, for example, the Caucasian rebels in *Hadji Murad* are more historically grounded. Tolstoy also had many more long-term social interactions with Roma than did other authors. His brother had several children with a Romani woman before the family allowed them to marry. (I thank Paul Friedrich for pointing out this contrast.)

15 Another exception is the film *Tsyganka Aza,* adapted from a work by the Ukrainian author Mixail Startits, in which a Romani man takes a Ukrainian woman—here, too, though, their union ends in tragedy.

16 See Pesmen 1998 on expansiveness as one of the tropes for the Russian soul.

17 On parallel images of northern "small peoples" in both tsarist and Soviet state-building mythology, see Slezkine 1994a.

18 Such characterizations of Gypsy musicality deny their creativity as musicians because they "borrow from" the musical traditions of others (see Tong 1995:33–56; and Silverman 1996a). But as any musician knows, *all* musical practice and creation involves such "borrowing."

19 On the Russian romantic, imaginary alignment with other imperial non-Russians in the Caucasus, Siberia, or Central Asia, against the West, see also Layton 1994.

20 Aristotle and his school formulated the dramatic ideal of the three unities, based mainly on Sophocles' tragedies. The unities dictate that time and space on stage should converge with actual time without breaks in duration. Unity of action includes unity of tone (not unlike Bakhtin's monologism [1984] or Voloshinov's auctorial context [1978]) and unity within the hero's consciousness; that is, the hero cannot contradict himself or his motives.

21 In Moldova, some Roma traveled but many were enserfed. During a three-week period in the summer of 1821, Pushkin was the guest of K. E. Ralli, a Romanian landowner. Ralli's son recalls in his memoirs that Ralli, on the way with Pushkin to visit his estate in Dolna, stopped at the settlement of his Romani serfs (Druts and Gessler 1990:172). Pushkin apparently visited several times and sketched those visits. But it is entirely unclear how he communicated with them, since he knew neither Moldovan nor Romani and the Roma had had no chance to learn Russian, Moldova having been ceded only recently. Shteinpress (1934:27) asserts that the Roma Pushkin encountered were in fact Romani house serfs, Lautari entertainers.

22 Mirsky (1958:93), for instance, writes, "The Gypsies of Bessarabia are not treated realistically, but merely as ideal representatives of a natural state of human society. The subject is the tragic inability of sophisticated and civilized urban man to throw away his convention-bred feelings and passions, especially the feeling of ownership of his mate. The poem is, on the face of it, a strong affirmation of freedom. . . . It is obviously and patently a plea for anarchism, and has been commented on in this sense by Dostoevsky (in his famous Pushkin Address)."

23 See, for instance, a fabricated account of wedding customs in the memoirs of Elizaveta Frantseva published in *Russkoje Obozrenije* (quoted in Druts and Gessler 1990: 173–178).

24 A cousin of Lev Tolstoy. One could add to Manush's list a range of scenes devoted to Gypsies or Gypsy choir performances from the great novels: Tolstoy's *War and Peace* and *Two Hussars;* and Dostoevskii's *Brothers Karamazov.*

25 From the 1980s until the mid 1990s, most press about Roma was written by ethnographers, not by journalists, or else at the very least press articles always contained authoritative interviews with the ethnographers.

26 A press interview a few years later with the ethnographer contains similarly worded statements: "In the area of culture there can be no conception of small or large nations—all are interwoven [*perepleteny*] into a common, world culture" (Demeter 1989).

27 Native ethnographers in the USSR—those who studied their "own" groups—had some role in fixing the categories and canons (see Balzer 1995). But Soviet institutes of ethnography were themselves already constructed along principles of segmentary nationality, and, wherever possible, native ethnographers were hired in the available slots—a Latvian ethnographer for Latvian peoples, and so on.

28 On such uses of Pushkin and the Russian classics in assimilation literature about other minorities, see Slezkine 1994a:357.

29 I gathered many of the texts while living in Russia. In addition, in 1995–96, I worked in Prague at the Open Media Research Institute, where clipping services delivered articles about Roma, and whose workers had maintained clippings on Roma for the previous decade, so I consider my press sample from 1991–96 fairly complete.

30 "Oj Romaly [*sic*], Oj Chavaly [*sic*] . . . ili Gavrilov-Jamskie Tsygane kak oni est'" (Oh, Roma, Oh, Romani Sons . . . or the Gavrilov-Jamskie Gypsies as They Really Are"), *Gubernskije Vesti,* May 14, 1996. The (mistransliterated) title deploys the few emblematic words in Romani known to most Soviets, locative forms of "Roma" and "Chjave."

31 Although some ethnographers served in state ministries on national and ethnic issues, or testified in court cases, others dropped out of public view as expert authorities. As throughout the Soviet period, they could not conduct autonomous fieldwork; they still shared expeditions and offices. Moreover, ethnographic fieldworkers were lower in status—often female and "native"—while ethnological theorists tended to be male.

32 "Tsygane shumnoju tolpoju" *Lipetskaja Gazeta,* February 10, 1996.

33 *Nezavisimaja Moldova* (Kishinev), April 2, 1996.

2 Roma, Race, and Post-Soviet Markets

1 As a foreigner, Walter Benjamin is another who describes Moscow street characters as flavored by their market activity (1986: passim).

2 On the opposition of byt to spiritual categories in Russian conceptions of the nation, see Boym 1994; and Pesmen 1998.

3 It has been contended widely that the Russian language has no word for "privacy." In fact, however, many Russian terms signify various senses of "private," for which English speakers use only one lexical item; one might thus argue that privacy was in fact important enough that Russian developed fine semantic distinctions to speak about it. Indeed, all places in Soviet Russia did not melt together into totalitarian space. The value of what Soviets distinguished as on-

tologically public or private — what actions and relations they coded as belonging to which sort of realm — is the crucial question. However, because ideals of individual property have been less salient to marking those realms than ideals of relational transcendence, non-Soviets overlook the local distinctions. On coding the "private" in socialist Hungary, see Gal 1996.

4 See also Gallagher 1986 on ways the bodies of female street peddlars in England were defined by and explicitly identified with the "dirt" of market milieu — and thus also indirectly with the "shameful," reasons they presumably left employment in bourgeois houses for the streets.

5 See also Stewart, in Hann 1993.

6 See Appadurai 1992 on the ways places and cultures come to stand for each other.

7 Though not necessarily. On how visual detail (in a text) can elide social pragmatics, see Crapanzano 1992.

8 On violence in Ukraine, see the report on Ukraine by the European Roma Rights Center (1997). In Russia, see press accounts by Pashkov (1991) and Mikeladze (1991) as well as commentary by Plotnikov (1991).

9 The Western press mistranslated the word glossed here as guestworker, *gastroljeri,* as "Gypsies." Although Roma, like other non-Russians, in practice were also subject to document checks, Mayor Luzhkov did not utter "tsygane." The translation appears to impose the Anglo sense of "Gypsy" as "Traveler." Still, the Russian press certainly reinforced any such connections visually in broadcast shots of guards and dogs searching Metro cars, the camera lingering on Romani beggars.

10 ORT, July 12, 1996.

11 On residence registrations, avoidance of registration, and the consequent inability to gain access to urban services (medical care, food rations, etc.), see Buckley 1995.

12 For studies of Soviet "nationality" and its terminologies, see Bennigsen and Wimbush 1979 and Conquest 1960.

13 Stuart Hall, for instance, perhaps emphasizing subjectivity more than had my interlocutor, remarks, "What this [cultural construction of race] brings into play is the recognition of the immense diversity and differentiation of the historical and cultural experiences of black subjects" (1992:254).

14 See Slezkine 1996 on the several sea changes the state went through over the validity of racialized criteria, from banning ethnography and condemning area studies scholars for "zoological nationalism" (851) to reasserting genealogy and racial analysis as valid methods to excavate the roots of ethnicities (*ethnogenesis*) and establish hierarchies based on national essences. See also Hirsch 1997 on the debates among experts responsible for devising and compiling the Soviet census over whether to include "physical type" as a criteria for constructing the category "nationality." The recurrence of these debates at high levels suggests that race was indeed a salient "commonsense" category.

15 For instance, Scherbakova (1984:35) cites V. I. Dal, who in 1898 describes a Gypsy caravan: "At first glance it seemed to be something incredibly gaudy and many-colored, although most of it was all disheveled; swarthy, black-complexioned drivers shouted at the horses and at each other somehow wildly, not with the words or voice of an ordinary driver." See also the article "Tsigane" in *Zhivopisnnyj Albom'* (1880:229): "[The Gypsy's] eyes are big and black, and shine one minute with wildness and fear, another with cleverness and cunning." On nineteenth-century references to dark skin and the description of the so-called racial degeneration of tsarist Russians who mingled with or married non-Russians in Siberia, see Sunderland 1996. On the popular imagery of non-Russians in the Empire, see Brooks 1984.

16 "Chjernyje" and "chjernozhopyje" were not applied to Africans, who were ascribed their own slurs, not rooted in local class structures of slavery as in the United States, but slurs nonetheless. Contrary to the experiences of African Americans who visited the USSR, such as William Anti-Taylor and Paul Robeson, many Russians disdained the African students who began studying in Moscow in the 1950s and 1960s. Several of my post-Soviet consultants remembered that African students were nicknamed *negativy* (a reference to photographic film reversal) and were singled out for other kinds of abuse.

17 On links between race, reproduction, and national ideologies of European prestige in colonial societies, and especially on the complex and always shifting criteria of racial boundaries and the ways these can align with state or commercial interest, see Stoler 1991.

18 See Simis 1982 for anecdotal accounts. For social thought on similar phenomena in other socialist states, see Verdery 1991; Sampson 1987; and Gabor 1979.

19 See especially Russian Federation legislation of January 29, 1992.

20 See Hessler 1996.

21 Hessler describes markets during the war years: "Constrained by the ability to pay for the expensive 'necessities' of the market, Soviet citizens experienced market 'freedoms' as a lack of control, lawlessness, and disorder" (1996:66).

22 See issues of *Den'* 1992 and 1993, for some of the more virulent public attacks on "blacks" and "speculators."

23 On nineteenth-century images of the trader, see Rieber 1982. For a contemporaneous critique of anti-Semitism in Russia and parts of Ukraine, see Leskov 1986. Written in 1884 in small pamphlet form for state officials, the critique argues for tolerance while nevertheless reproducing stereotype. Leskov had previously written viciously anti-Semitic stories and continued to publish caricatured, if mellowed, sketches of clever and mercenary Jewish characters (as in "Fish Soup without Fish," 1886) even after 1884.

24 For an account of similarly romanticized parallels in the Americas, especially on the idea of "blood memory," see Strong and Van Winkle 1996.

25 Elsewhere, on other "alienable" markings of race, see Cohn 1989 on images of clothing in colonial racial tropes, Gell 1996 on hair and the "Sikh" look. See also

Lutz and Collins 1993:92, 247 on clothing as marker of authentic identity or ostensible cultural deracination.

26 Several Russian consultants claimed to me that Gypsies summon the devil to help them make money in this way.

27 See also Druts and Gessler 1990:64–72.

28 See Rom-Lebedev 1990; Leskov's "The Enchanted Wanderer" (1961).

29 See Blok, "Faina," "Harps and Violins," "Karmen" (1907–1914, collected in 1927), the last based on his infatuation with a Russian singer who played the Gypsy in Bizet's opera, the two others on evenings in St. Petersburg nightclubs.

30 New tropes were opposed to those of earlier periods, when exchange was seen to be practiced by kin and circumscribed by familiar tradition; in contrast, the "formless, characterless nature of the money form became a recurring motif" (Agnew 1998:9; cf. Simmel 1991).

31 Cf. Herzfeld 1991 on the ways that Cretan villagers tried to outsmart Gypsy traders, offering "outrageously low prices just for fun" (167). For these Cretans, bargaining was "associated with cultural inferiority."

32 This term in Russian is not as derogatory as the English slur "nigger" or the patronizing "Negro," and has a different history of use.

33 Roma throughout Eastern Europe commonly interpret their social positions by comparing them with American race relations. In Czech Republic, I saw Roma carry placards of Martin Luther King in rallies against racism, and in Macedonia, where many Roma follow Islam, they identify with Muslim American blacks. Muslim Roma in Skopje, for instance, admire Mohammed Ali (Victor Friedman, personal communication).

34 For deconstructions of such imagery in Soviet literature and ethnography see the essays published in Diment and Slezkine 1993.

35 Humphrey (1993) describes post-Soviets who misrecognize Tadjik and other refugees at train stations and other public places, telling her that they were "Gypsies."

3 "What Is Your Nation?"

1 On tropes of penetration and secrets throughout ethnography, see Gable 1997.

2 Zsolt Csalog, a Hungarian writer and scholar (1992), blames German firms for raising the Romani unemployment rate in some areas of the country to 80 percent, the average rate in Hungary at that time being between 12 and 13 percent.

3 In Yugoslavia, Roma had "nationality" status since 1981, though separate republic governments often treated them as ethnic minorities (Fraser 1992a:281).

4 In 1989 there were officially 262,015 tsygane in the USSR, 152,939 of whom were in Russia (Goskomstat, USSR). By contrast the 1989 census counted only 102,938 Abxazians—who had their own autonomous republic, even though they were a minority within it.

5 See Hymes 1974:47: "Were the standard languages removed from above them, a

mapping of Europe's linguistic units would look much more like native North America."

6 For structural analyses of pollution in North America, see Sutherland 1997; and Miller 1968 and 1975. On Vlax pollution categories and social distinctions in Eastern Europe, see Stewart 1997. On how American Kelderash women use pollution rules in political and gender conflicts, see Silverman 1981; and Sutherland 1986.

7 Among the few who do contest Indic origins of Romani are Judith Okely (1983:27), who objects on the grounds that appealing to them to identify authentic Gypsies (here conceived to include English and Irish Travelers) is specious. She argues instead that Romani is not an Indic language but was merely a lingua franca along the Silk Road, and that numerous traveling groups began to be singled out as "foreign" at the fall of feudalism. However, just because *some* Traveler groups may not speak historically Indic languages, this fact does not mean that Romani is not Indic.

8 The name of this theology student was Ishtvan Valyi, and he passed his information on to formal linguists. For the first scholarly explication of Romani as Indic, see Rudiger 1790.

9 For early accounts tracing the paths of Romani to Europe, see Miklosich 1872–1880. See Turner 1927 for an argument tracing Romani to central India; Sampson 1968 for speculation that several dialects merged. See Pott 1844 on the link to Sanskrit. For studies comparing or connecting Romani and Sanskrit, see Paspati 1862; Pobozniak 1964; Friedman 1991; and Hamp 1990. Grellman argued in 1783 to link Romani to Hindustan (and Roma to the Shudra castes).

10 This was the message printed on anti-Roma leaflets in Belgrade in 1995 (Tanjung News Agency, September 23, 1995).

11 Here the author mistakenly overlays Russian grammar onto Romani, analyzing *sinte* as *s* (Russian particle "from") + *Indii* (Russian genitive for "India").

12 Acton and Gheorge (1995) remark that such Soviet-bloc categories derived from tsarist and Ottoman practices.

13 The term "narod" is defined quite vaguely. As Slezkine remarks (1994a), it could reference anything between "tribe" and "nation."

14 Nor do they always include groups traditionally considered Vlax into one head category: Olga Demeter-Charskaja, in her autobiography (1997), classes "various Gypsies" as "Russian, Ukrainian, Crimean, Hungarian and also Machvaja." "Hungarian" here includes Lovara and Kelderara (10).

15 On the relativity of naming among Roma and other Travelers throughout Europe, see also Liegeois 1994:62–64.

16 See also Appiah 1992:63: "In Zaire we find that a sweeping linguistic division (between Lingala and Swahili) is a product of recent history, an outcome of worker stratification imposed by the Belgian administration."

17 But see Guy 1998:41: "'Tribal' settlements in Slovakia . . . are far more ob-

viously the direct product of their historical situation than an age-old Romani tradition." See also Kaminski 1980.

18 In Vlax dialects spoken in Russia, certain mono- and disyllabic nouns (usually animate) have a plural with a zero marker (thus "Roma" = "Rom"). The brothers P. S. Demeter and R. S. Demeter note this form in their grammar of the Kelderari dialect in Russia (1990:291).

19 The word seems to bear this meaning only in dialects of this region. See Bartosz and Mroz 1988:20. Sergievskij and Barranikov's 1938 *Gypsy-Russian Dictionary* ("northern Russian" dialect) gives *xelado* for "soldier."

20 See Andronikova 1970 for a detailed description of Romani tent dwellings reconstructed from oral histories, as well as description of later home and apartment interiors. For earlier accounts, see Ranking 1911a, 1991b, and 1912–13.

21 Romologists debate whether all Wallachian Roma were enslaved or whether some were enserfed. Advertisements for sales of lots of Romani slaves (see Hancock 1987) would testify that many were being bought and sold apart from land. Soviet sources cite eye-witness accounts of such sales. Barranikov (1929) cites Palauzov's 1859 report on Wallachia and Moldova, where he remarks of Gypsies that "nowhere their condition is so pitiable as here, where slavery in all its shocking, immoral form weighs on 25,000 of these unfortunate souls" (223). German, in an article for the atheist journal *Bezbozhnik* (1922:11–13), cites an 1864 newspaper advertisement: "The sons and heirs of Serdar Nikolaj Niko of Budapest offer for sale 200 Gypsy families." There is also debate about the significance of emancipation in Wallachia and Moldova for triggering Vlax-Romani migrations, some arguing that the migrations had begun as a steady trickle earlier (cf. Acton 1993; and Fraser 1992c).

22 Ploxinskji claims that, even in 1765, the year Romani atamans in Ukraine were stripped of local authority and Roma were required to register with military regiments, "settled Gypsies were relatively numerous" (1890:99).

23 For an answer to such accusations from a Romani intellectual in Poland, see Mirga 1997.

24 On post–World War II restrictions on occupation and movement that created conflict among Roma, expressed in discourse of pollution, see Kaminskii (1980:299–304), who explains conflict exacerbated by the state, which set up a surveillance system creating "external leaders."

25 Some in India have claimed Roma for their own particular region. See Rishi 1976, 1980, and the journal *Roma,* especially on Indira Ghandi offering citizenship.

26 See Handler 1988. For an eloquent discussion of this dilemma, as pitched to the OSCE, see Acton and Gheorghe 1995. There are certainly examples of states that have justified themselves via ideologies about unifying "diverse" peoples, hierarchically ranked (see Segal 1995), as in Soviet multinationalism or in Hapsburg imperialism. In recent times this has not been the model for nationalism in Europe.

27 For comparison of such labeling policies across Europe and Eastern Europe, see Fraser 1992a:274–292.

28 For studies comparing or connecting Romani and Sanskrit, see Paspati 1862; Pobozniak 1964; Friedman 1991; Hamp 1990.

29 See also Grant 1995:53–54 on "artificial Indianizing," where non-Romani philologists padded Romani vocabularies with Indic words.

30 Many contemporary linguists concentrate instead on unraveling the actual and complex historical influences on Romani over the centuries. See, for instance, a recent collection of articles on Romani in contact with other languages (Matras 1995).

31 The equation of this lexicon with "the everyday" thus resembles the rhetoric of nation-building via journalistic and novelistic genres, with which "everyman" ostensibly identifies (Anderson 1983; for a critical reading of Anderson, see Silverstein 1994.

32 On Turkish lexical items and arguments for *not* eliminating them from a Romani standard, see Friedman 1990. For various views on the preferred lexical base for Romani standardization, see Friedman 1985; Cortiade 1990; Hancock 1993; Kochanowski 1995.

33 Cited in Hancock 1998a:117.

34 See Sampson 1968, for an etymology giving a Sanskrit root and Hindi examples.

35 Sources include accounts told by Roma in Europe. See "Hitler is, Sztalin is deportalta oket," in *Amaro Drom,* a Hungarian-language journal for Roma, 1991, no. 7. See also "Gypsies in New Russia," in *Moscow Tribune,* May 15, 1993.

36 Other socialist satellite countries, such as Hungary, Czechoslovakia, and Romania, followed suit with parliamentary acts and decrees settling Gypsies in 1958. Poland had such a statute in 1952, issuing another in 1964.

37 N. G. Demeter, quoted in a newspaper interview (*Nedelja,* September 4–10, 1989).

38 The largest Lovari immigration to Russia from Poland was in 1939, just before the war, some of these families being repatriated between 1956 and 1958 (Kaminskii 1987).

39 State Archive of the Russian Federation (GARF) f. 1235, op. 123, d. 27:3.

40 These songs were famous throughout Eastern Europe. Roma in the Czech Republic, for instance, could sing "Nane soxa" from Lotianu's 1976 film *Tabor Uxodit v Nebo.* A stage version of that film was produced in 1995 at the Slovak Romani Theater in Kosice. In Budapest that fall, at an international Romani festival, a group of Slovak Roma danced its choreography, while adolescent Russka performers visiting the festival remarked to me, "Russian Gypsies are the best."

41 See Hill 1985 on ambivalence about terms marked as borrowed from a dominant language and about code-switching that frames utterances as oriented to cultural hierarchy.

42   Demeter and Demeter 1981.

43   Stewart (1997:92) describes a similar performativity in crafting Romani/non-Romani identity: "Gypsy identity [w]as something that could be acquired and could therefore also be lost. It was not enough to be born to a Gypsy family—one had to continually reaffirm this identity by participating in activity together, by doing things in a similar manner." However, for Moscow Lovara, the issue was less that an individual's membership might be called into question than that certain vectors of affiliation could override some canonical divides.

44   For remarks on a roundup and resettlement of Vlax Roma camping "within 45 versts of Moscow" see Gerasimov, inspector for organizing Gypsy collectives, September 8, 1933, report to TSIK (Central Committee) in GARF f. 1235, op. 123, d. 28:161.

45   On patjiv and hospitality among Vlach-speaking Roma in America, see Miller 1994.

46   See Smirnova 1974, and especially the late Soviet "Economic Bases of Traditionalism," in Poljiakov 1992.

47   For the record, Kelderara do not like to spend the gold coins set aside for bride-price, and Lovara do not seem to understand this. Whether they have many such coins is hard to know—they displayed only one or two such tsarist coins at the weddings I attended, certainly not heaps and bags.

48   On the connections between kinds of cash and social categories and racial and national ideologies, see Lemon 1998.

49   See also Silverman 1988 for a discussion of how technological conveniences and popular culture have not "eradicated Romani culture in America, but have been co-opted in ways that allow Roma to maintain certain cultural forms and social ties more easily" (264).

50   Some Gypsiologists explain that the apron is meant as an extra layer of protection from pollution, worn only by married women over their skirts. However, when some Kelderari women had me don their clothes for a photograph, I saw that the bottom skirt did not wrap all the way to the front, to protect any material there. It did, however, make the skirt easier to put on without it going over your head, which would be polluting, without having to step through it, which could spoil the delicate fabric. It also makes the skirts easy to adjust for size, to go through pregnancy.

51   The *kaskad*: While tap-dancing rapidly, female dancers grasp the hem of a full skirt (at least three yards of material) and petticoat and flounce it so that the fabric rolls up and down in large waves.

52   On shame and the "civilizing process" see Elias 1978. Lewis (1987) outlines a progression in which leprosy is first a sign of pollution, then a sign of misfortune and shame, then one of sin and guilt. Opposing "shame" to "guilt," see also Dodds 1964 and Ricoeur 1967. American writing on Romani culture has emphasized ideas about "pollution" over those that Roma articulate about "shame."

This may be because most Roma in North America are Kalderash, but given that Kalderash in the United States connect their own discourses about pollution to broader cultural hierarchies differently than those in Russia do, this focus may have been part of a tendency to seek what is marked as most primitive.

4 The Gypsy Stage, Socialism, and Authenticity

1 Olga Demeter-Charskaya elaborates on this theme in her memoirs (1997:57): "The majority of Gypsies by nature can sing and dance. They all possess an excellent ear and sense of rhythm. But they do all this disregarding the rules of the stage. The music for dance has already started, but they start to dance whenever they feel like it. Or the music ends and they keep going. . . . Whenever we took a young Gypsy into our collective, we had to teach her the laws of the stage. It was about as tough as getting a bird into a cage."

2 A relative of Ilja Sokolov, director of Count Orlov's first Gypsy choir.

3 Gilliat-Smith (1922:58) corroborates this convention (simple black skirts and white blouses) in an account of a performance in Sofia by two Romani women, former choral singers, refugees from St. Petersburg.

4 Conducted by Vladislav Demeter, Marianna Seslavinskaja, and the author, February 1992.

5 See, for instance, the "village prose" of Rasputin and works by non-Russians such as Aitmatov in Kirgyzstan.

6 *Kinoglaz* 2 (1995), back page.

7 Interview with Petr Stepanovich Demeter, Romani composer, 1990.

8 At the same time, Romani political activists went to camps to report on any suspicious doings to the state. For instance, Gerasimov, a Russko Rom, inspector for the organization of Gypsy collectives, reported to TSIK (GARF, f. 1235, op. 123, d. 28, 1933:167–170) that there were "very many, not only Russian, but foreign Gypsies around Moscow," that these camps were "hiding White Guards" and were not all composed of "real Gypsies."

9 Still, nostalgia for socialist affirmative action grows more slowly among Roma in Russia than among those in Eastern Europe. In occupied parts of Eastern Europe during World War II, immense numbers of Roma were massacred, and after the war, when the region became socialist, most Roma were given jobs. In the USSR, the transition to socialism did not bring such striking contrasts for Roma.

10 GARF f. 1235, op. 123, d. 27:3. In contrast, during the 1990s in Hungary, schools were established where Roma and Beash Gypsies learned not "Gypsy" occupations, such as brick making, but computer skills.

11 See also Slezkine 1994a:135 on how professions were allocated by nationality in the far North. Russian polar bear hunters, for instance, were seen as anomalous, as either disturbing the environment or as exploiters.

12 On the relation of the "word of Lenin" to Soviet nationalities policy, see Lemon 1990.

13 This motive both resonated and contrasted with those behind plans to establish Nazi preservation camps for "pure Aryan Gypsies," briefly proposed only a few years later in Germany. And of course it resembled museum and "salvage ethnography" around the world (see Stocking 1983).

14 There had been tsarist attempts at assimilative agricultural schemes: in 1836, for instance, tsarist ministers established, in the newly acquired Moldovan territories, settlements named Faraonova (Pharoah's) and Kair (Cairo), names inspired by tales that Gypsies came from Egypt. See German (1930:29). See also Druts and Gessler 1990. For a summary of these sources in English, see Crowe 1995:151–74. Note also that similar policies were more broadly applied to Jews and others as well.

15 Several countries of Eastern Europe followed suit after World War II, though some soon switched to labeling them an "ethnic group" or even labeled Roma a "social category" (see Csalog 1992).

16 For accounts see Popova and Bril' 1932; Demeter and Cherenkov 1987; Druts and Gessler 1990. See also Lemon 1991; and Crowe 1995:174–194.

17 GARF, f. 1235, op. 15:140 [December 29, 1927].

18 See "Pervyj obrazets tsyganskoj pis'mennosti," in *Izvestija* 1926.

19 GARF, f. 1235 op. 123, d. 28:4 [1933].

20 These are catalogued in the Lenin Library in Moscow. German recorded them up to the year 1930 in his 1931 bibliography.

21 For retrospective commentary by a Romani intellectual, see Demeter 1989.

22 After 1937, nothing was published in Romani until a book of poems in the 1970s (Satkevich 1972); then came poems by Leksa Manush, collections of folktales and songs in the Russka dialect, many from films (Druts and Gessler 1988), a book of stories and proverbs in Vlax dialects (Demeter and Demeter 1981), a Kelderari-Russian dictionary (Demeter and Demeter 1990), and a lexicon combining Vlax and Russka, an attempt to create a new local standard (Maxotin 1993).

23 Depictions of this ideal have made their way into numerous performances, as in the film *The Gypsy Camp Takes to the Sky* (1976), when the heroine sings in Romani: *"Loli phabaj, me chinava—dopash tuke, dopash mange"* (I'll cut a red apple, half for you, half for me).

24 Druts and Gessler 1990:43.

25 See *Bednota* 1928:3. On the women of other Soviet nations as special targets of assimilation policy, see also Massell 1974; and Slezkine 1994a.

26 The Romani Theater modeled its first costumes on exaggeration of the colorful Kelderari skirt design, rather than the less exotic Russka attire, even though no Kelderara had yet performed there (Olga Demeter, personal communication 1992).

27 They took care to point out that the pronunciation differed from the Hungarian *Ishtvan*.

28 See interview published in *Exo Planety* with Nadezhda Demeter, Bernaskoni

1990:28. Her aunt, Olga Demeter, gives a different account: her father, fed up with avoiding families declared polluted, roused a group of men to make the rounds of the entire camp, polluting each and every family in turn, until "all the Gypsies were polluted, and everyone could be happy" (1997:19). Kalderash in Chicago likewise no longer discard fallen spoons and instead use strong combinations of bleach, soap, and hot water to salvage them. A difference is that in Chicago there was no official rhetoric or arena in which to claim that they had therefore "become civilized." Roma in Chicago thus do not ascribe to pollution rules that they practice the stigma that the Soviet state imposed upon such "patriarchal vestiges" scheduled for eradication.

29 For Soviet press reports, see, for instance, *Bednota* 1928 and 1929. For archival accounts, see GARF, f. 3316, passim.

30 GARF, f. 3316, op. 28, d. 794.

31 Muslim Xoroxane also suffered, especially because many had written "Tatar" as their "nationality" in their passports and were also resettled along with Chechens, Ingush, and other suspect nationalities after the war (Druts and Gessler 1991).

32 Russian Center for Deposit and Study of Documents for Recent History (RTSXIDNI), f. 17, op. 125, d. 570.

33 See Rom-Lebedev 1990; Druts and Gessler 1990; Rothstein 1980. See also Stites 1992 on waves of banning and coopting Gypsy music in the context of cultural politics affecting broader entertainment genres. For a contemporary argument against Tsyganshchina, see Shteinpress 1934.

34 Shteinpress (1934:33) remarks, "The corruption of the 'Gypsy artistic intelligentsia' by its Russian parasite-consumers is an indisputable fact. But the situation of Gypsy women differed little from that of their 'sisters in art' of other nationalities — say Russian or even French cafe-chanteuses."

35 Before the 1930s, some of the more famous and infamous have included Olga Vadina, the Poljakovy Gypsy Trio, and Tamara Tseretelli; in the 1990s, Tanja Filamonova, and the Trio Romen led by Valetina Panamonova.

36 On the distinction between "Gypsy" and "Romani music" as "true folk songs" in state taxonomies, and for contextualization of the ban of tsyganshchina within attacks on other musical styles, see Rothstein 1980:374.

37 TSGALI, f. 2928, op. 1, d. 473, *Doklad Novitskogo na proizvodstvennom soveshchanii rabotnikov Teatra*, 1934–35: p. 23.

38 Ibid., p. 28.

39 On the distinction between "great-power chauvinism" and oppressed-nation nationalism, and the need to encourage the latter under socialism, see Lenin 1965:41, 61–62, 113–114.

40 Born Nadezhda Kiseljova, Ljalja Chernaja had been a popular singer before the Revolution. Her mother was a "half-Russian, half-Gypsy" singer who was married briefly to a Count Golytsyn, himself the son of the senior Count Golytsyn and another Romani woman, Aleksandra Gladkova.

41 Tokmakov, born to Romani parents in the Urals, entered the party in 1918 and was responsible for organizing Gypsy collectives. In a biographical sketch of Tokmakov, Druts and Gessler write (1990:284–289) that he died a prisoner of the Nazis in 1942, having joined the Red Army because he was not able to bear seeing the Gypsy collectives in occupied territories destroyed.

42 GARF, f. 1235, op. 123, d. 28:4.

43 TSGALI, f. 2928 op. 1, d. 473, *Doklad Novitskogo na proizvodstvennom soveshchanii rabotnikov Teatra,* 1934–35: p. 24.

44 In contrast, the Yiddish theaters, first established in 1919 (there were twenty at their peak in the 1930s) performed in Yiddish until 1952, when the last one perished for lack of funding and various persecutions. The last Yiddish newspaper ceased publication in 1949. See Sandrow 1977. On the training of other non-Russian actors in Moscow, see the Ministry of Culture Anthology, *Vospitanije akterov v natsional'nyx studijax* (1979).

45 GARF, f. 1235, op. 123, d. 28:4. Protokol December 1933 Mosgorispolkom.

46 TSGALI, f. 2928 op. 1, d. 473, *Doklad Novitskogo na proizvodstvennom soveshchanii rabotnikov Teatra,* 1934–35: pp. 10–15.

47 On the perceived danger of "bourgeois ethnographers" and the attacks on ethnology, see Slezkine 1994a:246–264. On conflicts permeating academia in general, see Fitzpatrick 1978. Such criticisms are also more broadly familiar: On realism and "ethnographic authority," see Stocking 1983 and Clifford 1988.

48 TSGALI f. 2928, op. 1, d. 473, *Doklad Novitskogo na proizvodstvennom soveshchanii rabotnikov Teatra,* 1934–35: p. 23.

49 See also Robertson 1995 on imperial theater in Japan: "One aspect . . . that paralleled the colonial project was the process of locating and containing the gendered or ethnically marked other within, and thereby assimilating it—but sometimes purging parts of it" (973) and "enabling a broad spectrum of Japanese to think they were familiar with, knowledgeable about, and superior to manifold cultures" (974).

50 When Moscow was evacuated, the company could not return until 1943. Most remaining Romani performers fled to Tashkent on their own. On wartime concert tours, see Rom-Lebedev 1990; and Demeter-Charskaya 1997. On wartime and just postwar, see Radzinsky 1945 and 1947.

51 *"Ptichka bozhija ne znaet ni zaboty, ni truda, xlopotlivo ne svivaet, dolgovechnogo gnezda"* ("God's little bird knows no worries and no work, does not bustle to weave a sturdy nest," Pushkin 1956:40).

52 See also Bruner and Kirshenblatt-Gimblett 1994 on Maasai performers who collude with bosses and landlords to "mask modernity," to produce what the tourists expect.

53 On Bakhtin's interest in indeterminacy and free will in "open time," see Morson 1993.

54 Indeed, policy organized diasporic minority cultural institutions as if their needs and positions were analogous. For instance, many performers of the Romani

Theater recall that, during World War II, the Romani and Hebrew Theaters together always were evacuated last. Once stranded on the same barge, they endured sniping together from enemy planes. In the 1990s, some Roma expressed resentment that the Moscow Children's Gypsy Ensemble shared space with a Jewish group in the same House of Culture.

55 A film company, Romafilm, was established in 1994 by Roma from the theater.

56 The pair-part response to a greeting such as *"Sar san?"* or *"T' as baxtalo!"* or *"So Kerdjan?"* is often *"Shukar"* (great) or *"Mishtes"* (well), but *"So bikines?"* does occur as a greeting in an old Balkan Romani text (Friedman and Dankoff 1991).

57 Some Romologists in Russia assert that Kelderara have no indoor plumbing because of pollution taboos that ban a bathroom inside the house. However, Kalderash in Chicago all have bathrooms, and all Roma in Russia who could afford it had indoor plumbing — if they lived in a region where it could be installed.

58 This is parallel to pan-European film genres featuring Gypsies. The 1994 film *Latcho Drom* uses almost exclusively outdoor shots.

59 See also Nandy 1983 on ways of internalizing the discourses of the colonist.

5 The Hidden Nail

1 Ficowski also claimed (1982:168) that Roma do not remember the Holocaust, basing his conclusion on some amazing stretches of logic. The women still wear skirts, he remarks, assuming that if they truly remembered their suffering, they would try harder to assimilate. The women show "high fertility," which he considers unlikely in holocaust survivors. And the group he visits sing him "only two songs" recalling the camps.

2 All names in this chapter are pseudonyms.

3 September 8, 1993, report to TSIK and MOSO, GARF f. 1235, op. 123, d. 28:166.

4 See Martin 1996 on distrust of, and deportation and resettlement of, Soviet diasporic and border minorities in the 1930s and 1940s.

5 On constructivism and ethnic particularity, see Slezkine 1994b and Grant 1995.

6 See Slezkine 1992:61. Slezkine cites the 1928 chapter of the Criminal Code of the Russian Soviet Federative Socialist Republic (RSFSR), "Crimes that Constitute Survivals of Tribalism. "For versions of this logic in the 1960s, see Soia-Serko 1971, on a 1969 RSFSR Supreme Court resolution "On Judicial Practice in Cases of Crimes Comprising Vestiges of Local Customs." The article concentrates on the crimes of vendetta, polygamy, and marriage by abduction. On late 1920s assaults on tribal law and Islamic courts, see also Massell 1974:204–6.

7 "By a resolution of the Central People's Committee of the RSFSR of 10/27/1925, the All-Russian Gypsy Union was allotted 5,000 rubles. In 1925–26, the Gypsy Union spent around 4,000 rubles of that sum, mainly paid out as salary to the president and the secretary, but in the course of a year nothing was done to organize the Gypsy masses in Moscow" (GARF, f. 1235, op. 15:140 [December 29, 1927]). The investigation accused the union presidents of keeping

sloppy dues accounts, giving books away, and not keeping proper records of expenditures. But, as others have noted, simply throwing money at assimilation and "organization" rarely yielded results fast enough to satisfy the state. Briefly mentioned was a forged Gypsy union stamp, used by "tribal chiefs" to expedite requests from local authorities. However, such acts were hardly unusual ways of dealing with Soviet bureaucracy and would not have been particular to Roma.

8 GARF, f. 1235, op. 123, d. 27:1, "From the Procurator to the Central Committee," 1932.

9 Resolution of the Presidium of TSIK and SNK of the USSR of October 1, 1926, and the resolution of VTSIK of February 20, 1928, "On the distribution of land to Gypsies transferring to a working, settled way of life."

10 GARF, f. 1235, op. 123, d. 27(1). "From the Moscow Oblast' Procurator to the Department of the Nationalities, Presidium of the Soviet Central Committee, 1932."

11 Mirga (1993) reports similar policies later in Poland, where Roma were required to register their cooperatives, which trapped metal-working Roma into a cycle of low quotas and wages, the gray market, and criminal accusations.

12 GARF, f. 1235, op. 123, d. 27(1).

13 The work censured other practices, such as pollution rules, marriage practices, funeral and baptismal rites. Demeter argued that the Revolution had improved life by convincing Kelderara to drop most such customs, "although not without the maintenance of numerous negative survivals, which are still worth overcoming" (1988:20).

14 GARF, f. 1235, op. 123, d. 27(1).

15 The problem of actually drawing distinctions between Gypsy kulaks and Gypsy masses was certainly not peculiar to Roma (see Fitzpatrick, 1991).

16 On the persistence of stereotype in ethnography of Roma as illiterate, see Hancock (1988).

17 GARF, f. 1235, op. 123, d. 27(1).

18 GARF, f. 1235, op. 123, d. 27:206b.

19 GARF, f. 1235, op. 123, d. 27:211b.

20 On negotiating judge selection, Weyrauch and Bell (1993:355) cite Lee 1987 and Gropper 1975. My consultants insisted that judges never should be selected by the parties themselves, although both parties must agree to them. For an overview of the literature on Romani *krisi,* see Weyrauch and Bell 1993. For descriptions of Vlax-Romani *kris* procedures in other countries, see Yoors 1947; Lee 1987 and 1971; Sutherland 1986; and Gropper 1975.

21 Many authors describe long-term *magerdo* (pollution) sentences as social death. Weyrauch and Bell (1993:359) cite Clebert 1967:124–25 and Sutherland 1986: 98–99.

22 For a comparative survey of sources on Romani law, a description of it as "private law" within a model of conflict between state and private law, see Weyrauch and Bell 1993.

23 GARF, f. 1235, op. 23, d.27(1):211b.

24 Ibid., 204.

25 Ibid., 202–203b.

26 As Herzfeld remarks, "On Crete, I was often told that the role of co-godparent was closer, if not holier than that of a brother. Such reallocations of affect away from the state-as-family and the family-as-foundation allow considerable flexibility in negotiating personal and household relationships with the state itself" (1992:77).

27 The same anecdote appears in a contemporaneous article published about Roma by the Romani intellectual and writer Aleksandr German in *Bezbozhnik (The Godless)* in 1922.

28 Daranes was familiar with Barranikov and relies on him for authority: "For the baptism of the Ukrainian and South Russian nomad Gypsy children Barranikov gives the same sordid reason, but says that this motive does not play any part among the settled Gypsies" (1936: 205).

29 See Fraser 1992:60–78. Accusations of mercenary religiosity were not peculiar to Gypsies in Russia; see Slezkine 1994a:11–45 for such depictions of Arctic northerners.

30 Such implications are usually erased; for instance, Kusturica's film, *Time of the Gypsies,* set in Shutko Orizari near Skopje, gives not a hint of Islam in what is a predominantly Islamic Romani community.

31 The requested name stuck as a nickname. Sutherland (1994) writes that Vlax Roma have multiple names because of cultural expectations in tightly knit extended families; sharing lives, they share multiple American names. However, in Soviet Russia, Vlax Roma needed permanent internal passports for all important benefits transactions, and these passports were not so easily changed as American drivers' licenses or other IDs. Moreover, the practice of name changing is not unique to Gypsies; Slezkine (1994a:21) notes that tsarist servitors complained that tribute-paying northerners "change their names at the time of payment almost every year." And elsewhere, in the Czech Republic, for instance, foreign residents must use Czechified names on all documents issued by the state, on postal addresses, and so on.

32 The sixteenth-century church in fact recommended equivocation as a strategy in the face of repressive force. The church still does not regard "mental reservations" as sin, and catechisms give examples of acceptable social lies.

33 Under the tsars, peasants would get drunk at Easter and stage pogroms, justifying them with the belief that Jews consumed blood at Passover. (I thank Victor Friedman for this observation.)

34 On reading accounts left by state agents who themselves had limited knowledge of a "fragmented social reality," and on the impulse to "fill in incoherencies," see Stoler 1992:131.

35 In most Romani dialects *pomana*. I report a local variant perhaps influenced by Russian *pominka*.

36 Roma, like Jews, were assigned certain kinds of surnames by some states, and one had to pay to receive a higher status or better-sounding name.

37 Vlax Roma in Romania recall similar confiscations, as well as deportations (*The Independent*, March 7, 1990).

38 Compare to versions in Kenrick and Puxon 1972; Groome 1899.

39 Some versions give four nails.

40 See, for instance, Groome 1899.

41 The problem of the subaltern voice is a grave methodological issue for historians, but a methodological problem need not be extended to assumptions that "marginals" have not the capability to understand or communicate the structural constraints in which they find themselves. The question is how far they have access to amplifying infrastructures, such as media.

42 The kris is virtually ignored by the U.S. state, perhaps because Roma are much less visible in North American cities than they are in Central and Eastern Europe and in Russia.

43 Weyrauch and Bell (1993:356–357) also cite a variety of descriptions of the power of the oath at Krisi and the convention of swearing before icons and to the dead from Clebert 1967:130–31; Yoors 1947:177–179; Gropper 1975:83; and Lee 1987:28–29.

44 See Smart 1993: "[T]he state can define as bribes exchanges that the participants see as supporting a relationship rather than as inducements to anything improper."

6 "Roma" and "Gazhje": Shifting Terms

1 As evidence, she depicts Cale as always cadging favors from each other, as if therefore begging from non-Cale were an extension of an internal "culture." Mass media accounts of Gypsy begging as a form of artful resistance, fantastical stories about Gypsy beggar criminal clans (Emil Kustarica's *Time of the Gypsies,* 1989) are common. Such tales discount late-twentieth-century events that have driven Roma refugees from Romania and former Yugoslavia to Western capitals.

2 This is not to say that structuralism itself circulated in that direction. Quite the opposite: Jakobson, a founder of the Prague school whose lectures influenced Lévi-Strauss, was a Muscovite.

3 Wolff (1998) notes that Fortis, an eighteenth-century ethnographer of Dalmatia who ranked peoples culturally according to their treatment of women, singled out this very discursive practice: "[Even] the most civilized Morlacco, having to mention his wife, always says, '*Da, prostite, moja zhena*'" ("Yes, excuse me, my wife . . .").

4 Stewart (1997:52) states that "in part male bias is rooted in Romani language itself." Stewart would be right to stress that local language *use* (e.g., men called "brother" and women called "daughter") *can* reflect or perform social hierarchies (egalitarianism amongst men, male superiority to women). However,

the key lies not in semantics or grammar but in discursive practice and its inter-sections with other gendered ideologies and practice. Stewart argues that among Vlax Roma in Hungary, gazhje outsiders are both polluting and authoritative. Thus, given that a tradition of virilocality renders wives conceptual outsiders, wives are likened to gazhje, are polluting. Romani identity is thus based on the more hermetic category "brotherhood," and since sisters cannot be wives (and visa versa), women are thus excluded from Romanipe (Romaniness, Romani social world). However, in Moscow, while Romani intellectuals voiced male-defined notions of identity, not all my Romani consultants did so. Further, virilocality was not universal, and multiple kin ties entailed that wives *could* be seen also as insiders. Finally, names and images of female kin *were* often deployed to metonymically represent community: the words for "brotherhood" were not the only gendered ways to describe Romaniness, ideal or experienced.

5 Indeed, in Vlax-Romani dialects, grammar distinguishes post-Greek borrowings from earlier layers of vocabulary by phonological and morphological means; for example, post-Greek borrowings into Romani do not have final stress. On the morphological level, post-Greek nouns have separate plurals (Romanian plural suffixes *-urjal-ura* rather than Indic *-a/-i*) and there are separate conjugational parallels. But other Romani dialects do not have this system — and languages such as Russian also distinguish some later borrowings in similar ways.

6 See various Radio Free Europe/Radio Liberty (RFERL) and Open Media Research Institute (OMRI) reports through the 1990s.

7 Fascination with foreign things was not limited to commodities from the West; Indian films were also popular in Soviet Russian, and these had a dual attraction for Roma — in addition to being images of opulence from "abroad," they were a reminder of Indian origins.

8 On similar transpositions of forms that would, from some vantages, seem con-formist, compare Abu-Lughod 1990:50: "These Egyptian songs and stories . . . are oppositional within the young Bedouins' strategies of resistance to their elders, but unlike the old forms of Bedouin poetry or even folktale, they are not oppositional discourses within their original social context."

9 Both take on James Scott's theory that the "hidden transcripts" of the weak are opposed to "public transcripts," which are known to the weak but are controlled by the powerful (1990:15). Humphrey (1994) points out that clear distinctions between weak and powerful were not visible in Mongolia, where there were few racial markers of power, and social networks intersected at all levels of authority. In state-socialist countries, the line between "us" and "them" was not always so clear.

10 Generally these women have low-paying regular jobs or none at all, and Lovara give them supplemental income and occasional meals. Kelderara in Russia, by contrast, generally do not have maids (although Kelderash in America may).

11 This was the only Romani family I knew, from Chicago to the Urals, who traveled such a long distance.

12 This practice of screening windows and doors marked Lovari houses from those of their Russian neighbors, who kept windows closed, save for a tiny casement or transom, to avoid a dangerous draft *(skvoznjak)*. The casement, however, still allowed mosquitoes to flit inside. Lovara also made gauze cones to keep flies off food, a technique other Soviets seemed not to know or deploy.

13 Victor Friedman reports that this is also a preferred arrangement in the Balkans (personal communication).

14 Compare to Hanks 1990:105–106.

15 Much as can a jibing "Look at that chick!" or similar in English, or *"Smotri!"* in Russian.

16 A text of this song appears in Demeter and Demeter 1981.

17 See Tong 1983. On ideologies that hierarchize languages and on linguistic divisions of labor, see Hill 1993; and Irvine 1989.

18 On mock usages of language as an expression of racism, see Hill 1993.

19 It also entered Hungarian slang (Miklós Vörös, personal communication). To this Russian the word "lové" was metonymic of all Gypsies, and in knowing it, he seemed to assume that he knew everything else about who and what they were.

20 Note that "zakon" is a Slavic loan word.

21 On similar reversals in North America and in Europe, see Silverman 1988 and Salo 1977.

22 Lovara disdain Russians for what they see as *misplaced* hyperpropriety as well: while Russian women are too brazen about how they move past men, they are too timid in how they speak. And, for instance, they display their legs but seem overly modest about their breasts.

23 That is, "Our drinks taste bitter, sweeten them!" Russian newlyweds then must kiss on demand while the guests count — some Russians explain that each second wards off a year of bitterness. Others say it is a reversal, so as not to jinx *(sglazit')* the couple by crying "Sweet!" (as a kiss should be).

24 Stewart (1997) makes a compelling case for such an argument.

25 Silverstein (1993) illuminates how real-time social hierarchies emerge when interlocutors calibrate relative spatial and temporal deictics ("here," "there," "then") to cultural and social hierarchies (the ranking of "this school," to "that" or of "education back then" to "now").

26 Paul Friedrich (1986:81), writing about the connection between the dreamer's imagination and culture, concludes that many "dreams . . . are fundamentally political. They are *about* ethnic and racial conflicts, war, the vendetta, threats of fascism and so forth. These and similar types of conflict may be contextualized in the here-and-now of a neighborhood, party, even a family."

27 For a juxtaposition of different modes of dream interpretation, see Mannheim 1991: "From my perspective as an ethnographer, the narrative reflects deeply rooted anxieties about non-Quechaus. . . . But the dreamer herself interpreted the dream indexically, as an augury . . . [and] most of the narrative was discarded for a single detail" (50–51).

28 See Mannheim, who acknowledges that his own interpretation as ethnographer necessarily "treats the dream narrative intertextually" and that while useful for translation, is likely to be "irrelevant to interpretation of isolated images as omens for the day" (1991:49).

29 Paul Gilroy remarks that critics of Richard Wright's later works, which did not address experiences of American slavery, "dismiss Wright's entitlement to hold a view on modernity at all" and maintain "a view of Wright in Paris as a remote and deracinated author" (1993:156).

BIBLIOGRAPHY

Abu-Lughod, Lila. 1990. "The Romance of Resistance: Tracing Transformations of Power through Bedouin Women." *American Ethnologist* 17, no. 1:41–55.

Acton, Thomas. 1974. *Gypsy Politics and Social Change: The Development of Ethnic Ideology and Pressure Politics among British Gypsies from Victorian Reformism to Romany Nationalism.* London: Routledge and Kegan Paul.

———. 1979. "Academic Success and Political Failure." *Ethnic and Racial Studies* 2, no. 2:231–241.

———. 1993. "Rom Migrations and the End of Slavery: A Rejoinder to Fraser." *Journal of the Gypsy Lore Society (JGLS)* ser. 5, vol. 3 (August): 77–89.

———. 1997–98. "Mediterranean Religions and Romani People." *Journal of Mediterranean Studies* (University of Malta) 7, no. 1 (1997–98):37–51.

Acton, Thomas, and Nicolae Gheorghe. 1995. "Dealing with Multiculturality: Minority, Ethnic, National and Human Rights." *OSCE/ODHIR Bulletin* 3, no. 1:28–45.

Agnew, Jean-Cristophe. 1998 [86]. *Worlds Apart: The Market and the Theater in Anglo-American Thought, 1550–1750.* Cambridge: Cambridge University Press.

Alt, Betty, and Silvia Folts. 1996. *Weeping Violins: The Gypsy Tragedy in Europe.* Kirksville, Mo.: Thomas Jefferson University Press.

"A Gypsy Concert in Moscow." 1864. *All the Year Round* (London) 11:56–161.

Anderson, Benedict. 1983. *Imagined Communities: Reflections on the Origin and Spread of Nationalism.* London: Verso.

Andrew, Joe. 1990. "'I Die Loving': Narrative, Desire and Gender in Pushkin's *The Gypsies.*" In *Semantic Analysis of Literary Texts,* ed. Eric de Haard, Thomas Langerak, and William G. Weststeijn, 13–23.

Andronikova, I. M. 1970. "Evoljutsija zhilishcha russkix tsygan" ("The Evolution of the Dwellings of Russian Gypsies"). *Sovjetskaja Etnografija* 4:31–45.

Appadurai, Arjun. 1992. "Putting Hierarchy in Its Place." In *Rereading Cultural Anthropology,* ed. George E. Marcus, 34–47. Durham, N.C.: Duke University Press.

Appiah, Anthony. 1992. *In My Father's House: Africa in the Philosophy of Culture.* New York: Oxford University Press.

Austin, John L. 1975 [1962]. *How to Do Things with Words.* New York: Oxford University Press.

Bakhtin, M. M. 1984. *Problems of Dostoevsky's Poetics.* Ed. and transl. Caryl Emerson. Minneapolis: University of Minnesota Press.

———. 1986. *Speech Genres and Other Late Essays.* Trans. Vern McGee. Austin: University of Texas Press.

———. 1994 [1981]. *The Dialogic Imagination: Four Essays.* Austin: University of Texas Press.

Balzer, Marjorie, ed. 1995. *Culture Incarnate: Native Anthropology from Russia*. Armonk, N.Y.: M. E. Sharpe.

Barany, Zoltan. 1994. "Living on the Edge: The East European Roma in Postcommunist Politics and Societies." *Slavic Review* 53:321–344.

Barinov, Mark. 1967. "How Real Are Those Gypsies?" *Sputnik*, no. 6.

Barranikov, Aleksej Petrovich. 1928. "On the Term 'The Gypsies of Russia.'" *Comptes Rendus de l'Académie des Sciences del 'URSS* 10:211–217.

———. 1929. "Ob izuchenii tsygan SSSR" ("On the Study of Gypsies in the USSR"). *Izvestija Akademii Nauk SSSR*, Leningrad, 7 ser., otdel gumanitarnykh nauk, no. 5:369–398/no. 6:457–478.

———. 1931a. *Tsygane SSSR (Gypsies of the USSR)*. Moscow: Tsentrizdat.

———. 1931b. "W. I. Philonenko: 'The Crimean Gypsies,'" *JGLS*, 3d ser. 10, no. 2:144–46.

———. 1932. "On the Russian Gypsy Singers of Today." *JGLS*, 3d ser. 11, nos. 3–4:187–192.

———. 1934. *The Ukrainian and South Russian Gypsy Dialects*. Leningrad: Akademija Nauk.

Barth, Fredrik. 1969. "Introduction." In *Ethnic Groups and Boundaries: The Social Organization of Cultural Difference*, ed. Fredrik Barth, 9–38. London: George Allen and Unwin.

Bartosz, Adam, and Lech Mroz. 1988. "Roma in Poland." *Roma*, no. 29:19–27.

Basso, Keith. 1979. *Portraits of the White Man*. London: Cambridge University Press.

Bateson, Gregory. 1972. "A Theory of Play and Fantasy." In *Steps to an Ecology of Mind*, 177–193. New York: Ballantine.

Bauman, Richard. 1977. *Verbal Art as Performance*. Prospect Heights, Ill.: :Waveland Press.

———. 1993. "Disclaimers of Performance." In *Responsibility and Evidence in Oral Discourse*, ed. Jane Hill and Judith Irvine, 182–196. Cambridge: Cambridge University Press.

Bauman R., and Charles Briggs. 1990. "Poetics and Performance as Critical Perspectives on Language and Social Life." *Annual Review of Anthropology* 19:59–88.

Bednota. 1928a. "Nadelenije zemlej tsygan, perexodjashchije k trudovoj zhizni" ("Distribution of Land to Gypsies Shifting to a Working Life"). July 13.

———. 1928b. "Obo vsem" ("About Everything"). July 17.

———. 1929. "Tsyganskije kolxozy" ("Gypsy Collective Farms"). July 18.

Benjamin, Walter. 1986 [1926]. *Moscow Diary*. Ed. Gary Smith, trans. Richard Sieburth. Cambridge, Mass.: Harvard University Press.

Bennigsen, Alexandre A., and S. Ender Wimbush. 1979. *Muslim National Communism in the Soviet Union: A Revolutionary Strategy for the Colonial World*. Chicago: University of Chicago Press.

Bernaskoni, Elena. 1990. "Narod vetra i ognja" ("People of Wind and Flame"). *Exo Planety*, no. 7:26–34.

Blok, Aleksandr. 1928. *Dnevniki (1917–21) (Diary)*. Ed. Pavel N. Medvedev. Leningrad: Izdatel'stvo pisatelej.

Boas, Franz. 1966 [1896]. "The Limitations of the Comparative Method of Anthropology." In *Race, Language and Culture*, 270–280. New York: Free Press.

Bobri, V. 1961. "Gypsies and the Gypsy Choruses of Old Russia." *JGLS*, 3d ser. 40, nos. 3–4:112–120.

Bogartyrev, Oleg. 1996. "Ne xodi s tolpoj tsyganok za kibitkoj kochevoj" ("Don't Walk Off with a Crowd of Gypsy Women behind Their Nomadic Tent"). *Moja Gazeta* (Samara), February 24–January 3, 3.

Bogomazov, Sergej. 1945. "Moscow Gypsy Artists in Wartime." *JGLS*, 3d ser. 24, nos. 1–2:60–61.

Boretsky, Norbert. 1994. *Grammatik des Kalderash mit Texten und Glossar*. Osteuropa Institut and Freien Universität Berlin. Balkanologische Veroffentlichungen. Wiesbaden: Harrassowitz.

Bourdieu, P. 1984. *Distinction: A Social Critique of the Judgement of Taste*. Trans. Richard Nice. Cambridge, Mass.: Harvard University Press.

———. 1986. "The Forms of Capital." In *Handbook of Theory and Research for the Sociology of Education*. New York: Greenwood Press.

Boym, Svetlana. 1994. *Common Places: Mythologies of Everyday Life in Russia*. Cambridge, Mass.: Harvard University Press.

Brah, Avtar. 1992. "Difference, Diversity and Differentiation." In *"Race": Culture and Difference*, ed. James Donald and Ali Rattansi, 126–145. London: Sage Publications.

Braham, Mark. 1993. *The Untouchables: A Survey of the Roma People of Central and Eastern Europe*. Report of the Office of United Nations High Commissioner for Refugees. New York: U.N. High Commissioner for Refugees.

Briggs, Charles L. 1984. "Learning How to Ask: Native Metacommunicative Competence and the Incompetence of Fieldworkers." *Language in Society* 13:1–28.

———. 1988. *Competence and Performance: The Creativity of Tradition in Mexicano Verbal Art*. Philadelphia: University of Pennsylvania Press.

Brooks, Jeffrey. 1984. *When Russia Learned to Read: Literacy and Popular Culture, 1861–1917*. Princeton, N.J.: Princeton University Press.

Bruner, Edward, and Barbara Kirshenblatt-Gimblett. 1994. "Maasai on the Lawn: Tourist Realism in East Africa." *Cultural Anthropology* 9, no. 4:435–471.

Buckley, Cynthia. 1995. "The Myth of Managed Migration: Migration Control and Market in the Soviet Period." *Slavic Review* 54, no. 4:896–916.

Butler, Judith. 1990. *Gender Trouble: Feminism and the Subversion of Identity*. New York: Routledge.

———. 1998. *Excitable Speech: A Politics of the Performative*. New York: Routledge.

Cameron, Deborah. 1990. "Demythologizing Sociolinguistics: Why Language Does Not Reflect Society." In *Ideologies of Language*, ed. John E. Joseph and Talbot J. Taylor. London: Routledge.

Cheboksarov, N. N. 1967. "Problems of the Typology of Ethnic Units in the Works of Soviet Scholars." *Sovetskaja Etnografija*, no. 4:94–109.

Cherenkov, Lev Nikoleavich. 1987. "Tsyganskaja Literatura." In *Literaturnij entsiklopedicheskij slovar'*, ed. Vadim M. Kozhevnikov and Petr A. Nikolaev. Moscow: Sovjetskaja Entsiklopedija.

Chinyaeva, Elena. 1997. "Hostages of Their Own Music." *Transitions* 4, no. 4:38–41.

Clebert, Jean-Paul. 1967. *The Gypsies*. Trans. Charles Duff. Harmondsworth, England: Penguin Books.

Clark, Katrin. 1995. *Petersburg: Crucible of the Cultural Revolution*. Cambridge, Mass.: Harvard University Press.

Clifford, James. 1988. *The Predicament of Culture: Twentieth-Century Ethnography, Literature, and Art*. Cambridge, Mass.: Harvard University Press.

——. 1994. "Diasporas." *Cultural Anthropology* 9, no. 3:302–338.

Cohn, Werner. 1973. *The Gypsies*. Reading, Mass.: Addison-Wesley.

Cohn, Bernard. 1989. "Clothes, Clothing and Colonialism." In *Cloth and Human Experience*, ed. A. B. Weiner and J. Schneider. Washington, D.C.: Smithsonian Institution.

Comaroff, John. 1987. "Totemism and Ethnicity." *Ethnos* 52, nos. 3–4:301–323.

Condee, Nancy. 1995. "The ABC of Russian Consumer Culture." In *Soviet Hieroglyphics: Visual Culture in Late Twentieth Century Russia*, ed. Nancy Condee, 130–172. Bloomington: Indiana University Press.

Conklin, Beth. 1997. "Body Paint, Feathers and VCRs: Aesthetics and Authenticity in Amazonian Activism." *American Ethnologist* 24, no. 4:711–737.

Connerton, Paul. 1988. *How Societies Remember*. Cambridge: Cambridge University Press.

Conquest, Robert. 1960. *The Soviet Deportations of Nationalities*. London: Macmillan.

Cortiade, Marcel. 1990. "Romani and Gadzhikani: Where Is the Boundary?: A Typological Approach to the Lexical Intercourse between a Minor Tongue and the Surrounding Linguistic Milieu." In *100 Years of Gypsy Studies*, ed. Matt Salo. Publication no. 5. Cheverly, Md.: Gypsy Lore Society.

Cotten, Rena. 1954. "Gypsy Folktales." *Journal of American Folklore* 67:261–266.

Crapanzano, Vincent. 1992. *Hermes' Dilemma and Hamlet's Desire: On the Epistemology of Interpretation*. Cambridge, Mass.: Harvard University Press.

Crowe, David. 1995. *A History of the Gypsies of Eastern Europe and Russia*. New York: St. Martin's Press.

Crowe, David, and John Kolsti, eds. 1991. *The Gypsies of Eastern Europe*. Armonk, N.Y.: M. E. Sharpe.

Crowley, Tony. 1989. "Bakhtin and the History of Language." In *Bakhtin and Cultural Theory*, 68–90. Manchester, England: Manchester University Press.

Csalog, Zsolt. 1992. "'We Offer Our Love': Gypsies in Hungary." *New Hungarian Quarterly* 33, no. 127:70–80.

Daniel, E. Valentine, and John C. Knudsen, eds. 1995. *Mistrusting Refugees*. Berkeley: University of California Press.

Daranes. 1936. "Baptismal Benefits." *JGLS*, 3d ser. 13, no. 4:200–221.

De Certeau, Michel. 1984. *The Practice of Everyday Life.* Trans. Stephan Rendall. Berkeley: University of California Press.

Deleuze, Gilles, and Felix Guatarri. 1987. *A Thousand Plateaus: Capitalism and Schizophrenia.* Minneapolis: University of Minnesota Press.

Demeter, Nadezhda Georgjevna. 1977. "Nekotoryje cherty semejnogo byta tysgan kelderari, konets XIX–XX vv. ("A Few Features of Family Daily Life of Kelderari Gypsies, from the End of the 19th to the Beginning of the 20th Century"), *Polevyje issledovanija.*

———. 1988. *"Semejnaja obrjadnost' tsygan kelderari, konets XIX–XX vv."* ("Family Rituals of the Kelderari Gypsies, from the End of the 19th to the Beginning of the 20th Century"). Precis to Candidate Dissertation, Institute of Ethnography, USSR Acadamy of Sciences.

———. 1989. "Tygane." *Nedelja,* September 4–10:12.

Demeter, Nadezhda, and Georgi Demeter. 1985. "Prirody bednyje syny"? ("Nature's Poor Sons"?). *Pravda,* July 15.

Demeter, N., and Lev Nikolaevich Cherenkov. 1987. "Tsygane v Moskve" ("Gypsies in Moscow"). In *Etnicheskyje gruppy v gorodax evropejskoj chasti SSSR (Ethnic Groups in the Cities of the European Part of the USSR).* Moscow: USSR Academy of Sciences, 40–49.

Demeter R. S., and P. S. Demeter. 1981. *Obraztsy fol'klora tsygan Kelderari (Folklore of the Kelderari Gypsies).* Moscow: Eastern Literatures.

———. 1990. *Tysgansko-russkij i russko-tsyganskij slovar': Kelderarskij dialekt (Gypsy-Russian and Russian-Gypsy Dictionary: Kelderari Dialect).* Moscow: Russian Language Press.

Demeter-Charskaja, Olga. 1997. *Sud'ba Tsyganki (Fate of a Gypsy Woman).* Moscow: Published by author.

Derrida, Jacques. 1988 [1977]. *Limited, Inc.* Evanston: Northwestern University Press.

Diment, Galya, and Yuri Slezkine, eds. 1993. *Between Heaven and Hell: The Myth of Siberia in Russian Culture.* New York: St. Martin's Press.

Dirks, Nicholas. 1992. "Castes of Mind." *Representations* 37:56–78.

Dodds, E. R. 1964 [1951]. *The Greeks and the Irrational.* Berkeley: University of California Press.

Dostoevsky, F. M. 1880. "Rech' o Pushkine" ("Speech on Pushkin"). Delivered on June 8, 1880, *Dnevnik Pisatelja,* August.

———. 1984. "Pushkin (Ocherk)." In *Polnoe Sobranie Sochinenii (Collected Works),* 26:146–147. Leningrad: Nauka.

Douglas, Mary. 1966. *Purity and Danger.* London: Praeger.

Druts, Efim, and Aleksei Gessler. 1985. *Skazki i pesni rozhdennyje na doroge (Stories and Songs Born on the Road).* Moscow: Nauka.

———. 1988. *Narodnyje pesni russkix tsygan (Folk Songs of Russian Gypsies).* Moscow: Sovetskii Kompozitor.

———. 1990. *Tsygane: Ocherky (Gypsies: Notes)*. Moscow: Sovietskii Pisatel.

———. 1991. *Skazki Tsygan SSSR (Stories of the Gypsies of the USSR)*. Moscow: Nauka.

———. 1993. "Outlaws." *Nezavisimaja Gazeta (The Independent)* 4, nos. 12–13.

Dudarova, N., and N. Pankov. 1928. *Nevo drom — bukvarjo vash bare manushenge (The New Road: A Primer for Adults* [Romani]). Moscow: Tsentrizdat.

Dunham, Vera. 1976. *In Stalin's Time: Middle-Class Values in Soviet Fiction*. Cambridge: Cambridge University Press.

Duranti, Alessandro, and Charles Goodwin. 1992. *Rethinking Context: Language as an Interactive Phenomenon*. Cambridge: Cambridge University Press.

Ekran. 1929. "Akademija poshlosti" ("Academy of Banality"), no. 7:12.

Elias, Norbert. 1978. *The History of Manners: The Civilizing Process*. New York: Pantheon Books.

European Roma Rights Center (ERRC). 1997. *The Misery of Law: The Rights of Roma in the Transcarpathian Region of Ukraine*. Budapest: ERRC.

Evans-Pritchard, Edward Evan. 1971 [1940]. *The Nuer: A Description of the Modes of Livelihood and the Political Institutions of a Nilotic People*. New York: Oxford University Press.

Fabian, Johannes. 1990. *Power in Performance: Ethnographic Explorations through Proverbial Wisdom and Theater in Shaba, Zaire*. Madison: University of Wisconsin Press.

Ferguson, William. 1933. "Russian Gypsy Singers." *JGLS*, 3d ser. 12, no. 2:108.

Ficowski, J. 1965. *Cyganie na Polskich Drogach*. Krakow: Wydawn, Literackie.

———. 1982. "The Fate of Polish Gypsies." In *Genocide and Human Rights*, 166–177. Lanham, Md.: University Press of America.

Fitzpatrick, Sheila. 1978. "Cultural Revolution as Class War." In *Cultural Revolution in Russia, 1928–1931*, ed. Sheila Fitzpatrick, 8–40. Bloomington: Indiana University Press.

———. 1991. "The Problem of Class Identity in NEP Society." In *Russia in the Era of NEP*, ed. Sheila Fitzpatrick, A. Rabinowitch, and R. Stites. Bloomington: Indiana University Press.

———. 1994. "Signals from Below: Soviet Letters of the 1930s." Paper presented at the conference "The Practice of Denunciation," University of Chicago, April 29–30.

Fonseca, Isabel. 1995. *Bury Me Standing: The Gypsies and Their Journey*. New York: Knopf.

Frake, Charles. 1975. "How to Enter a Yakan House." In *Sociocultural Dimensions of Language Use*, ed. Mary Sanches and Ben G. Blount, 25–40. New York: Academic Press.

Fraser, Angus. 1992a. *The Gypsies*. Oxford: Blackwell.

———. 1992b. "Looking into the Seeds of Time." *Tsiganologische Studien*, nos. 1–2:135–66.

———. 1992c. "The Rom Migrations." *JGLS* 2, no. 2:131–145.

Friedman, Victor A. 1985. "Problems in the Codification of a Standard Romani

Literary Language." In *Papers from the Fourth and Fifth Annual Meetings, Gypsy Lore Society,* ed. Joanne Grumet, 56–75. Cheverly, Md.: Gypsy Lore Society.

——. 1988. "National Language and Linguistic Nationalism in the Balkans." In *Sprakforholden pa Balkan og i Ost Europa.* Skriftserie Nr. 32, Serie A:1–16. Universitet I Bergen Institutt for fonetik og lingvistik.

——. 1990. "On the Turkish Lexical Component in Romani Dialects and Their Relationship to Language Planning." In *100 Years of Gypsy Studies,* ed. Matt Salo, 137–143. Cheverly, Md.: Gypsy Lore Society.

——. 1991. "Case in Romani: Old Grammar in New Affixes." *JGLS* 1, no. 2:85–102.

Friedman, Victor, and Robert Dankoff, 1991. "The Earliest Texts in Balkan [Rumelian] Romani: a Passage from Evliya Chelebi's Seyehat-name. *JGLS* 1, no. 1:1–20.

Friedrich, Paul. 1966. "Structural Implications of Russian Pronomial Usage." In *Sociolinguistics,* ed. W. Bright, 214–259. The Hague: Mouton.

——. 1986. *The Language Parallax: Linguistic Relativism and Poetic Indeterminacy.* Austin: University of Texas Press.

——. 1989. "Language, Ideology and Political Economy." *American Anthropologist* 91, no. 2:295–312.

Friedrich, Paul, and Norma Diamond, eds. 1994. *Encyclopedia of World Cultures,* vol. 4: *Russia and Eurasia/China.* Boston, Mass.: G. K. Hall.

Gable, Eric. 1997. "A Secret Shared: Fieldwork and the Sinister in a West African Village." *Cultural Anthropology* 12, no. 2:213–233.

Gabor, R. Istvan. 1979. "The Second (Secondary) Economy." *Acta Oeconomica,* nos. 3–4:291–311.

Gal, Susan. 1987. "Codeswitching and Consciousness in the European Periphery." *American Ethnologist* 14:637–653.

——. 1989. "Language and Political Economy." *Annual Review of Anthropology* 18:345–367.

——. 1991. "Bartok's Funeral: Representations of Europe in Hungarian Political Rhetoric." *American Ethnologist* 18, no. 3:440–458.

——. 1995. "Language and the 'Arts of Resistance'" (book review of *Domination and the Arts of Resistance* by James Scott). *Cultural Anthropology* 10, no. 3:407–424.

Gallagher, Catherine. 1986. "The Body versus the Social Body in the Works of Thomas Malthus and Henry Mayhew." *Representations* 14:86–106.

Gates, Henry Louis. 1988. *The Signifying Monkey: A Theory of Afro-American Literary Criticism.* New York: Oxford University Press.

Gell, Simeran Man Singh. 1996. "The Origins of the Sikh 'Look.'" *History and Anthropology* 10, no. 1:37–83.

German, Aleksandr. 1922. "Tsygane." *Bezbozhnik* (Moscow), no. 1, December 21: 11–13.

——. 1930. *Bibliografija o tsyagnax: pokazatel' knig i statej ot 1780–1930 (A Bibliogra-*

phy on Gypsies: A Directory of Books and Articles from 1780 to 1930). Moscow: Tsentrizdat.

———. 1932. *Romano Teatro, khelybena (Romani Theater, Plays)*. Moscow: Gosizdat xudozehstvennaja literatura.

Gilliat-Smith, Bernard. 1922. "Russian Gypsy Singers." *JGLS* 3d ser. 1:58–64.

———. 1932. "The Dialect of the Gypsies of Northern Russia." *JGLS,* 3d ser. 15, no. 2:71–87.

Gilman, Sander. 1993. *Freud, Race and Gender.* Princeton, N.J.: Princeton University Press.

Gilroy, Paul. 1993. *The Black Atlantic: Modernity and Double Consciousness.* Cambridge, Mass.: Harvard University Press.

Ginsberg, Faye. 1994. "Embedded Aesthetics: Creating a Discursive Space for Indigenous Media." In *Cultural Anthropology* 9, no. 3:365–382.

Gitlits, Ilya. 1972. "Gypsies in the USSR." *Sputnik,* no. 9:90–99.

Goffman, Erving. 1986 [1974]. *Frame Analysis: An Essay on the Organization of Experience.* Boston, Mass.: Northeastern University Press.

———. 1981 [1979]. "Footing." In *Forms of Talk,* 124–159. Philadelphia: University of Pennsylvania Press.

Goricha, V. 1931. *Vechernaja Moskva (Evening Moscow),* December 31.

Gorky, Maxim. 1959 [1892]. "Makar Chudra." In *Selected Short Stories,* trans. B. Isaacs. New York: Frederick Ungar Publishing, 9–21.

Grant, Anthony P. 1995. "Plagiarism and Lexical Orphans in the European Romani Lexicon." In *Romani in Contact,* ed. Yaron Matras, 53–68. Amsterdam: John Benjamins Publishing.

Grant, Bruce. 1995. *In the Soviet House of Culture.* Princeton, N.J.: Princeton University Press.

Grellman, H. M. G. 1783. *Die Zigeuner: Ein historischer Versuch über die Lebensart und Verfassung, Sitten und Schicksale diese Volkes in Europa nebst ihrem Ursprunge.* Dessau.

Grigorjev, Apollon. 1915. "Russkije narodnyje pesni s ix poeticheskoj i muzykal'noj storony." ("Russian Folk Songs from Their Poetic and Musical Side"). In *Sobranie Sochinenii Apollona Grigorjeva (Collected Works of Apollon Grigorjev),* ed. V. F. Sadovnik. 14th ed. Moscow: Tip. Kushnerov.

———. 1988 [1862–64]. *Vospominanija (Memoirs).* Moscow: Nauka.

Grishin, D. V. 1974. *Rech' Dostoevskogo o Pushkine (Dostoevsky's Speech on Pushkin).* Dept. of Russian Languages and Literatures, University of Melbourne.

Groome, Francis Hindes. 1899. *Gypsy Folk Tales.* London: Hurst and Blackett.

Gropper, Rena. 1975. *Gypsies in the City: Culture Patterns and Survival.* Princeton: Darwin Press.

Guy, Will. 1998 [1975]. "Ways of Looking at Roma: The Case of Czechoslovakia." In Tong, *Gypsies,* 13–68.

Haley, William J. 1934. "The Gypsy Conference at Bucharest." *JGLS,* 3d ser. 13, no. 4:182–190.

Hall, Stuart. 1990. "Cultural Identity and Diaspora." In *Identity: Community, Culture, Difference*, ed. Jonathan Rutherford. London: Lawrence and Wishart.

Hall, Kira, and Mary Bucholtz. 1995. *Gender Articulated: Language and the Socially Constructed Self.* New York: Routledge.

Halliday, W. R. 1925. "Russian Gypsies." *JGLS*, 3d ser., no. 3:143.

Hamill, Alfred E. 1943. "Gypsies in and about Russian Literature." *JGLS*, 3d ser. 22, nos. 1–2:57–58.

Hamp, Eric P. 1990. "The Conservatism and Exemplary Order of Romany." In *100 Years of Gypsy Studies*, 151–155. Cheverly, Md.: Gypsy Lore Society.

Hancock, Ian. 1976. "Romance vs. Reality: Popular Notions of the Gypsy." *Roma* 1, no. 2:7–23.

———. 1985. "Non-Gypsy Attitudes towards Rom: The Gypsy Stereotype." *Roma* 9, no. 1:50–65.

———. 1987. *The Pariah Syndrome: An Account of Gypsy Slavery and Persecution.* Ann Arbor: Karoma Publishers.

———. 1989. Review of *Familiar Strangers: Gypsy Life in America* by Marlene Sway. *Roma* 13, no. 1:41–48.

———. 1991. "The East European Roots of Romani Nationalism." In *The Gypsies of Eastern Europe*, ed. Crowe and Kolsti, 133–150.

———. 1993. "The Emergence of a Union Dialect of American Vlax Romani, and Its Implications for an International Standard." *International Journal of the Sociology of Language*, ed. Jeff Sigel, 91–104.

———. 1995a. *A Handbook of Vlax-Romani.* Columbus, Ohio: Slavica Press.

———. 1995b. "On the Migration and Affiliation of the Domba: Iranian Words in Rom, Lom and Dom Gypsy." In *Romani in Contact: The History, Structure and Sociology of a Language*, ed. Yaron Matras, 25–52. Amsterdam: John Benjamins Publishing.

———. 1996. "Responses to the *Porrajmos:* The Romani Holocaust." In *Is the Holocaust Unique? Perspectives on Comparative Genocide*, ed. Alan S. R. Rosenbaum, 39–64. Oxford: Westview Press.

———. 1998a [1996]. "Duty and Beauty, Possession and Truth: 'Lexical Impoverishment' as Control." In Tong, *Gypsies*, 115–125.

———. 1998b. "The Struggle for the Control of Identity," *Transitions* 4, no.4:36–53.

———. 2000. "The Emergence of Romani as a Koine outside of India." In *Scholarship and the Gypsy Struggle—Commitment in Romani Studies: Essays in Honour of Donald Kenrick*, ed. Thomas Acton. Hatfield, England: University of Hertfordshire Press.

———. [No date]. *A Grammar of the Hungarian-Slovak (Carpathian, Bashaldo, Romungro) Romani Language,"* unpublished manuscript.

Handler, Richard. 1988. *Nationalism and the Politics of Culture in Quebec.* Madison: University of Wisconsin Press.

Handler, Richard, and Jocelyn Linnekan. 1984. "Tradition, Genuine or Spurious." *Journal of American Folklore* 97, no. 385:273–290.

Handler, Richard, and Daniel Segal. 1989. "Serious Play: Creative Dance and Dramatic Sensibility in Jane Austin, Ethnographer." *Man,* new ser. 24, no. 2:322–339.

Hanks, William. 1987. "Discourse Genres in a Theory of Practice." *American Ethnologist* 14, no. 4:668–692.

———. 1990. *Referential Practice: Language and Lived Space among the Maya.* Chicago: University of Chicago Press.

Hann, C. M. 1993. *Socialism: Ideal, Ideologies and Local Practice.* London: Routledge.

Herzfeld, Michael. 1987. *Anthropology through the Looking Glass: Critical Ethnography in the Margins of Europe.* Cambridge: Cambridge University Press.

———. 1991. *A Place in History: Social and Monumental Time in a Cretan Town.* Princeton: Princeton University Press.

———. 1992. *The Social Production of Indifference: Exploring the Symbolic Roots of Western Bureaucracy.* Chicago: University of Chicago Press.

Hessler, Julie. 1996. "Soviet Bazaars and the Politics of Value." In "Culture of Shortages: A Social History of Soviet Trade," Ph.D. diss., Department of History, University of Chicago.

Hill, Jane. 1985. "The Grammar of Consciousness and the Consciousness of Grammar." *American Ethnologist* 12, no. 4:725–737.

———. 1993. "Hasta la Vista, Baby: Anglo-Spanish in the American Southwest." *Critique of Anthropology* 13, no. 2:145–176.

Hill, Jane, and Bruce Mannheim. 1992. "Language and World View." *Annual Review of Anthropology* 21:381–406.

Hirsch, Francine. 1997. "The Soviet Union as a Work in Progress: Ethnographers and the Category 'Nationality' in the 1926, 1937, and 1939 Census." *Slavic Review* 56, no. 2:251–278.

Hubschmannova, Milena. 1993. "Three Years of Democracy in Czecho-Slovakia and the Roma." *Roma,* nos. 38–39: 130–49.

———. 1998 [1984]. "Economic Stratification and Interaction: Roma, an Ethnic Jati in East Slovakia." In Tong, *Gypsies,* 232–267.

Hubschmannova, Milena, and Anna Sebkova. 1991. *Romsko-cesky a cesko-romsky kapesni slovnik (Romani-Czech and Czech-Romani Pocket Dictionary).* Prague: Státni pedagogické Naklada telství.

Hugo, Victor. 1947. *Notre Dame de Paris.* New York: Dodd, Mead.

Human Rights Watch-Helsinki. 1995. *Crime or Simply Punishment? Racist Attacks by Moscow Law Enforcement,* no. 12. Helsinki: Human Rights Watch.

Humphrey, Caroline. 1989. "'Janus Faced Signs': The Political Language of a Soviet Minority before Glasnost." *Sociological Review* 36:145–175.

———. 1993. "Myth-Making, Narratives and the Dispossessed in Russia." Paper presented to the Society of the Anthropology of Europe at the 1993 meeting of the American Anthropological Association, Washington, D.C.

———. 1994. "Remembering an 'Enemy': The Bogd Khan in Twentieth-Century Mongolia." In Watson, *Memory, History and Opposition,* 21–44.

———. 1995. "Creating a Culture of Disillusionment: Consumption in Moscow, a Chronicle of Changing Times." In *Worlds Apart: Modernity through the Prism of the Local,* ed. Daniel Miller. Routledge: New York.

Hymes, Dell. 1974. *Foundations in Sociolinguistics: An Ethnographic Approach.* Philadelphia: University of Pennsylvania Press.

Irvine, Judith. 1989. "When Talk Isn't Cheap: Language and Political Economy." *American Ethnologist* 16:248–267.

———. 1996. "Shadow Conversations: The Indeterminacy of Participant Roles." In Silverstein and Urban, 131–159.

Ivy, Marilyn. 1995. *Discourses of the Vanishing.* Chicago: University of Chicago Press.

Jakobson, Roman. 1960. "Concluding Statement: Linguistics and Poetics." In *Style in Language,* ed. T. A. Sebeok, 350–377. Cambridge, Mass.: MIT Press.

———. 1971 [1957]. "Shifters, Verbal Categories, and the Russian Verb." In *Selected Writings of Roman Jakobson,* 139–47. The Hague: Mouton.

Janicki, Joel. 1989. "Gypsies." In *The Modern Encyclopedia of Russian and Soviet Literature,* vol. 9, ed. George J. Gutsche. Gulf Breeze, Fl.: Academic International Press.

John, Augustus E. 1909. "Russian Gypsy songs." *JGLS,* old ser. 2:179–199.

Kalinin, A. V. 1991 [1966]. *Tsygan: Roman (Gypsy: A Novel).* Moscow: Molodaja Gvardija.

Kaminskii, Igancy-Marek. 1980. *The State of Ambiguity: Studies of Gypsy Refugees.* Gothenburg, Sweden: University of Gothenburg, Dept. of Social Anthropology.

———. 1987. "The Dilemma of Power: Internal and External Leadership. The Gypsy-Roma of Poland." In Rao, 323–355.

Kapralski, Slawomir. 1997. "Identity Building and the Holocaust: Roma Political Nationalism." *Nationalities Papers* 25, no. 2:269–283.

Kaprow, Mirian Lee. 1982. "Resisting Respectability: Gypsies in Saragossa." *Urban Anthropology* 11, nos. 3–4:399–431.

Kenedi, Janos. 1986. "Why Is the Gypsy the Scapegoat and Not the Jew?" *East European Reporter* 2, no. 1:11–14.

Kenrick, Donald, and Grattan Puxon. 1972. *The Destiny of Europe's Gypsies.* New York: Basic Books.

Khanzhanov, A. 1989. "Drama in a Gypsy Camp near Moscow." In *Silent Witnesses: Russian Films 1908–1919,* ed. Paolo Cherchi Usai and Yuri Tsivian. London: British Film Institute, 46–48.

Kobak, Annette. 1995. "The Gypsy in our Souls" (review of Fonseca, *Bury Me Standing*). *New York Times Book Review,* October 22, 16.

Kochanowski, Vania de Gila. 1959. "N. A. Pankov." *JGLS,* 3d ser. 38, nos. 3–4:159–160.

———. 1965. *"Mashkir Romende* (Among Gypsies): The Views of a Latvian Gypsy." *JGLS* 3d ser. 44, nos. 3–4:137–140.

———. 1968. "Black Gypsies, White Gypsies." *Diogenes* 63:27–47.

———. 1979. "Roma—History of Their Indian Origin." *Roma* 4, no. 1:16–32.

———. 1982. "Demystification." *Roma* 6, no. 2:17–39.

———. 1995. "Romani Language Standardization." *JGLS* 5, no. 2:97–108.

Kruchinin/Xlebnikov, N. N. 1955. "Pesni tsygan iz dramy L. N. Tolstogo ("Gypsy songs from Tolstoy's Drama"). In *Zapis' i obrabotka.*

Kuprin, Aleksandr. 1964. "Faraoanova plemja" ("Pharoah's Tribe"). In *Collected Works.* Moscow: Pravda.

Layton, Susan. 1994. *Russian Literature and Empire: Conquest of the Caucasus from Pushkin to Tolstoy.* Cambridge: Cambridge University Press.

Lee, Benjamin. 1997. *Talking Heads: Language, Metalanguage, and the Semiotics of Subjectivity.* Durham, N.C.: Duke University Press.

Lee, Ronald, 1971. *Goddam Gypsy: An Autobiographical Novel.* Indianapolis: Bobbs Merrill.

———. 1987. "The Kris Romani." *Roma* 11, no. 2:19–34.

Lemon, Alaina. 1991. "Roma (Gypsies) in the USSR: The Moscow Romani Theater." *Nationalities Papers* 19:359–372.

———. 1998. "'Your Eyes Are Green Like Dollars': Counterfeit Cash, National Substance, and Currency Apartheid in 1990s' Russia." *Cultural Anthropology* 13, no. 1:22–55.

———. 2000. "Talking Transit and Spectating Transition: The Moscow Metro." In *Altering States: Ethnographies of Transition,* ed. Daphne Berdahl, Matti Bunzl, and Martha Lampland. Ann Arbor: University of Michigan Press.

Lemon, Alaina, and Midori Nakamura. 1994. *T'an Baxtale!* Video. Romani and Russian with English subtitles. 75 minutes.

Lenin, V. I. 1965. *Voprosy natsional'noj politiki i proletarskogo internatsionalizma (Questions of national politics and proletarian internationalism).* Moscow: Politizdat.

Lermontov, Mikhail Yurevich. 1966. *A Hero of Our Time.* Trans. Paul Foote. London: Penguin Books.

Leskov, Nikolaj. 1961. "The Enchanted Wanderer." In *Selected Tales,* trans. David Marshack. New York: Farrar, Strauss and Cudahy, 51–211.

———. 1969. "Deception" and "Fish Soup without Fish." In *Satirical Stories of Nikolaj Leskov,* trans. William B. Edgerton. New York: Pegasus Press.

———. 1986. *The Jews in Russia: Some Notes on the Jewish Question.* Trans. Harold Schefski. Princeton, N.J.: Kingston Press.

Levy, Anita. 1991. *Other Women: The Writing of Class, Race and Gender, 1832–1898.* Princeton, N.J.: Princeton University Press.

Lewis, Gilbert. 1987. "A Lesson from Leviticus." *Man* 22, no. 4:593–612.

Liegeois, Jean-Pierre. 1994. *Roma, Gypsies, Travellers.* Strasbourg: Council of Europe Press.

Lipetskaja Gazeta. 1996. "Tsygane shumnoju tolpoju" ("Gypsies in a Noisy Crowd"). February 10, 7.

Liszt, Franz. 1926. *The Gypsy in Music.* Trans. Edwin Evans, 149–155. London: William Reeves.

Lockwood, William. 1986. "East European Gypsies in Western Europe: The Social and Cultural Adaptations of the Xoraxane." *Nomadic Peoples* 21, no. 22:63–70.

Loginova, N. 1992. " . . . i moja zhena—tsyganka" (" . . . and My Wife is a Gypsy"). *Zhurnalist* 8:33–36.

London Independent. 1990. "Ceaucescu Is Dead. The Gypsy King Lives!" March 7.

Lutz, Catherine, and Jane Collins. 1993. *Reading National Geographic.* Chicago: University of Chicago Press.

Malkki, Lisa. 1997. "National Geographic: The Rooting of Peoples and the Territorialization of National Identity among Scholars and Refugees." *In Culture, Power, Place: Explorations in Cultural Anthropology,* ed. Akhil Gupta and James Ferguson. Durham, N.C.: Duke University Press, 52–74.

Malnick, Bertha. 1959. "The Moscow Gypsy Theater, 1957–58." *JGLS,* 3d ser. 38, nos. 3–4:81–85.

Mandel, Ruth. 1989. "Constructing Difference: The Production of Ethnicity in the Context of Migration." Unpublished manuscript.

———. 1990. "Shifting Centres and Emergent Identities: Turkey and Germany in the Lives of Turkish Gastarbeiter." In *Muslim Travellers: Pilgrimage, Migration and the Religious Imagination,* ed. Dale F. Eikelman and James Piscatori. Berkeley: University of California Press. 153–171.

Mannheim, Bruce. 1991. "*After* Dreaming: Image and Interpretation in Southern Peruvian Quechua." *Etnofoor* 4, no. 2:43–79.

Manush, Leksa. 1985. "K probleme muzykal'nogo fol'klora tsygan" (istoki tsyganskoj muzyki v Evrope) ("On the Problem of Gypsy Musical Folklore" [Sources of Gypsy Music in Europe]). *Sovetskaja Etnografija* 5:46–56.

———. 1990. "Pesennaja poezija tsygan Voevodina" ("The Sung Poetry of the Gypsies of Voevodina"). *Sovjetskaja Etnografija* 1–2:160–165.

Marcus, George. 1995. "Ethnography in/of the World System: The Emergence of Multi-Sited Ethnography." *Annual Review of Anthropology* 24:95–117.

Martin, Terry. 1996. *The Soviet Nationalities Policy, 1923–38.* Ph.D. diss., Department of History, University of Chicago.

Marushiakova, E., and Vesselin Popov. 1997. "The Romanies in the Balkans during the Ottoman Empire." *Roma,* no. 1: 47:63–72.

Massell, Gregory J. 1974. *The Surrogate Proletariat: Moslem Women and Revolutionary Strategies in Soviet Central Asia, 1919–1929.* Princeton, N.J.: Princeton University Press.

Matras, Yaron, ed. 1995. *Romani in Contact.* Amsterdam: John Benjamins Publishing.

Maximoff, Mateo. 1946. "Germany and the Gypsies: From the Gypsy's Point of View." *JGLS* 25, nos. 3–4:104–108.

Maxotin, Djuri. 1993. *Adzhutipe pre romani club (A Guide to Romani).* Tver: Poligrafreklamizdat.

Mayall, David. "Lorist, Reformist, and Romanticist: The Nineteenth-Century Response to Gypsy Travelers." *Immigrants and Minorities* 4, no. 3:53–67.

Mikeladze, N. 1991. "Bitva nad Pskovom" ("Battle over Pskov"). *Komsomolskaja Pravda,* August 17.

Mixailov, Semion. 1932. *Tzyganskaja Zarja (Gypsy Dawn).* Moscow: Literatura i Voina.

Miklosich, F. 1872–80. *Uber die Mundarten und die Wanderungen die Zigeuner Europas.* Denkschriften der kaiserlichen Akademie der Wissenschaften, Philosophisch-historiische Klasses, vols. 21–31. Vienna.

Miller, Carol. 1975. "American Rom and the Ideology of Defilement." In *Gypsies, Tinkers, and Other Travellers,* ed. Farnum Rehfisch, 41–54. London: Academic Press.

———. 1968. "Machwaya Gypsy Marime." MA thesis, University of Washington, Seattle.

———. 1994. "Respect and Rank among the Machwaia Roma." *JGLS* 4, no. 2:95–110.

Ministry of Culture of Soviet Russia. 1979. *Vospitanije akterov v natsionalnyx studijax. Sobranije statej. (The Training of Actors in the National Studios: A Collection of Articles).* Moscow: Gosizdat.

Mirga, Andrzej. 1993. "The Effect of State Assimilation Policy on Polish Gypsies." *JGLS* 3, no. 2:69–76.

———. 1997. "Reply to Yaron Matras' Review of 'The Roma in the Twenty-First Century: A Policy Paper." Romnet [Internet News Group], January 15.

Mirga, Andrzej, and Niklolaj Ghoerghe. 1997. *The Roma in the Twenty-First Century: A Policy Paper.* Project on Ethnic Relations (PER). Princeton, N.J.: Project on Ethnic Relations.

Mirsky, D. S. Prince. 1958. *A History of Russian Literature from Its Beginnings to 1900.* New York: Vintage Books.

Morath, Inge. 1989. "Lyala Kuznetsova's Scenes of Gypsy Life." *Aperture* (fall):34–39.

Morson, Gary. 1993. "Strange Synchronies and Surplus Possibilities: Bakhtin on Time." *Slavic Review* 52, no. 3:477–493.

Moskovskaja Pravda. 1932. "Kto otvechajet za razval tsyganskogo kolxoza" ("Who Answers for the Breakdown of the Gypsy Collective Farm"). July 26.

Mullaney, Stephen. 1988. *The Place of the Stage: License, Play and Power in Renaissance England.* Chicago: University of Chicago Press.

Müller-Hill, Benno. 1988. *Murderous Science: Elimination by Scientific Selection of Jews, Gypsies, and Others, Germany 1933–45.* Trans. George R. Frase. Oxford: Oxford University Press.

Myers, Fred. 1994. "Culture-Making: Performing Aboriginality at the Asia Society Gallery." *American Ethnologist* 21:679–699.

Nandy, Ashis. 1983. *The Intimate Enemy: Loss and the Recovery of Self under Colonialism.* Delhi: Oxford University Press.

National Magazine (London). 1859. " . . . Gipsy and other Choirs." Vol. 6:43–47.

Nazarov, K. K. 1982–83. "Contemporary Ethnic Development of the Central Asian Gypsies (Liuli)." *Soviet Anthropology and Archaeology* 21, no. 3:3–28.

Nevo Drom (New Road). 1931. Moscow: Tsentrizdat Narodov SSSR.

Novosti. 1926. "Pervij obrazets tsyganskoj pismennosti" ("The First Example of Gypsy Writing").

Okely, Judith. 1983. *The Traveller-Gypsies.* Cambridge: Cambridge University Press.

O'Malley, Michael. 1994. "Specie and Species: Race and the Money Question in Nineteenth-Century America." *American Historical Review* 99:369–395.

Ortner, Sherry. 1995. "Resistance and the Problem of Ethnographic Refusal." *Comparative Studies in Society and History* 37, no. 1:173–193.

Pankova, Olga. 1934. *Syr Romenge Dzhindjpe dre Rossija* (How Roma Educated Themselves in Russia). Moscow: Tsentrizdat Narodov SSSR.

Papazjan, V. I. 1901. "Armjanskaja Bosha (Tysgane): Etnografcheskij Ocherk" (Armenian Bosha [Gypsies]: Ethnographic Sketch). *Etnografcheskoje Obozrenije* 49, no. 2:93–158.

Parker, R. 1983. *Miasma: Pollution and Purification in Early Greek Religion.* Oxford: Clarendon Press.

Pashkov, A. 1991. "Vystrely v Alapajevske" (A Gunshot in Alapajevsk). *Izvestija*, July 29.

Paspati, A. G. 1862. "Memoir on the Language of the Gypsies, as Now Used in the Turkish Empire." Trans. C. Hamlin. *Journal of the American Oriental Society* 7:143–270.

Patkanoff, K. P. 1908. "Some Words on the Dialects of the Trans-Caucasian Gypsies—Bosha and Karachi." *JGLS*, new ser., 1, no. 3:229–257.

Peirce, Charles S. 1961. *Collected Papers of Charles Sander Peirce.* Ed. Charles Hartshorne and Paul Wiess; vols 7–8, ed. Arthur Burks. Cambridge, Mass.: Harvard University Press.

Pesmen, Dale. 1998. "The Russian Soul: Ethnography and Metaphysics." Ph.D. diss., Department of Anthropology, University of Chicago.

Plotnikov, Sergej. 1991. "S drekol'em—na tsygan?" *Rossija*, October 1–8.

Ploxinskij, M. 1890. "Tsygane staroj malorossii" ("The Gypsies of Old Little Russia"). *Etnografcheskoje obozrenije* (Moscow), ed. N. A. Janchuka, no. 4:95–117.

Pobozniak, T. 1964. *Grammar of the Lowari Dialect.* Krakow: Polska Akademia Nauk, Panstwowe Wydawnictvo Naukowe.

Poljiakov, Sergej. 1992. *Everyday Islam: Religion and Tradition in Rural Central Asia.* Trans. Martha Brill Olcott. Armonk, N.Y.: M. E. Sharpe.

Popkin, Kathy. 1992. "Chekov as Ethnographer." *Slavic Review* 51, no. 1:36–51.

Popova, E., and M. Bril'. 1932. "Tsygane v SSSR" ("Gypsies in the USSR"). *Sovjetskoje Stroitel'stvo* no. 2.

Pott, August. 1844. *Die Zigeuner in Europa und Asien: Etnographisch-linguistische Untersuchung Vornehmlich ihrer Herkunft und Sprache.* Halle: Heynemann Verlag.

Pushkin, Aleksandr. 1956 [1824]. *Tsygany*, 35–59. In *Poemy*. Moscow: Gosizdat Detskoj Literatury.

Puxon, Grattan. 1976. "Gypsies: Blacks of East Europe." *The Nation*, April 17: 460–464.

Radzinsky, Stanislav. 1945. "A Stirring Play at the Moscow Gypsy Theater." *JGLS*, 3d ser. 24, nos. 3–4:120–121.

———. 1947. "Moscow's Gypsy Theater." *JGLS*, 3d ser. 26, nos. 3–4:173.

Ranking, Devey Fearon de l'Hoste. 1911a. "The Gypsies of Central Russia: Introduction." *JGLS*, new ser. 4, no. 3:195–217.

———. 1911b. "The Gypsies of Central Russia: The Gypsies of Kiselevka." *JGLS*, new ser. 4, no. 4:245–258.

———. 1912–13. "The Gypsies of Central Russia: Manners and Customs." *JGLS*, new ser. 6, no. 2:90–110.

Rao, Aparna. 1987. *The Other Nomads: Peripatetic Minorities in Cross-Cultural Perspective*. Koln: Bohlau Verlag.

Rieber, Alfred. 1982. *Merchants and Entrepreneurs in Imperial Russia*. Chapel Hill: University of North Carolina Press.

Ricoeur, Paul. 1967. *The Symbolism of Evil*. New York: Harper and Row.

Rishi, W. R. 1976. *Roma: The Panjabi Emigrants in Europe, Central and Middle Asia, the USSR and the Americas*. Patiala, India: Punjabi University.

———. 1980. *Romani Punjabi Conversation Book*. Patiala: Punjab Language Department.

Roback, A. A. 1979 [1946]. *A Dictionary of International Slurs (Ethnophaulisms)*. Waukesha, Wis.: Maledicta Press.

Robertson, Jennifer. 1995. "Mon Japon: The Revue Theater as a Technology of Japanese Imperialism." *American Ethnologist* 22, no. 4:970–996.

Romano Racs, Sandor. 1994. *Karpati Cigany — Magyar/Magyar-Karpati Cigany: Szotar es Nyelvtan (Carpathian Gypsy-Hungarian/Hungarian-Carpathian Gypsy Dictionary and Grammar)*. Budapest: Balassi Liado.

Rom-Lebedev, Ivan. 1990. *Ot tsyganskogo xora do teatra "Romen" (From the Gypsy Choir to the Romani Theater)*. Moscow: Iskusstvo Press.

———. 1992. *Tabornaja tsyganka (Gypsy Women of the Camp)*. Moscow: Olimp.

Rossi, Jacques. 1992 [1987]. *Spravochnik po gulagu (Gulag Handbook)*. Moscow: Prosvet.

Rothstein, Robert. 1980. "The Quiet Rehabilitation of the Brick Factory: Early Soviet Popular Music and Its Critics." *Slavic Review* 39, no. 3:373–88.

Rudiger, Johann. 1782. *Neuster Zuwachs der teutschen, fremden, und allgemeinein Sprachkunde in eigenen Aufsatzen*, part 1, 37–84. Leipzig.

———. 1790. *Von der Sprache und Herkunft der Zigeuner aus Indien*. Hamburg: Buske.

Russian National Union. 1995. "O trebovanijax k tem, kto nameren sozdat' sem'ju" ("On the Demands on Those Intending to Start a Family"). *Shturmovik*, no. 3:1.

Said, Edward. 1978. *Orientalism*. New York: Vintage Books.

Salo, Matthew. 1977. "The Expression of Ethnicity in Rom Oral Tradition." *Western Folklore* 36:33–56.

——, ed. 1990. *100 Years of Gypsy Studies*. Cheverly, Md.: Gypsy Lore Society.

Sampson, John. 1968 [1926]. *The Dialect of the Gypsies of Wales*. London: Oxford University Press.

Sampson, Stephen. 1987. "The Second Economy in Eastern Europe and the Soviet Union." *Annals of the American Association of Political and Social Science* 493:120–136.

Sandrow, Nahma. 1977. "The Soviet Yiddish State Theaters: GOSET." In *Vagabond Stars: A World History of Yiddish Theater*, 222–250. New York: Harper and Row.

Sanarov, V. J. 1970. "The Siberian Gypsies." *JGLS* 49, nos. 3–4:126–137.

Sarat, Austin, and Roger Berkowits. 1994. "Disorderly Differences: Recognition, Accommodation, and American Law." *Yale Journal of Law and the Humanities* 6:285–316.

Satkevich, Nikolaj. 1972. *Struny (Strings)*. Tula, Russia: Priokskoje Knizhnoje Izdatel'stvo.

Scott, James. 1990. *Domination and the Arts of Resistance: Hidden Transcripts*. New Haven: Yale University Press.

Scheiffelin, Edward. 1985. "Performance and the Cultural Construction of Reality." *American Ethnologist* 12, no. 4:707–724.

Shcherbakova, T. 1984. *Tsyganskoje muzykal'noje ispolnitel'stvo v Rossii (Gypsy Musical Performance in Russia)*. Moscow: Muzyka.

Schindler, Debra Lee. 1990. "The Political Economy of Ethnic Discourse in the Soviet Union." Ph.D. diss., Department of Anthropology, University of Massachusetts, Amherst.

Schneider, David. 1968. *American Kinship: A Cultural Account*, Englewood, N.J.: Prentice-Hall.

Segal, Dan. 1995. "Living Ancestors: Nationalism and the Past in Postcolonial Trinidad and Tobago." In *Remapping Memory*, ed. Jonathan Boyarin, 221–239. Minneapolis: University of Minnesota Press.

Sergijevskij, M. V., and A. P. Barranikov. 1938. *Tsygansko-Russkij Slovar' (Gypsy-Russian Dictionary)*. Moscow: Gosizdat Inostrannyx i natsionalnyx slovarej.

Seton, Marie. 1935. "The Evolution of the Gypsy Theatre in the USSR." *JGLS*, 3d ser. 14, no. 2:65–73.

Shandler, Jeffrey. 1997. "The Other Other" (review of *Bury Me Standing* by Isabel Fonseca). *Tikkun* 11, no. 5:92–94.

Shteinpress, Boris. 1934. *K istorii 'tsyganskogo penija' v Rossii (Toward a History of Gypsy Song in Russia)*. Moscow: Gosudarstvennoje Muzykal'noje Izdatel'stvo.

Silverman, Carol. 1981. "Pollution and Power: Gypsy Women in America." In *The American Kalderash: Gypsies in the New World*, ed. Matthew Salo, 55–70. Hacketstown, N.J.: Gypsy Lore Society.

———. 1986. "Bulgarian Gypsies: Adaptation in a Socialist Context." *Nomadic Peoples* 21, no. 22: 51–62.

———. 1988. "Negotiating 'Gypsiness': Strategy in Context." *Journal of American Folklore* 101:261–75.

———. 1996a. "Music Marginality: The Roma (Gypsies) of Bulgaria and Macedonia." In *Retuning Culture: Musical Change in East Europe,* ed. Mark Slobin. Durham, N.C.: Duke University Press.

———. 1996b. "Who's Gypsy Here?: Reflections at a Rom Burial." In *The World Observed: Reflections on the Fieldwork Process,* ed. Bruce Jackson and Edward Ives. Urbana: University of Illinois Press.

Silverstein, Michael. 1976. "Shifters, Linguistic Categories and Cultural Description." In *Meaning in Anthropology,* ed. Keith Basso and Henry A. Selby, 11–55. Albuquerque: University of New Mexico Press.

———. 1979. "Linguistic Structures and Linguistic Ideology." In *The Elements: A Parasession on Linguistic Units and Levels, April 20–21,* ed. Paul Kline et al., 193–247. Chicago: Chicago Linguistic Society.

———. 1993. "A Minimax Approach to Verbal Interaction: Invoking 'Culture' in Realtime Discursive Practice." Paper presented at the conference "Language, Cognition and Computing," Fundacio Catalana per al la Recerca. Barcelona, November 25–26.

———. 1999. "Whorfianism and the Linguistic Imagination of Nationality." In *Regimes of Language: Ideologies, Identities, and Polities,* ed. Paul V. Kroskrity. Santa Fe: School of American Research Press.

Silverstein, Michael, and Greg Urban, eds. 1996. *Natural Histories of Discourse.* Chicago: University of Chicago Press.

Simmel, Georg. 1991 [1900]. *The Philosophy of Money.* London: Routledge.

Simis, Konstantin M. 1982. "The Underground Business World." In *USSR: The Corrupt Society: The Secret World of Soviet Capitalism.*

Sinjavskij, Andrej [aka Abram Tertz]. 1975. *Progulki s Pushkinom (Walks with Pushkin).* London: Overseas Publications Interchange, in association with Collins.

Slezkine, Y. 1992. "From Savages to Citizens: the Cultural Revolution in the Soviet Far North, 1928–38." *Slavic Review* 51, no. 1:52–76.

———. 1994a. *Arctic Mirrors: Russia and the Small Peoples of the North.* Ithaca: Cornell University Press.

———. 1994b. "The USSR as Communal Apartment, or How a Socialist State Promoted Ethnic Particularism." *Slavic Review* 53, no. 2:414–452.

———. 1996. "N. Ia. Marr and the National Origins of Soviet Ethnogenetics." *Slavic Review* 55, no. 4:826–862.

Slichenko, Nikolaj. 1984. "From Campfire to Footlights: Gypsies in the Theater." *Unesco Courier* (October): 26–28.

Smart, Alan. 1993. "Gifts, Bribes and *Guanxi:* A Reconsideration of Bourdieu's Social Capital." *Cultural Anthropology* 8, no. 3:388–406.

Smirnova, A. Ja. 1974 [1962]. "New Features in the Adygej Wedding." *Introduction to Soviet Ethnography,* ed. Stephen Dunn and Ethel Dunn, 291–309. Berkeley, Calif.: Highgate Road Social Science Research Station.

Southhall, Aidan W. 1970. "The Illusion of Tribe." *Journal of Asian and African Studies* 5, nos. 1–2:28–50.

Sovjetskaja Kul'tura. 1980. "My druzhilis' v Tjumene" ("We Made Friends in Tiumen"). 4, no. 4:3.

Spivak, Gayatri. 1988. "Can the Subaltern Speak?" In *Marxism and the Interpretation of Culture,* ed. Cary Nelson and Lawrence Grossberg. Urbana: University of Illinois Press.

St. John, Bayle. 1853. "The Gypsy Slave of Wallachia." *Household Words* 185:139–142.

Stallybrass, Peter, and Allen White. 1986. *The Politics and Poetics of Transgression.* Ithaca: Cornell University Press.

Stanislavskii, Constantin. 1983 [1936]. *An Actor Prepares.* New York: Theater Arts Inc.

Stewart, Michael. 1993. "Gypsies, the Work Ethic and Hungarian Socialism." In *Socialism: Ideal, Ideologies and Local Practice,* ed. C. M. Hann, 187–203. London: Routledge.

———. 1997. *The Time of the Gypsies.* Boulder, Colo.: Westview Press.

Stites, Richard. 1992. *Russian Popular Culture: Entertainment and Society since 1900.* Cambridge: Cambridge University Press.

Stocking, George. 1983. *Observers Observed: Essays on Ethnographic Fieldwork.* Madison: University of Wisconsin Press.

Stoler, Ann. 1991. "Carnal Knowledge and Imperial Power." *Gender at the Crossroads of Knowledge: Feminist Anthropology in the Post Modern Era,* ed. Michaela di Leonardo, 51–101. Berkeley: University of California Press.

———. 1992. "'In Cold Blood': Hierarchies of Credibility and the Politics of Colonial Narratives." *Representations* 37:151–289.

The Story of Karl Stojka: A Childhood in Birkenau: Exhibition at the Embassy of Austria. 1992. Catalogue of the exhibit, April 30–May 29. Washington, D.C.: United States Holocaust Memorial Museum.

Strathern, Marilyn. 1980. "No Nature, No Culture: The Hagen Case." In *Nature, Culture, and Gender,* ed. Carol P. McCormack and Marilyn Strathern. Cambridge: Cambridge University Press.

Strong, Pauline Turner, and Paul Van Winkle. 1996. "'Indian Blood': Reflections on the Reckoning and Refiguring of Native North American Identity." *Cultural Anthropology* 11, no. 4:547–576.

Sunderland, Willard. 1996. "Russians into Iakuts? 'Going Native' and Problems of Russian National Identity in the Siberian North, 1870s–1914." *Slavic Review* 55, no. 4:806–825.

Sutherland, Anne. 1977. "The Body as Social Symbol among the Rom." In *The Anthropology of the Body,* ed. John Blacking, 375–90. New York: Academic Press.

———. 1986a. "Gypsy Women, Gypsy Men: Cultural Paradoxes and Economic

Resources." In *Papers from the Sixth and Seventh Annual Meetings,* ed. Joanne Grumet. New York: Gypsy Lore Society, 104–113.

———. 1986b [1975]. *Gypsies: The Hidden Americans.* Prospect Heights, Ill.: Waveland Press.

———. 1994. "Gypsy Identity, Names and Social Security Numbers." *Political and Legal Anthropological Review* 17, no. 2:75–84.

Szuhay, Peter. 1995. "Constructing a Gypsy National Culture." *Budapest Review of Books* 5, no. 3:111–120.

Tanjung News Agency. 1995. Belgrade, September 23.

Taussig, Michael. 1993. *Mimesis and Alterity.* New York: Routledge.

Tolstoy, Lev Nikolaevich. 1949 [1912]. *Zhivoj Trup (The Living Corpse).* Leningrad: Iskusstvo.

Tong, Diane. 1983. "Language Use and Attitudes among the Gypsies of Thessalonika." *Anthropological Linguistics* 25, no. 3:375–385.

———. 1995. *Gypsies: A Multidisciplinary Annotated Bibliography.* New York: Garland.

Trumpener, Katie. 1992. "The Time of the Gypsies: A 'People without History' in the Narratives of the West." *Critical Inquiry* 18, no. 4:843–884.

Tserushkin, B. 1992. "Tsygan za zhenu platit zolotom" ("The Gypsy Pays Gold for His Wife"), *Argumenty i Fakty,* no. 7.

"Tsygane." 1880. In *Zhivopisnyj Albom: Narody Rossii (A Pictorial Album: The Peoples of Russia).* St. Petersburg.

Tumarkin, Nina. 1983. *Lenin Lives! The Cult of Lenin in the Soviet Union.* Cambridge, Mass.: Harvard University Press.

Turner, R. L. 1927. *The Position of Romani in Indo-Aryan.* Gypsy Lore Society Monographs, no. 4. Edinburgh: Edinburgh University Press.

Turner, Victor. 1987. *The Anthropology of Performance.* New York: PAJ Publications.

Tyrnauer, Gabrielle. 1989. *Gypsies and the Holocaust: A Bibliography and Introductory Essay.* Montreal: Centre Interuniversitaire d'Études Européennes.

Urciuoli, Bonnie. 1991. "The Political Topography of Spanish and English: The View from a New York Puerto Rican Neighborhood." *American Ethnologist* 18:295–310.

———. 1995. "Language and Borders." *Annual Review of Anthropology* 24:525–546.

Velexova, Nina. 1972. "Tajny tsyganskogo penija" ("Mysteries of Gypsy Song"). *Teatr* 4:84–95.

Ventsel', T. V. 1964. *Tsyganskij jazyk: Severno-russkij dialekt (The Gypsy Language: Northern Russian Dialect).* Moscow: Nauka.

Verdery, Katherine. 1991. "Theorizing Socialism: A Prologue to 'Transition.'" *American Ethnologist* 10, no. 3:419–438.

———. 1993. "Ethnic Relations, Economies of Shortage, and the Transition in Eastern Europe." In *Socialism, Ideals, Ideologies and Local Practice,* ed. C. M. Hahn, 172–186. London: Routledge.

Voloshinov, V. N. 1978 [1930]. "Reported Speech." In *Readings in Russian Poetics,* ed. Ladislav Matejka and Krystyna Pomorska, 149–175. Ann Arbor: University of Michigan Press.

Vowles, Judith. 1993. "Marriage à la Russe." In *Sexuality and the Body in Russian Culture,* ed. Jane Costlow, Stephanie Sandler, and Judith Vowles. Stanford, Calif.: Stanford University Press.

Watson, Rubie S. 1994. *Memory, History, and Opposition under State Socialism.* Santa Fe, N.M.: School of American Advanced Research Press.

Weinerova, Renata. 1994. *Romanies—In Search of Lost Security?: An Ethnological Probe in Prague 5.* Prague Occasional Papers in Ethnology, no. 3. Prague: Institute of Ethnology and Journal Český lid.

Weyrauch, Walter Otto, and Maurene Bell. 1993. "Autonomous Lawmaking: The Case of the 'Gypsies.'" *Yale Law Journal* 103, no. 2:323–399.

Willis, Paul E. 1977. *Learning to Labor: How Working Class Kids Get Working Class Jobs.* Westmead: Saxon House.

Wixman, Ronald. 1984. *The Peoples of the USSR: An Ethnographic Handbook.* New York: M. E. Sharpe.

———. 1986. "Applied Soviet Nationality Policy: a Suggested Rationale." In *Turco-Tatar Past, Soviet Present: Studies Presented to Alexandre Bennigsen,* ed. C. Lemercier-Quelquejay et al. Louvain: Editions Peeters, 449–468.

Wolff, Janet. 1993. "On the Road Again: Metaphors of Travel in Cultural Criticism." *Cultural Studies* 7, no. 2:224–239.

Wolff, Larry. 1998. "Morlacchi: Ethnographic Identity, Enlightened Anthropology, and the Idea of Eastern Europe." Paper presented at the conference "Vocabularies of Identity in Russian and Eastern Europe," April 3–4, University of Michigan, Ann Arbor.

Woolard, Kathryn. 1989. *Double Talk: Bilingualism and the Politics of Ethnicity in Catalonia.* Stanford: Stanford University Press.

Yoors, Jan. 1947. "Lovari Law and Jurisdiction." *JGLS* 26, nos. 1–2.

———. 1987 [1967]. *The Gypsies.* Prospect Heights, Illinois: Waveland.

Films

Andrej Rubljev (Russia, USSR), dir. Andrej Tarkovskii, 1966.

Greshnyje Apostoly Ljubvi [*Sinful Apostles of Love*] (Russia), dir. Moscow Gypsy Center Romale, 1995.

Latcho Drom [*Good Road*] (France), dir. Tony Gatlif, 1993.

Posdlednij Tabor [*The Last Camp*] (Russia, USSR), dir. M. I. Goldblatt, 1935.

Shirli-Myrli [*Topsy-Turvy*] (Russia), dir. D. Menshov, 1995.

T'an Baxtale!: Roma in Russia (USA, in Russian and Romani with English subtitles), dir. Alaina Lemon and Midori Nakamura, 1994.

Tabor Uxodit v Nebo [*The Gypsy Camp Takes to the Sky*] (Moldovan SSR), 1976, dir. Emil Lotianu, 1976.

Time of the Gypsies (Yugoslavia), dir. Emil Kusturica, 1989.

Tsygan (Russia, USSR), dir. Evgenii Matveev, 1966.

Tsygan for television (Ukraine, USSR, Odesskoj Kinostudio), dir. Aleksandr Blank, 1979.

Tsyganka Aza (Ukraine, USSR), dir. Grigorij Zil'berman, 1987.

Uvidet' Parizh I Umirat' [*To See Paris and Die*] (Russia), dir. Aleksander Proshkin, 1993.

Zhestokij Romans [*A Cruel Romance*] (Russia, USSR), dir. L. Gaidaj and Risto Orko, 1980.

INDEX

ALAINA LEMON is Assistant Professor in the Department of Anthropology, University of Michigan.

Library of Congress Cataloging-in-Publication Data

Lemon, Alaina

Between two fires : Gypsy performance and Romani memory from Pushkin to post-socialism / Alaina Lemon.

p. cm.

Includes bibliographical references and index.

ISBN 0-8223-2456-3 (alk. paper)

— ISBN 0-8223-2493-8 (pbk. : alk. paper)

1. Gypsies — Russia (Federation) — History. 2. Russia (Federation) — Ethnic relations. 3. Performing arts — Russia (Federation) I. Title.

DX241.K46 2000

947'.00491497 — dc21   99-056926